IS NATURE EVER EVIL?

Moral names are often flung at nature. From Noah's Flood to Shakespeare, from anthropomorphic magic to religious concepts of creation and redemption, nature has been praised as a totem of order, goodness, beauty and hope, and castigated for its harshness, disorder and indifference. Culture has long imputed ethical and moral purpose to nature, though in tangled and contradictory ways. But can we in all scientific seriousness call nature evil – or good? Is life a dog-eat-dog affair, where value-judgements have no place, or is there a place for judgements as to what 'ought to be', and not as to what 'just is'? If nature is dangerous, or haphazard, or faulty, can we hold it morally to blame? And what can science – a universal but strangely neutral way of looking at the world – say on this matter?

From a compellingly original premise, under the auspices of major thinkers including Arnold Benz, John Brooke, Lindon Eaves, Philip Hefner, Mary Midgley, Holmes Rolston, and Keith Ward, *Is Nature Ever Evil?* examines the value-structure of our cosmos and of the science that seeks to describe it. What moral strategies can science give for understanding the human experience of our world? Science, says editor Willem B. Drees, claims to leave moral questions to aesthetic and religious theory. It rarely considers the nature of nature: it does not ask about evil. But the supposed neutrality of a scientific view masks a host of moral assumptions. How does an ethically transparent science arrive at concepts of a 'hostile' universe or a 'selfish' gene? How do botanists, zoologists, cosmologists and geologists respond to the beauty and ferocity of the universe they study, reliant as it is upon catastrophe, savagery, power and extinction? Then there are the various ways in which science seeks to alter and improve nature, medically and technologically – to redefine nature's remit down to the smallest cells of the living frame. What do prosthetics and gene technology, cyborgs and dairy cows say about our appreciation of nature itself? Surely science, in common with philosophy, magic and religion, can aid our understanding of evil in nature – whether as natural catastrophe, disease, predatory cruelty or mere cosmic indifference?

Is Nature Ever Evil? marks a fascinating contemporary return to a persistent cultural debate, considering the different ways in which reality is understood by the disciplines of ethics, religion and science. Focusing on the ethical evaluation of nature itself, it re-ignites the wider questions of hope, responsibility and possibility in nature that these conflicts of value imply.

Willem B. Drees is Chair in Philosophy, Religion and Ethics at Leiden University in the Netherlands. He is a physicist, theologian and philosopher whose publications include *Creation: From Nothing until Now* (Routledge, 2002), *Religion, Science and Naturalism* (CUP, 1996) and *Beyond the Big Bang* (Open Court, 1990).

IS NATURE EVER EVIL?

Religion, science and value

Edited by Willem B. Drees

LONDON AND NEW YORK

First published 2003
by Routledge
11 New Fetter Lane, London EC4P 4EE

Simultaneously published in the USA and Canada
by Routledge
29 West 35th Street, New York, NY 10001

Routledge is an imprint of the Taylor & Francis Group

Typeset in Sabon by Taylor & Francis Books Ltd
Printed and bound in Great Britain by TJ International Ltd, Padstow, Cornwall

British Library Cataloguing in Publication Data
A catalogue record for this book is available from the British Library

Library of Congress Cataloging in Publication Data
Is nature ever evil?: religion, science, and value / edited by Willem B. Drees.
Includes bibliographical references and index.
1. Philosophy of nature. 2. Nature–Moral and ethical aspects. 3. Science–Moral
and ethical aspects. 4. Nature–Religious aspects–Christianity. 5. Christian
ethics. I. Drees, Willem B.

BD581 .I595 2002
111'.84–dc21   2002068159

ISBN 0-415-29060-0 (hbk)
ISBN 0-415-29061-9 (pbk)

CONTENTS

CONTENTS

FIGURES

CONTRIBUTORS

Arnold Benz is Professor of Astrophysics at the Swiss Institute of Technology (ETH) in Zurich, Switzerland. Among his books are *Plasma Astrophysics* (Kluwer 2002), *The Future of the Universe* (New York: Continuum, 2000) and *Würfelt Gott?* (Düsseldorf: Patmos, 2000).

Martien E. Brinkman is Professor of Ecumenical Theology at the Vrije Universiteit, Amsterdam, the Netherlands. He has written on creation and the sacraments, including *Progress in Unity? Fifty Years of Theology within the World Council of Churches* (Louvain: Peeters, 1995) and *Sacraments of Freedom* (Zoetermeer: Meinema, 1999).

John Hedley Brooke is Andreas Idreos Professor of Science and Religion at the University of Oxford. Among his books are *Science and Religion: Some Historical Perspectives* (Cambridge UP, 1991) and (with G. Cantor) *Reconstructing Nature: The Engagement of Science and Religion* (T & T Clark, 1998; Oxford UP, 2000).

Eduardo R. Cruz is Professor of Religious Studies at the Pontifical Catholic University of São Paulo and the author of *A Theological Study Informed by the Thought of Paul Tillich and the Latin American Experience: The Ambivalence of Science* (Mellen University Press, 1997).

Jacobus J. De Vries is Professor of Hydrogeology in the Faculty of Earth and Life Sciences of the Vrije Universiteit, Amsterdam. He is also a member of the UNESCO working group on the history of water and civilization.

Kris Dierickx is Guest Professor at the K.U. Leuven (Belgium) and a Postdoctoral Fellow of the National Fund for Scientific Research (NFWO). In 1999 a monograph of his on ethical and social aspects of genetic testing was published in Dutch by Intersentia Publishers.

Willem B. Drees is Professor of Philosophy of Religion and Ethics in the Department of Theology, Leiden University, and President of ESSSAT, the European Society for the Study of Science and Theology. He is the author of *Religion, Science and Naturalism* (1996) and *Creation: From Nothing until Now* (Routledge, 2002).

Lindon B. Eaves is Distinguished Professor of Human Genetics and Psychiatry, and Director of the Virginia Institute for Psychiatric and Behavioral Genetics, Richmond, USA. He is also an ordained Anglican/Episcopalian priest. In 2000 he received from the Vrije Universiteit, Amsterdam, an honorary doctorate for his studies on twins.

Henk G. Geertsema holds the extraordinary chair dedicated to the philosophy of Herman Dooyeweerd at the Vrije Universiteit in Amsterdam. He is Extraordinary Professor of Reformed Philosophy at the universities of Utrecht and Groningen. His dissertation considered philosophical aspects of Jürgen Moltmann's theology of history.

Philip Hefner is Professor of Systematic Theology Emeritus at the Lutheran School of Theology in Chicago and Editor-in-Chief of *Zygon: Journal of Religion and Science*. He is author of *The Human Factor* (Fortress Press, 1993) and *Natur, Weltbild, Religion* (Munich: Institut Technik-Technologie-Naturwissenschaft, 1996).

Mathew Illathuparampil is completing his PhD in moral theology at the Catholic University of Leuven, Belgium. His dissertation investigates the role of moral imagination in dealing with ethical ambiguities regarding technology.

Leo P. ten Kate is Professor of Clinical Genetics and Human Genetics at the Vrije Universiteit Medical Center in Amsterdam. His inaugural address in 1994 dealt with disputes over religious boundaries on genetic research and applications.

Jozef Keulartz is Associate Professor at the University of Wageningen, the Netherlands. He has published on political philosophy, environmental ethics and nature policy, including *Die verkehrte Welt des Jürgen Habermas* (Junius Verlag, 1995) and *The Struggle for Nature: A Critique of Radical Ecology* (Routledge, 1998).

Edwin Koster studied mathematics and theology at the Vrije Universiteit (Amsterdam), Madrid and Princeton. He is preparing a PhD thesis (Amsterdam, VU) on the rationality of narrative traditions.

Anne Kull is Lecturer in Systematic Theology and head of the Department of Systematic Theology, University of Tartu, Estonia. She studied at the Lutheran School of Theology in Chicago, taking a PhD in 2000 on 'A Theology of Nature Based on Donna Harraway and Paul Tillich'.

Joachim Leilich studied philosophy, linguistics and catholic theology at the J.W. Goethe University in Frankfurt, Germany. He teaches philosophy at the University of Antwerp (UFSIA), Belgium. Among his publications are *Die Autonomie der Sprache* (1982) and, as editor, books on Kant and Wittgenstein (in Dutch).

Neil A. Manson is Visiting Assistant Professor at Virginia Commonwealth University, Richmond, USA. He is the editor of *God and Design: The Teleological Argument and Modern Science* (Routledge, 2003). He has been Gifford Research Fellow in Aberdeen, Scotland, and Postdoctoral Fellow at the University of Notre Dame, USA.

Ronald Meester is Professor of Probability Theory at the Vrije Universiteit, Amsterdam. He is also interested in philosophical aspects of probability theory. A book, in Dutch, on the interpretation of probability in relation to religious faith is to appear.

Mary Midgley was formerly Senior Lecturer in Philosophy at the University of Newcastle on Tyne in the UK. Among her books are *Beast and Man* (1978), *Science as Salvation* (Routledge, 1992) and *Science and Poetry* (Routledge, 2001). She is currently working on the meaning of the concept of Gaia.

Arthur C. Petersen is a physicist, philosopher and atmospheric scientist. He is currently a Senior Social Scientist at the Office for Environmental Assessment, RIVM, in the Netherlands. Until January 2002 he worked in the Faculty/Department of Philosophy, Vrije Universiteit, Amsterdam, on the role of computer simulations in science and politics.

Hans Radder is Associate Professor of Philosophy of Science in the Faculty of Philosophy at the Vrije Universiteit, Amsterdam. His publications include *In and about the World* (SUNY Press, 1996) and, as editor, *The Philosophy of Scientific Experimentation* (University of Pittsburgh Press, 2003).

Holmes Rolston, III is Professor of Philosophy at Colorado State University. Among his books are *Genes, Genesis and God* (Cambridge UP), *Philosophy Gone Wild* (Prometheus Books), *Environmental Ethics* (Temple University Press) and *Science and Religion* (Random House, McGraw Hill, Harcourt Brace).

Angela Roothaan is Assistant Professor in Philosophy at the Vrije Universiteit in Amsterdam. She is currently working on a study of the relevance of the human experience of nature for ethics. Her thesis dealt with Spinoza's *Tractatus Theologico-Politicus*.

Claudia Sanides-Kohlrausch is a member of the research group on philosophy of nature at the Ruhr-Universität in Bochum. She has studied biology, philosophy and the history of science. She has a special interest in the philosophy of nature and culture, scientific realism, and the history and philosophy of Darwinism.

Peter Scheers is currently finishing a doctoral degree in the Philosophy Department of the Vrije Universiteit, Amsterdam. His research is concerned with perfectionism as a perspective on human existence, work and nature.

Jan Smit is a geophysicist at the Vrije Universiteit in Amsterdam. He is one of the world's foremost experts on the catastrophic events that led to the extinction of the dinosaurs at the end of the Cretaceous period. He is a member of the Royal Netherlands Academy of Arts and Sciences (KNAW).

Fred Spier is Senior Lecturer in World History at the University of Amsterdam. Among his publications are *Religious Regimes in Peru: Religion and State Development in a Long-term Perspective and the Effects in the Andean Village of Zurite* (Amsterdam UP, 1994) and *The Structure of Big History: From the Big Bang until Today* (Amsterdam UP, 1996).

Jair Stein studied biology at the Vrije Universiteit, Amsterdam, where he developed a special interest in the biological basis of religion; he wrote an MSc thesis on this topic. Presently he works as science editor with VPRO Noorderlicht Radio, the Netherlands.

Wessel Stoker teaches Philosophy of Religion at the Vrije Universiteit, Amsterdam. Among his publications are *Is the Quest for Meaning the Quest for God?* (1996), and *Verhulde waarheid* (with H.M. Vroom, 2000). *Een geloofsverant-woording: Geloof, rede en ervaring* is to appear in 2003.

Mladen Turk is finishing his PhD at the Lutheran School of Theology in Chicago with a dissertation on concepts of truth related to sociobiological theories of religion and their theological interpretations. He is the co-author of an introductory book on logic (published in Croatian).

Nico M. van Straalen is Professor of Animal Ecology at the Vrije Universiteit, Amsterdam. He teaches evolutionary biology, ecology and ecotoxicology. His research group studies the ecology of soil invertebrates. He is director of the national graduate school Socio-Economic and Natural Sciences of the Environment.

Tatjana Visak works as a junior researcher and teacher in the Center for Bio-Ethics and Health Law at Utrecht University and in the faculty of medical ethics in the Erasmus Medical Center in Rotterdam. She studied political sciences at Leiden University.

Silvia Völker is Professor of Laser Physics of (Bio-)molecules at the Vrije Universiteit, Amsterdam, and heads a research group on molecular physics at the Huygens Laboratorium, Leiden University, the Netherlands.

Keith Ward is Regius Professor of Divinity at the University of Oxford. He wrote a 4-volume comparative theology *Religion and Revelation, Religion and Creation, Religion and Human Nature* and *Religion and Community* (Oxford University Press, 1994–2000). In 2000 he received an honorary doctorate from the Vrije Universiteit, Amsterdam.

THIS VALE OF TEARS – THE BEST OF ALL POSSIBLE WORLDS?

Willem B. Drees

Fifty slices of buttered toast were placed on the table. I pushed them over the edge one by one. Forty-nine dropped on the floor with the buttered side down. The fiftieth I saved, by eating it. This experiment raises a deep existential question:

Why does buttered toast always fall on the floor with the buttered side down?

Well, why does it? It has to do with the flip the toast makes when it is shovelled over the edge. And the flip has to do with the strength of gravity and the height of the table. To make a full turn, the table would have to be over three metres high. We would have to be about five metres tall for such a table to be useful. However, unstable bipeds as we are, we are better off not getting so tall since we would damage our heads severely when falling over. The mix of gravity (fall) and chemical bonds (risk of breaking bones) results in a maximal length for healthy bipeds of about three metres. Given the strength of gravity and electromagnetic forces (chemical bonds), a biped on any planet would face a similar fate: his (her) buttered toast will fall upside down. Thus, the answer to our question is:

Buttered toast falls upside down because the universe has the properties it has. The universe is to blame for our bad luck.

This could be taken as an example of Murphy's law, the idea that if anything can go wrong, it will go wrong. And it will do so at the place which is most difficult to access, with the parts for which you do not have spares, at a time that does not suit you at all (and so on). A couple of years ago Robert Matthews went through the details of the buttered toast problem (Matthews 1997). He concluded that there is an *anthropomurphic* principle at work; our universe is such that it is bound to generate bad luck.

By speaking of an anthropomurphic principle, Matthews implicitly criticizes those who speak of an *anthropic* principle. This refers to a far more optimistic view of our universe. Our life depends on many features of our world: the availability of a star like the Sun (and hence nuclear fusion), of a planet like the Earth with a solid crust and a protective atmosphere, of the rich variety of a chemistry based on water and organic carbon compounds, and so on. That all these conditions have turned out well says something about the universe we find ourselves in. If one were to attempt to design a slightly different universe, as a thought experiment, with gravity slightly weaker, a somewhat heavier electron, or whatever, it turns out to be quite a different universe. The universe would be so different that it would be unable to bring forth and sustain our kind of life. There seems to be a significant and meaningful correlation between our existence and the properties of the universe; we are at home in the universe. Some have moved on from such arguments to the conclusion that there must have been a creator who created the universe with these particular properties and constants of nature for the sake of the emergence of life, and especially of human life.

Two contradictory interpretations of the world as we know it. Is reality hospitable to our existence, to be appreciated as something valuable? Or is the universe a vale of tears, optimized for generating bad luck, with the emergence of humans as nothing but a marvellous accident? These two different attitudes – praising and criticizing the cosmos – can be discerned in various responses to the natural sciences: evolution as progress, as increasing complexity, but also as endless suffering, red in tooth and claw; the Second Law of Thermodynamics as the running down of a clock, bringing us to ultimate doom, or as the basis for life, for persistent order out of chaos.

In this introduction we will briefly consider four different responses by scientists, four different ways of understanding their own discipline. This will serve as a background to a preview of the chapters of this volume.

Scientists facing a hostile universe

Steven Weinberg wrote in 1977 a small book, *The First Three Minutes*, on the early stages in the development of our universe. At the end of this book he concludes that 'the more the universe seems comprehensible, the more it also seems pointless'. Whether the universe is to expand forever or will collapse again in some billions of years, ending in ice or in fire, there is no indication of a humane human destiny. Weinberg moderates his conclusion by writing in the final sentence of his book that our efforts to understand the universe, and hence the exercise of fundamental science, 'is one of the very few things that lifts human existence a little above the level of farce, and gives it some of the grace of tragedy'.

Biology too seems a fertile basis for sobering views on the meaning of existence. Richard Dawkins describes humans in his *The Selfish Gene* as survival machines, robots blindly programmed by our genes. Culture isn't much better; there we have the tyranny of 'memes', of ideas which spread like infectious diseases, not because they are right or good, but because they are contagious – and the most contagious ideas survive, just like the most selfish genes. But Dawkins too ends on the final page with a positive note. Our ability to look ahead, to simulate the future – and this is in particular the ability of the scientist – gives us the power to resist the selfish genes we are born with, and if necessary the selfish memes with which we are indoctrinated – a call to rebel against the tyranny of our genes and memes.

The biologist George C. Williams argues that reality is not just meaningless, but clearly immoral. Perhaps one might describe physical reality as indifferent, but in biology the main point of the process is to get more copies of your genes into the next generations than copies of your neighbour's genes; morally, this is to be condemned. The analogy of the golden rule in morality (to treat your neighbour the way you would like to be treated yourself) is that you ought not to cheat on your neighbour, unless you may expect to benefit from it (Williams 1997, 213f.). There is only one source of hope: the biological process is not only immorally bad, but also abysmally stupid. That gives us some room for hope; we, thanks to our intelligence, can fight evil. We ought to face the situation as it truly is and analyse the consequences of various scenarios – precisely what may be expected from scientists.

The patriarch of this attitude among scientists may well be Thomas H. Huxley, a younger contemporary of Charles Darwin. In 1893 his lecture 'Evolution and Ethics' appeared. 'Thus, brought before the tribunal of ethics, the cosmos might well stand condemned. The conscience of man revolts against the moral indifference of nature.' Moral nature may have emerged out of nature, but ought not to follow nature. Nature is a formidable opponent, but with intelligence and self-restraint we may change the conditions of existence. The same intelligence that has converted the wolf into a dog that takes care of our sheep should also be able to correct our barbarian instincts.

Authors such as these suggest that the true scientist ought to face reality as it really is, in all its hostility.

Scientists called to improve nature

Carl Sagan titled his last book *The Demon-Haunted World: Science as a Candle in the Dark*. Not only does science reveal our loneliness and the meaninglessness of the process. Science is also called upon to free us from fear by exposing various forms of animism and magical expectations. In a world perceived as being haunted by demons, science liberates. Science is like a candle in the dark – not a merciless flashlight. Science itself is vulnerable, in need of protection. The images Sagan's title evokes are less military, less individualistic than those indicated above, even though there is also significant affinity. The focus is more pastoral, more on the care and comfort that science might provide.

Science is about *understanding* reality. For sciences such as cosmology and paleobiology (the study of fossils) understanding is by the nature of the subject the only aim. Other sciences, however, are not only about understanding but also about *transforming* reality. An archetype may be chemistry, which has its roots in the search of alchemists for the philosopher's stone and the transformation of lead into gold. Doctors seek to heal patients, engineers seek to improve the world or, at least, particular aspects of the world, such as materials, civil hygiene and transportation systems. To see the world as open to improvement suggests not only that there is no reason to be fatalistic, but also that this world is not 'the best of all possible worlds'.

Science revealing that nature is not that bad after all

Romantics tend to see nature differently. Sunlight in a forest in autumn, ice on fields in winter, the first flowers of spring, the fullness of summer: beauty can be found in all seasons. Science can testify to the grandeur of nature as well. Aren't the same forces that make the toast fall upside down also the basis of our existence? Evolution has led to the emergence of complex creatures – and hence to the flight of the eagle, the sonar of the bat, the shape of the dolphin. And to humans, who can see and observe all of this, think and talk about it, wonder about it all. In cosmology, this has been debated under the heading of the 'anthropic principle'. Even more so than among active scientists, there seems to be a longing for harmony between science and a positive, normatively loaded view of reality among the theologians, religiously interested philosophers and retired scientists who populate current debates on religion and science.

Science's neutrality

There are scientists like Weinberg who look out of the window and see how meaningless it all is. There are doctors – like Leo ten Kate, as revealed by his contribution to this volume – who out of compassion with 'victims of nature' seek to help, to relieve suffering. And there are some who, appealing to Ilya Prigogine and others, prefer a more positive understanding of the interplay of natural processes. But most scientists are arbiters who argue that the whole discussion is misguided. Science does not rule on beauty or ugliness, good or evil. Science describes the way things are; no judgement of value is involved.

In the philosophy of science there have been various debates concerning the ideal of value-neutral science. Studies have revealed the role of cultural and political values and interests in the development of the natural sciences. As Philip Kitcher has argued in his study *The Advancement of Science*, there nonetheless seems to be the possibility of speaking of progress in science. Absolute objectivity is an illusion, but in the process of consensus formation cultural boundaries and personal preferences are left behind. Michael Ruse, philosopher and historian of biology, described this process recently in his *Mystery of Mysteries: Is Evolution a Social Construction?* That Erasmus Darwin, grandfather of Charles, opted for an evolutionary view can be understood on the basis of his social values. Charles Darwin himself was not a 'pure' scientist, though the role of data had significantly expanded. In our time there is still an interplay between cultural and other values shaping science. But over time those particular cultural values have become dominant that promote the quality of knowledge by supporting epistemic values such as consistency and coherence, precision and predictive accuracy. In that sense, one can well argue for the neutrality of professional science, not as a given but as an ambition that is being realized to an ever increasing extent.

Let us return to our central theme. The issue is not primarily whether science is neutral, but how we value our world, the reality we are part of. This question puts us squarely within the debate on world views and religions.

Creation or redemption – an issue in theology?

A brief, stylized and simplified history: despite all the horrors in the emerging cities (e.g. outbreaks of the plague), people in the Middle Ages may perhaps still have seen our world as God's good creation. Mixed feelings can be found, however, in various ages. In 1611, a time of turmoil in Europe, John Donne wrote in a poem the often quoted line 'And new philosophy calls all in doubt'. Stephen Toulmin referred to this line in his book *Cosmopolis* in order to exemplify the uncertainties created by the collapse of the social and moral order. Well over a century later, in 1755, Voltaire wrote a poem on the earthquake that destroyed Lisbon (see Sanides-Kohlrausch in this volume), which he subtitled 'an investigation into the axiom "All is well"'. The theme returns in his novel *Candide ou l'optimisme* (1759). The more philosopher Pangloss argues that this world is the best of all possible worlds, the less convincing his case becomes. Another example, a further century later, can be taken from Dostoyevski's book *The Brothers Karamazov*. One of the brothers wants to return his ticket for heaven. Earthly suffering is not justified by any heavenly reward or meaning.

Such changes in the appreciation of our world have had their consequences for theology. This is most explicit with respect to theologians who have abandoned the theistic concept of God as the divine King who created this world and rules over it day and night. Instead, they seek to articulate an understanding of God as the companion of those who suffer, of the poor. The 'death of God' debate in the 1960s has to do with a greater emphasis on human autonomy, but also with an increased sensibility to cruelty and suffering in this world.

In theology, this is not a new debate. The first – and arguably most significant – heretic of Christian history was Marcion, in the second century CE. He stressed the tension between the idea of God as the creator of this ambivalent world and God as the loving father of Jesus Christ. Whereas the Creator has a proportional sense of justice (an eye for an eye), the father of Jesus Christ is associated with grace and forgiveness. Marcion concluded that the biblical stories are about two different gods – a Creator and a Redeemer. The Christian tradition has rejected this; confessional statements affirm again and again that God as known via Jesus is the Creator of heaven and earth. In medieval theology the continuity of nature and grace was a common assumption; God's grace does not abandon nature but perfects it. The protestant reformers had more hesitations about this continuity; their theology is more coloured by the tension between nature and grace, between this world and the world to come; a contemporary reflection of such theological differences can be discerned in this volume in the response by Martien Brinkman to Keith Ward. One consequent articulation is that God's grace is not to be found in nature – as when Dietrich Bonhoeffer writes in his letters from prison that we ought not to look for God in the limitations of our knowledge. We live in a secular world, a world in which God is not manifest – but in this world we live before God. We are left with a radical sense of responsibility because we have been set free.

Religion and science

What consequences may there be from this diversity of opinions on reality and value for current discussions on religion and science? Conferences, books and projects often seem to be aimed at *causal* issues. Is it possible to speak in a sensible way of divine action in the world as we know it? Is there any divine involvement in the first instance, referred to as 'the Big Bang', or throughout the processes that shape and constitute our world, say in quantum indeterminacy or the flexibility of chaotic processes? Does the complexity of the living cell emerge spontaneously, or is there a need for guidance? Some debates do not so much focus on divine involvement as on human identity: is our behaviour merely a consequence of genes and circumstances? Is morality nothing but a veiled and subtle form of self-interest, and hence egoism? Is there anything 'else' involved in religious experience, or is it projection?

The *appreciation* or valuation of reality is considered far less explicitly in debates on religion and science, even though it is implicitly present in concepts of God assumed. This issue, of our various valuations of the world and their relation to science, is central to this volume.

Is nature ever evil? A preview of this book

This volume results from a conference held at the Vrije Universiteit in Amsterdam, October 23–25, 2000, organized by the Bezinningscentrum of the Vrije Universiteit in collaboration with Dr. Antje Jackelén of the CTNS Science and Religion Course Program in Europe and sponsored also by the Council for the Humanities of the Netherlands Organization for Scientific Research (NWO). The title of the conference in Amsterdam was 'Is Nature Ever Evil, Wrong, or Ugly? Neutrality and Engagement in the Scientific Study of Reality'. There were eight invited contributors (resulting in most of the substantial essays in this volume), each followed by responses, often from the faculties of the sciences, theology and philosophy (resulting in various brief comments in this volume), and workshops with, mostly, younger scholars contributing.

The central question, 'Is Nature Ever Evil?', triggered a variety of reflections. The first part of the book, 'Nature, science and value', considers some fundamental issues regarding our concept of nature and our view of the contribution science might make. In the first essay the philosopher Mary Midgley takes to task scientific critics of the cosmos. Other essays in this section question and explore various methodological issues relating to moral pronouncements regarding the nature of reality.

The second part opens with an essay by the philosopher Holmes Rolston, arguing (to summarize it all too briefly) that evil is an intrinsic part of any reality that is interesting; creation is 'cruciform'. Subsequent contributions in this part explore similar issues concerning the justification for belief in the ultimate goodness of reality in the light of catastrophic processes in reality.

Central to the third part are the essays by the historian John Brooke and the theologian Philip Hefner. Brooke surveys discourses on 'improving nature', which implicitly suggest that nature is not as good as it could be. Hefner moves further on in a theological exploration of the 'human co-creator', assessing the active role of humans in creating culture and technology. Other essays respond to their contributions and delve into particular issues of health and disease, the drive for perfection, and technology.

The final part begins with an essay by the theologian Keith Ward, arguing for the co-existence of explanations in terms of physical processes and in terms of personal intentions and values, and hence for the irreducibility of a theistic understanding of our world. The geneticist and Episcopalian priest Lindon Eaves deals extensively with current research in behavioural genetics and its consequences for our understanding of human nature, including the normative dimension we experience, and thus brings us to ask how the 'ought', the values embedded in religious and humanist traditions, is related to the 'is' of the processes uncovered by science. As the title of this section asks 'Values as explanation or values explained?', the essays here raise the issue of whether a theistic theology with its value-laden notions of purpose and intention offers a framework for understanding 'reality, science and values', or whether reality as seen through the sciences is the framework through which we can understand our values.

References

Dawkins, R. (1976) *The Selfish Gene*, New York: Oxford University Press.

Huxley, T.H. (1893) 'Evolution and Ethics', reproduced in J. Paradis and G.C. Williams (eds), *Evolution and Ethics: T.H. Huxley's 'Evolution and Ethics', with New Essays on Its Victorian and Sociobiological Context*, Princeton: Princeton University Press, 1989.

Kitcher, P. (1993) *The Advancement of Science*, New York: Oxford University Press.

Matthews, R. (1997) 'The Science of Murphy's Law', *Scientific American* 276 (4 April): 72–5.

Ruse, M. (1999) *Mystery of Mysteries: Is Evolution a Social Construction?*, Cambridge, Mass.: Harvard University Press.

Sagan, C. (1996) *The Demon-Haunted World: Science as a Candle in the Dark*, New York: Random House.

Toulmin, S. (1990) *Cosmopolis*, New York: Free Press.

Weinberg, S. (1977) *The First Three Minutes*, New York: Basic Books.

Williams, G.C. (1997) *Plan and Purpose in Nature*, London: Orion Books.

Part I

NATURE, SCIENCE AND VALUE

Introduction to Part I

Willem B. Drees

Is the universe hostile to human interests? The British philosopher Mary Midgley challenges in her essay scientists who criticize or praise the cosmos: What might be the basis for their judgements? Is the language appropriate? From what perspective can one make such evaluations? The biophysicist Silvia Völker concurs with the criticism of scientists who speak with authority on issues far outside their own domain; nonetheless, she underlines the element of chance in existence – an element which does not bring us to any particular interpretation, but does need to be taken into account. In his response, the philosopher Hans Radder agrees with Midgley's criticisms too, but questions her own constructive proposal as too much indebted to an individualistic understanding of science. The social dimension of science which Radder stresses is also central to the reflections of Joachim Leilich on Max Weber, the great thinker on values and science. Leilich argues that nature is not evil (nor is it good), since moral pronouncements become appropriate only when mind is involved. This view highlights one of the recurrent issues in this volume, namely the understanding of the concept of 'nature'. How wide is the concept? Does 'nature' encompass the whole of reality, involving minds as well as human culture and technology? Or is 'nature' limited to the biological realm (which may include human influences), or even further limited to pristine nature, untouched by humans? What about dairy cows? Tatjana Visak considers this example in her reflections on the concept 'naturalness' and its normative significance. Philosopher Angela Roothaan continues the dialogue on the human contribution to any interpretation of nature, and proposes to emphasize under the concept 'nature' not 'order' or 'spontaneity' but rather 'alterity'. More specifically in relation to the interpretation of animals, philosopher Peter Scheers also argues for a benevolent hermeneutics which recognizes and appreciates otherness in animals.

1

CRITICIZING THE COSMOS

Mary Midgley

The question about what it means to say that 'nature is evil' is many-sided. Among its sides, I would like to concentrate on questioning the meaning of certain strong accusations of this kind which have actually been made by distinguished scientists. As often happens with extreme manifestos, these accusations seem to me to cast a useful light on the other, more cautious, parts of the controversial scene. In particular, I would like to consider how these attacks relate to the 'official neutrality of a scientific view of reality', which is an important part of our topic in this book.

Trouble about tribunals

Thomas Carlyle was once told that a lady had said, 'I accept the universe'. He replied, 'By God, she'd better' .... And it is indeed hard (isn't it?) to say what it would be like *not* to accept the universe – to reject it. Where, outside the universe, does one stand to perform this difficult feat?

As it happens, another great Victorian – Thomas Henry Huxley – did try to do this. What he said on the subject is interesting because the line that he took has had a great effect on our thinking today. Huxley wrote:

> Ethical nature, while born of cosmic nature, is necessarily *at enmity with its parent* .... The ethical process is in opposition to the principle of the cosmic process, and tends to the suppression of the qualities best fitted for success in this struggle .... Thus, brought before the tribunal of ethics, the cosmos might well seem to stand condemned. The conscience of man revolts against the moral indifference of nature .... [Man must therefore be] perpetually on guard *against the cosmic forces, whose ends are not his ends.* Laws and moral precepts are directed to the end of *curbing the cosmic process.*
>
> (Huxley 1893: viii, 44, 182. Emphases mine.)

The concerns of this book invite us to ask a particular question about this kind of manifesto, namely: is it part of science? Was Huxley speaking as an impartial scientist? Does his stance express 'the official neutrality of a scientific view of reality'?

To this, the answer must surely be no. Huxley's colourful, highly personal imagery does not fit that neutrality. Both his Oedipal suggestion of an ethical process 'at enmity with its parent', and his military language of putting us 'on guard against the cosmic forces' which have their own 'ends', unmistakably imply a human opponent. So, too, does the image of the tribunal. But there is something ludicrous about this language because these human conflicts provide much too small a model for what he is trying to convey. The project of turning against the entire nature of things and 'curbing' it is on a quite different scale from just opposing one's parent or arresting a malefactor or taking part in a tribal feud. And this inadequate imagery indicates a deeper trouble. It is not at all clear how 'we' could somehow stand so far outside the whole cosmic process as to oppose it.

Huxley's language here shows that he is still what may be called an Animist. Though he brings in no gods, he personalizes nature, enduing it with a kind of consciousness and will which still place it in some social relation to our own – namely a hostile one. Since his time, theorists who have noticed the oddity of this personification have seen this difficulty and have made great efforts to make the same kind of point without personifying. They still want to express essentially the same depressed, alienated view of our relation to the cosmos but to depersonalize it in a way that annihilates animism. They want to objectify this demolition job so that it can count as part of science. Thus Jacques Monod:

> It is perfectly true that science attacks values. Not directly, since science is no judge of them and *must* ignore them; but it subverts every one of the mythical or philosophical ontogenies upon which the animist tradition, from the Australian aborigines to the dialectical materialists, has based morality, values, duties, rights, prohibitions.
>
> If he accepts this message in its full significance, man must at last wake out of his millennary dream and discover his total solitude, his fundamental isolation. He must realize that, like a gypsy, he lives on the boundary of an alien world; a world that is deaf to his music, and as indifferent to his hopes as it is to his sufferings and crimes.
>
> (Monod 1974: 160. Author's emphasis.)

Here again, however, the social imagery undermines the attempted impersonality. Why does Monod speak of gypsies rather than Eskimos or Arctic explorers? Gypsies do not live in a non-human world that has no views about them. They live among hostile human beings, or at least ones who dislike them. This imagery, again, describes a bad social relation, a bad drama, not an absence of social relations. And that social twist becomes even more striking in Monod's image of the cosmic casino.

> Immanence is alien to modern science. Destiny is written as and while, not before it happens .... The universe was not pregnant with life nor the biosphere with man. Our number came up in the Monte Carlo game. Is it surprising that, like the person who has just made a million at the casino, we should feel strange and a little unreal?
>
> (Monod 1974: 158)

For Monod, then, the universe is no longer (as Huxley supposed) a bad parent. It has ceased to be our parent at all. It was not pregnant with us. We are quite unrelated to it. In his efforts to make this story of our detachment look plausible, Monod takes a quite extraordinary view of how both life and the human species have come into being. He dismisses both these big changes as sudden, unaccountable events, cut off from all that went before them by the same sort of artificial disinfecting process that is used to isolate one spin of the wheel from another in a casino. This causal isolation is meant to make us essentially solitary beings, alien to everything around us in the physical cosmos. Thus, as Monod says, we are left alone to pursue 'an anxious quest in a world of icy solitude' (*ibid.*, p. 158).

Once more, however, the attempt at impersonality fails. The casino image still represents nature as standing in a social relation to us, though a strange one. Nature has now become a croupier – an anonymous functionary whom we do not know personally and to whom we could owe no gratitude, a stranger who just happens to hand us a fortune. But this story too implies a social context. Money from the casino does not come out of the blue. It is still human money. In fact it is other people's money, channelled to us by their greed, their excitability, their wild hopes, their despair and our own decision to gamble. This is the social background which would make the winner feel 'a little unreal'.

The picture of detachment from the world which Monod is trying to paint here cannot really be made clear because it is such an extraordinary one for any biologist to conceive. It clashes radically with that insistence on the continuity of evolution which lies at the heart of post-Darwinian biology. It is especially hard to reconcile with the Darwinian insistence on bringing *Homo sapiens* within that continuity. Monod's language raises the urgent question: what kind of beings does he take *us* to be, these beings who are radically cut off from the rest of nature?

The answer to that must surely be sought not in biology but in philosophy. This dramatic view of human standing is surely drawn from

Jean-Paul Sartre, and before him from Descartes' conception of the independent soul. It is the Existentialist vision of the human will as solitary
and independent, disconnected from the body, an uncaused cause that
owes nothing to our natural feelings, a heroic Ajax asserting its freedom
by defying the cosmic lightning.

The physicist Steven Weinberg displays a similar drama:

> It is almost irresistible for humans to believe that we have some
> special relation to the universe, that human life is not just the
> more-or-less *farcical* outcome of a chain of accidents reaching
> back to the first three minutes, but that we were somehow built in
> from the beginning .... It is very hard to realize that all this is just
> part of an *overwhelmingly hostile universe* .... The more the
> universe seems comprehensible, the more it also seems *pointless*.
>
> (Weinberg 1977: 154. Emphases mine.)

Overwhelmingly hostile and laughing at us? Is this a natural way to
describe the universe that has made us and has given us everything that we
have? What is so hostile about that?

Weinberg cites a number of grievances against this universe. He
complains (1) that it does not give us a long enough life, (2) that it is too
big, so that it makes us feel small, (3) that it is too temporary, since it
cannot support us and our descendants for ever, (4) that it is too contingent, because it does not show us to be necessary, and (5) that it is too
pointless, because it does not aim centrally at our interests. This remarkable series of complaints presupposes that something much better could
have been expected – that the universe ought to have been much more
suited to our interests. Again, this surely puts us back into a social context,
treating the world once more as a bad parent or other human on whom we
have unfulfilled claims. That is the mood in which (as A.E. Housman put
it) unhappy people

> curse
> Whatever brute or blackguard made the world.
>
> (*Last Poems*, no. ix)

But this language is only available to theists. Unbelievers who want to say
such things are reduced to complaining, with Sartre, 'The Bastard! He
doesn't exist!'

Neutrality and objectivity

What, however, about our central theme of Scientific Neutrality? Monod's
and Weinberg's stories surely do not rank high on this spectrum. It seems
clear that they belong to ethics and to metaphysics, not to science, and also

that they are highly emotional. Though these passages occur in the last chapters of scientific books and are presented as science, they do not offer scientific conclusions. Instead, they express possible moral attitudes and possible emotional responses to the facts of the world. These attitudes and responses are not forced on us by science. They are options for us to consider alongside others that are available to us. Sartre, after all, was not trying to write science. Nor is it easy to see how his world-picture can be brought into any intelligible relation with it.

For Monod, these proposals centre on the concept of objectivity. He insists that nature has now been scientifically discovered to be *objective*, by which he officially means only 'the *nonexistence* anywhere in nature of a purpose, of a pursued end' (*op. cit.*, p. 31). This might seem to mean simply the absence of a single ruling cosmic purpose behind creation. But, as the passages just quoted show, he actually means by objectivity something much stronger and stranger than this. He is saying that we ought to view natural things – such as plants and animals – just *as objects* – that is, as inert, lifeless items not having their own purposes, beings that are unrelated to us and therefore intrinsically valueless. It is not clear whether we ourselves are included in this category of purposelessness, whether our own purposes too – including the purpose of pursuing this argument – are being dismissed as illusory. But the continuity of evolution would suggest that this must be so.

In order to induce us to accept this highly unbiological programme Monod offers chiefly an appeal to our vanity. He asks us to join the elite number of those who are virile enough to receive it.

> We understand why so many thousand years passed before the appearance, in the realm of ideas, of those presenting objective knowledge as the only source of truth.
>
> Cold and austere, proposing no explanation but imposing an ascetic renunciation of all other spiritual fare, this idea could not allay anxiety; it aggravated it instead. It claimed to sweep away at a stroke the tradition of a hundred thousand years, which had become assimilated to human nature itself .... With nothing to recommend it but a certain puritan arrogance, how could such an idea be accepted? It was not; it still is not.
>
> (Monod 1974: 158)

Only exceptionally heroic people (that is) are tough enough to go on this starvation diet – austere enough to lock themselves up in this refrigerator and live there. Monod invites us to show our heroism by joining them. But the shakiness of his reasons for doing this comes out in the telltale phrase *objective knowledge*. The general message of the book is that this means physical science. Yet the arguments of the book itself are of course not part of physical science. They are metaphysical propaganda – discussions of the general presuppositions of our reasoning, of the way in which we should interpret our data and of our system of values. In listing these values, which he claims to have swept away wholesale, Monod suddenly reveals a surprising exception. There is, it now appears, one value after all that can survive the deluge, namely the value of science itself:

> True knowledge is ignorant of values, but it has to be grounded on a value-judgement, or rather on an *axiomatic* value .... By the very loftiness of its ambition, the ethic of knowledge might perhaps satisfy this craving for something higher. It puts forward a transcendent value, true knowledge, not for the use of man, but for man to serve from deliberate and conscious choice .... As for the highest human qualities, courage, altruism, generosity, creative ambition, the ethic of knowledge both recognises their sociobiological origin and affirms their transcendent value in the service of the ideal it defines.
>
> (*Ibid.*, pp. 163–4. Author's emphasis.)

Does it also recognize its own sociobiological origin? We are not told. At the end of the book we are simply asked to accept this moral conclusion – for which no moral arguments have been given – that in the realm of values the king is dead and therefore long live the king, who is now Science, to which all other aims and ideals must be subservient. Weinberg draws a similar conclusion, describing research in astrophysics as being 'one of the very few things that lifts human life a little above the level of farce and gives it some of the grace of tragedy'. Very few things? He doesn't say what he thinks the others are, nor how the human race managed to occupy itself during the long, long centuries before it, very recently, invented this kind of work.

Huxley and the Social Darwinist demons

I have started this discussion by considering Huxley's, Monod's and Weinberg's somewhat hostile views of nature because they seem often to be respected today and taken as specially authoritative. They are believed to be Scientific – sometimes even viewed as being the typical, authorized conclusions of Science. Even people who dislike these ideas and are frightened of them often have an uneasy sense that they carry the stamp of scientific authority – that they will eventually have to be accepted because they are somehow impartial statements of scientific facts. And it is not surprising that the public gets this impression because these writers undoubtedly share it. It is easy for them, just as it is for their audience, to think of these ideas as scientific simply because they are the ideas of an eminent scientist. They see the authority of specialists in discussing their own field as extending to these vaster and more general background questions. And today's scientists have often been so narrowly educated that – even when they are distinguished in their own field – they may well not be aware that they have taken this step away from solid ground into a quagmire of unfamiliar questions. This commonly happens because, somewhere far out in the quagmire, they have seen an opinion which they want to oppose. They are then struck by what seems to be a simple way of opposing it, and in they go.

T.H. Huxley did not, of course, have this disadvantage of a narrow twentieth-century scientific education. But his natural enthusiasm and pugnacity made him hasty and his hastiness landed him in the strange views that we have seen. The target of Huxley's fury was Herbert Spencer's complacent evolutionary ethic, which taught that evolution not only was always for the best but also was the sole guide for morals. Evolution (said Spencer) was infallible. Right conduct simply was conduct that furthered evolutionary progress. This conduct always produced 'the survival of the fittest' – a disastrously ambiguous phrase which was, of course, Spencer's coinage, not Darwin's. Evolution, left to itself, could be relied on as an escalator which would carry the human race up to celestial heights in the future. (This faith too was, of course, Spencer's and Lamarck's contribution, not Darwin's.) Accordingly (Spencer explained), it was always wrong to interrupt evolution by helping the unfit poor. They should simply be allowed to perish:

> The whole effort of nature is to get rid of such, to clear the world of them and to make room for better .... If they are sufficiently complete to live, they do live. If they are not sufficiently complete to live, they die, and it is best that they should die.
>
> (Spencer 1864: 414–15)

Rightly horrified by this, Huxley simply reversed the ethic, saying instead that this heartless evolutionary process was immoral and should be hotly resisted. It did not occur to him to question the whole idea of such a one-sided process – to point out that evolution is not actually just a simple sequence of dog eating dog, that co-operation is just as important in it as competition. Evolution is a much wider process which has produced sociality, generating love and altruism just as much as competition. If it had not done so (he could have said), there would never have been a human 'ethical process'. That process is every bit as much a product of evolution as its contrary is.

Huxley simply did not notice that Spencer's drama had no roots in real biology – that essentially Spencer (who was primarily a political theorist) had simply projected his exaltation of capitalism on to the cosmic scale. Huxley failed to spot this because – again unlike Darwin – he himself knew very little about the behaviour of non-human animals and was not interested in it. For all he knew, these animals might indeed all be ravening monsters, embodied vices, as the mythical tradition suggested. Though anatomical arguments had convinced him that he was physically descended from the apes, he always saw that as a most disturbing fact. His only suggestion about how we could come to terms with this painful and tragic discovery was that we could take even more pride in the achievements of civilized *man* than we otherwise would, when we saw from how humble and indeed disgusting a source he had contrived to raise himself.

Huxley was also, of course, appalled to see how Spencer's 'Social Darwinist' message was catching on with the public. Its crude simplicity made it readily intelligible both to those who liked it and to those who hated it. Being much easier to understand than Darwin's real views, it was widely accepted as simply representing them. Spencer, who did not himself grasp the difference between their positions, always represented himself as forwarding Darwin's ideas, and he did this most notably in successful lecture tours all over America. The result was the widespread identification of 'Darwinism' with these indefensible moral positions. This confusion has persisted to the present day and is largely responsible for the anti-Darwin sentiment which makes some people reject the whole idea of evolution. As Stephen Jay Gould has pointed out, today's vigorous Creationist movement arose out of the horrified reaction of people like William Jennings Bryan to the Social Darwinist propaganda that was circulating in the 1920s.

Huxley had good reason, then, to object to Social Darwinism. But objecting rightly to something does not mean that one has found the right position to take instead of it. You cannot uproot a position while you are still sitting firmly on one of its central presumptions.

The quest for alien status

What, then, is now the target of Monod's and Weinberg's controversial campaigns? What are they denying?

Weinberg denies 'that we have some special relation to the universe ... that we were somehow built in from the beginning'. Monod speaks of destroying the 'animist covenant' supposedly uniting us to a supposedly purposeful world.

What do these vague phrases mean? They could cover any of a great range of views. The most obvious target of both writers is, of course, traditional religion. But Monod ostentatiously shoots much more widely, claiming to reject 'every one of the mythical philosophical ontogenies on which the animist tradition, from the Australian aborigines to the dialectical materialists, has based morality, values, duties, rights, prohibitions'.

18

It is this apparent comprehensiveness that made his book so striking and that has caused it to remain so influential. He seems to call for a blank rejection not just of outside sanctions for morality but of all explanation within it, a wholesale retreat from the entire business of moral reasoning. The idea of such a rejection and such a retreat was, of course, not his invention. It was already the declared policy both of Existentialist ethics and of English-speaking academic anti-naturalism during the middle part of the twentieth century. It is not, however, actually a very impressive programme. The most glaring weakness of this policy lay – as it does with most forms of supposedly radical scepticism – in the sort of inconsistency that I have just pointed out in the case of Monod. These sceptics, being themselves moralists, could not avoid breaching their own declared standards in order to accommodate their particular favoured ideals – in Monod's case, scientific knowledge, in Sartre's, the ideal of individual freedom.

This is not, however, just a matter of chance and incompetence. Under this *ad hominem* objection lies the deeper fact that the whole campaign is invalidated by gross exaggeration. Of course it is true that the reasons brought in support of various moral views have often been irrelevant, and that it is often quite hard to find clear standards of relevance by which to prevent this. But since we constantly have to find some way of dealing with moral conflicts and dilemmas, we cannot meet this difficulty by just washing our hands of the whole enterprise. There is not – as Sartre and Monod suggest – a single predominant value which will resolve our difficulties by always taking precedence. This means that we have no choice but – somehow – to work out ways of expressing the various considerations that arise and weighing them against one another. We also need to keep developing these concepts so as to make them more effective. The suggestion that we should abandon all this effort in favour of direct intuition or – what comes to the same thing – pure, unformulated 'choice' does not really make any sense at all.

Anthropic?

In the 1970s, after Monod published his book, another view about the cosmos appeared which would certainly have furnished him with a suitable target for his attacks, had he known about it. This view is relevant to our theme because, while it differs radically from those that we have just considered, it, like them, has been put forward as carrying a scientific seal of approval. It is the view that the universe does indeed have a central purpose, namely, the exaltation of *man*. This idea is currently expressed in scientific terms in the Strong Anthropic Principle, which regards the perfection of Intelligent Life (that is, of us and our successors, some of whom will be machines) as the ruling aim of the whole cosmos. Its supporters tell us that this terminus will eventually be consummated, at the Omega Point, by our successfully colonizing the entire physical universe through intelligent machines:

> At the instant the Omega Point is reached, life will have gained control of *all* matter and forces, not only in a single universe but in all universes whose existence is logically possible; life will have spread into *all* spatial regions in all universes which could logically exist, and will have stored an infinite amount of information, including *all* bits of knowledge which it is logically possible to know. And this is the end.
>
> (Barrow and Tipler 1986: 677. Author's emphasis.)

Lest this should seem not to be enough, a footnote adds: 'A modern-day theologian might wish to say that the totality of life at the Omega Point is omnipotent, omnipresent and omniscient!'

The interesting thing is that this view, too, is presented as a scientific one. Its authors are two highly respected cosmologists and (again) it occurs in the last chapter of a book rich in equations and much of which is devoted to astrophysics, evolutionary biology, quantum mechanics and biochemistry, all designed to support this conclusion.

Plainly, however, this too is a book of moral and metaphysical propaganda. Its starting point is a dizzyingly high valuation of the importance of 'intelligence' – conceived, rather oddly, as the power to gather information – within human life. It then simply projects that valuation on to the cosmic screen and proceeds to work out ways in which the cosmos might be supposed to accommodate it. The original value-judgement itself is never discussed or defended against other possible judgements of importance. The moral and metaphysical questions that it raises are by-passed. But (again) there is a public hungry for this myth, because computers, and dealings in information generally, are venerated today as forces which will be able to succour us and stave off the dangers of our age.

When Weinberg denies that we have 'some special relation to the universe', he may have in mind this kind of extreme claim. Or he may merely be thinking of the more modest status that Christian thinking gives to humanity as God's steward. But rejecting either of these views does not in any way call for the strange suggestion – which he surely draws from Monod – that we are cut off from the rest of the physical world in a way that forces us to see it as hostile and pointless. Nor does his claim that we were not 'somehow built in from the beginning' make his argument any clearer. According to the determinist point of view which most scientists endorse for much of the time, we surely *were* so built in, just as surely as toads and thunderstorms and bacteria were. On that common assumption, our development has indeed been inevitable, as has that of every other creature. And even a looser, less deterministic view of this development still roots us deeply in the whole sequence of organic life. Nor does invoking quantum indeterminacy alter this situation. It cannot possibly supply the sudden large-scale break in causation that Monod's story seems to imply, both for the dawn of life and for the rise of *Homo sapiens*.

It is hard to see any reasonable justification for simply denying the continuity of nature in this way. The objection to doing so does not depend on a religious belief in God as Creator, though it is quite compatible with that belief. It rests simply on our kinship with the rest of the natural world around us. On this matter, real Darwinian thinking agrees closely with widespread human tradition in taking us to be an integral part of that world, so that our natural tendency to love and revere it is a wholly appropriate part of our emotional constitution. We are not alien invaders in this world. We are at home in it.

This is the large and obvious truth which Monod and Weinberg reject. And their rejection of it is what prevents them from effectively attacking the anthropolatrous arrogance embodied in the Anthropic Principle. Like Thomas Huxley, they share a vital presumption with their proposed target. At heart, they seem to be just as convinced as these cosmologists are that humans are essentially non-terrestrial beings, pure wills or intelligences, radically cut off from the rest of nature. And they also share the cosmologists' view that the quality which cuts humans off in this way is the calculating intellect, the capacity to seek theoretical knowledge. The only difference between their two positions lies in their varying degree of hopefulness about the future. The cosmologists claim that the human intellect is destined for an eventual apotheosis in which it will separate itself entirely from everything earthly and go on to colonize and command the whole universe. The Monod school, understandably unconvinced by this prediction, replies that, on the contrary, it can only expect a tragic and desolate existence alone in a world with which it has nothing in common.

As we have seen, this whole world-view rests on Monod's central 'postulate of objectivity', stating 'the non-existence anywhere of a pursued end' is 'consubstantial with science' (*op. cit.*, p. 31). He dates this postulate from 'the formulation by Galileo and Descartes of the principle of inertia'. This is unhistorical. What Galileo did was simply to remove purposive argument from physics. He did not demonstrate that it makes no sense elsewhere. Descartes, and many seventeenth-century thinkers who followed him, did indeed try to establish that the simplifying, mechanistic methods of current physics were the only ones that would be needed throughout the physical sciences (though not, of course, for understanding the soul). This ambition for comprehensive simplicity in science long fascinated scholars and it still does today, generating talk of 'Theories of Everything'. It has, however, long been obvious that the subject matters of

21

the other sciences are complex and require different and more complex methods to deal with them.

On top of this, during the twentieth century physics itself deserted this simple, mechanistic paradigm and physicists now recognize the need for different ways of thinking at different levels – ways which cannot in principle be reduced to any single model. Reductionist practitioners of other sciences, however, still follow Monod's example in singing from the seventeenth-century hymn book. Thus Peter Atkins declares that:

> Inanimate things are innately simple. That is one more step along the path to the view that animate things, being innately inanimate, are innately simple too.
>
> (Atkins 1987: 53)

What about values?

All these strange world-pictures come from reputable scientists and are supposed to be scientific. If we ask 'can they be considered value-free?', our answer must surely again be no. These last chapters of books obviously express moral visions, suggested attitudes to life which may have their own value but which cannot possibly be treated as literal facts about the physical world. Their mere variety makes this clear. If we tried to take them all as parts of science, science would seem to be at variance with itself in an extraordinary way.

As I remarked at the outset, I have deliberately picked out rather striking examples of this genre, simply in order to make that point clear. But I have not cheated in doing so by picking cases that are unreal or atypical. All the doctrines I have mentioned have a great deal of influence in the modern world. They owe this influence partly to their dramatic imagery, but partly also to their simplicity. In a confusing world, violent colours and flat blacks and whites are at a premium.

It is not surprising, either, that these visions now often emerge out of the practice of science. Of course very simple factual questions in the sciences would not give rise to them. Scientists who are asking those questions within a clear and accepted framework do not have to go beyond what that framework provides for. But in the devising of new frameworks, and in the adaptation of old ones, new ideas constantly come in, and they are naturally ones which are active in the background culture of the time. This is particularly obvious with respect to imagery.

The machine imagery that fascinated the seventeenth century has had enormous influence on our thinking ever since, an influence that has often been found to be misleading – as in the case of modern particle physics. And again, the economic imagery of the Victorian age has pervaded thought about evolution (not only in Social Darwinism) and still does so, often doing a good deal of damage, notably in the area of sociobiology. Each of the striking, simple visions which produce such imagery may contain some truth, but they all need to be judged in the context of a wider whole. Because the real world is complex, we need to treat them soberly as a range of possible contributions to our lives – pictures suggesting new useful angles on the real complexity – not to expect any one of them to provide universal guidance.

Scientists who move away from detailed questions towards larger issues of principle are using ideas from the wider culture around them. They are also making suggestions which can affect those ideas. They therefore need, at this stage, to become responsible on such matters – to grow conscious of the current trends that they are using and to which they in their turn are contributing. It was one great virtue of the Marxist polymaths who arose in science before the Second World War – men like J.B.S. Haldane and J.D. Bernal – that they were aware of this need. They made great efforts to do justice to these issues in their doctrines. But the general discrediting of Marxist thought since that time has led to an unfortunate neglect of such wider problems, which is why Monod, in drawing on Existentialist ideas, did not feel any need to analyse them or to defend them against obvious objections. At the same time, an increased respect for science in our age has secured a large public ready to listen to the confident preachings of scientists on general subjects. The charismatic, ideological Last Chapter of scientific books has therefore now become accepted as an appropriate pulpit for these preachings, which sometimes pervade the rest of the book as well.

Conclusion

All this seems to me to lead to a rather important conclusion. This is that Monod's project failed not on account of any incompetence in him, but because what he aimed at is impossible. There is no way in which we humans can resolve the difficulty of finding an appropriate emotional attitude to the cosmos that we live in by simply refusing to have any such emotional attitude. We cannot – as he wished – take up a relation to the entire world around us which is purely cognitive, treating it quite dispassionately, merely as an object of enquiry. We cannot do this because we ourselves are part of it. We are not pure intellects but vulnerable, dependent creatures deeply involved in that world. Indeed, I do not think that it is clear that there could in principle be any such pure enquiring intellects, creatures moved only, or even primarily, by curiosity about particular facts. I doubt whether the idea of them makes sense. But whether it makes sense or not, we ourselves are certainly not such beings.

Two things follow. The first is that any attempt to produce this emotional neutrality by simply suppressing our natural reactions to the world will fail dangerously. It will not result in an emotional blank but, instead, in a different, and usually less suitable, emotional state, one drawn from another part of our social repertoire. As Bishop Butler noted, this is what tends to happen when sages try to suppress their natural human affections towards other people:

> Experience will show that, as want of natural appetite to food supposes and proceeds from some bodily disease, so the apathy the Stoics talk of as much supposes, or is accompanied with, somewhat amiss in the moral character, in that which is the health of the mind. Those who formerly aimed at this upon the foot of philosophy appear to have had *better success in eradicating the affections of tenderness and compassion than they had with the passions of pride and resentment.* These latter at the best were but concealed, and that imperfectly too.
>
> (Joseph Butler: *Sermon 5*, Section 11. Emphasis mine.)

The same thing surely holds with regard to the cosmos. Of course we can, if we wish, stop viewing the natural world around us with the mixture of awe, fear, respect and gratitude which has been the typical response found in most human cultures. And since the Enlightenment many people in our culture have indeed made great efforts to drop this kind of response in the name of 'disenchantment', as if this kind of awe were a superstition. But it is not open to us to avoid replacing it with other equally human emotional attitudes, for instance with envy, resentment, blank terror or pure predatory greed. The choice between these attitudes is a moral choice. It is the choice of a way of life, a choice of which attitude we think it good to live with. It is not a cognitive choice between various scientific hypotheses about the facts, so it cannot be determined by science.

The second point concerns personification. Since we are deeply social beings, our emotional attitudes always tend to take a personal form, even when they are not actually focused on our fellow human beings. We have just seen how this has happened in the case of the theorists that I have been discussing. And awe, respect and gratitude are attitudes that do naturally seem to demand some kind of a personal object. Obviously, this is one great source of religion. But in the various religions, personification plays very varying parts. Buddhism and Taoism play it down. Even within Christianity, there is a wide spectrum from believers like Kierkegaard who insist on 'the God of Abraham, Isaac and Jacob' to mystics who reject all such humanization. More widely, the notion of a guiding purpose in nature can be expressed on a similar spectrum running from a literal notion of Jehovah's creation to a vague and highly abstract conception of evolving forces of life. Most of us do not formulate any such idea at all clearly. But something like it is surely a general background assumption that underlies a great deal of our thinking.

The important thing here is that we should recognize the limitations of our powers and of our emotional language. In all the great religions, and no doubt in paganism too, serious people recognize that they are talking symbolically on these matters. They know that in regarding gods and goddesses as parents they are casting out a tiny net into a vast ocean of meaning. Nevertheless, that particular way of thinking does capture something of enormous importance – namely, that we are part of, and profoundly dependent on, a huge system which, in spite of its dangers, we do right to view as akin to us and as essentially benign. This has to be the best view because the alternatives – viewing it as malign, or as a dead, alien object – are seriously misleading and dangerous. Any errors which we may make as a result of respecting that system are (therefore) much less disastrous than those that would follow from viewing it as, in general, evil or alien to us. And viewing it with respect does tend to involve some kind of personification.

This point has come up interestingly lately in the response of the scientific community to James Lovelock's concept of Gaia – of life on earth as a self-maintaining system. Lovelock named his theory after the Greek earth-goddess, mother of gods and men, in the hope of bringing its meaning home to his audience. With the wider public this caught on quite quickly; many people found this imagery acceptable. Orthodox scientists, however, were so gravely disturbed by the imagery that they refused for a long time to look at the perfectly respectable scientific arguments which Lovelock brought forward for his detailed conclusions. After a time, however, these arguments began to be heard. Many of them are now accepted. But the scientific community still ducked the theory's name and associations. In his autobiography, Lovelock comments:

> As you now read, there are few scientists who doubt that the climate and chemical composition of the earth are coupled with the metabolism of the organisms that inhabit it, and the German systems scientist, John Schellnhuber, called it, in a *Nature* article, a new Copernican revolution .... In the thirty-five years of Gaia's existence as a theory, the view of the earth has changed profoundly. Yet so far only a tiny minority of scientists realize how much Gaia theory has helped to change their view. They have adopted my radical view of the earth without recognizing where it came from, and they have forgotten the scorn with which most of them greeted the idea of a self-regulating earth.
>
> (Lovelock 2000: 392)

It is interesting that this resistance came from a scientific community that was perfectly happy with the mass of lurid economic imagery that surrounded sociobiological concepts such as the selfish gene, a community that had also gladly received Monod's striking metaphors. These people did not object to colourful imagery as such. Metaphors did not bother them, so long as they were metaphors expressing the familiar clichés of Enlightenment individualism. The trouble with Lovelock's concept was that it contradicted those clichés. It called attention to an entity – the earth – which was not a voter, not a party to the social contract, not a standard, fully rational, adult human being operating on the stock exchange, but a wider whole, within which these adults are only tiny parts, a whole on which they are wholly dependent. This imaginative challenge was extremely frightening to contemporary Western thought. The easiest way to evade it was to simply declare that it was 'not science'. And indeed in the narrow sense of science as meaning merely the discovery of particular, 'value-free' facts, it was not. But that discovery never stands alone on the intellectual scene. It grows out of, and feeds into, a much wider landscape of imaginative visions, visions which determine the direction of our attention and the way we act. When we try to grapple with the problem of evil, these are the visions of which we need to be aware.

My point is not, of course, that scientists ought not to speak about things outside the detailed questions of 'normal science'. They cannot avoid doing that, because those questions are never isolated from their conceptual background. Larger issues are inevitably always coming up. Even the selection of topics always proceeds from a wide variety of reasons, so that there can be no such thing as total 'value freedom'. What is needed is that, when they do range into wider matters, these scientists should pick up the elements in background thought which are relevant to what they want to say and do justice to the questions that arise there. They should not depend on the authority that they have simply *as scientists* as a licence to settle questions which range far outside their discipline. Without some such caution there is surely a real danger today that this kind of casual theorizing can seriously erode the respect that is due to the authority of real science.

References

Atkins, P. (1987) *The Creation*, Oxford and San Francisco: W.H. Freeman.

Barrow, John D. and Tipler, Frank R. (1986) *The Anthropic Cosmological Principle*, Oxford: Oxford University Press.

Butler, Joseph *Sermons*.

Housman, A.E. *Last Poems*.

Huxley, T.H. (1893) *Evolution and Ethics*, London and New York: Macmillan.

Lovelock, James (2000) *Homage to Gaia: The Life of an Independent Scientist*, Oxford: Oxford University Press.

Monod, J. (1974) *Chance and Necessity*, trans. A. Wainhouse, London: Fontana.

Spencer, H. (1864) *Social Statics*, New York: D. Appleton.

Weinberg, S. (1977) *The First Three Minutes*, London: Andre Deutsch.

2

RESPONSE TO MARY MIDGLEY'S 'CRITICIZING THE COSMOS'

Silvia Völker

Let me begin by saying that I wholeheartedly agree with Mary Midgley's final conclusion that 'the authority that they have simply *as scientists*' is not 'a licence to settle questions which range far outside their discipline' and, I quote again, that 'this kind of casual theorizing can seriously erode the respect that is due to the authority of real science'. All too often the validity of this conclusion is illustrated by letters on the opinion pages of our daily newspapers, letters on socio-economic problems signed by persons flaunting their full academic titles earned in other fields, say Professor Doctor Engineer Nitwit. This, similarly, should be a warning for me when commenting on Midgley's thought-provoking contribution on the relation between man and nature: I am a down-to-earth physicist and unqualified as a philosopher of science. I am, therefore, going to be brief.

I agree with her that the last chapters of books by reputable natural scientists, in which they venture into the quicksand of philosophy, are not their most convincing. In particular, the animist tendency to personalize nature I reject.

Actually, to be sure what we were talking about in the symposium this book emerged from, I took a dictionary and looked up the three adjectives in its title ('Is Nature Ever Evil, Wrong or Ugly?'). According to *Webster's* their principal meanings are:

Evil: morally reprehensible; arising from bad character or conduct

Wrong: not according to the moral standard

Ugly: frightful. This word stems from the old Norse 'uggr', which means fear.

Clearly, an impersonal nature has no morals and thus cannot be qualified as either evil or wrong. But it very well can be ugly, as I have felt, for instance, on a stormy ocean with its fearsome breaking waves, or in the

27

mountains of Patagonia, where, as implied by the name, certain people ascribe human qualities to them, such as vanity and fickleness.

Coming back to the speaker's talk, I, as a physicist, want to stress that there is an important common aspect in the messages of both Monod and Weinberg: the element of chance in the processes that led to the appearance of mankind on earth.

Charles Darwin stated that natural selection depended on the accidental occurrence of variations in a species that were favourable to its interaction with the particular environment. Evolution is the result of a near-infinite sequence of such accidental events.

Accordingly, Weinberg concludes that human life is the outcome of a chain of accidents reaching back to the first three minutes, or in Monod's words: 'our number came up in the Monte Carlo game'. I think this stochastic point of view is scientifically correct. But once we humans had arrived here, it tells us nothing about our relation with the surrounding world. Thus, I do not agree with Monod when he says that 'we are radically cut off from the rest of nature'.

Like bees and other animals, our ancestors have developed a pattern of social conduct and moral values that suited the interaction with the environment. I think one should make a clear distinction between events that are unpredictable and events that are unaccountable.

The long-term dynamic behaviour of the majority of complex systems is essentially 'chaotic' by nature. Or more precisely, as Professor Benz points out in his contribution, it obeys non-linear equations. That is, in simple words: two systems that are very nearly equal at the beginning may be totally different after a length of time, even though they are governed by the same laws of physics. That evolution is such a chaotic process is well illustrated by the striking variations in the development of birds and insects on different islands, noted by both Alfred Wallace and Darwin.

That we humans are here and able to discuss these issues can be accounted for by the theory of evolution. But our presence could not be predicted from the conditions prevailing after Weinberg's 'first three minutes' or at some other early geological time.

3

MARY MIDGLEY ON SCIENCE, NATURE, METAPHYSICS AND ETHICS

Some comments

Hans Radder

I enjoyed reading Mary Midgley's straightforward and well-written critique of scientific critics of the cosmos. Her discussion of the world-views of Thomas Huxley, Jacques Monod and Steven Weinberg goes right to the heart of the matter. She convincingly questions the claimed neutrality of Monod's and Weinberg's scientist accounts of the relationship between humans and nature. Moreover, her alternative view – according to which human beings are necessarily embedded in, and essentially dependent on, nature – certainly has much to recommend it.

Yet, the issue of 'science, nature and human beings' is both complicated and delicate. For this reason, some of Midgley's arguments require further differentiation, while some others leave room for different conclusions. In this spirit, I would like to offer some brief comments on her paper in order to stimulate further discussion.

First, I would like to point to an important tension in Monod's approach, which is not taken into account in Midgley's discussion but which may serve to reinforce her main conclusion. On the one hand, Monod portrays human beings as 'totally solitary and fundamentally isolated'. As essentially disembodied and independent souls, they are necessarily alienated from the natural world. In this respect, Midgley rightly refers to the views of Sartre and Descartes.

On the other hand, a closer look at the quotations from Monod shows that what he opposes to nature is not individual human beings but 'morality, values, duties, rights and prohibitions'. Such terms, however, do not primarily characterize individuals but rather human communities and traditions. For example, defining human beings in terms of their values implies that they are seen as basically social beings, as living in and from the communities and traditions in which those values are embedded and embodied. Hence, it is misleading to describe them at the same time as being totally solitary and fundamentally isolated. Put differently, taking seriously our dependence on community and tradition is compatible with a nature–culture divide, but hardly with a Sartrean or Cartesian mind–body dichotomy. In Midgley's account, those two issues are not sufficiently distinguished either.

The underlying mistake is the slippage between characteristics of humanity as a whole and characteristics of individual human beings. The point is worth emphasizing, since the mistake is committed quite often, both by professional philosophers and by philosophizing scientists.

One of the major issues in Midgley's paper is the relationship between science and metaphysics or ethics. Regarding this issue two lines of argumentation can be found. The first seems to posit a straightforward opposition of science to metaphysics and ethics. Thus, Monod's and Weinberg's views are said to belong to metaphysics and ethics rather than science. In the same vein, Barrow and Tipler's arguments for a strong anthropic principle are criticized as being non-scientific, moral and metaphysical propaganda. Finally, Spencer's sociobiological moral views are claimed to lack any roots in real biology. All this suggests a strong contrast between 'real science' on the one hand and metaphysics and ethics on the other.

In spite of this, the paper contains a second and more differentiated approach to the issue of the relationship between science and philosophy. According to the last two sections in particular, value-laden points of view are unavoidable in, and ineliminable from, scientific practice. Even normal science is always practised against a broader background that includes certain metaphysical and ethical premises. More generally, the claim is that dispassionate inquiry is impossible in principle because scientists are not purely intellectual beings.

Hence, this second approach admits that science and philosophy are not fully separate and cannot be simply opposed. Now, however, Midgley's point is that science does not *dictate* its own metaphysics or ethics. This means that we need to argue for a particular metaphysical interpretation or a specific ethical position. Some arguments are better than others, however, and good metaphysical or ethical arguments need to employ the acknowledged skills and insights of philosophy. Hence, scientists who embark on this terrain should be aware of this and be philosophically knowledgeable and accountable.

I think that the second approach to the issue of the relationship between science and metaphysics or ethics is much more promising than the first. Within this approach, Midgley goes on to claim that Monod's and Weinberg's metaphysics is bad philosophy, and that the view she advocates constitutes the best alternative: nature is akin to us and it is essentially benign. Her alternative is based on the premise that, according to post-Darwinian evolutionary biology, there is a continuity between nature and human beings. A kinship exists between humans and (other) animals, and perhaps even between humans and non-living things.

As such, the statement that 'humans are part of nature' is surely correct. Yet, as it stands it is rather vague as well, and it certainly needs further articulation. For instance, when Midgley moves from 'our dependence on nature' to 'our kinship with nature' and from there to the claim that 'nature is essentially benign', she takes two crucial steps that are hardly argued for. But in which sense precisely is nature akin and benign to us and what exactly does this imply with respect to the character and role of morality, values, meaning, etc.? More generally, the critical question is whether or not morality, values and meaning can be *fully* derived from, and justified by, our evolution as physical and biological organisms? In this respect, it is unclear how much naturalism Midgley is willing to endorse.

The point is important because human beings may both be part of nature and transcend nature in certain respects. After all, one may plausibly argue that (natural and cultural) evolution has produced genuine novelty, in particular mind and language. On the basis of their mental and linguistic competence human beings are able to reflect on their own existence vis-à-vis the universe. This capacity for self-reflection enables them to be aware of their mortality and finiteness and to give meaning to events and processes over and above their physical or biological significance. While mind and meaning are certainly constrained by natural processes, it is highly questionable whether they ever will or can be fully explained in naturalistic terms. For this reason, although I agree that humans are part of nature, I also think that the general intuition underlying the views of Monod and Weinberg is dismissed a bit too quickly. The challenge is to develop a differentiated view that takes account of the various ways in which we are simultaneously embedded in and go beyond the natural world.

In sum, while most of Midgley's criticisms of the scientistic critics of the cosmos are pertinent, her own solutions to the problems in question are not always sufficiently clear and well developed to be fully convincing. Without further articulation her basic premise that we are part of nature is as undifferentiated and hence as unhelpful as the presupposition of her adversaries that we are opposed to nature.

4

MIND AND VALUE

Reflections on Max Weber

Joachim Leilich

To the title of this book – *Is Nature Ever Evil?* – my spontaneous reaction was no. When I reflected on the reason why I thought that the answer should be no, the reason which seemed to me most convincing was that in nature there is no mind, and that where there is no mind there can't be value (moral or aesthetic) either. I asked myself whether – for example – in a world in which survived the music of Bach's Goldberg variations but in which there was no longer a mind to listen to it, this beautiful music would have a value. It seemed to me that this couldn't be the case. Could – to take another example – a flower be beautiful if there are no longer eyes to look, nor noses to smell? Could in a world without a conscious mind there be something like a beautiful object or something having an aesthetic value? My spontaneous reaction told me that this 'obviously' couldn't be the case. The next step in my reflection was that the realm of nature is free of mind. Of course this thesis is problematic but I will try to give a rather trivial interpretation of it later. But now, if (1) the realm of nature is free of mind, and if (2) the possibility of value presupposes mind, then (3) in nature (as far as it is viewed not in connection with externally imposed values) there can't be value. The result of this preliminary reflection seems to be an anthropocentric view on values. Without something like a human (or human-like) mind there can't be value. But isn't relating everything to our human interests and values not just one of the reasons that nature is endangered? Don't we need a concept of value which is free from human interests and human points of view in order to have, for example, a true environmental ethics?

Value-freedom and the social sciences

In the full title of our book there is something like a shift of focus between the main title and the subtitle. In the first part of the title – *Is Nature Ever Evil?* – the subject we are speaking about is *nature*. In the second part of the title – *Religion, Science, and Value* – the subject matter is the *science* of nature. The title makes a connection between nature and the study of nature. The question is whether nature should (or could) be studied with the ideal of value-free objectivity. (To my ears the title even suggests – intentionally or not – that only if the answer to the first question is 'yes', could we answer to the second question that natural science shouldn't be exercised in a 'neutral' manner.) This discussion, of course, has a famous forerunner: the dispute about value-freedom in the social sciences. The classic author here is Max Weber and his well-known – but not always well-understood – postulate of value-freedom, that is the demand that social scientists should abstain from value-judgements about their subject matter (that is social reality). Here the suspicion from the so-called critical social science was (or is) that such neutrality would be bad for social reality itself, because such a neutral stance would affirm what is not just in society. Such a value-neutral social science would not, as social scientists wrongy think, describe or explain in a neutral manner what is the case, but would contribute to an unjust society which they (the scientists) think they only describe. From this 'critical' point of view neutral social science becomes guilty. The analogy to nature and natural science from this point of view is whether a natural scientist who subscribes to the ideal of objectivity or neutrality becomes guilty of the destruction of nature. So, I hope, throwing in a view on the social sciences may perhaps help us to become more clear about our issue: nature and natural science.

Weber's doctrine is so often misrepresented and misunderstood that it seems necessary to remind ourselves what Weber's doctrine amounts to (see Weber 1968), as described in the important papers 'Die "Objektivität" sozialwissenschaftlicher und sozialpolitischer Erkenntnis' (1904) and 'Der Sinn der "Wertfreiheit" der soziologischen und ökonomischen Wissenschaften' (1918). Surely Weber's doctrine does not imply – as is sometimes stated (Schmidt 1974: 537) – that scientists should be indifferent to whether the results of science have bad or good consequences, as if – for example – Weber wanted to say that in genetic research we shouldn't bother about the risks. This was surely neither Weber's opinion nor an unintended consequence of his thought. Reminding ourselves that Weber was a defender of an ethics of responsibility (*Verantwortungsethik*) should be argument enough that Weber didn't want to release scientists from (social) responsibility. I shall try, as briefly as possible, to make clear what Weber's thesis of value-freedom means and what it does not mean.

Value-free science does not mean (Weber 1968: 499) that science itself is something to which no value can be assigned. Treating something in a scientific spirit, being objective, etc. are of course themselves (scientific) values. Weber's thesis doesn't deny that scientific activities themselves are value-laden. Nor does value-freedom mean that what we study or investigate should or could be chosen in the spirit of value-freedom. We do, for example, medical research because we want to struggle against dangerous diseases. Here health obviously functions as a value. Perhaps we study social psychology because we want to fight against racism, or we study economic mechanisms because we want to reduce unemployment, or maybe we choose a theme because it is neglected in the history of our discipline. Insofar as the question is 'What do we want to study (and why)?', value-freedom is impossible. So we shouldn't use such considerations as arguments against the possibility of value-freedom.

Weber's conception of social science is much more critical than most of its critics think. Even from the point of view of value-free social science, the social scientist has an important critical function. This critical function is exercised within the context of means and ends. The (social) scientist can (and should) criticize means, if he has good reasons to think that by those means the intended end is not reached. Judgements like 'with these means you won't stop inflation' or 'with these laws you can't stop this kind of criminality' are fully compatible with the postulate of value-freedom as understood by Weber. Even more, from Weber's point of view the scientists are obliged to direct our attention to unintended consequences of the means we use. It is not forbidden for a value-free scientist to say, for example, that the construction of a new airport near the sea will endanger or destroy a certain species of waterbird or that the 'Schengen agreements' about abolishing border controls will facilitate some criminal actions (for example, drug trafficking). If the scientists didn't have the right to say things in this spirit, they couldn't be responsible – and of course, even according to Weber (1968: 149ff), they should be.

What the postulate of value-freedom amounts to is simply that the scientist can't say (as a scientist) which values we should favour or violate, and which not (Weber 1968: 149ff). Take the example of the construction of a new airport. There are reasons to construct new airports and of course, inevitably, they have to do with values. There can be so much traffic that there is a risk to the life of the passengers. By constructing an airport a city can become more attractive for investments, which will increase prosperity. With a second airport there will be less noise at the first, and so on, so constructing the second airport favours some values. But inevitably it also endangers other values: there will be more noise in other parts of the country, more traffic means more pollution, more pollution means more danger for some species, and so on. By taking decisions we always create a conflict of values. If we decide that abortion should be legal, we favour the value of individual autonomy of mothers, who can decide themselves whether they want to continue with a pregnancy or not. But with the same decision we violate the value of unborn human life. So the problem for Weber is this: which function does the scientist have if there is a conflict of values (and such a conflict always arises if we take decisions and act). Value-freedom means that scientists can only make us aware of which values are served and which values are violated if we decide for or against something. But because the question as to which of the opposing values we should serve isn't a scientific question, scientists must be silent concerning the question of what we must do. They say: if you do A, you serve this value and you violate the other. But as scientists they can't say more. If they do say more, then, and only then, they act against the postulate of value-freedom. The social scientist speaks about values in the sense of preparing a balance (the pros and cons), but he or she doesn't articulate value-judgements. What we want to do is a question of will, not of science. But of course science will have an influence on what we want to do. Often we no longer want something once we are informed about the risks or consequences. And here, of course, lies the important critical function of scientists as specialists. But this critical function is fully compatible with Weber's view that science should be value-free.

Nature, culture and value

The main theme in my reflection on Max Weber lies elsewhere, however. Let us ask whether we can transfer Weber's discussion of value-freedom from the social sciences to the natural sciences. It seems to me we can't, and the answer to the question of why we can't leads to my central topic, 'Mind and Value' (and gives the clue to what I mean if I say that nature is a realm which is free of mind). It seems to me that it is not by accident – for example, because he was a social scientist – that Weber confines himself to the discussion of the social sciences. From Weber's point of view a problem of value, and by consequence a problem of value-freedom, can't even arise in the natural sciences. In order to plead for this standpoint, I shall use a very general distinction, which lies from my point of view – and probably from Weber's too – at the basis of the discussion about value. The general distinction I want to discuss is the one between that which is dependent on the human mind and that which is not. A lot of objects are mind-dependent in the sense that they are intentional actions or the result of action. Trivially, without mind there wouldn't be action, because we only call action that which is intentional (a hiccough is unintentional and that's why it isn't action; writing a paper is intentional and is therefore true action). The existence of works of art is dependent on action and consequently on intentional mind. All kinds of institutions, for example parliaments, courts of justice or conferences, depend on human purposive intention. The same is the case with large parts of history, language and economics. Here we are dealing with the realm called *Geisteswissenschaften* or the realm of cultural sciences. (Weber was at home in the discussions about methodological differences between natural science and humanities, mainly through neo-Kantian influences.) The distinction I propose (of course it isn't my invention, I simply propose to use it) is the distinction between culture and nature (the objects of the social sciences, society, law, economics, are of course products of culture, which means products of mind).

The difference between culture and nature is a good starting point for a discussion of the problem of value and mind. If we use this distinction, there is a quite natural way to understand why in nature there is no mind (and no value) but in culture there is. If we are confronted with the results of human intentional or purposive action, we always have the *conceptual* possibility of raising questions of value. We can ask meaningfully whether a law is just, whether a piece of literature is so good that we should read it, whether the minister has taken a good decision, whether it would be better to sell stocks now, and so on. Such questions have to do with values of different sorts (aesthetic, ethical, rational ones). We can't avoid such questions and that's why the problem of value-freedom exists in the humanities and the social sciences. Social science, according to Weber, should be value-free just because the objects of the social sciences are value-laden. (If there wasn't value in acting and deciding, questions of value couldn't meaningfully arise.)

But now consider nature. Take a natural law, for example the law that says something about the connection between heat and pressure in a gas. That pressure increases with temperature is a fact, but this fact doesn't depend on mind. And because it doesn't depend on mind, there is no conceptual possibility of discussing questions of value. Should we praise nature because its laws are beautiful? Calling laws beautiful seems something like a category mistake. Should (or better could) we blame (or praise) nature because there is a lawful connection between heat and pressure? Should (or could) we call nature rational because it is governed by laws? Should we call light rational because it takes the shortest route? It seems to me that conceptually we don't have these possibilities. Nature can't be wrong. (And of course it can't be right either. If you can't be wrong, you can't be right.)

In Weber's thought the central category is the will (1968: 157). The realm of culture and of society exists because there is the phenomenon of will. And where there is will, there is the phenomenon of value too (they come together). And will, of course, is an aspect of mental life, an aspect of mind. If we were to conceptualize nature as a result of will, the difference between nature and culture would break down. For example, if we think laws of nature exist because God created them for some purpose, we could immediately use value-laden categories. We could praise this god as we can praise a craftsman for his work, or we might blame him because there are earthquakes. If behind the phenomena of lightning and thunder there was a god-like mind, then of course we had better not provoke it. From this point of view, the price of having values in nature would be to turn the history of science back to a pre-scientific mentality. But, of course, the world of the natural sciences is a disenchanted (*entzauberte*) world, to use Weber's famous words.

There is another, more trivial, way to introduce the possibility of speaking of values in nature. I am thinking of cases where the human mind uses nature for its own purposes. If you want to make good wine, weather conditions should be favourable. The climate of Amsterdam probably isn't good enough for winemakers, and nor is the climate in the Sahara. We can say that a natural phenomenon – for example weather – is good (or bad) if we put it into the means–end relation of human purposive action or more general human values. But being good here means not being good in itself, but being good insofar as it serves human ends. (I will return later to this point in discussing the question of whether we can speak of purposes in nature without any relation to an evaluating mind.)

The upshot of all this is that value is *conceptually* related to mind and that, therefore, in the realm of nature (conceptualized as a realm which is free of human intentions or intentional minds) we have no conceptual possibility of speaking of values. The language game of appraisal only functions in human contexts; not for the trivial reason that humans are the only ones who can 'appraise' someone or something, the only ones who can formulate value-judgements, but because, so to speak, values are ontologically mind-dependent. Value-*judgements*, of course, are mind-dependent, because there is no judgement without mind. What I mean is that the values we speak about are mind-dependent too. My point is a *conceptual* one. It's not at all my intention to defend forms of anthropocentrism or species egoism. My point is that the use of a certain concept (in this case, value) presupposes the possibility of using other concepts that have essentially to do with mind. There is a 'conceptual connection' between the two concepts (value and mind) and using the one necessitates the possibility of using the other.

The result of the discussion so far is that in nature there is no intentional or purposive mind – and therefore no value either. A consequence of this is that in the natural sciences we can't have value-judgements because there is no subject matter which could correspond to those judgements. This point of view is only plausible if we make a sharp distinction between natural science and technology. Technology, of course, belongs to the realm of culture and is value-laden. We can ask which values are served by which technology, and we can and should give warnings if we have reason to think that some technologies are dangerous. Technology has to do with means and ends – i.e. a mind's means and ends – and so values come into play. We can use the pressure of a gas for an end (as in some sprays), the pressure of a gas can be useful if we use it instrumentally, but in pressure itself, without relation to a mind, there is no value. Nature is value-free, technology isn't, because in the first there are no means and ends, but in the second there are. Of course the central question now is whether we are really unable to speak of ends in nature, ends which are independent of human ends and human minds. I'll finish my paper with a discussion of this problem.

Taking Bach's cantatas seriously

A lot of people who work in the field of environmental ethics or ecological movements think that such a view as I have articulated lies at the core of our nature-destroying forces, because we think too anthropocentrically; we think that the only values are our values. My conceptual investigation doesn't necessarily imply an anthropocentric vision (with its negative, species-egoistic connotation). But it is certainly an anthropogenic argument. (For the difference between anthropocentric and anthropogenic, see Rolston 1994.) All values are rooted in a context in which there is a relation to a mind (and so far in evolutionary history only we humans possess a mind of the appropriate sort). But in nature it seems there are phenomena which give us the possibility of speaking about value without the human mind. (Again, to speak you need a mind of course – the question is whether the phenomenon you speak about is possible without mind.) We are used to thinking about natural processes in terms of needs and purposes, mainly in biological contexts. The flower needs water for its existence. Water is a value for flowers. It would be bad for the flower, if we were to disturb its life by denying it water. Some organisms need hearts to survive, and a heart which doesn't function well is not a good heart. Isn't nature wrong if it gives an organism a heart that doesn't serve its purpose? Lions suffering from heart problems will have trouble hunting.

Do we not have in (mind-independent) nature processes which can be translated into the language of purpose, the language of means and ends, do we not need a teleological vocabulary to do justice to nature? Roots of plants and hearts don't have minds, but they serve purposes. But does a heart, in order to serve its purpose, need a relation to a mind?

It seems that the possibility of applying the concept of natural, non-intentional purposes is sufficient to give us the possibility of speaking of values in a manner which is 'mind-free'. A mixture of sunshine and rain is good not only for winemakers, but also for the plants, independent of our human purposes. Hearts that are insufficient are bad for the lions themselves, independently of our own values and our minds. Of course, as we all know, after Darwin the notion of purposes in natural processes is dubious and probably most scientists tend to eliminate all teleological terminology in favour of pure efficient causality.

John Searle in his *The Construction of Social Reality* (1995) has given an analysis of natural purposiveness that can serve in our context as an argument in favour of the 'anthropogenic' view (the view that all value is mind-dependent). For Searle the difference between the (mind-free) causal story and the (mind-laden) teleological story has do to with the fact that in the teleological story a description is given by imposing a value to a causal fact. As the terminology already says, the value is imposed, which has to be done by someone. As a value it can't exist without the imposing mind. Let's look at how Searle sees this relation.

According to Searle, functions – as, for example, the function of the heart to pump blood – 'are never intrinsic to the physics of any phenomenon, but are assigned from outside by conscious observers and users' (1995: 14). Causality belongs intrinsically to physics. Causal events in nature happen independently of our thought. The heart pumps blood whether or not we think or know it does. The question is whether a heart can have the *function* to pump blood independently of thought. Following Searle, if we speak about functions, we do more than merely report some causal processes. If we say it is the heart's function to pump blood, 'we are situating these facts relative to a system of values that we hold' (1995: 15). Searle's point is that causality plus values, added from outside, yields talk of functions (or teleology/purposiveness). This is very plausible and not at all problematic where we make use of something. I use, for example, wood to make fire. The burning of the wood and the heat are the causal aspects. But, of course, trees don't naturally have the function to serve as burning material. If I impose this function on trees, then we can say that certain pieces of wood are good because they serve the purpose better. The value-judgement that the wood is good can't be independent of the function I impose on it. If I impose on my trees the function not to serve as burning material but to serve for the production of fruits, then it is surely not good if the trees are used as burning material.

So we have on the one hand value-free causal talk, but by imposing a function values come into play. I chose the tree example so that we would not be inclined to think that trees naturally serve the purpose to burn. But what about the fruits and the roots? Is the teleology of the life of plants imposed by us or intrinsic to nature? Is the function of the heart (which makes it possible to speak of good or bad hearts) imposed by us or intrinsic? Astonishingly, Searle sees no fundamental difference. We can only speak of the function of the heart because *we value* life and we can only speak of good or bad hearts because we value survival and health. If we really longed for death – as in some of J.S. Bach's beautiful cantatas, such as 'Ich habe genug' (BWV 8 and 82) and 'Komm, o süsse Todesstunde' (BWV 161) – then we could say that it is the function of heart diseases to bring us nearer to the goal and good hearts would be bad because they prevent the death we are longing for. Life is no more an intrinsic goal of nature than death. It's only if we value the one more than the other that we can speak of hearts which do the work of pumping better or worse.

Of course this analysis fits well my intention to argue that when we speak of values, there is always a more or less hidden reference to mind.

Taking Bach's cantatas seriously – and why shouldn't we? – demonstrates that the strategy of introducing non-anthropogenic values with the help of the notion of natural purposes is not without problems. I don't want these remarks to be understood as a form of relativism or subjectivism. Pleading that there is a necessary connection between value and mind doesn't automatically mean that something is only a value because we value it.

References

Rolston III, H. (1994) *Conserving Natural Value*, New York: Columbia U.P.

Schmidt, H. (ed.) (1974), *Philosophisches Wörterbuch*, lemma 'Rationalismus', 16th edn, Stuttgart: Kröner.

Searle, J.R. (1995) *The Construction of Social Reality*, London: Penguin.

Weber, M. (1968) *Gesammelte Aufsätze zur Wissenschaftslehre*, Tübingen: Mohr.

5

THE MORAL RELEVANCE
OF NATURALNESS

Tatjana Visak

'How natural is a dairy cow?' Participants in the seminar kept repeating this question after it was put forward from the audience during one of the first lectures. This seemingly odd question touches some of the central issues. (1) What is 'nature' or 'natural'? We are in need of a workable definition of these central terms. (2) Does it matter morally whether something is 'natural' or not? We need to know whether the label 'natural' can ever be of moral relevance and – if so – when. Most of the contributors were in one way or the other confronted with these questions. They had to take a stance. Rarely, however, did any of the contributors attempt to answer these questions in an explicit way. In the present paper an explicit attempt is made to deal with these issues.

What is natural?

During the seminar there was great confusion about the question 'What is natural?' While nature was a central issue of the seminar, it was not at all clear what nature actually is. While everyone may have some implicit ideas about what nature is, during the seminar not a single definition of nature was given. Some contributors claimed that nature no longer exists, not at any rate in the Netherlands. Everything seems to be influenced by human beings. Even so called 'nature reserves' are really parks planned and managed by people. On the other hand, it was claimed that everything is natural. Human beings as an animal species are as natural as the rest of nature and it is natural for humans to influence or even 'recreate' nature. Thus, bombs made by humans are as natural as beavers and their dams. In one way nothing and in another way everything seems to be natural. How can one make sense of this paradox?

It is important to be aware of the conceptual difference between what we call 'nature' and what we call 'natural'. Evidently, the first is a noun and the second is an adjective. 'Nature' refers to something specific. As with all nouns, we use 'nature' for a class of things with certain characteristics. A possible characteristic of nature may be that it blossoms spontaneously. ('Blossom' here doesn't imply a value-judgement. It stands for all spontaneous development, thus also for what we call 'decay'.) Spontaneous blossoming can happen at different levels. There might be trees that grow and develop spontaneously in a forest that as such has been planned and managed. There might be a tree that was planted but which from this point on shows spontaneous growth and development. In this sense nature still exists, even in the garden called 'the Netherlands'. Human beings can be classified as nature, insofar as (on certain levels) they (as 'things out there') blossom spontaneously. The adjective 'natural' can be used in several ways. It may refer to what is made from nature or what is happening in nature.

One particular definition of 'natural' that was also used during the conference may be 'species-specific'. All kinds of human behaviour can be considered 'natural' in the sense of being 'species-specific', as they may be part of the way in which humans deal with their environment. Humans as an animal species have certain characteristics which determine their species-specific way of being and living. It seems to be specific for our species that we can use tools and technology. In this sense it is natural that we (can) make bombs. It is also species-specific that we can use moral reasoning. As humans we show our species-specific way if we are allowed to be and live freely. It should be clear that a human being kept in chains in a dark room for a long period couldn't show much of his or her species-specific ways. With this adjective, as with the noun, there are several levels of naturalness. The human being mentioned above can show a species-specific way of coping with that extraordinary situation. But that is far removed from any self-realization. On a more profound level, this human being cannot be and live in a species-specific way. If all humans were kept like this, it wouldn't even be clear what the species-specific way of humans really is.

Non-human animals, like humans, have their species-specific ways of living. Besides, the fact that something is species-specific for one species doesn't mean that it cannot (to any extent) be species-specific for another species as well. We can get to know their species-specific ways if we watch these animals in their natural (species-specific) environment. For sparrows it is species-specific to fly around and for pigs it is species-specific to wallow in mud. What, however, is the natural behaviour of species that are as such not wholly natural? The so-called 'dairy cow' can serve as an example. It follows from what has been said above that the dairy cow blossoms spontaneously only to a limited degree. She did not appear spontaneously, but her birth was timed and planned. (This does not analogically imply that human babies that are timed and planned are less natural than ones that are not. It is the species-specific way of humans and not of cows to time and plan and, more importantly, the criteria that lie at the basis of that timing and planning are human criteria.) Even at the level of her genes the dairy cow's spontaneity is limited by way of selective interbreeding and/or genetic engineering. Some aspects of the cow are still 'natural', which means that in these respects the cow is blossoming spontaneously. Even a cow as a semi-artefact can be and live in a more or less species-specific way. Her species-specific way can be determined by what her free (and less artificial) counterparts do. Another possibility of finding out her species-specific way would be to constrain her as little as possible in order to learn how she would behave normally.

In what sense is 'naturalness' morally relevant?

As with the question 'What is natural?', there is great confusion about when – if at all – naturalness can be morally relevant.

Referring to something's naturalness is very often misplaced with regard to morals. In the search for moral guidelines for our behaviour, it does not make any sense to say 'Bombs are natural'. It may be debated as to whether they show spontaneous blossoming and whether they are made from natural ingredients. It may be said that it is part of our species-specific way that we can think and use tools and thus make bombs. However, the capability of moral reasoning is species-specific for us as well. Holmes Rolston rightly says that we are called *Homo sapiens* – the wise species – and that as such we may appear to be a threat. But, as Rolston points out, we are the 'ethical species' as well. Without reference to further norms cotton is not better than plastic. The justification that 'genetic engineering' happens in nature doesn't imply that human scientists ought to do it as well. Thus, even if we *can* make bombs and even if they are natural in one sense or other, we must still decide whether we *ought to* make them or not. It makes little sense to claim that humans are or are not 'natural' or to claim that in Holland there is nothing natural anyway. Even if these claims were right, the question would be 'So what?' It is problematic to refer to nature as a moral example and to equate 'natural' with morally good and 'unnatural' with morally bad.

There is one way, however, in which the pointing to naturalness can be morally relevant. It can be morally relevant to refer to 'naturalness' in the sense of 'species-specific way'. If we want to show any respect for others we should at least pay attention to their species-specific way. As humans we can use our capability of sympathy and moral reasoning. As for non-human animals, their species-specific way can serve as a point of reference when we choose how to treat or not to treat them. 'Naturalness' in the sense of 'species-specific way' appears to be very appropriate as a moral guideline. More than other guidelines it helps us with the setting of goals and limits for *our* species-specific way of using technology. Respect for the species-specific way of other beings can even guide our human tendency to recreate nature.

Take, for instance, the example of the dairy cow: it follows that it is not appropriate to call a dairy cow 'natural' in any normative sense. The whole idea of a cow being a dairy cow indicates a lack of understanding of what a cow really is. If a cow has been pregnant she produces milk, just as a human female does. Naturally she is no more a 'dairy cow' than a human female is a 'milk woman'. Claiming that it is natural for her to fill a bucket with milk because 'a cow can be very successful in this', as the primatologist Van Hooff said at our conference, is to argue from either an anthropocentric or a reductionist point of view. A cow that is forced to give milk by humans is usually doing no more than coping in her species-specific way with the strains that are put on her. In order to take 'naturalness' seriously as a moral guideline we should interpret it as holistically as possible. The spontaneous blossoming of the cow should not be reduced to the meaningless level of some of her bodily functions. The functioning of the cow should not be evaluated from an anthropocentric point of view (as functional for us). Finally, the species-specific way should be seen as a given fact and not as something to be manipulated at human will.

The assumption that the species-specific way should be respected as a given fact is in line with what Rolston prescribes as 'building our culture in intelligent harmony' with nature. This is of special importance for scientists who consider themselves 'co-creators', trying to improve nature (see the contributions by Brooke, ten Kate and Hefner). In order to take the role of a co-creator it would be necessary to know the ultimate aim of creation. How anthropocentric or self-centred would the co-creators be? How much understanding and overview would they really have? Van Hooff's claims about the effectiveness (and thus 'naturalness') of a cow giving milk may show that without a proper understanding of the species-specific way of the cow there cannot be proper respect.

Acknowledgement

I am very much indebted to Thijs Visser and Henk Verhoog. They discuss the moral relevance of naturalness in Visser, M.B.H. and Verhoog, H. (1999) *De Aard van het Beestje – de Morele Relevantie van Natuurlijkheid*, Den Haag: NWO Ethiek en Beleid.

6

THE EXPERIENCE OF NATURE
A hermeneutic approach

Angela Roothaan

In this paper I want to reflect on the concept of nature from the point of view of human experience. What kind of experiences are being expressed in the scientific, as well as in the everyday, concept of nature? How does this concept function in the orientation of human beings in their life-world? How is such an orientation structured? And, what does this mean for the concept of nature in contemporary culture? These questions indicate the direction of what follows.

I will start with a general discussion of how 'experience' and 'orientation' can be connected. The idea outlined here is that human orientation has three central aspects: a moral, a spiritual and an epistemic one. In these aspects human experience of life is sedimented. Subsequently, I will narrow down my reflection to the different meanings 'nature' has had in Western cultural and intellectual tradition. I will propose an articulation of the concept of nature in which 'alterity' is introduced. This expresses, in my opinion, present-day experience of nature more adequately. With this concept of nature in mind, I will look into the moral and spiritual aspects of the scientific knowledge of nature. To conclude, the connection of the three aspects will be investigated in a case study from a field where science and everyday experience meet: medical technology. There the consequences of adopting the proposed view of nature are illustrated.

Experience of life and epistemic orientation

When we reflect on human beings as beings who interact with each other and with their non-human surroundings, we may notice that this interaction presupposes that human beings are able to orientate themselves in the network of potential relations that is their world. For a person to relate to his or her world, he or she has to have some kind of mental and emotional map that contains information on important spots and persons, on how things work, on ways of going about projects and shortcuts. This map reflects the human being's orientation.

A very important aspect of this orientation is the epistemic aspect. A person's map has to consist of knowledge. This knowledge may be scientific, based on science, or based on what we have learned from others and from everyday experience. I will put forward the view that, besides the epistemic aspect, human orientation also has a moral and a spiritual aspect. This means that a person's knowledge of the world is intertwined with an orientation of one's actions towards what one believes to be morally good, and also with an intimate personal orientation on what one holds to be good and true in life.

Here I will deal primarily with the epistemic aspect of human orientation. This aspect is about building theories and assessing facts. This may concern everyday facts and theories like the knowledge that it will not rain every single day of the year or the theory that children learn by making mistakes. It may also concern facts and theories which are developed and tested scientifically. In the following I will initially refrain from discriminating between these two kinds of epistemic orientation and ask how such an orientation functions in human life.

When people are in the process of drawing their epistemic map of the world, they orientate themselves in terms of what I call their experience of life. When we say that someone has a lot of experience, this does not mean that this person has simply undergone many life-changing events, but, rather, that he or she has interpreted life's events in such a way that he or she has gained a frame of meaning which makes it possible to deal with past as well as with future events. This is shown by the fact that another common term for experience of life is 'wisdom', which in turn comes close to the traditional philosophical concept of 'prudence'. Prudence is a concept which stems from Aristotelian practical philosophy, meaning knowing from experience what to do at what moment. Like this Aristotelian concept, our 'experience of life' has a relation to an individually or a commonly held idea of 'the good life'.

Experience of life can be understood as ordered around highs and lows. While living one's life, one goes through events that make an impression, that change one's life, such as the loss of a beloved person, the experience of being loved, or of being frustrated in an important life-project. Such interpreted experiences provide one with a frame to make sense of other experiences. I consciously write here about *interpreted* experience, for I think that the moment of interpretation not only changes the experience but is also necessary to turn it into a point of reference that can be a constitutive element of a frame of meaning. To give an example, losing someone by death changes in aspect from the moment that one says to oneself 'now I am alone in this world', or, if the person restricted me, 'now I am free to go my own way'. The brief story one tells oneself, or that one tells to other persons, is the start of an interpretative process, in which the importance of the event is diminished or extended, romanticized or neutralized.

That I write here of the importance of the interpretative moment does not mean that I could organize or invent my 'life story' in an arbitrary manner. Events come to me independently of my wish, and it is not in my power to choose what will make a large impression on me or what will change my life. In telling others what happened to me, or even in telling myself (like at the point in time in which I 'decide' to label this particular unnerving feeling as 'having fallen in love'), however, I change things in such a way that they now have gone through my reflection. By having told the story, I have changed things effectively, not just psychologically. If, for instance, I tell a friend that 'I am in love', my relationships with several people (the friend, the object of the infatuation and myself; even with others, for instance with my spouse, or, if I am a young person, with my parents, etc.) change, as well as the way I behave towards them.

Overwhelming experiences may be turned into a frame which makes it possible to give meaning to other experiences. Take the case of a man who thinks: 'Since the death of my father, when I was a child, I have lost my direction in life. Breaking up with my wife, changing my field of study two times, and changing jobs every three years, these were all instances of this insecurity that started with the death of my father.' In the same manner, interpreted experience will function as a frame of meaning when one has to express and interpret new experiences. Thus a person's experience of life forms the instrument by which one classifies and evaluates the knowledge which will make up one's epistemic orientation.

It is important to stress that experience as it is talked about here is experience that has already been interpreted and expressed in language (be it mentally, spoken, written or typed). This means that my approach to epistemic orientation combines elements from two 'continental' philosophical movements, namely from phenomenology and hermeneutics. Let us try to characterize these movements very briefly. If we had to do this in one word, we could link the first one with the word 'experience' and the second one with 'interpretation'. Historically, in its development by Husserl, phenomenology was designed as a method which was to provide philosophy with the means to get into contact with objective experience, with 'things themselves'. The idea was that the philosopher should confront himself with reality as such, in order to arrive at a kind of scientific philosophical knowledge. The aim of this project was to present an alternative to philosophy (as it was often considered in those days) as a world-view, as a system of meaning.

Hermeneutics, by contrast, is, through its development, concerned with meaning, expressed as it is in texts, in texts of law, in the text of the Bible, and in cultural symbols as such. The hermeneutical investigator looks for intentions, rather than for phenomena. This does not of course make his or her work necessarily less scientific. Neither does it make his or her philosophy express a world-view. The difference is that the perspective of hermeneutics is not directed towards objectivity, but towards elucidation of intended, subjective meaning.

There are those who see hermeneutics as an interpretation of human experience which may disclose the intrinsic value of things. This is, in fact, a phenomenology which has incorporated the hermeneutic act as a moment of the phenomenological process. As may be clear, I took the element of experience from phenomenology and the element of interpretation from hermeneutics, but by using an element from a third philosophical movement, from deconstructivism, my approach differs from the 'intrinsic value' one.

This third element lies in the observation that all interpretation is embodied in some form of material symbolic expression, that is, in language. Symbolic expression makes use of material signs, which can only function as bearers of meaning because we interpret them. This interpretation functions by way of shifts and transfers, which makes meaning unobtainable in a pure, unambiguous form. Therefore, deconstructivist philosophy stresses the potentiality of language to produce meaning as well as nonsense in any communication. In each transfer of meaning there is always a chance of being understood as well as of being misunderstood. Expressed meanings (may) take on slightly (or radically) different contents when taken up by other people. And, in fact, this is not a failure of communication, but rather the precondition for transferring meaning at all.

For the theme of this section, the relation between experience of life and epistemic orientation, this means that we explain shifts in meaning not only from new experiences, but also from the symbolic expression of these interpreted experiences. To return to my previous example, suppose that a man who blames his loss of direction on the early death of his father later in life reads a book about 'direction in early twentieth century spiritual life' and consequently starts to give a negative meaning to the word 'direction', which in turn leads to a new evaluation of his life events and thus to another epistemic orientation, one in which he will no longer say 'I am a person who lacks direction', but rather 'I am a person who likes to try different things in life'. Also, if this person happens to be on a board which decides about funds for research, his orientation can change from favouring projects presented under the names of well-known professors to favouring original projects from unknown people.

This example shows not only how a shift in the interpretation of a symbolic expression may lead to a change in one's experience of life, and, therefore, to a change in one's epistemic orientation, but also how this orientation also consists of a moral and of a spiritual aspect. The spiritual aspect can be recognized in the *evaluation* which is inherent in this man's knowledge of himself. In the earlier phase of his life this evaluation is oriented towards what he holds to be good and true in personal attitude, namely 'being directed', in the later phase it is oriented towards the value of creativity. Morally, his change in outlook results in a change of actions in accordance with what he holds to be good, at first the furtherance of proven excellence, and later the furtherance of change and perhaps a more even distribution of funding.

Nature in human experience

To introduce the concept of experience of life, I started out from examples in the area of human relationships. But other interpreted experiences are no less important in the epistemic orientation of human beings. One can think of experiences with our own bodily existence, as this changes in form through the course of life. Changing from a childlike into an adult body, or changing from an active middle-aged person into an old person who needs increasing amounts of help from medical technology, constitute experiences which have to be turned into life stories and thus into frames of meaning.

One can also think of those experiences that have to do with everyday existence like driving to work, cooking food, cleaning oneself, etc. Normally, such events will be rather peripheral (but never absent) in one's life narrative, except of course for the more significant ones like moving house or suffering from a disease. Among the stories that make up a person's experience of life, there are also those which can be labelled as experiences of nature. What kind of experiences will be labelled thus, and on what grounds? That is the question which I will tackle here.

In ancient and medieval Western culture 'nature' was understood to refer to experiences of order. The cosmic order or the order of creation was seen in the distinctions between the species, between rulers and those ruled, between men and women in terms of their differing status. Nowadays such experiences of nature as order are not common. Since Westerners have called themselves modern, they have tried to improve social relationships according to political and cultural blueprints, and to preserve the term 'nature' for experiences of events which are out of our orderly control. Nature is no longer considered to be orderly in a moral or aesthetic fashion, it is at most considered orderly in its own non-human structural characteristics.

This change concerns the moral as well as the descriptive use of 'nature'. When the expression is used in a moral context, as in the sentence 'individuals should be allowed to follow nature', it refers, in present-day experience, to giving in to one's spontaneous drives, rather than to trying to develop one's 'true rational nature'. Also, when the term 'nature' is used in a descriptive sense, as when we speak of the natural growth of some cells in a test tube, we mean by this not the process of realizing the intended cosmological beauty, but rather the fact that we do not (yet) control every aspect of the developing process.

49

Here it is interesting to examine the historical development of modern and present-day (sometimes called postmodern) concepts of nature more closely. When we consider an early modern researcher of nature like Isaac Newton, we see that his frame of reference is still that of divinely created order (see Christianson 1984). His interest is in finding and articulating the eternal laws of a cosmos bestowed with beauty and goodness. At about the same time, in the seventeenth century, we see in philosophical reflection, as for instance in the works of René Descartes (1637), a rising awareness of the human factor in modern science. Descartes sees the importance of its systematic method in securing the clarity of its results. His contemporary Francis Bacon (1620) also stresses the importance of systematic inquiry, combined with a method for defining one's concepts, in finding the real distinctions in nature.

Apart from reflecting on the human input in creating reliable science, both thinkers were also very interested in the usefulness of this science for human life. According to Descartes, the goal of science was to provide the means to lead a healthy and comfortable life. When we look at present society we are tempted to think that he spoke farsighted words; many of the technologies through which the lives of humanity have been changed so radically indeed concern medical practice and everyday comfort: cars, washing machines, better means of food processing and storage, etc.

When the natural sciences really started to become technologically successful, in the nineteenth century, we see a remarkable change in the philosophical and general cultural reflection on nature. In what Taylor (1989) has called the 'expressivist turn', nature is no longer thought of as order, but as spontaneity. This marked the end of the mechanistic world-view, and the beginning of a more organicist view of nature. We could also put it the other way around: since the views of seventeenth-century (mechanistic) philosophers had become dominant, order in the scientific process, as well as in its results, was no longer seen as given, as natural, but rather as the effect of human reason. Since nature had become the object of the sciences, a thing which had to be understood and conquered, it was seen as wild and unstructured in itself.

In the twentieth century technologies resulting from scientific research impinged on life in its entirety. From preservatives to pain killers, the experience of the entire human course of life was changed. Also, through the mass media and mass killing methods, war as well as peace changed radically. In present-day culture this has created a general feeling of unlimited power.

In this atmosphere it becomes harder to determine anything as essentially natural, in the sense of showing spontaneous development. We are able to create a 'natural' forest; we are on the way to preserving wild species by impregnating lions with tiger embryos; we see humanity as responsible for changes in the global climate, etc. How would it make sense to keep on using the word 'nature' in postmodern culture? In my view the concept of nature can only be used meaningfully in our time, if we succeed in providing a novel articulation of the experience which it refers to. Such an articulation will be proposed in the following.

In looking for a new articulation of the concept of nature, it is useful to return to the roots of the concept of nature. In antiquity this concept was coined in a biological context, as an adverb to the Latin verb *nascor*, which is the translation of the Greek verb *gignomai*. It had two basic connotations. The verb referred to organic development in general, meaning 'to grow' (especially of plants), as well as to the specific form of mammalian coming into being, 'being born'.

When we look back to the historical development of the Western experience of nature, we can conclude that originally 'nature' expressed the experience that there were aspects to things that belonged to them originally, from their beginning (or from creation). Later on, the organic connotation (spontaneous growth) of nature predominated. I want to propose that an adequate articulation of present-day experience of nature should refer to those conditions of the experienced world that are connected with 'being born'. Here we could refer to the expression introduced in philosophy by Hannah Arendt (1958), 'natality'. When we reflect on 'natality', especially in our own, human, experience, its most significant aspect is what in postmodern philosophy is called 'alterity'. Being born means that one does not find one's origin in oneself, but in someone who is an other to me. My origin is in a sense strange to me, and uncontrollable.

When spontaneous growth becomes, in our experience, the exception, and the cosmic beauty of eternal order is not a common experience, I want to suggest that 'nature' can express more adequately experiences of uncontrollability and of strangeness in our world. If one is able to go along with this suggestion, the concept of nature will refer not only to extra-cultural processes and objects like weather, rocks, plants, etc., but also to things and processes which have been manipulated by human beings. Thus we could say that to the general user the not-understood software of a computer provides this person with an experience of nature. When it fails him or her, this person feels like the ancient farmer who hasn't foreseen a storm: helpless and frustrated.

Moral and spiritual aspects of scientific knowledge of nature

Until now I have spoken of 'epistemic orientation' and of the knowledge that constitutes it in a general manner. Now I will look at scientific knowledge as a kind of epistemic orientation with certain specific characteristics. Among those characteristics are the criteria which control the process by which this knowledge is gathered, such as the demand that the concepts used are as unambiguous as possible, and the demand that methods of experimentation are reproducible. In fact, these criteria are not entirely foreign to everyday knowledge either: when two reliable persons report a totally different outcome after using a cookery recipe, we will not trust the recipe. The difference, however, is that in science one tries to meet these demands systematically.

From the point of view of experience, however, scientific knowledge and everyday knowledge resemble each other very closely. When we first consider the function of this knowledge in the experiential relationship of human beings to their life-world, we notice that scientific knowledge, like everyday knowledge, functions as a frame of orientation through which we interpret novel events and explain events in the past. This view is not new but was introduced by the American pragmatist philosophers of the early twentieth century, of whom the most important are Charles Sanders Peirce, William James and John Dewey.

Secondly, we can say that the generation of scientific knowledge resembles that of everyday knowledge in the fact that it is partly steered by the experience of life of those who generate it. Here I want to refer to Bruno Latour's study *Science in Action* (1987), in which it was shown that science in the making is led by all kinds of non-epistemic factors, like relationships between scientists, funding and material aspects of the instruments with which scientists work. With hindsight it might seem that a theory or certain facts were already out there and just had to be discovered, but actually Latour stresses that, during the production of scientific knowledge, several competing views could still be realized, depending on the abovementioned factors.

There is, however, a blank in Latour's philosophical explanation, and that is that he doesn't recognize the role of human moral and spiritual intentionality. When we want to study the factors in the process of generating scientific knowledge, we should acknowledge that scientists and funders may also direct their actions towards what they consider to be (morally) good, and that they may also direct their personal attitude to what they hold to be good and true. In an earlier section I showed that the (re-)interpretation that makes up a person's life story, as well as his or her experience of life, has moral and spiritual aspects that are intertwined with the epistemic aspect. We should affirm the same multidimensionality in scientific knowledge, also when it regards nature.

In the foregoing section I hope to have convinced my readers that 'strangeness and uncontrollability' express adequately present-day experiences of nature. By connecting these explications of what postmodern philosophers call 'alterity' to the ancient meaning of the verb *gignomai* (Latin: *nascor*) as 'being born', I wanted to show how the expression of important present-day existential experiences of our world can be viewed as a further link in the chain of meanings transferred by the term 'nature'.

Let us now look more closely into the contemporary experience of 'nature' in relation to scientific knowledge and modern culture. In our time and in our, rich, region of the world, the growth in knowledge and communication is enormous. The remarkable thing, however, is that this growth produces at the same time an effect which could be named 'chaos'. When surfing the Internet, one can have an experience similar to that of wandering in a large forest. All the time one is prone to the temptation to turn into yet another path, because one never knows what new information it might provide. Also, in scientific research, specialization has progressed so far that information on most of the fields even within one's own discipline becomes foreign and uncontrollable. The scientific researcher is in a similar position to that of the Internet-surfer: there are so many directions to choose, and methods of research are so powerful, that one is likely to have produced new knowledge before one has meditated thoroughly on which direction to choose. Being thus unable to control satisfactorily the direction in which science is moving, an experience of 'nature' may be felt to creep into the very tools that human beings have developed to increase control and ownership.

According to this view, alterity accompanies the control we have gained in our relations to the world. This leads to an awareness of the contingency and the provisional character of our knowledge. Or, rather, to the awareness that the development of our knowledge can be furthered or threatened, or moved in different directions, by political, religious and economic struggles. This does not mean, however, that what we acknowledge to be true should be considered a subjective or a relative matter, but only that the direction and significance of our knowledge depends to some extent on the orientation which results from human experience of life. In line with my earlier reference to a Latourian view on science, I hold that a change in the experience of nature has as large an effect on everyday experience as it has on scientific experience. In science the growth of specialized knowledge and of efficient means of communication creates, as it were, an overflow of information, which in turn creates the effect that its practitioners lose their oversight of the broader field of knowledge.

Alterity

When people increasingly experience strangeness and uncontrollability in relation to their life-world, the content of the concept of nature, in the scientific as well as in the everyday domain, could better be designated as 'alterity' than as 'spontaneity'. Whereas 'spontaneity' retains in some way the idea of intrinsic good which was present in the ancient cosmological concept of nature (without, however, the metaphysical frame of reference to sustain this idea), this idea is not present in the concept of 'alterity'.

To illustrate these conclusions, it might be interesting to view a topic from the field of medicine, because in this field scientific knowledge and everyday experience touch each other, especially when we look at the question of how to evaluate new medical techniques from a moral point of view. The topic I have selected for this purpose is that of treating infertility by means of in vitro fertilization. I want to show that some arguments for and against IVF in public debate are lacking in persuasive power, because on both sides they seem to rest on the same, inadequate (romantic) idea of 'naturalness'.

In an age in which human beings possess the knowledge to intervene in the earliest stages of the growth of life, we cannot in a sensible manner defend or contest IVF with the aid of the concept of cosmological order, and indeed this doesn't happen. What does happen is that arguments pro and contra use the concept of nature in the sense of spontaneity. Some arguments in favour of IVF, for example, rest on the legitimacy of the desire of adult persons to have children, saying that it is natural to want children. Here 'nature' should be understood in some meaning of spontaneity: the spontaneous, given, desires of individuals (as long as they don't harm other individuals) are considered worthy or good in themselves. On the other hand, some arguments against IVF, stemming mostly from a Christian point of view, also seem to rest on the modern concept of nature as spontaneity. In these arguments the central idea of the sanctity or worthiness of all (even embryonic) life rests in part on the idea of the embryo's potential to grow spontaneously into a full human being, making the destruction of extra embryos resulting from IVF treatment morally objectionable.

As I have shown above, however, this concept of spontaneity can hardly express adequately contemporary experiences of nature, precisely because the power of science and its influence in everyday life have made spontaneity a thing which cannot be detected in a pure or authentic way. When we understand nature, however, as the experience of strangeness and uncontrollability, we include the 'unspontaneity' created by the power of modern science, as well as the awareness of the intrinsic limits of this power. To return to our case, when treating infertility by means of IVF neither the short-term effect of the procedure (whether it will work, and if so why), nor the long-term effect (on the 'products', the children) can be controlled or predicted. When we are aware of this uncontrollability, we can see a 'natural' (in the contemporary sense) factor in this medical technique as well as in the scientific knowledge on which it rests. Also, the moral status of extra-uterine embryonic life produced in the laboratory can hardly be decided upon by making use of the idea of nature as spontaneity. It seems possible, however, to reflect on the moral, spiritual and epistemic aspects of the procedure and its products, by expressing their features in terms of nature as alterity. Seeing the strangeness, the uncontrollability in them would make one aware of the limits of the power of humans to realize wittingly what they consider to be good (in this example, reducing the sorrow of infertile couples).

Consequently, the proposed expression of contemporary experiences of nature does not produce ready-made answers to the moral and spiritual dilemmas that modern science faces us with. It does, on the contrary, raise our awareness of the ambiguity which is inherent in our experience of nature, whether in its epistemic, moral or spiritual aspect. We cannot ever hope to be absolutely sure about the truth or goodness of our orientation. At the same time, however, this concept of nature shows that, since it does not recognize intrinsic goodness or truth 'out there', the moral and spiritual commitment of people is a relevant factor in their epistemic orientation. This means that questions like those concerning IVF should not be discussed without taking this commitment into account.

With this example I hope to have illustrated some interesting consequences of introducing alterity into our concept of nature. When we come to realize the contingency and the provisionality of what we can do and know, it can be considered good and illuminating to refer less, in public discussions about issues of modern science and everyday life, to the value of the spontaneous and given character of desires and/or living beings, and more to the moral, spiritual and epistemic ambiguity inherent in scientific knowledge. This could induce awareness of the need to further the sensibility for what can be experienced (in all its provisionality) as truth and goodness. This, then, could lead to an improvement in the quality of the decisions in our human orientation.

References

Arendt, H. (1958) *The Human Condition*, Chicago: University of Chicago Press.

Bacon, F. (1620) *The New Organon*, edited with an introduction by F.H. Anderson, Indianapolis: Bobbs-Merrill, 1960.

Christianson, G.E. (1984) *In the Presence of the Creator: Isaac Newton and His Times*, New York: Free Press.

Descartes, R. (1637) *Discourse on Method*, translated by J. Cottingham, R. Stoothoff, D. Murdoch, in *The Philosophical Writings of Descartes* (vol. I), Cambridge: Cambridge University Press, 1985.

Latour, B. (1987) *Science in Action: How to Follow Scientists and Engineers through Society*, Milton Keynes: Open University Press.

Taylor, C. (1989) *Sources of the Self: The Making of the Modern Identity*, Cambridge: Cambridge University Press.

7

HUMAN INTERPRETATION AND ANIMAL EXCELLENCE

Peter Scheers

In this chapter I introduce the hermeneutico-ethical figure of the benevolent interpreter. In its classical version this figure is concerned with human versions of otherness (other selves and/or their products and expressions, such as texts). It is important, however, to be open to benevolent interpretations of non-human versions of otherness. I will focus on animal being. In the following I propose, in the context of a benevolent interpretation, the idea of 'animal excellence'. I will take excellence in a broad way, not at all as identical with virtues and vices (which are typically human). Excellence is best associated with an original and successful way of being.

Moral and interpretational being

Let us begin by noting the fundamental reciprocity between moral and interpretational being. The moral attitude of a human self towards other persons is strongly influenced by interpretation. In particular, when we concretely interpret the other as someone with original meaning, we are prepared to develop and sustain a moral attitude involving respect, justice and care. Immoral behaviour often originates in negative or shallow interpretation. Misinterpretation is therefore a fundamental source of moral failure. Interpretation also assumes moral being. Only when we already have the moral virtues of honesty, tolerance, patience and fairness, are we able to undertake proper forms of interpretation. Someone without the virtue of patience, for example, would not manage to comprehend all the semantic layers of a novel or of the life story of another self. Interpretation takes time and virtues.

An interesting version of the reciprocity of interpretation and morality is expressed in the notion of the 'benevolent interpreter'. This notion refers back to the eighteenth century tradition in German hermeneutics, as exemplified in Georg Friedrich Meier (see Greisch 2001). Meier proposes the virtue of 'hermeneutische Billigkeit'. This virtue of hermeneutical fairness implies the demand to begin and to continue reading a text with the serious and sustained expectation of finding meaning and truth. Only when one really expects to find meaning, will one take the trouble to keep looking. In current literature the notion of a benevolent interpreter is connected only to humans. The benevolent interpreter, however, should at least be willing to probe the possibility of finding meaning and excellence in non-human others. Some may consider benevolence to be a kind of soft virtue, but it has its own radicality. An authentic benevolent interpreter would be inclined to extend the search for original meaning as far as possible. Capabilities may create duties. We are capable of interpreting nature. It would therefore be immoral not to try to interpret nature truthfully. The ethics of interpretation implies the duty to interpret.

(Mis)understanding animals

Striking, however, is the ubiquity of misunderstanding animals. We see some animals as monstrosities, while cats and dogs are almost human friends. It is conceivable that a person working in the meat-processing industry, where animals are literally squashed into products, comes home in the evening to take care of his or her pet. The same animal may be reduced to something without meaning or humanized, depending on mood and the time of day. The human awareness of animals is an obvious case of 'interpretational dissonance'. Together with interpretational dissonance, another feature complicates our awareness. More than a few people sense that animal being is an original realm which ultimately resists reduction, stigmatization and anthropomorphism. This awareness is a fragile form of interpretation, but it holds an important place. It tells us that reduction, stigmatization and humanization are forms of misinterpretation.

I am not sure whether awareness of animal originality as such allows the expression of clear and distinct concepts. What can be put into philosophical discourse, however, is the experience that not every lived experience invites concept and argument. This is already true in the human lived experience of oneself and of other human persons. Vladimir Jankélévitch (1957), a French Existential philosopher, speaks about the 'je ne sais quoi' ('I don't know what'). It is often possible to say that something is, but not what it is in its essence. Certain people, for example, radiate a particular grandeur. We may say that such is the case, but we cannot fully explain or describe what it is. Jankélévitch does not want to make human experience esoteric. He simply wishes to point to experiences that most of us have. In the case of human sensing of animal originality, we are often confronted with aesthetic experience – horses running in a field, the powerful eagle flying over its territory, the monumental body of the elephant. We are fascinated by animal beauty, which is a penetrating invitation to sense otherness of meaning. This experience will bring most of us to the conclusion that there is 'something' beyond our cultures and cities.

In some instances it is difficult to sense animal meaning. Who 'loves' rats, worms and parasites? One should never underestimate the antagonism that rules between humans and (some) animals. Not all is a matter of peace and tranquillity. Perhaps hermeneutical perseverance or imagination is at times highly necessary to overcome feelings of negativity and aversion. Quite an array of animals are 'expelled' from human aesthetic sensing. Then, of course, there is no bliss of sensing feeding a further process of interpretation. We should in such cases count on a longer labour of interpretation, which afterwards may perhaps lead to appreciation. And the hard work of interpretation is needed in any case, whether there is initial sensing or not. Sensing is itself a sudden form of interpretation. It makes us a believer in animal meaning. This belief, however, leaves us with a further task of comprehension, namely to understand better what is at hand in animal ways of being and to purify as much as possible our processes of interpretation. This is not a retraction of the former point that we cannot ultimately understand the 'je ne sais quoi' of animals; we have to accept the mystery of animal being and, at the same time, should continue the effort of understanding as far as possible. This process takes months and years. To believe in order to understand, to understand in order to believe. This version of the hermeneutical circle describes accurately what is at stake in the relation between sensing and extended interpretation. Sensing an elephant's originality is one thing, understanding its life is another. Think here of interpretation in the reading of texts. One can sense that a novel is precious, but it can take years to grasp its depths. Ethology is or should be an extended and generous reading of animal lives.

An epistemological problem pops up. We may be of good will and will the good, but perhaps we are so imprisoned by human categories, moods and perceptions that an interpretation of animals will always be 'too human'. We already know what the sceptic will say: we live in a world of human words, stories and constructions by which we have turned 'a barren wilderness of white noise into a habitable world' (Cupitt 1991: 99). So there is no objective and benevolent understanding of nature, whatever we try. I think, however, that the sceptic overstates his position. Obviously, we cannot leave human cognition, language and interpretation. But let us not ignore possibilities of human rationality and understanding. First, the play of concepts and metaphors is not static. We criticize and revise one metaphor by means of another. Second, we are all creatures of the Earth. It is therefore highly unlikely that we are completely cut off from the way of being of animals. The radical gap between man and animals is itself a rhetorical construction. Being-on-Earth in togetherness with other organisms perhaps constitutes the first principle of zoo-hermeneutics. Third, we of course cannot directly enter the being of bats, but we can at least become aware of how a bat moves and flies and screams. We know what it eats. In fact a bat provides us through its noises and movements with an expressive testimony of its power to be. It is, and it is in a particular way. We use human words and look with human eyes, but what we see is not human. We recognize non-humanity and differences between animals. The recognition of difference is a powerful hermeneutical tool that works in a double way (observation of differences between animals, human observation of differences between humans and varieties of animal being). But also the recognition of similarities between humans and animals, and between animals, is fundamental. Animals give food for thought or interpretation by way of offering differences as well as similarities.

It is interesting to probe a little further the hermeneutic importance of similarity for our understanding of other human selves as well as animal beings. In his phenomenology of interpretation Edmund Husserl highlights the productive role of similarity in the interpretation of human otherness (Ricoeur 1986). The other self is an intentional modification of the 'I'. While other human beings or texts do confront us with otherness, it is never an otherness so radical that there are no underlying identities and deep resemblances. Other selves speak like us. They have eyes, ears and hands like us, they drive cars, live in houses and go to work, exactly like us. I do not think Husserl's hermeneutics of similarity is a retraction of the theory of benevolent interpretation (which involves the search for meaning dissimilar to my own schemes of value and meaning). Obviously, we have to leave behind Husserl's 'egological' tendencies. But as a principal moment within a complex theory of the benevolent interpreter, the hermeneutics of similarity has a strategic role to play. Sensing and understanding difference is perhaps only possible by virtue of sensing and understanding certain similarities. Only the project of finding similarity will tell the interpreter when resemblance works and when it fails. Husserl also addresses the otherness of animal being and the role of similarity in human understanding of animals. Husserl is right to stress that we cannot but take ourselves as the beginning point in a confrontation with otherness, radical or not. This is an inescapable and productive hermeneutical mechanism. What we ourselves intimately know, for example, about eating and other organic acts must be considered helpful and constructive in our attempt to understand animals. We should, however, not follow Husserl in his view on certain animals as 'deviations' in relation to the human norm (Husserl 1992: 129 ; Cabestan 1995: 39–79).

According to Husserl, the more we leave the world of pets and higher animals, the more we are confronted with ways of being which are radically different from human existence. In comparison with human traits and capacities, these are 'shadows of normality'. Here, I expect the benevolent interpreter to opt for another strategy and to propose a plurality of vital norms. A bat's way of being contains similarities and radical differences. These differences, which we cannot fully grasp, are, considered with an eye on the vital norm of the bat's way of being, not deviations at all.

On the contrary, in a bat's cave we are the shadows of normality. In a snake's jungle we are the ones that seem lost. The hermeneutics of similarity has its limitations and should never become a simple evaluation of radical otherness from the perspective of one's own capacities and excellences. Every animal or animal species has its own way of being. For Heidegger (1983: 287), at least in some layers of his thought, each animal has its own perfection, beyond comparison: 'Jedes Tier und jede Tierart ist als solche gleich vollkomen wie die andere.' Between similarity and otherness, between shadows and originalities, I propose a space of human interpretation of animal otherness which is less secure perhaps than scientists would wish, but less hesitating than sceptics think, and far less arrogant than humanists would like – a space which, above all, is nourished by the moral and hermeneutic intention to find meaning and excellence in nature.

Excellence and animals

With the possibilities and moralities of interpretation in mind as I have sketched them, we can in the following come to one important interpretational/appreciative issue concerning the being of animals, namely the issue of 'animal excellence'. The language of excellence, in its broadest sense, is confined to the human realm. The classical definitions of being human automatically refer to a state of excellence (capacities, competences, perfections, functions). We are *animal loquens* (animals with the excellence of speech) or *homo faber* (entities which can make). And we are political, rational, narrative and interpretational animals. These dimensions and qualities are portrayed as, and believed to be, authentic excellences. It is good to have these qualities. When the idea of excellence is applied to the animal world, it is often only in the context of considering animals as proto-humans. Does this show us that it is perhaps best to confine qualities of excellence to human reality or is there a more subtle way to ascribe 'excellence' to animals? Let us consult two authors who – in opposite ways – address animal excellence, namely Eugen Fink and Maurice Maeterlinck. And let us afterwards try to find some middle ground.

It is interesting to refer to Eugen Fink's argument against animal excellence. Fink's stance is articulated in one of his main works, namely *Grundphänomene des menschlichen Daseins* (1979). He characterizes us humans as workers, players, lovers, fighters and mortals. Perhaps not all of these characterizations refer directly to excellence (think of death), but even then upon closer inspection excellence is confirmed; to be aware of the possibility of death implies certain interpretational and cognitive powers. The playing, loving and working self is quite directly an excellent self. We are confronted with 'excellences' of affection, relation, activity, imagination and creativity. In work we transform the world and produce artefacts. In love we celebrate the recognition of otherness. In play we create imaginative worlds and even works of art. Animals may confront us with ways of being which appear to be similar to human ways. We therefore speak of worker bees and of kittens playing in the grass. For Fink, however, we should resist the application of human terms. Animals have no consciousness concerning the future. They, therefore, do not know death as death. They simply cease to exist. Playing and working presuppose the capacity to plan, to conceive and be conscious of one's needs. Whatever the animal 'builds' or 'collects', it is not work, since animal temporality and initiative exclude planning in a human sense.

The Belgian author Maurice Maeterlinck received the Nobel Prize for Literature in 1911. In his 'animal books' we find a generous defence of animal excellence. For our purpose, it is sufficient to consider briefly Maeterlinck's fertile study on *La vie des abeilles* (1943). Maeterlinck underlines that the discovery of a sign of intelligence outside ourselves should produce in us something of the emotion Robinson Crusoe felt when he saw the imprint of a human foot on the sandy beach of his island. It is good to be less alone than we believed. Maeterlinck observes all kinds of excellences in bee existence. The individual bee is compelled to renounce the vice of independence (the urge to eat up all the eggs). Domestic bees live in a state of perpetual chastity and have a passion for work. They are architects, masons, wax workers and sculptors with skills of communication and cooperation. They persevere and are devoted to the future. Concerning his ascriptions of excellence to animals, Maeterlinck agrees that it is all a matter of human conjecture. But whatever conjectures we weave, there still remains the fact that 'something' is going on in animals and that we have to try to find words to match this. Some would perhaps say that animal excellence is reducible to anonymous instincts; it is not a matter of individual intelligence. Maeterlinck responds: why should general instincts not be admirable and wonderful as such? It is not because something is not individual that it is futile. This is a major reason for Maeterlinck to apply the language of excellence beyond humanity. Maeterlinck shows us full use of human language in the effort to speak about animals. His hermeneutical vice is perhaps 'overgenerous' interpretation. Also, the charge of human projection (which, ultimately, is the opposite of generosity) can be made.

Who to follow then, Fink or Maeterlinck? To express processes of meaning and excellence in animals we will have to look for words embedded in human dictionaries. And while using human words to describe animal processes, Fink's concerns and hesitations should not be ignored at all. On the contrary, as the temptation to project humanity on to animality continuously pops up, something like Fink's 'anti-projection stance' should regularly be taken towards one's efforts to express animal being. On its own, Fink's stance is perhaps not very fruitful, but situated within the effort to speak about animal meaning it actually has a valuable function. The point is to bring prudence and generosity together. The critical togetherness of Maeterlinck and Fink offers some suggestions for speaking about animals. To illustrate this, let us relate animal being to the 'excellences' of work, moral being, interpretation and life story.

Varieties of animal excellence

Maeterlinck describes the bee as worker. Fink denies the animal application of work. Traditional philosophies of work stress the dimensions of intention, planning, tools and production. In the same spirit Fink underlines, as we already know, that animals do not plan and, hence, do not work. Playing the 'Maeterlinck card' would mean looking for aspects in the lives of animals which are related to the idea of work. A beaver does something. A bird's nest is made in some way. No matter how much we want to doubt the conjectures we weave around these facts, something has happened and we simply cannot deny its qualities. The nest is there, and so is the beaver's dam. The fact that human work also concerns the construction of things used as shelter may be more significant than the suggestion that animals do not conceive and plan like humans. The fact that the nest is perhaps built as a result of animal instincts does not destroy the miracle of nest building. I would suggest that in the case of work there is more reason to apply the term to animals than not. In this case, Maeterlinck revises Fink, even while it is clear that animal work is not human work. There is a meaningful sense of work.

What about moral being? Fink would of course stand first in line to deny moral being in animals. Maeterlinck's theory of moral animals may find some support in ethological studies which underline social and even proto-moral behaviour. In animals, however, there seems to be no full sensing of otherness as otherness, and this awareness is essential for moral being as such (the full recognition of otherness as something other than me and my wishes and perceptions). But perhaps there is middle ground. One cannot speak of full recognition of otherness in animals – we are capable of feeling with others, of empathy, and such empathic capacities are missing in animals. Yet within the bounds of group sociality and species rules we have to remain open to mutual recognition between cat and kittens: not recognition of full otherness, but also not 'nothing'. Here we should be introduced to concrete ethological studies of what happens between animals. Inspired by Maeterlinck, but sobered up through Fink, we may want to try out reinterpretations of certain moral terms – for example, a cat 'caring' for its kittens; not human caring, but something that can only be expressed by the word caring, even if at the same time we mentally distil away certain human dimensions. In the case of moral terminology, perhaps, it is Fink who can limit some of Maeterlinck's generous descriptions ('chastity', 'renouncing the vice of independence').

Fink acknowledges that something must be going on in animals for them to be able to survive. He could have opened up a discussion, and his conclusion might have been that in animals there is indeed no planning of the human type, but that nonetheless there is 'something' in animal other-ness which becomes all too neglected when we radically block the application of human words to animals. Animals know their way around in their world. Maeterlinck speaks about animal knowledge. In the context of his metaphorical network there are many opportunities for him to go too far. But there is, I believe, some middle ground which is well illustrated in the 'Umweltlehre' of Jakob von Uexküll (1980). Interpretation is a partial, mediated, selective process of reception and appropriation of aspects of being. Human beings can interpret in highly complicated ways (for example, reading). But there is interpretation beyond reading. According to Uexküll, every animal species lives in its own constructed 'Umwelt' (subjective environment). A table for humans is a 'thing to lie under' for dogs. There is therefore a plurality of subjective environments. Every animal has its own excellence of interpretation.

The realm of stories is intimately associated with humanity and culture. We have the excellence of narrative complexity. We are able to listen to and produce narrative discourse – a discourse which symbolizes powers of synthesis, selection, expression and reflection. In stories we bring together – by way of a plot – friends, enemies, past, future, aims, obstacles, ideals, failures, successes, realities and fictions. Would it be odd to grant animals some kind of membership into the narrative community? We know what Fink would answer: animals do not tell anything, nor can they understand stories. Even Maeterlinck would not go so far. He stresses semiotic powers of communication in bees and other animals, but there are signs beyond language and narration (Peirce). One author, Wilhelm Schapp (a phenomenologist who, long before the recent narrative movement in the humanities, developed a narrative anthropology in the 1950s) writes that we can only really understand the lives of animals when we tell stories about them. Animals do not tell stories, but we do, and what happens in animal being can only be adequately described in narrative structure. Animals have untold life stories, which – so Schapp remarks – 'are blown into our direction like the sounds of distant music, which we cannot represent any more in music notes, but of which we can still say that it is music' (1976: 134). Perhaps we cannot say that animals have the active excellence of narrative being, but they are in any case to such an extent involved in lives of action, interpretation, conflict and flourishing that they necessarily invite human narration. Between the poles of Maeterlinck and Fink, animals can be considered as members of narrative being by virtue of their 'untold' life stories.

In this chapter I have tried to suggest the idea of animal excellence. Such a proposal is embedded in, and a logical outcome of, a broader theory of the benevolent interpreter. It may all come down to the role of human beings as interpreters of what happens on Earth. Scientists often take the side of reduction and minimalism. Poets (Rilke for example, but also Maeterlinck) trust human language to be able to express nonhuman realms. Such a trust certainly invites the vice of human projection, but resisting the use of and search for adequate language will simply have more devastating effects: not to speak about animals will lead us to ignore them. Not that animals in themselves need humans. The best we can do, surely, is to leave nature alone. Perhaps we should, as human species, simply withdraw from certain quarters of the earth. But to convince ourselves that we should eventually withdraw, we have to know that animals are original projects of excellence. This can only happen by virtue of human expression.

The duty not to be silent is a moral task which holds a central position in any ethical system, also in environmental ethics. We need many benevolent interpreters who dare to speak about animal excellence.

References

Cabestan, P. (1995) 'La constitution de l'animal dans les Ideen', *Alter. Revue de Phénoménologie* 3 : 39–79.

Cupitt, D. (1991) *What Is a Story?*, London: SCM.

Fink, E. (1979) *Grundphänomene des menschlichen Daseins*, Freiburg: Alber.

Greisch, J. (2001) 'Le principe d'équité comme âme de l'herméneutique', *Revue de Métaphysique et de Morale* 1: 19–42.

Heidegger, M. (1983) *Die Grundbegriffe der Metaphysik*, Frankfurt am Main: Klostermann.

Husserl, E. (1992) *Gesammelte Schriften Edmund Husserl*, volume 8 (*Cartesianische Meditationen*), Hamburg: Meiner.

Jankélévitch, V. (1957) *Le je-ne-sais-quoi et le presque-rien*, Paris : Seuil.

Maeterlinck, M. (1943) *La vie des abeilles*, Brussels: Ed. du Rond.

Ricoeur, P. (1986) 'Phénoménologie et herméneutique', in P. Ricoeur, *Du texte à l'action*, Paris : Seuil, 39–73.

Schapp, W. (1976) *In Geschichten verstrickt*, Wiesbaden: Heyman.

Von Uexküll, J. (1980) *Kompositionslehre der Natur*, Frankfurt am Main: Ullstein.

Part II

EVIL EVOLUTIONARY JUSTIFIED?

Introduction to Part II

Willem B. Drees

Can evil ever be justified in the context of our scientific understanding of reality? In theology the effort to explain how belief in God's goodness may be combined with experiences of suffering is called a 'theodicy', more specifically 'a theoretical theodicy'. Without indulging in too much explicit theology, that is the issue around which various arguments in this section circle. How do various forms of evil we experience shape our understanding of reality? The American philosopher Holmes Rolston argues for 'cruciform creation': in order to have the creativity we value, nature has to be a domain of finitude, death and suffering. Comments on his arguments are given by the geophysicist Jacob J. de Vries and the philosopher Jozef Keulartz. Jan Smit, a paleobiologist who was one of the co-discoverers of the catastrophic events that resulted in the extinction of the dinosaurs some sixty-five million years ago, considers the significance of catastrophic events in the evolutionary history of life. The recognition of the importance of these events has been slow to emerge within the scientific community, as the Darwinian evolutionary understanding has been tied to a uniformitarian view in geology. However, with his emphasis on catastrophic events, Smit stays well within the boundaries of regular science; the underlying laws of physics are never suspended. The philosopher Arthur Petersen and the world historian Fred Spier offer some comments and additional insights. Claudia Sanides-Kohlrausch offers an interesting essay on the impact of a major catastrophe in Europe, the Lisbon earthquake of 1755, on European philosophy and theology. The Swiss astrophysicist Arnold Benz explores in his contribution the history of our universe, and the grounds for hope with respect to its future. Grounds for such hope are not found, according to him, in scientific understanding, but neither are they excluded. Ultimately, it is a matter of faith whether one believes in a future as something new, an Easter beyond all decay. Eduardo Cruz, a theologian from Brazil, offers further thoughts on the notions of 'tragedy' and 'hope' as used by Benz. The philosopher Neil A. Manson considers the parameters that make our reality the way it is. He argues in a carefully crafted essay that not only design arguments (including those about 'anthropic principles') but also their main competitor, 'multiple universe' scenarios, implicitly assume that there is something of value to be explained, namely life.

8

NATURALIZING AND SYSTEMATIZING EVIL

Holmes Rolston, III

A common approach de-naturalizes evil – takes the evil out by claiming that natural things just *are*, without value being either present or absent. If one asks whether a tree is sad or glad, one is misunderstanding trees. If one asks whether evolution is good or evil, one is using irrelevant categories. Nature is a neutral substrate. Natural processes and products have the standing possibility of valuation or disvaluation when humans come on the scene. But matters of fact have to be kept in a different realm from matters of value.

This view is plausible for moral evil, in the strong sense of culpably depraved. Neither is nature morally praiseworthy. We humans do not take our moral standards from nature, nor should we fault nature as though it were moral. That is a category mistake.

My inquiry is about nonmoral evil, in the weaker sense, of events and processes, which, though not culpable agents, are bad, harmful, cruel, injurious. Here, too, often nature just is. When Comet Shoemaker-Levy crashed into Jupiter in 1994 and upset the flow bands, I was not prompted to ask questions of good and evil. There does not seem to be anything evil out there in space. The place to look is here on Earth. Orcas catch sea lions for food, and play with them, tossing the struggling lions into the air, prolonging their agony. I do not fault the killer whales, but I might ask whether the nature is evil that, through natural selection, results in the nature of such beasts.

I am not asking whether this is the best possible world, but more modestly whether this Earth is systemically prolific at increasing biodiversity and biocomplexity, and whether the evils here integrate well into those powers. Perspective is crucial.

Physics and biology

But there is another side to this. Agreeing that there is bad in biology, physicists reply that their nature is not value free, but quite valuable. Looking at nature systemically, we have discovered a 'fine-tuned' universe from astrophysics to nuclear physics, and a messy one from evolutionary and ecosystemic biology. Physics has made dramatic discoveries at astronomical and submicroscopic ranges. This universe originated fifteen billion years ago in a 'big bang' and has since been expanding. From the primal burst of energy, elementary particles formed, and afterward hydrogen, the simplest element, which serves as fuel for the stars. In the stellar furnaces all the heavier atoms were forged. Some stars subsequently exploded (supernovae). The heavier elements were collected to form, in our case, the solar system and planet Earth.

Physics has discovered that startling systemic interrelationships are required for these creative processes to work. Recent theory interrelates the two levels; astronomical phenomena such as the formation of galaxies, stars, and planets depend critically on the microphysical phenomena. In turn, the mid-range scales, where the known complexity mostly lies (on Earth, in ecosystems or human brains), depend on the interacting microscopic and astronomical ranges.

Change slightly the strengths of any of the four forces that hold the world together (the strong nuclear force, the weak nuclear force, electromagnetism, gravitation), change critical particle masses and charges, and the stars would burn too quickly or too slowly, or atoms and molecules, including water, carbon, and oxygen, or amino acids (building blocks of life) would not form or remain stable.

Astrophysicists and microphysicists have joined to discover that, in the explosion that produced our universe, what seem to be widely varied facts really cannot vary widely, indeed that many of them can hardly vary at all, and have the universe develop life and mind. We find a single blast (the big bang) fine-tuned to produce a world that produces us, when any of a thousand other imaginable blasts would have yielded nothing.

How the various physical processes are 'fine-tuned to such stunning accuracy is surely one of the great mysteries of cosmology,' remarks P.C.W. Davies. 'Had this exceedingly delicate tuning of values been even slightly upset, the subsequent structure of the universe would have been totally different.' 'Extraordinary physical coincidences and apparently accidental cooperation ... offer compelling evidence that something is "going on." ... A hidden principle seems to be at work' (1982: 90, 110). Maybe we will need to draw theological conclusions, maybe not. But naturalistically, at least cosmologically, this seems to be a good system, not value free at all, but valuable, value-able, able to generate value.

In biology, by contrast, the history of life on Earth is a random walk with much struggle and chance, driven by selfish genes, although biologists have also found that in this random walk order is built up over the millennia across a neg-entropic upslope, attaining in Earth's natural history the most complex and highly ordered phenomena known in the universe, such as ecosystems, organisms, and, above all, the human mind.

So systemically we have a case of cognitive dissonance, a physical world that seems value free in some perspectives, valuable in others, and a biological world that seems fertile but clumsy, maybe evil.

Order and disorder

Perhaps the reason why all the good is in physics and the bad in biology is that all the order is in physics and all the disorder in biology. But the matter is complex. We are not going to get, and do not want, any law that says: order, more order, more and more order. Logically and empirically, there must be an interplay of order and disorder if there is to be autonomy, freedom, adventure, success, achievement, emergents, surprise, and idiographic particularity. In a world without chance there can be no creatures taking risks, and the skills of life would be very different, if indeed life – as opposed to mechanism – were possible.

But sceptics are not so sure. Yes, molecular biology is impressive for the order it has discovered. But no, when we turn to evolutionary biology, the processes get much more disordered. Evolutionary history has located the secret of life in natural selection operating over incremental variations, with the fittest selected to survive. The process is prolific, but no longer fine-tuned. On the contrary, it is make-shift.

The evolutionary course, far from being a directionally ordered whole, or having headings anywhere in its major or minor currents, rather wanders. It wanders in the first instance due to atomic and molecular chance (both relative and absolute) and, given these chancy mutational possibilities provided from the lower levels, it wanders in the second instance due to the nonselection for anything but mere survival, without bias toward progress, improvement, or complexity. The process is aimless, so it can bring evil as readily as it does good. Biologists survey the staggering array of fossil and surviving life forms, see it as full of struggling, chance, zigzag, and groping omnidirectionality, some trials happening to work, most failing, a very few of them eventuating in the ascent of neural forms.

Nevertheless, systemically, what most needs to be explained in biology is not the disorder, but the neg-entropic ascent. Biologists are much troubled by what account to give of any systemic, constructive forces that give a slope to evolution. (One might say that, at this point, the discipline is in disorder about order.) The physical world overall moves thermodynamically downhill, but now in bioscience we need an overall upslope force, or set of forces, a sort of biogravity that accounts not only for a survival drive but for the assembling and conservation of more diverse and also more advanced forms. With the passage of time and trials, there will, by ever more probability, be ever more salient constructions of life, enormous distances travelled upward.

Systemically, there seems a mixture of inevitability and openness, so that one way or another, given the conditions and constants of physics and chemistry, together with the biased earthen environment, life will somehow both surely and surprisingly appear. Manfred Eigen, a thermodynamicist, concludes 'that the evolution of life ... must be considered an *inevitable* process despite its indeterminate course' (1971: 519). Life is destined to come, yet the exact routes it will take are open and subject to historical vicissitudes.

Now we can get the biology back together with the physics. Despite the fine-tuned and systemically well-ordered nature we were sketching, there is disorder too in physics, the quantum indeterminism. Often that has no import for our native ranges of experience. Any uncertainty will be statistically, or systemically, masked out. A macro-determinism remains, despite a micro-indeterminism. Stochastic processes at lower levels are compatible with determinate processes at upper levels.

But perhaps there are sometimes gross effects. In genetics, events at the phenotypic level are profoundly affected by events launched at the genotypic level, as with point mutations or genetic crossing over, affected by radiation subject to quantum effects. This may affect regulatory molecules, as when allosteric enzymes, which amplify processes a million times, are in turn regulated by modifier molecules, of which there may be only a few copies in a cell, copies made from a short stretch of DNA, where a few atomic changes can shift a whole reading frame. Indeed, by the usual evolutionary account, the entire biological tale is an amplification of increments, where microscopic mutations are edited over by macroscopic selective processes. These increments are most finely resolved into molecular evolutions.

If we turn from the *random* to the *interaction* possibilities in physics, we gain a complementary picture. Nature is not just indeterminate in random ways but is plastic enough for an organism to work its program on. An organism can coagulate affairs this way and not that way, in accord with its cellular and genetic programs. The macromolecular system of the living cell is influencing by its interaction patterns the behaviour of the atomic systems. The organism is fine-tuned at the molecular level to nurse its way through the quantum states by electron transport, proton pumping, selective ion permeability, DNA encoding, and the like. The organism via its information and biochemistries participates in forming the course of the micro-events that constitute its passage through the world.

The organism is responsible, in part, for the micro-events, and not the other way round. The organism has to flow through the quantum states, but the organism selects the quantum states that achieve for it an informed flow-through. The information within the organism enables it to act as a preference sieve through the quantum states, by interaction sometimes causing quantum events, sometimes catching individual chance events which serve its program, and thereby the organism maintains its life course.

The organism is a whole that is program-laden, a whole that executes its lifestyle in dependence on this looseness in its parts. There is a kind of downward causation which complements an upward causation, and both feed on the openness, if also the order, in the atomic substructures. The microscopic indeterminism provides a looseness through which the organism can steer itself by taking advantage of the fluctuations at the micro levels.

These organisms, over time, maintain themselves in their species lines. Adaptation is imperfect, but if it were perfect evolution would cease, nor could life track changing environments, nor could we have evolved to where we are. It is the imperfection that drives the world toward perfection, the disvalue that is necessary in the search for more value. Natural selection requires disvalues in its exploration for values, but selects against them, to leave the values in place, so far as this is possible under local genetic and ecological constraints.

Now a different perspective on this earthen stew strikes us. Complexity requires multiple distinct parts with multiple connections. Too much distinctness yields disorder, chaos, contingency. Too much connection yields rigidity, determinism, order. Complexity must be situated between order and disorder, or 'at the edge of chaos,' or, we might say, 'on the edge of evil' on either side. A spontaneously organizing system (= 'self'-organizing) is one in which, over time, such complexity has appeared, is maintained, and may continue into the future.

This churn of materials, perpetually agitated and irradiated with energy, is not some problematic, indifferent, value-free substrate, but the prolific source. The neg-entropy is as objectively there as the entropy. Nor is the disordering entropy always bad, because in a world of perpetual construction there must be perpetual deconstruction. Systemically, the achievements are as real as the drifting cycles and random walks. Genetic organisms have been making biological discoveries superposed on the geomorphic and astronomical givens. Against the indifference, the results have been prolific, five million species flourishing in myriads of diverse ecosystems.

Life makes matter count. It loads the dice. Biological events are superintending physical ones. Biological nature takes advantage of physical nature. We gain space for the higher phenomena which physics had elected to leave out.

Law and history

What the random walk omits is the cybernetic, hereditary capacity of organisms to acquire, store, and transmit new information over historical time. Organisms start simple and some of them end up complex; there are trends over longer-range time scales because something is at work additionally to tracking drifting environments. The life process is drifting through an information search, locking onto discoveries. With such a conclusion we pass from a law-like world into a historical world, or more technically from a nomothetic system to an idiographic system.

The highest values are in story, not law, in history not repeatability. Only in a spontaneously generating story can there be such adventure and novelty. The familiar scientific word for this is 'evolution,' but the better word is 'history.' In physics and chemistry one seeks laws and initial conditions with which one can predict the future. But in biology any such laws become only regularities, subject to surprises. The novel discoveries, coded in the genetics, have not only revised the initial conditions, they have also revised the previous regularities. The disorder and openness generate history. The future is not like the past; there are developing story lines.

Frances Crick complains that biology has no 'elegance.' Organisms evolve happenstance structures and wayward functions that have no more overarching logic than the layout of the Manhattan subway system (Crick 1988: 6, 137–42). Stephen Jay Gould insists that the panda's thumb is evolutionary tinkering and that orchids are 'jury-rigged' (Gould 1980: 20). Evolution works with what is at hand, and makes something new out of it.

But what is so disvaluable about that? The achievements of evolution do not have to be optimal to be valuable; and if a reason that they are not optimal is that they had to be reached historically along story lines, it is more valuable to have history plus value as storied achievement than to have 'elegant' optimal solutions without history or autonomy. Organismic vitality is better than regimented simplicity. The elegance of the thirty-two crystal classes is not to be confused with the elegance of an old-growth forest.

Take Figures 8.1 and 8.2 on the following pages and suppose they looked instead like Figures 8.3 and 8.4.

Such a world would be impressive, but rather boring, less interesting than the world in which we in fact find ourselves. It would have too much system and too little adventure, too much law and no history.

Something is increasingly learned across evolutionary history: how to make more kinds and more complex kinds. This may be a truth about natural history, even if neo-Darwinism is incompetent to say much about how this happens. Cold and warm fronts come and go, so do ice ages. There are rock cycles, orogenic uplift, erosion, and uplift again. But there is no natural selection there, nothing is competing, nothing is surviving, nothing has adapted fit, and biology seems different. All those climatological and geomorphological agitations continue in the Pleistocene period more or less like they did in the Precambrian, but the life story is not the same all over again. Where once there were no species, now there are five

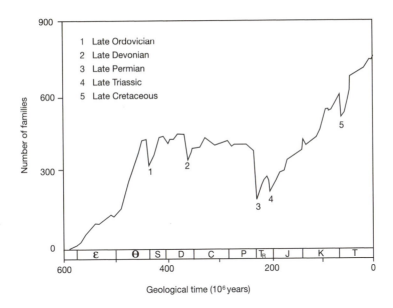

Figure 8.1 Standing diversity through time for families of marine vertebrates and invertebrates, with catastrophic extinctions

Source: Reprinted with permission from Raup and Sepkoski, 1982, p. 1502. Copyright 1982 American Association for the Advancement of Science.

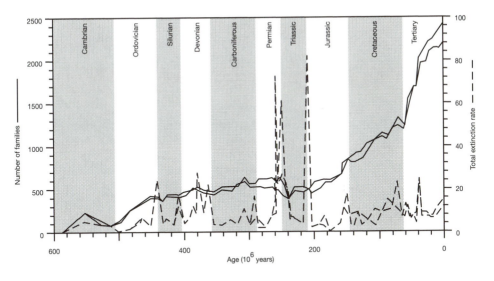

Figure 8.2 Proliferation of number of families on Earth, continuing through major extinctions. The double lines in both the number of families and the extinction rate represent maximum and minimum estimates.

Source: Reprinted with permission from Myers, 1997, p. 598, based on Nee and May, 1997. Copyright 1997 American Association for the Advancement of Science.

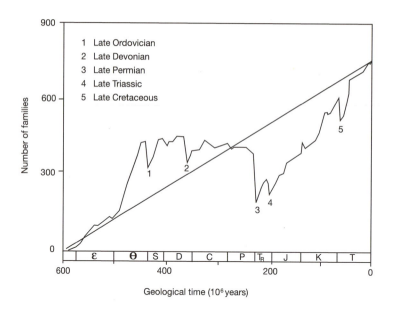

Figure 8.3 Supposed linear development of marine diversity

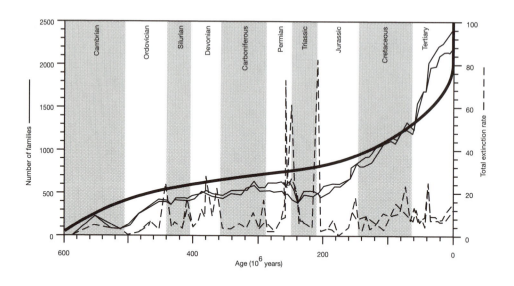

Figure 8.4 Supposed more orderly proliferation of life on Earth

to ten million. On average, and environmental conditions permitting, the numbers of life forms start low and end high.

J.W. Valentine concludes for marine environments: 'A major Phanerozoic trend among the invertebrate biota of the world's shelf and epicontinental seas has been towards more and more numerous units at all levels of the ecological hierarchy. ... The biosphere has become a splitter's paradise' (Valentine 1969: 706). There is 'a gradually rising average complexity' (Valentine 1973: 471). The story of terrestrial life is even more impressive, because the land environment is more challenging. Reptiles can cope in a broader spectrum of humidity conditions than amphibians. Mammals can cope in a broader spectrum of temperature conditions than reptiles. Genetic and enzymatic control is surpassed by neural networks and brains; there are increases in sentient capacity, locomotion, acquired learning, communication, language acquisition, and in manipulation.

There are increases in capacities for centralized control (neural networks, brains that surpass mere genetic and enzymatic control), increases in capacities for sentience (ears, eyes, noses, antennae), increases in locomotion (muscles, legs, wings), in capacities for manipulation (arms, hands, opposable thumbs), increases in acquired learning (feedback loops, synapses, memory banks), increases in communication and language acquisition. Nothing seems more evident over the long ranges than that complexity has increased, developing historically. In the Precambrian there were microbes; in the Cambrian Period trilobites were the highest life form; the Pleistocene Period produced persons.

Francisco J. Ayala concludes: 'Progress has occurred in nontrivial senses in the living world because of the creative character of the process of natural selection' (Ayala 1974: 353). Some will find that this is a 'law' of evolution. If so, this is a startling law: incessantly generate more biodiverse and complex kinds. Such law passes over into history.

Self and community

There are 'selves' – biological organismic identities to be preserved. No such selves exist, except in communities, ecosystems. It is difficult to imagine much life without a cellular character, difficult to imagine much biodiversity or biocomplexity without life being multicellular. It is difficult to imagine much organismic differentiation and specialization of functions and skills without a characteristic 'self.' To optimize a vital 'self' with a unique genetic self over a landscape of challenges, stabilities, and contingencies is really to develop a story line.

Further, one 'self' cannot do it all. No 'self' has 'aseity' (total self-containment). A lot of diversity, with autonomy, will mean a lot of interdependencies, feedback loops, feed forward loops, indeed a lot of feed loops. Systemically, it seems impossible – on this Earth at least – to have animal biology without 'feeding,' value capture, biotic resources such as energy and structural materials that were preformed outside oneself. It cannot be a bad thing for an organism to depend on another for skills or metabolisms it lacks, or else humans (who cannot photosynthesize) eating plants (which can) would be an evil. All heterotrophs of spectacular evolutionary achievement live in dependence on plants. A photosynthetic world would be a largely immobile world. In turn, autotrophs quite depend on animals for their carbon dioxide. Cycles and hypercycles build up.

The heavens are fine-tuned, and we are happy about the beauty and regularity there. But the heavens are also a world in which there is no caring. Earth, with its selves, is a world in which things can get hurt. You cannot be helped in a world where you cannot be hurt; you cannot live biologically in a world in which you cannot die; you cannot succeed in a world in which you cannot fail. Notice too that there is no community on the moon, on Mars, Jupiter, no interdependence of selves in community – and they are, comparatively, boring.

This self-impulse is the vital life impulse, the principal carrier of biological value. An organismic self is not a bad thing, nor is the defense of it, not *ipso facto* empirically or logically. Systemically put, the question is: are these good products the resultant of a bad process? If there is systemic disvalue, this must lie in an overextension or aberration of the self-impulse.

Every organism is full of 'selfish genes,' Richard Dawkins (1989) tells us. George Williams decries evolutionary nature because it 'can honestly be described as a process of maximizing short-sighted selfishness' (Williams 1988: 385). But a process that produces selves, and interrelates them in communities, need not be bad, nor one in which these selves reproduce their kinds, actualizing their own values.

The system evolves organisms that attend to their immediate somatic needs (food, shelter, metabolism) and that reproduce themselves in the very next generation. They have to be 'short-sighted.' In the birth-death-birth-death system a series of replacements is required. The organism must do this, it has no options; it is 'proper' for the organism to do this (Latin *proprium*, one's own proper characteristic). Somatic defense and genetic transmission are the only conservation activities possible to most organisms; they are necessary for all, and they must be efficient about it. The alleged selfishness is really the key to the systemic conservation of value intrinsic to the organism in the only manner possible and appropriate to it. Any particular organism, in the subroutines of this system, actualizes its own values and transmits these to the next generation (with variations). Although the organism is engaged in a short-range reproduction of its kind, the systemic processes are neither short-range and nor do they selfishly maximize only one kind. The system is three and a half billion years old; it has steadily produced new arrivals, replacements, and elaborations of kinds, going from zero to five (or ten) million species, through five (or ten) billion turnover species in a kaleidoscopic panorama. The result is a quite dramatic story, the history we were celebrating.

The genes seek only survival, but the story is of arrivals. The environmental system in which these selfish genes are embedded not only irritates them, producing an agitated effort at competitive survival, but also induces them, sometimes, to pass over into something higher. Species increase their kind; but ecosystems increase kinds.

In this kind of system, there will be, by logical and empirical necessity, bad things that happen to individuals. If an animal has one hundred available actions (locating a prey, stalking a prey, catching it, killing it, defending its place in the dominance hierarchy), and the animal needs to sequence ten of these, there are 100^{10} combinations available, an astronomical number. Unfolding such possibilities, it is inconceivable that such creatures will not make mistakes and have accidents, some of them tragic.

In the woods one comes upon the lovely nest of an ovenbird, built on the ground of grasses folded over like an old-fashioned oven. Inside are the chicks, but, alas, crushed, for they have been stepped on by a passing deer. That can seem a gratuitous evil. The deer gains nothing by the accident; had it stepped elsewhere nothing would have been really different for it. The bird has only lost.

But in a world where ovenbirds are on their own, and deer are free-ranging, these trajectories are sometimes going to clash. A world with creaturely integrities could not be otherwise, though a less valuable world of marionettes might. Windblown seeds fall, some on rock or unsuitable ground. Some get eaten. Some sprout to get killed by a frost; some die when the rains fail. But some succeed, and their species lines perpetuate in their communities. It cannot be otherwise in the prolific combination of order and disorder, law and history, self and community we enjoy on Earth.

But the caring self is on its own in a nature that doesn't care. Yes, and the same nature provides life support. As a species, organisms get selected for those functions and skills that enable them to do better in their niches, and what is so uncaring about that? Selection for adapted fit is a strange kind of indifference.

Conflict and resolution

In a world in which there are 'selves,' there are going to be conflicts between these 'selves,' as surely as there must be some cooperation among them. There are going to be winners and losers. If the environment can be good, that brings also the possibility of deprivation as a harm. To be alive is to have problems. Things can go wrong just because they can also go right. Organisms will hit limits, and these limits are, from the viewpoint of that organism, 'bad' for them. But these limits are not necessarily a bad thing, but rather are likely to be a good thing systemically, and even good for the species of which the organism is a member.

If irritability seems at first an unwelcome, adventitious intruder into the life project, by a switch of gestalts it becomes part of the biologic and logic of meanings. All advances come in contexts of problem solving, with a central problem in sentient life the prospect of hurt. We do not really have available to us any coherent alternative models by which, in a painless world, there might have come to pass anything like these dramas of nature that have happened. There is none of this on Mars, Jupiter.

Injury, harm, disease, and misfortune will come to individuals as a logical and empirical result of the character of the system. Sceptics will attempt a case by case analysis, and have little problem finding this or that event that is counterproductive, hurt with no beneficial result. It would have been a better world if the deer had not crushed the ovenbird's nest. Yes, you can sneak out such events here and there and not make any difference, systemically. But it is logically and empirically impossible systemically to eliminate all such events, or even foundationally significant numbers of such events, and have autonomous selves in the system. You cannot take out this class of events and have the richness of lives that has eventuated on Earth.

The system summarizes the lives of individuals in their conflict and resolution, using this to innovate by spinning out the biodiversity and biocomplexity we treasure. Failure in this system is 'evil' for each individual, but the summarizing and innovating system has not failed, not yet at least for 3.5 billion years.

Still, sceptics will insist: the relentless struggle to survive is an evil in the system. Adapted fit seems a good thing, but the shadow side is how each organism is doomed to eat or be eaten, to stake out what living it can in competition with others. Perhaps there is more efficiency than waste, more fecundity than indifference, but each organism is ringed about with competitors and limits, forced to do or die. Each is set as much against the world as within it. Physical nature, from which are wrested the materials of life, is brute fact and brutally there, caring naught and always threatening. Organic nature is savage; life preys on life. Predation of the orcas on the sea lions is difficult to watch without wincing.

Nature as a jungle does not mean that there are no valuers in the wild; it portrays too many claimants contesting scarce worth. Perhaps the most we can conclude is that local achievements of value are wrested out of a disvaluable place? But systemically, the truth lies deeper. The context of creativity logically and empirically requires this context of conflict and resolution. An environment entirely hostile would slay us; life could never have appeared within it. An environment entirely irenic would stagnate us; advanced life, including human life, could never have appeared there either. Oppositional nature is the first half of the truth; the second is that none of life's heroic quality is possible without this dialectical stress. Take away the friction, and would the structures stand? Would they move? Muscles, teeth, eyes, ears, noses, fins, legs, wings, scales, hair, hands, brains – all these and almost everything else comes out of the need to make a way through a world that mixes environmental resistance with environmental conductance. Half the beauty of life comes out of endurance through struggle.

What is this struggle but a history of transvaluing disvalues into values? Both are objectively present in nature, nor is the struggle a zero sum game, nor null of value; rather, the struggle is prolific creativity. Systemically, there is as much reason to think that the outcome of all this struggle is a good thing as a bad thing, especially if seen as a struggle for adapted fit and to thrust life on. Charles Darwin felt this keenly. The process is 'clumsy, wasteful, blundering, low, and horribly cruel' (quoted in De Beer 1962: 43). But Darwin concluded his *Origin of Species* by finding a 'grandeur in this view of life' (1872: 484).

John Stuart Mill cursed nature as an 'odious scene of violence' ([1874] 1969: 77, 398). Thomas Huxley admonished: 'Let us understand, once for all, that the ethical process of society depends, not on imitating the cosmic process, still less on running away from it, but in combating it' ([1893] 1946: 82). George Williams hates nature: 'Mother Nature is a wicked old witch!' (1993). Over evolutionary history, with the diversity, complexity, and creativity we have celebrated, there emerges the capacity to suffer. Indeed the story could be titled, perversely, 'The Evolution of Suffering.' Each seeming advance – from plants to animals, instinct to learning, ganglia to brains, sentience to self-awareness, herbivores to carnivores – steps up the pain. Struggle deepens through time into suffering. In chemistry, physics, astronomy, geomorphology, meteorology nothing suffers; in botany life is stressed, but only in zoology does pain emerge. Is not this the evolution of increasing disvalue? A more adequate answer is that struggle is the dark side of creativity. The system, from the perspective of the individual, is built on competition and premature death. Seen systemically, that is the generating and testing of selves by conflict and resolution, such values required to be both prolific and adapted fits.

Generate and test

The standard account is that evolution is blind. Random variations bubble up from the genetic level. Those few that are accidentally useful are selected; most, worthless, are discarded; some, to which even natural selection is blind, since they produce no differential survival rates, remain and result in genetic drift. Zig here, zag there, organisms stumble onto a life program. 'The evolutionary process,' says George Williams, 'is abysmally stupid' (Williams 1988: 400).

But genetic creativity is really quite startling in what it has produced: many millions of species all the way from microbes to persons, coded for coping in all kinds of environments, and we may want to think further about whether it is something more than a random walk. Genetic vitality may be in fact a sophisticated problem-solving process.

In reproduction, the genetically originated novelties are formed in a shuffle that is far from chaotic. Only those variations are tested and selected that are more or less functional. The organism typically only probes the nearby space for possible directions of development. Mutators and antimutators increase or trim the mutation rates as a function of population stresses. Repair mechanisms snip out certain genetic errors, and thus eliminate some variation. Individual genetic sets are adept at pumping out their own disorder. But they do not pump out all novelty; that would cease evolutionary development and lead to extinction (Gardner 1975: 267–303).

Specific mutations are non-directed, but the rate and place at which they occur is partially regulated. There is a tendency for genes to sort in blocks, often pre-tested blocks (Mayr 1976). There is a shake-up of the genes under environmental stress, so that the fastest evolution toward variant forms, often more highly organized forms, takes place almost explosively after major geologic crises.

These trials and ancestral forms are subject to optimizing pressures and tested for their performances. What nature conserves is the best of its constructions within a particular ecological niche. Mutation scans for new 'ideas,' and natural selection throws out the trash and saves the gems. Evolutionary achievement is a rudimentary form of cognition. In terms of human imagination and logic, it is not always a waste but sometimes an index of creativity to cast forth a thousand ideas so as to sort out the single best one.

Systemically, the gestalt begins to change. The evolutionary process, far from being irrational, is a prototype of the only kind of rationality that we know. There is a logic to it, not only to its information conservation, but to its random exploration and problem solving. The speciation process is drifting through an information search, and edited for its discoveries of information. This editing is for survival, but it also scans and produces new arrivals on a climb toward complexity, sentience, and, eventually, mind. It is the production of errors that produces knowledge. The whole system is a context of instruction. Natural selection at its critical turnings will select those mutations that are superior and reproduce them. It tends in that direction, even though it does not intend it. Thus the seeming absurdity of the random element can be put in a more intelligible gestalt, where it becomes a precondition of epistemic development.

Contemporary geneticists are insisting that we misperceive this process if we think of it as blind. There is a vast array of sophisticated enzymes to cut, splice, digest, rearrange, mutate, reiterate, edit, correct, translocate, invert, and truncate particular gene sequences. John H. Campbell concludes: 'Cells are richly provided with special enzymes to tamper with DNA structure,' enzymes that biologists are extracting for genetic engineering. But this 'engineering' is already going on in spontaneous nature. 'Gene-processing enzymes also engineer comparable changes in genes in vivo. … We have discovered enzymes and enzyme pathways for almost every conceivable change in the structure of genes. The scope for self-engineering of multigene families seems to be limited only by the ingenuity of control systems for regulating these pathways.' These pathways may have 'governors' that are 'extraordinarily sophisticated.' 'Self-governed genes are "smart" machines in the current vernacular sense. Smart genes suggests smart cells and smart evolution, … the promise of radically new genetic and evolutionary principles' (Campbell 1983: 408–10, 414).

So far from disparaging the blind groping of genes, computer scientists may deliberately seek to imitate a similar process on their unconscious computers. Some sophisticated programs use what are called 'genetic algorithms' (Goldberg 1989; Mühlenbein, Gorges-Schleuter and Krämer 1988). Such algorithms involve recombining partial solutions to a problem in order to generate improved solutions. Genetic problem solving, then, does not seem so tinkering, jury-rigged, and blind. On the contrary, it is remarkably like what some of the smartest scientists are doing. There is valuable problem solving taking place. Maybe there is more elegance than we first thought. Certainly there are remarkable success stories.

Nature and grace

Biology and religion have increasingly joined in recent years in admiration for this marvellous planet. We see in nature, beyond any natural laws, a kind of grace. Grace, most will think, belongs in the theological tradition, where goodness appears that one has no cause to expect, a salvation that one has not merited, a favour that one does not deserve. But in nature too there is surprising goodness, something given that has no justification in law or logic, even if there does seem some heading or destiny filling up the world with these wonders.

Classical theology frequently separated nature and grace, a sometimes useful contrast. But today, systemically in natural history, we can combine nature and grace at new levels of insight and intensity. Life is a kind of gift. There is startling fertility, genesis. This is among the best established facts. This creativity we inherit, and the values this generates, are the ground of our being, not just the ground under our feet. Nature is grace, whatever more grace may also be. Earth is an expression point of a mysterious power in cosmic nature.

Life persists because it is provided for in the evolutionary and ecological Earth system. Earth is a kind of providing ground, where the life epic is lived on in the midst of its perpetual perishing, life arriving and struggling through to something higher. When J.B.S. Haldane was asked whether he had concluded anything about the character of life from his long studies in biology, he replied that the marks of biological nature were its 'beauty,' 'tragedy,' and 'inexhaustible queerness' (1932, 1966: 167–9).

This beauty approaches the sublime; the tragedy is perpetually redeemed with the renewal of life, and the inexhaustible queerness recomposes as the numinous. If anything at all on Earth is sacred, it must be this enthralling creativity that characterizes our home planet. So the secular – this present, empirical epoch, this phenomenal world, studied by science – urges us on a spiritual quest. If there is any holy ground, any land of promise, this promising Earth is it. Today we say: life is generated 'at the edge of chaos.' Yesterday, John said: 'The light shines in the darkness, and the darkness has not overcome it' (John 1:5).

Annie Dillard rebels against Earth: 'I came from the world, I crawled out of a sea of amino acids, and now I must whirl around and shake my fist at that sea and cry shame' (Dillard 1974: 180). But if I were Aphrodite, rising from the sea, I think I would turn back to reflect on that event and raise both hands and cheer. And if I came to realize that my rising out of the misty seas involved a long struggle of life renewed in the midst of its perpetual perishing, I might well fall to my knees in praise. Out of physical premises one derives biological conclusions, and, taking these as premises in turn, one derives psychological conclusions, which, recompounded again, yield spiritual conclusions. This kind of logic seems more story than argument; the form of argument is not so much rational as, to use a religious word, incarnational, since each step has to be embodied. Story is a better category than law, much less randomness, when one wants to get more out of less. If one tries to interpret the world as law plus initial conditions, there is little plot. If one tries to interpret the world as statistical probabilities, there is little story.

Science has disenchanted natural history, but this only increases the mystery. The story is quite fantastic, except that it is true. Maybe the best category, systemically updated, is that of miracle. Moses thought that the burning bush, not consumed, was quite a miracle. We hardly believe any more in that sort of supernatural miracle; science has made such stories incredible. But what has it left instead? A self-organizing photosynthesis driving a life synthesis that has burned for millennia, life as a strange fire that outlasts the sticks that feed it. This is hardly a phenomenon less marvellous, even if we no longer want to say that it is miraculous. Indeed, in the original sense of 'miracle' – a wondrous event, without regard to the question whether natural or supernatural – photosynthesis and the life it supports is the secular equivalent of the burning bush.

The bush that Moses watched was an individual in a species line that had perpetuated itself for millennia, coping by the coding in its DNA, fuelled by the sun, using cytochrome-c molecules several billion years old, and surviving without being consumed. To go back to the miracle that Moses saw, a bush that burned briefly without being consumed, would be to return to something several orders of magnitude less spectacular.

Thanks to the molecular biologists and geneticists, we increasingly know how this works; but is this an account that de-mystifies what is going on? The account we have is, if you like, a naturalistic account, but this nature is pretty spectacular stuff, a remarkable 'given,' even if you dislike thinking it might be a 'gift.' Yes, there is this spinning round of trillions of molecules, organizing themselves into a code for life, and executing this in a coping individual; but is there anything that suggests that such prolific nature is its own self-sufficient explanation?

Every life is an unceasing adventure in endowment and risk, and all organic being is constituted – to employ a scientific metaphor – in a mixture of environmental conductance and resistance, where the world is both resource and threat. To adapt the Psalmist's religious metaphor, life is lived in green pastures and in the valley of the shadow of death, nourished by eating at a table prepared in the midst of its enemies.

Cruciform creation

The root idea in the word 'nature' is 'birthing,' of a woman in labour (Greek *natans*, giving birth). Birth is a transformative experience where suffering is the prelude to, the principle of, creation. There is struggling through to something higher. Death *in vivo* is death ultimately; death *in communitatis* is death penultimately but life regenerated ultimately: life, death, and regeneration. Life is the first mystery that comes out of earthen nature, and death a secondary one. But death comes as surely as life to all higher organisms. Even the lower forms that reproduce by cell fission or by generating offshoots may and do die. So the great value, life, is countered by the great disvalue. For each organism, the last word is destruction.

But we are trying to see nature systemically, where death is not the last word – at least it has never yet been across three and a half billion years. Death is the key to replacement with new life. If nothing much had ever died, nothing much could have ever lived. Just as the individual overtakes, assimilates to itself, and discards its resource materials, so the evolutionary wave is propagated onward, using and sacrificing particular individuals, who are employed in, but readily abandoned to, the larger currents of life. Thus the pro-life evolution both overleaps death and seems impossible without it. Death is part of the life cycle, not life part of the death cycle.

The death of the organism feeds into the non-death of the species. Only by replacements can the species track the changing environment; only by replacements can they evolve into something else. Species sometimes do die, go extinct without issue, but they are often transformed into something else, new species; and, on average, there have been more arrivals than extinctions – the increase of both diversity and complexity over evolutionary history.

These experiences of the power of survival, of new life rising out of the old, of the transformative character of suffering, of good resurrected out of evil, experiences of the harshness of nature invite us systemically toward a natural theology, and one congenial with Christian theology. Christianity seeks by a doctrine of providence to draw all affliction into the divine will. This requires penetrating backward from a climaxing cross and resurrection to see how this is so. Nature is intelligible. Life forms are logical systems. But nature is also *cruciform*. The world is not a paradise of hedonistic ease, but a theatre where life is learned and earned by labour. Life is advanced not only by thought and action, but also by suffering, not only by logic but also by pathos.

The Greek word is 'pathos,' suffering, and there are pathologies in nature, such as the diseases of parasitism. But pathology is only part of the disvalue; even in health there is suffering. Life is indisputably prolific; it is just as indisputably pathetic, almost as if its logic were pathos, as if the whole of sentient nature were pathological. This pathetic element in nature is seen in faith to be at the deepest logical level the pathos in God. God is not in a simple way the Benevolent Architect, but is rather the Suffering Redeemer. The whole of the earthen metabolism needs to be understood as having this character. The God met in physics as the divine wellspring from which matter-energy bubbles up, as the upslope epistemic force, is in biology the suffering and resurrecting power that redeems life out of chaos. All have 'borne our griefs and carried our sorrows.'

The abundant life that Jesus exemplifies and offers to his disciples is that of sacrificial suffering through to something higher. There is something divine about the power to suffer through to something higher. The Spirit of God is the genius that makes alive, that redeems life from its evils. The cruciform creation is, in the end, deiform, godly, just because of this element of struggle, not in spite of it. There is a great divine 'yes' hidden behind and within every 'no' of crushing nature. Redemptive suffering is a model that makes sense of nature and history. So far from making the world absurd, suffering is a key to the whole, not intrinsically, not as an end in itself, but as a transformative principle, transvalued into its opposite. The capacity to suffer through to joy is a supreme emergent and an essence of Christianity. Yet the whole evolutionary upslope is a lesser calling of this kind, in which renewed life comes by blasting the old. Life is gathered up in the midst of its throes, a blessed tragedy, lived in grace through a besetting storm.

Biblical writers rejoice in nature; they also speak of nature labouring in travail. 'Travail,' 'birthing,' in fact, is a key to understanding these evils.

Paul writes that 'the whole creation has been groaning in travail together until now' (Romans 8:22). That is archaic in the antique sense, and equally archaic in the foundational sense: a cruciform creation. But note that Paul nowhere says – what is usually understood, indeed what Paul may also have believed – that this subjecting to suffering was a result of human sin. 'Groaning in travail' is in the nature of things from time immemorial. Such travail is the Creator's will, productive as it is of glory.

We have tried to see into the depths of what is taking place in natural history. The view here is not panglossian; it is a sometimes tragic view of life, but one in which tragedy is the shadow of prolific creativity. That *is* the case, and the biological sciences – evolutionary history, ecology, molecular biology – can be brought to support this view, although neither tragedy nor creativity are part of their ordinary vocabulary. Since the world we have, in its general character, is the only world logically and empirically possible under the natural givens on Earth – so far as we can see at these native ranges that we inhabit – this world that *is*, *ought* to be. A world without blood would be poorer, but a world without bloodshed would be poorer too, both less rich in biodiversity and less divine.

References

Ayala, F.J. (1974) 'The Concept of Biological Progress', in F.J. Ayala, T. Dobzhansky (eds.), *Studies in the Philosophy of Biology*, New York: Macmillan, 339–55.

Campbell, J.H. (1983) 'Evolving Concepts of Multigene Families', in [no named ed.] *Isozymes: Current Topics in Biological and Medical Research, Volume 10: Genetics and Evolution*, New York: Alan R. Liss, 401–17.

Crick, F. (1988) *What Mad Pursuit: A Personal View of Scientific Discovery*, New York: Basic Books.

Darwin, C. (1872) *The Origin of Species*, New York: Collier Books.

Davies, P.C.W. (1982) *The Accidental Universe*, New York: Cambridge University Press.

Dawkins, R. (1989) *The Selfish Gene*, new edition, New York: Oxford University Press.

De Beer, G. (1962) *Reflections of a Darwinian*, London: Thomas Nelson and Sons.

Dillard, A. (1974) *Pilgrim at Tinker Creek*, New York: Bantam Books.

Eigen, M. (1971) 'Selforganization of Matter and the Evolution of Biological Macromolecules', *Die Naturwissenschaften* 58: 465–523.

Gardner, E.J. (1975) *Principles of Genetics*, 5th edition, New York: John Wiley.

Goldberg, D. (1989) *Genetic Algorithms in Search, Optimization, and Machine Learning*, Reading, MA: Addison Wesley.

Gould, S.J. (1980) *The Panda's Thumb*, New York: W.W. Norton.

Haldane, J.B.S. (1932, 1966) *The Causes of Evolution*, Ithaca: Cornell University Press.

Huxley, T.H. [1893] (1946) 'Evolution and Ethics,' in T.H. Huxley and Julian Huxley, *Evolution and Ethics*, London: Pilot Press.

Mayr, Ernst (1976) *Evolution and the Diversity of Life*, Cambridge, MA: Harvard University Press.

Mill, J.S. (1874) 'Nature', in *Collected Works*, vol. 10, Toronto: University of Toronto Press, 1969, pages 1963–77.

Mühlenbein, H., Gorges-Schleuter, M. and Krämer, O. (1988) 'Evolution Algorithms in Combinatorial Optimization', *Parallel Computing* 7: 65–85.

Myers, Norman (1997) 'Mass Extinction and Evolution', *Science* 278: 597–8.

Nee, Sean and May, Robert M. (1997) 'Extinction and the Loss of Evolutionary History', *Science* 278: 692–4.

Raup, David M. and Sepkoski, Jr., J. John (1982) 'Mass Extinctions in the Marine Fossil Record', *Science* 215: 1501–3.

Valentine, J.W. (1969) 'Patterns of Taxonomic and Ecological Structure of the Shelf Benthos during Phanerozoic Time', *Paleontology* 12: 684–709.

—— (1973) *Evolutionary Paleoecology of the Marine Biosphere*, Englewood Cliffs, NJ: Prentice-Hall.

Williams, G.C. (1988) 'Huxley's Evolution and Ethics in Sociobiological Perspective', *Zygon: Journal of Religion and Science* 23: 383–407.

—— (1993) 'Mother Nature is a Wicked Old Witch', in Matthew H. Nitecki and Doris V. Nitecki (eds.) *Evolutionary Ethics*, Albany: State University of New York Press, 217–31.

9

COOPERATION OR
COMPETITION
Comments on Rolston

Jacobus J. de Vries

Holmes Rolston argues that our world is the best of all possible worlds and, in view of the fine-tuning of basic physical laws and parameters, perhaps the only possible world, this in spite of the inherent aspect of disvalue or evil that is caused by the struggle for life (or the struggle to survive) through competition and selection with suffering as a side-effect. This mechanism of biological evolution out of chaos seems a prerequisite for development ('progress') and a necessary adaptation to changing conditions within the physical evolution of the Earth. In other words, Rolston reasons that evil is inevitable because it is part of natural selection, which in turn is an inherent part of the evolution process.

There are evolutionary biologists who – in contrast – consider symbiosis and cooperation as the dominant mechanisms in the evolutionary process. Well-known advocates of this theory are Lynn Margulis and Dorion Sagan (1997). They argue, partly following the theories of Ivan E. Wallin (1927), that the vehicle of evolution is the fusion of different organisms into a symbiotic system which subsequently created new bodies, organs and species. Moreover, nearly all organisms live in some kind of symbiosis and show relicts of earlier symbiosis. Examples are the mitochondria in the human cell, which used to be independent bacteria. In fact, the basic substance of cells consists of bacterial nucleo-cytoplasma.

Others (e.g. Augros and Stanciu 1987) have investigated the behaviour of present day life and concluded that natural selection and competition are not omnipotent on Earth. All species have their own niche and nature makes use of all kinds of ingenuity to avoid competition, or at least its negative effects. Within species, there seems hardly any struggle or killing on a large scale. Moreover, there is no proof that natural selection has caused more than rather superficial adaptations within species. This of course does not mean the absence of the disvalue of suffering by illness, death and disasters, partly because of competition. But if evolution is characterized by cooperation rather than by competition, one wonders if evil is part of an evolutionary strategy.

Competition and selection are perhaps more important in the history of mankind, where we find similar mechanisms to those in biological evolution. Cooperation, competition, selection, accumulation of information, increasing complexity and the associated adverse effects of war, genocide and environmental destruction are inherent aspects of the progress of civilization. This process can be explained and summarized in the aphorism: '*That man wants to be who he is not, and wants to have what he does not have, is the source of all progress and all evil.*'

We can distinguish between technical and social aspects in the history of civilization. Technical progress evolved by competition as well as cooperation, and obviously human manipulation of the earth surface was driven by the wish to improve God's creation, to make it a better place to live, or just to cope with changing conditions. However, the physiographic structures are chaotic, self-organizing systems and very robust to changing natural conditions. Human interference, by harnessing natural systems, has disturbed the regulating feedback processes and often led to destabilization and human-induced disasters. This is evident in my profession, hydrology and water management. From the dawn of civilization, man has applied irrigation and drainage to improve agricultural production and has built structures for protection against floods, for power generation, to ensure the availability of drinking water and to improve sanitation. At present, more than three-quarters of agricultural production is dependent on water management, which means that the majority of people are in one way or another dependent on manipulation of their environment. All these wonderful technological and scientific achievements, however, have created the adverse effects of overpopulation, pollution, destabilization and environmental destruction and have put mankind in a dependable and vulnerable position.

But not just technological measures have caused harm; socio-economic and political manipulation might be considered even more destructive, with the excesses of communism and fascism as clear examples, the former by trying to eliminate competition and the latter by enhancing competition and selection. Both systems can be characterized by a lack of flexibility and natural feedback, which have caused accumulated evil side-effects and eventually resulted in collapse. Apart from these large-scale manipulations, mankind has continuously suffered from competition for space and political and economic domination.

Fortunately, humans are aware of the moral aspects of their striving to change and progress, which has very often resulted in suppression and destruction of the weakest and ended with losers on both sides. They therefore acquired or developed ethical principles of compassion and cooperation as a counterbalance. Whether these ethics are an evolutionary product because they proved an advantage to the survival of the group, or whether they have a supernatural (or transcendent) origin as suggested in most religions, is not relevant in this respect, although endorsement of ethical behaviour is certainly promoted by a transcendent legitimization. Cooperation is often an advantage in an evolutionary sense, but care and compassion may also have evolutionary roots.

My conclusion is that both cooperation, with altruistic costs, and competition, the latter with suffering as a side-effect, are inherent and unavoidable components of the biological world. With respect to civilization, one may argue that mankind, in its attempts to improve living conditions, has applied the principles of biological evolution of cooperation as well as competition and natural selection. Humans have accordingly produced progress with the evil of social as well as environmental destruction as adverse effects. One may speculate as to whether humans will eventually (as a side-effect of civilization) destroy each other and/or their habitat, making civilization one of the many experiments within the evolutionary process which fails to survive in the long term.

References

Augros, R. and Stanciu, G. (1987) *The New Biology*, Boston: Shambhala Publications.

Margulis, L. and Sagan, D. (1997) *Slanted Truths: Essays on Gaia, Symbiosis and Evolution*, New York: Copernicus Books.

Wallin, I.E. (1927) *Symbiotism and the Origin of the Species*, Baltimore: Williams & Wilkins.

10

ROLSTON

A contemporary physico-theologian

Jozef Keulartz

Rolston tells a grand narrative, under the heading 'The Way of Nature is the Way of the Cross', and adds, with self-assurance: 'The story is quite fantastic, except that it is true.' In doing so he shows courage but also a certain degree of obstinacy. Since Kant, modern philosophy has taken the road from unity to plurality, to difference, dissemination, deconstruction and discontinuity. Instead of the one grand narrative there is a multitude of narratives, language-games, discourse-genres and vocabularies. To quote Richard Rorty, 'there are many descriptions of the world and of ourselves possible, and the most important distinction is that between those descriptions which are less and those which are more useful with respect to a specific purpose' (1999: 27). My main questions will be: what kind of discourse-genre does Rolston's story represent and which problems are connected with this genre. To answer the first question I will proceed in three steps.

First, Rolston places himself explicitly in the tradition of so-called 'providentialism'. This eighteenth-century movement strove to reconcile the theological truths of Christianity with the scientific findings of natural history research. The best-known work in the providentialist tradition was written by the Anglican canon William Derham and published under the title *Physico-Theology* in 1713. The book was intended to provide proof of the existence of God and to deduce His qualities from Creation. Derham's book was so successful that all future providentialist literature was presented as physico-theology. The providentialist literature bears the character of a 'theodicy'. A theodicy tries to answer the question of how God's goodness is reconcilable with the evil in the world. In physico-theology the evil that results from the 'struggle for life' is portrayed as an essential element of natural harmony. This struggle between species, notably between predators and prey, guarantees that a balance will be maintained among the various species.

Second, Rolston makes a powerful appeal to Darwin. It is under Darwin's influence that Rolston situates the struggle for life not so much between as within species. Therefore Rolston's story is all about natural selection. As John Brooke argues in his contribution, Darwin's evolutionary biology offered new prospects for a theodicy: 'If the working of natural selection required struggle and competition for limited resources then one might see animal and human pain not as features of Nature to be deplored but as the necessary concomitants of a creative process.' A fairly exact description of Rolston's position.

Finally, Rolston's account is indebted to the holist movement. The holist movement manifested itself in the 1920s and 1930s in the work of philosophers such as Alfred North Whitehead and Adolf Meyer-Abich, and ecologists like William Morton Wheeler, Warder Allee, Karl Friederichs and August Thienemann. Following Aldo Leopold, Rolston himself defends a weak organic holism – communitarian holism. The political message of holism is that a community's chances of survival are totally dependent on the unconditional subservience of its members to the greater whole, of their readiness to exercise self-discipline, self-denial and self-sacrifice. Rolston interprets the natural occurrence of suffering and sacrifice in the light of the New Testament. I quote: 'The abundant life that Jesus exemplifies and offers to his disciples is that of a sacrificial suffering through to something higher. ... The cruciform creation is, in the end, deiform, godly, just because of this element of struggle, not in spite of it. ... suffering is a key to the whole.'

In summary, Rolston's story represents a specific type of physico-theology, a mixture of providentialism, Darwinism and holism. Now let's turn to the question: what is problematic about this story?

From a theological point of view Rolston's story can be criticized in at least two ways. First, the most radical criticism can be derived from the work of Karl Barth. According to Barth, God is the complete Other, about which we can neither learn nor experience anything on the basis of our knowledge of the world. Influenced by Kierkegaard, Barth opposed any form of rational or natural theology. Instead, he defends a theology of revelation: anything and everything we can learn about God we owe to his self-revelation in Christ.

Second, the criticism of Immanuel Kant is less radical. His opposition does not concern rational or natural theology in general, but only one specific type of these, namely physico-theology. Physico-theology is not a fully fledged theology, according to Kant, because it does not step outside nature and consequently cannot answer the questions of what the purpose and goal of nature itself are. Rolston also fails to provide an answer to these questions. In the course of evolution, he states, life becomes more and more diverse and complex. However, biodiversity and biocomplexity are morally neutral terms. A fully fledged theology can only come into being, according to Kant, if physico-theology is complemented by an ethico-theology which takes as its starting point not the natural but the moral order. The distinction between physico- and ethico-theology goes back to the distinction between nature and freedom, between *Sein* and *Sollen*. As a contemporary physico-theologian, Rolston is forced to deny the importance of this distinction. In many places in his work he therefore resists the idea of a gap between 'is' and 'ought', and the idea that someone who reasons from facts to values commits a naturalistic fallacy. On this point, however, Rolston has to deal with a serious problem. This problem manifests itself in his anthropology, as expounded in his main work *Environmental Ethics*.

On the one hand, Rolston understands humans as the ecosystem's most sophisticated products. 'They have the highest per capita intrinsic value of any life form supported by the system' (Rolston 1988: 73). On the other hand, however, he considers them to be misfits in the system. Except perhaps for primitive tribes, human activities only degrade the system. According to Rolston, humankind is the great terror and humans are super-killers. It is an evil for humans to be like beasts, propagating only their kind. To fit in the system humans have to transcend their own interests. Different from animals, humans are actually capable of doing this. 'Animals are wholly absorbed into those niches in which they have such satisfactory fitness, but humans can stand apart from the world and consider themselves in relation to it. Humans are eccentric to the world. ... So humans can begin to comprehend what comprehends them; in this lies their paradox and responsibility' (Rolston 1988: 71). There is indeed a paradox here: man, the ecosystem's most sophisticated product, owes his existence to a process of natural selection, but should abandon the further development of this process in order not to destroy the ecosystem once and for all. The question is: where does man find the moral strength to put the process of natural selection out of action and to transcend his own interests? Here it becomes painfully obvious that physico-theology only has eyes for the natural order and is blind to the moral order of the world.

Another serious problem Rolston has to contend with concerns the ecological basis of his physico-theology. Rolston's ecosystem theory is indebted to early twentieth-century holism. In this theory the whole, which is greater than the sum of its parts, is interpreted in a realistic way. In postwar system ecology this realistic interpretation is replaced by a nominalistic interpretation in which the whole merely serves as a scientific working hypothesis and as a methodologically useful construct. However, even this kind of methodological holism is under discussion at the moment. Among ecologists there is no consensus about such central notions as 'ecosystem' or 'community'. And as Shrader-Frechette and McCoy have concluded: 'Building a general ecological theory on notions of "community" or "ecosystem" that are ambiguous, inconsistent and unclear is like building a skyscraper on sand' (1994: 112). It is not surprising, then, that ecosystem theory has now lost much of its appeal. I quote Donald Worster (1995: 283): 'A survey of recent ecology textbooks shows that the concept [of "ecosystem"] is not even mentioned in one leading work and has a much diminished place in the others.' From the mid-1970s the holistic approach in ecology has increasingly given way to an individualistic approach.

These remarks make it clear that any appeal to 'the' ecology is highly deceptive and misleading. It ignores the fallible and contingent nature of this science and, what is more, it ignores the fact that ecology, too, is a battlefield of competing paradigms and research programmes. In short, there are many visions of nature at work within ecology; there is not just one story, one Earth narrative. There are different stories, which more often than not contradict each other. I must conclude, therefore, that Rolston's physico-theology is highly debatable, both from a physical and from a theological point of view.

References

Rolston, H. (1988) *Environmental Ethics*, Philadelphia: Temple University Press.
Rorty, R. (1999) *Philosophy and Social Hope*, New York: Penguin Books.
Shrader-Frechette, K.S. and McCoy, E.D. (1994) 'How the Tail Wags the Dog: How Value Judgments Determine Ecological Science', *Environmental Values* 3: 107–20.
Worster, D. (1995) 'The Ecology of Order and Chaos', in C. Pierce and D. VanDe-Veer (eds), *People, Penguins, and Plastic Trees: Basic Issues in Environmental Ethics* (2nd edn), Belmont, CA: Wadsworth: 280–88.

11

ARE CATASTROPHES IN NATURE EVER EVIL?

Jan Smit

Catastrophes such as the one that took place at the Cretaceous–Tertiary boundary (in short, the K/T boundary) 65 million years ago wipe out large standing stocks of living creatures. These catastrophes are contingent upon the presence of natural 'threats', if one so wishes, of various kinds. These threats are well identified, but it seems that only those that happen on historical timescales, i.e. those that are experienced by mankind, undergo ample treatment and are considered worthy of intense scientific scrutiny (and proper funding). I do not consider here the disasters that mankind imposes upon himself, such as the Second World War, although the next major extinction event since the K/T boundary is likely to be contingent upon the ubiquitous presence of our species over the entire world (Ward 1993). A successful species does not tolerate the presence of a competitor. And animals, if not subjected to our use, are by definition competitors to mankind. Thus, as a purely hypothetical prediction: the next intelligent species will appear on Earth only when mankind totally disappears or is kept in cages or reserves where it poses no threat to the then prevailing intelligent species. A similar thing happened to mammals: they had already been there for over 120 million years during the reign of the dinosaurs, but only the disappearance of the dinosaurs made their successful evolution and proliferation possible.

Well-known contingent threats are (in a geological perspective) the eruption of volcanoes, the occurrence of huge earthquakes, the possible (inevitable) rise of sea level by several centimetres after the melting of the continental ice masses, the deep freeze for Western Europe when Younger Dryas conditions return. The Younger Dryas is the short geological period that started about 12,700 years ago and ended 11,400 years ago, when northern Europe suddenly, in a matter of years, became tundra again, although the last ice age had been over for several thousand years. If this happens today, no crops will grow in what is now Western Europe (see *www.theatlantic.com/issues/98jan/climate.htm*). Note that all these catastrophes may only be disastrous for mankind. Nature itself will probably not be influenced significantly, and does not care, unless such phenomena are scaled up until the climatic effects become global and the abundant, cosmopolitan, species start to disappear.

Let's have a look at a few catastrophes in the geological past.

Earthquakes occur only locally. In order to shake the earth globally one needs to speculate about possible Earth–core–mantle boundary heating mechanisms that might trigger an unprecedented acceleration of the movements of the plates of the lithosphere. There is ample evidence that contradicts the idea of such enormous deviations of a uniformitarian Earth: plate-tectonics has proceeded for hundreds of millions of years in a slow and steady fashion.

Similarly, volcanic eruptions (often put forward as the causal mechanism for major extinction events) cannot be scaled up indefinitely. There are two kinds of volcanism that pose a threat: 1) The explosive type, for example the 1994 Pinatubo eruption in the Philippines, and 2) the non-explosive type that cause fissure eruptions over a wide area, e.g. the Laki eruption of 1783 on Iceland. Again, this kind of environmental threat is a disaster only from a human perspective; nature does not care. Scaling Pinatubo up to the maximum is not easy. Computer modelling can help, but the models available are not yet satisfactory. It is simpler and more reliable to look back in geological time and observe what is the maximum the Earth has ever experienced. The Krakatoa (1883), Pinatubo (1991) and Tambora (1815) eruptions are catastrophic from the human, historical perspective but do very little to influence the biosphere. The largest volcanic eruptions observed in geological history were more devastating by two orders of magnitude. The most recent, and one of the largest, the Toba lake eruption in northern Sumatra, occurred about 75,000 years ago. The ashes are found almost 2,000 km away in Sri Lanka but, as far as geological evidence shows, there have been no long-lasting effects on the biosphere, although on a local scale northern Sumatra must have been sterilized.

Large fissure eruptions (plateau basalts) are a non-explosive type of basalt outflow, often occurring in enormous quantities. In geological history (none has happened in human history) there are episodes where kilometre-thick piles of such basalts have accumulated; in places in excess of 2,000 km^3 of basalts must have been extruded in a matter of weeks. Such eruptions might have influenced the composition of the atmosphere for a short time, and have led to environmental stress sufficient to cause extinction(s) of species. There is some flimsy evidence for this at the end of the Cretaceous period, when large amounts of lava, known as the Deccan traps, covered the Indian peninsula. But nothing more is known than that this occcurred at roughly the same time as, for instance, the disappearance of the reefs formed by large oyster-like clams, rudists, in the Cretaceous.

Also, the 'mother of mass extinctions' at the Permian/Triassic boundary has recently been shown to be coincident with the extrusion of the Siberian trap lavas, about the same size as the Deccan traps. However, other such plateau lava events, though known to be quite extensive, do not coincide with extinctions.

A recent addition to the list of geological catastrophes is the intriguing theory of 'snowball earth' (Hoffman and Schrag 2000). Low CO_2 concentrations and a lesser solar energy output are invoked to explain the presence of ice masses covering all the continents, even at equatorial latitudes, at several times during the Precambrian (2500–800 million years ago). The latest of these snowball episodes occurred shortly before the Cambrian explosion of multi-cellular life; the phenomenon has not returned since. The snowball earth gives rise to all kinds of interesting speculations about the interaction of the biosphere with the climate on Earth. It may be that multi-cellular life could only exist, and persist, when such snowball episodes do not occur any more due to feedback mechanisms in the biosphere itself. The return of the Gaia hypothesis?

Last but not least, the Earth is subject to influences from outer space, and these are the most promising cause of global catastrophes leading to loss of species. The K/T boundary extinctions are firmly related to the impact of a large meteorite, probably a primitive asteroid-like object. But even here it is difficult to pinpoint the environmental stresses that led to the demise of all these species, although several scenarios have been developed that relate the impact to the mass extinctions. Additionally, even in hindsight, it is still not possible to say accurately for what reason which species went extinct and which not, presumably because the fossil record contains only a very small fraction of the total number of species extant at K/T boundary times.

The last major impact(s) happened within a time span of 20,000 years some 35 million years ago. One created the 100-km-diameter Popigai crater in Siberia, the other a slightly smaller crater near Washington, D.C., the 80-km diameter Cheasapeake Bay crater. In contrast to the K/T boundary, no extinctions are connected with these impacts. However, there is some evidence from the helium isotope record that these impacts were part of a longer-lasting shower of cometary matter. Around the same time, the Earth started to cool down from a warm greenhouse world of the early Eocene, 50 million years ago, when no continental ice masses existed, to the present day ice-house world.

Prevailing theories connect the beginning of the cooling to the thermal isolation of Antarctica, caused by the plate-tectonic separation of Antarctica from Australia. It is tempting, however, to invoke a role for the comet showers as well.

Large supernova explosions belong to the list of potential species killers, but as yet not a trace of evidence for these has been found in the geological record. But astrophysicists have predicted that on timescales of hundreds of thousands of years such supernova explosions happen close enough to the Earth to be potentially harmful.

Catastrophes are contingent happenings on Earth. They are part of nature, have happened in the past and will happen again, but are hard if not impossible to predict, just as it is impossible to predict when the next 'Elfstedentocht' will take place, the 200-km Dutch skating tour, although it is a near certainty that one or more will take place in the next thirty years.

Catastrophes also play a renewing role in the biosphere. Evolution of species is 'accelerated' after catastrophes that wipe out otherwise stable ecosystems that would normally prevent the proliferation of 'mutant' species. However, the species to become extinct may just have been unlucky, in the wrong place at the wrong time, such as the dinosaurs at the end of the Cretaceous. Species now in existence, such as the large mammals, whales and other rare species, are also in the wrong place at the wrong time, because the ever-growing human population will not allow them to remain here any more.

References

Hoffman, P.F. and Schrag, D.P. (2000) 'Snowball earth', *Scientific American* 282: 68–75.

Ward, P.D. (1993) *On Methuselah's Trail: Living Fossils and the Great Extinctions*, New York: Freeman.

12

CONTINGENCY AND RISK

Comment on Smit

Arthur C. Petersen

Jan Smit has given us an interesting description of some global-scale catastrophes that are experientially unfamiliar to us. The catastrophes with the largest impact probably have been caused by large meteorites. A large meteorite could have caused something like the K/T boundary extinctions 65 million years ago, although there still are uncertainties about the precise mechanisms that led to the extinctions. The last time a really significant meteorite fell on our predecessors' heads was some 35 million years ago – which event, by the way, was not accompanied by a mass extinction of species. Can we predict when the next major impact will be and what the consequences will be? No, at this moment we cannot. We can only say with confidence that some time in the next few tens of millions of years another major meteorite impact will happen and probably that not *all* life will disappear from Earth after such an event. Maybe even humans – if still around – may survive.

Note that relatively little public attention and funding are being focused on the kind of global-scale catastrophes just described, as opposed to more familiar natural disasters. Much more research is being done on topics such as hurricanes, floods, droughts, landslides, avalanches, extra-tropical storms, tsunamis and storm surges, tornadoes, sand and dust storms, extreme temperatures, weather-related fires, severe local storms, volcanoes and earthquakes than on meteorites. The explanation is simple: every year about 250,000 lives are lost worldwide directly or indirectly as a result of familiar natural disasters, and economic losses amount to billions of euros each year. The possible impact of meteorites seems to be too abstract for most people to bother about. However, there are changes in sight (and there are new opportunities for the meteorite research community). An increasing amount of money is being reserved for monitoring the skies and searching for objects that might fall on our heads. And I can imagine that at some time in the future NASA and the nuclear weapons laboratories will announce a research and development plan for space vehicles that can deliver a hydrogen bomb to the surface of a comet in order to alter its course by means of a nuclear explosion. Of course one has to think about the question of whether such a strategy would be a wise one. I will briefly comment on that at the end of my response to Smit.

But first I would like to address the general question: 'Are catastrophes in nature ever evil?' The answer Jan Smit is suggesting is that although catastrophes may be considered evil for individual people, or even for entire species in the case of global-scale catastrophes, there is generally a positive side to catastrophes as well. For instance, in the wake of the impact 65 million years ago the dinosaurs disappeared (which was evil for them), but mammals that had already been around for 150 million years grabbed the opportunity to further evolve and proliferate (the same catastrophe was good for them and ultimately for us). Furthermore, a dominant theme in Smit's chapter is the contingency of such events. One of the thinkers on nature and evil that has stressed both the contingency of evil, and the opportunities generated by it, is Alfred North Whitehead.

Let me very briefly discuss Whitehead's position here, using a new interpretation that is different from standard process theology. A major characteristic of present-day process theology that is often criticized is the view that not God but a mythological Chaos causes evil. A further criticism of process theology could be that God is practically unable to do anything against it. In her book *Does God Matter?* (published in Dutch in 1998) Palmyre Oomen presents an interpretation of Whitehead's philosophy which is far more nuanced and complex with respect to the question of evil than the dominant view among both followers and critics of Whitehead. One of the things Oomen stresses is that Whitehead does not see all evil as abject, since opportunities arise from evil (think of the destruction of the dinosaurs and the eventual evolution of humans; think also of the regeneration mentioned by Holmes Rolston in his contribution).

Furthermore, according to Whitehead evil originates from the clash among a 'plurality of aims'. For example, the contingent aim of a certain comet or asteroid could be to hit the Earth. This aim clashes with the contingent aims of humans, whose lives are likely to be disrupted if not destroyed by the meteorite impact. Now, a crucial question about evil is: what is the role of God in this clash of aims? Suffice it to say that, according to Whitehead, initial aims are given by God. In the context of comets and asteroids this means that these objects are obeying the laws of gravity, and we should not expect significant deviations from these laws. And if these objects are going to impact the Earth, the God-given aim is indeed to hit the Earth. We humans have other aims, and being hit by a large meteorite would constitute evil for us. Oomen emphasizes the positive aspect of things and humans having their ground in God. This ground does not disappear when aims get into conflict with each other.

God has a consequent nature as well; besides being an 'unmoved mover', he is also a 'moved mover'. Sufficiently complex sentient beings, such as humans, are able to be inspired by the same God to recognize that there may be alternative futures which are more just and less evil than the collision course the world may be currently following. Criticism of nature and criticism of culture can have their ground in God as well. A vision of the future derived from the consequent nature of God might motivate people to prevent themselves, other people and even the rest of nature from being hit by a meteorite or from suffering too much from it. God is not indifferent to what happens to Earth, but we have a responsibility to do something about it.

To conclude, I promised to evaluate the idea of avoiding evil by actively searching for extraterrestrial objects that are on a collision course and using spacecrafts and nuclear bombs to alter the future. I am frightened by the hubris of our current large-scale technological projects and can see evil creep into such projects, whatever the noble or just intentions with which these projects are initially set up. What are the risks of launching space-crafts with nuclear bombs on board? How much exposure to risk will there be during the development and testing phases of such projects? Will the technology eventually work? How about a nuclear-weapons free world? I do not have the answers to these questions, but I think it is important to think about them and also to come up with alternative options. Besides, the use of nuclear weapons for this purpose has been crit-icized as not being effective (even if the technology 'works'): an early 'push' (by hitting the object with a space vehicle, functioning as a cannon-ball) could reduce the risk of impact more effectively than a larger 'push' shortly before impact. But, of course, this only works if the risk is known long enough in advance.

To finally answer the question 'are catastrophes evil?', I would say 'typi-cally yes'. We should therefore continue on the path of making society more resilient and less vulnerable to natural disasters. With respect to our vulnerability to meteorite impacts, it may seem that we need not hurry, but nature is unpredictable in this respect and, although the chances are high that nothing serious will happen within the next few million years, we should start to think seriously about dealing with the meteorite-impact risk.

Reference

Oomen, P. (1998) *Doet God er toe? Een interpretatie van Whitehead als bijdrage aan een theologie van Gods handelen*, Kampen: Kok.

13

NATURE DOES NOT CARE INDEED, BUT HUMANS DO

A commentary

Fred Spier

Why would humans care?

I would like to start by saying that Jan Smit raised many excellent points with which I wholeheartedly agree. I will therefore concentrate on raising a few questions and discussing a minor point of disagreement.

Jan Smit noted in passing that 'nature does not care'. Most of nature is dead anyway, so this statement is true to a large extent. However, humans do care about their own well-being and, by extension, about major aspects of non-human nature that help or hinder them in surviving in reasonable prosperity. And humans are part of nature, too.

This raises some big questions: 1. Is this an exclusively human characteristic? 2. How did the human attitude come about?

Is caring about nature exclusively human?

It seems obvious that, in one way or another, most if not all animals care about their own well-being. Since we cannot sufficiently communicate with most other animals, we do not know whether, or to what extent, these beasts judge the rest of nature according to its beneficial or damaging effects. However, it seems beyond question that such judgements exist, given the expression of fear (and, more rarely, of satisfaction) that many animals exhibit.

In a long learning process of how to survive, most animals have developed a certain amount of knowledge, genetically based and/or culturally transmitted, indicating which parts of nature should be considered friendly and pleasant, and which aspects of the natural surroundings should be feared and avoided. However, it seems unlikely that most animals would share abstract concepts such as nature being evil, wrong or ugly.

How did the human attitude concerning nature come about?

Like most animals, the primary concern of humans is their own well-being. In my opinion, any judgement about nature being either good or bad can only be properly understood within this context.

Human history spans perhaps between two and four million years. For most of this period humans lived in small bands on the basis of scavenging, gathering and hunting. This means that they were utterly dependent on the surrounding natural environment. It seems likely that, as a result, they would have viewed nature in very emotional ways, as all modern gatherers and hunters as well as peasant societies do today.

The slow but sure development of more elaborate ways of communicating and of coordinating their behaviour allowed humans to find ways of becoming less dependent on their direct environment. However, the idea that most of nature is dead and does not care is a rather recent Western European view. Even today, most humans living on this planet would probably not agree. Only people who have reached a stage in which they can live comfortably without having to worry too much about how to make a living from their direct environment would be willing to think in such ways. And even for quite a few of them, in the wake of a natural catastrophe, big or small, it may be hard to maintain the view that nature does not care .

In sum, humans' moral views of nature first of all arise out of concern for their own well-being. Since humans are better able to think and communicate than any other animal, they have developed more abstract concepts to express these concerns.

Chance and necessity

Jan Smit emphasized that many catastrophes cannot be predicted. Within this context, he used the example of the Dutch 'Elfstedentocht'. This 'Eleven-city tour' is a long-distance skating race in the northern province of Friesland, which can only be held when the canals and lakes freeze over sufficiently to allow all the participants to take part safely. This happens only rarely. Every winter, however, there is a great deal of speculation about whether the conditions will be suitable for holding this event, considered very exciting by many native Dutch.

I agree that the next 'Elfstedentocht' cannot be predicted with any great certainty. However, in June 1997 I discovered a curious trend.[1] There seems to be a clear correlation between the winters during which these tours have been held and the sunspot activity of that period. At that time I was reading three different books on the correlation between sunspots and climate (Hoyt and Schatten 1997; Friedman 1986; Calder 1997). Most of the information about sunspots and climate which I present below comes from these books.

Sunspots are explosions on the surface of the sun. To earthly observers they appear as black spots. As far as we know, they were first discovered around 400 BC in ancient Greece by Meton, who noticed a correlation between the occurrence and number of such spots and rainy weather, based on a twenty-year record he kept. However, it was not until the early seventeenth century that European scientists began to make careful long-term observations.

Around 1650, however, very soon after their European rediscovery, the sunspots almost completely disappeared. This phenomenon, now known as the Maunder Minimum, corresponded with the 'Little Ice Age', the period during which the famous Dutch winter landscapes were painted and Londoners held fairs on the frozen River Thames. Around 1720 the spots reappeared in considerable numbers. They have been observed ever since. The re-emergence of solar activity signalled the end of the 'Little Ice Age'.

Much later it was recognized that the sunspots also exhibit a cyclical pattern lasting about eleven years. There are years in which there are hardly any spots. Then their numbers increase steadily. About five to six years later they reach a maximum, only to decrease towards a minimum again.

Although there is good evidence for correlations of various kinds between the number of sunspots and climate change on Earth, the scientific community does not agree about the mechanism that would explain the sunspots' influence on our planetary weather.

In January 1997 the 'Elfstedentocht' was held again, for the last time to date. While considering the possible influence of sunspots on the climate, it struck me that this was the period of the lowest sunspot activity in the eleven-year cycle. Was this coincidence or part of a larger pattern?

Thanks to the arrival of the Internet, I could do a quick search on sunspots. From the NASA website I downloaded a graph with sunspot counts during the past two centuries. The website of the organizers of the 'Elfstedentocht' provided me with the historical data I needed for a correlation. The result, updated for the year 2000, is shown in Figure 13.1.

The graph shows very clearly that no 'Eleven-city tours' were held during all the periods when the sunspot count was fifty or higher. Over the last decades only solar minima were occasions for this Friesian and Dutch skating event.

Of course, many factors are at play here. They include a possible warming up of the climate, perhaps due to human action; increasing numbers of sunspots during the twentieth century; the industrialization of the Netherlands, leading, among other things, to the discharge of more warm water into the canals and lakes of Friesland; a greater tendency to break up the ice to allow shipping to continue to move during cold periods; greater numbers of potential participants and, as a result, the need for thicker ice; the state of the organization which is responsible for the tour, etc.

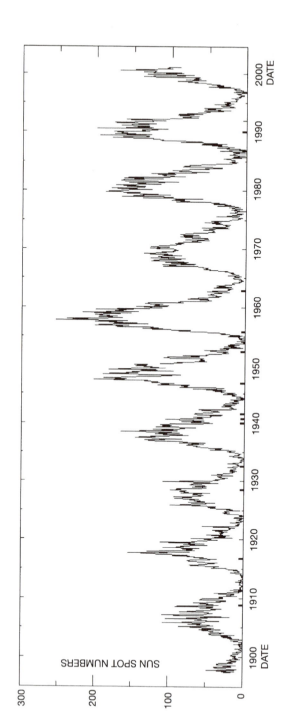

Figure 13.1 The number of solar spots in the last century. The small vertical bars indicate the years in which the 'Eleven-city Skating Tour' was held.

Source: The graph of solar spots is used with permission from David Hathaway/NASA/ NSSTC.

But whatever role these interactions may play, clearly the number of sunspots sets a limit on the possibility of holding this event. It is possible to predict that no tours will be held for as long as the sunspot counts are fifty or higher.

This may be a trivial example, but it raises a serious question: might we be able to discover similar links for catastrophes caused by nature, such as earthquakes and volcanic eruptions, if we start looking for unusual correlations? Of course, I am not suggesting that earthquakes are brought about by sunspots. But who knows what unexpected mechanisms might cause them?

Chance and necessity

Jacques Monod's book *Chance and Necessity* is discussed in various essays in this volume. Attention is often focused on the importance of chance events in nature. This would explain why nature is often viewed as evil. The 'Elfstedentocht' example may help to explain Monod's view of why both chance and necessity are important in understanding nature. By themselves the sunspot numbers do not cause the 'Eleven-city tour'. Clearly, there is a great deal of chance involved in producing the human constellation on Earth which results in these tours. But, apparently, the sunspot numbers set an upper limit. This is where necessity plays a role.

All of human history is characterized by these two aspects: a combination of chance effects and a number of limits posed by natural circumstances. If greater numbers of humans were to understand this better, they might view nature less as a good or evil thing and more as the inevitable condition we are all part of.

Note

1 In the meantime, I have found that at least two persons preceeded me in discovering the relationship between low sunspot activity and the Elfstedentocht: Evert van Brummelen in 1985 and C.P.J. Dommisse in 1995. However, they only published their findings in 1997 on their own websites; these discoveries did not show up when I did my search.

References

Calder, Nigel (1997) *The Manic Sun: Weather Theories Confounded*, London: Pilkington Press.

Friedman, Herbert (1986) *Sun and Earth*, New York: W.H. Freeman & Co.

Hoyt, Douglas V. and Kenneth H. Schatten (1997) *The Role of the Sun in Climate Change*, Oxford: Oxford University Press.

Monod, Jacques (1972) *Chance and Necessity: An Essay on the Natural Philosophy of Modern Biology*, translated from the French by A. Wainhouse, New York: Vintage Books.

14

THE LISBON EARTHQUAKE, 1755

A discourse about the 'nature' of nature

Claudia Sanides-Kohlrausch

The aim of this chapter is to examine the discourse about different meanings of nature (e.g. whether nature is good or bad or neutral) with the help of a historical case study, namely an analysis of the philosophical reactions to the Lisbon earthquake of 1755. At the beginning of this chapter a brief account of the Lisbon earthquake will be given. Thereafter, the positions taken by three prominent philosophers, namely Voltaire, Kant and Rousseau, with respect to the earthquake and nature in general will be described. Their philosophical statements about nature are then placed in the eighteenth-century context. The weaknesses of the traditional reasoning about nature, which persist in philosophical and/or theological discussions, will also be discussed. And at the end of the chapter proposals concering contemporary approaches of *culturalistic* philosophy are made in order to evaluate if and how we can overcome the old problems inherent within the discourse about the 'nature' of nature.

Introduction: why start with the Lisbon earthquake?

It is still thought by historians of science and of theology, as well as by many biologists (especially in the camp of sociobiology), that the doctrine of a well-ordered, balanced and *good* nature as taught by natural theology or physico-theology was challenged by the publication of Darwin's *Origin of Species* in 1859 (see, for example, Cosslett 1984: 7–8; Mayr 1982; Dawkins 1976, 1995, 1996; Desmond and Moore 1991). However, as I will illustrate by means of the following two very different examples, this simple view cannot be supported by nineteenth-century contemporary sources concerning the reception of Darwin's book:

(a) In two famous British critiques of the *Origin of Species* by two prominent contemporaries of Darwin, namely one of his old friends and colleagues, the geologist Adam Sedgwick (1785–1873) and Bishop

Samuel Wilberforce (1805–73) – both dedicated to the ideas of natural theology – the idea that Darwin had laid bare the cruel aspects of nature, and thereby undermined the doctrines of natural theology, did not play a role. It is not even mentioned in their long and elaborate critiques. They criticize Darwin's thesis of evolution by natural selection only by methodological arguments. They suspect that Darwin's scientific work had not been carried out properly relative to the well-established scientific standards within the British scientific community (Sedgwick 1860; Wilberforce 1860).

(b) After the failure of the German March Revolution in 1848, many of the leading intellectuals were searching for a more convincing programmatic foundation for their ideas of social development and progress in order to be able to agitate more successfully in the future. When Darwin's work was published, the 'message' (or at least what they *thought* to be Darwin's central message) was enthusiastically welcomed. In their view, Darwin's work had *proved* the progressive character of nature, therefore supplying not only an optimistic perspective on nature but also a scientifically based justification for social progress (Weingarten 1998).

Thus, even if in some circles Darwin's book has been regarded as supporting a pessimistic view of nature, this view cannot and should not be generalized. Darwin's book stimulated optimistic views of nature as well, and also discussions about the 'proper scientific method' to evaluate the true character of nature.

In contrast, historians who study the period of the Enlightenment in general, regard the Lisbon earthquake of 1755, the most prominent natural disaster of the eighteenth century, as *the* challenge to the optimistic portrait of nature painted by the physico-theological doctrine. In contrast to the reception of Darwin's *Origin*, the historical sources are undisputed here: very soon after the earthquake had happened and been reported in the newspapers all over the European continent, it was transformed into *the* exemplary model for a theological and/or philosophical discourse about the 'nature' of nature. It was intensely debated whether the character of nature is indeed evil or economical, whether the balance between nature and culture is appropriate, what the standards for appropriate moral and technical human conduct should be, and how the *utility* of science, at *that* time not yet a well-established profession, should be demonstrated. The arguments developed in this discourse were much more elaborate than anything that has been written about the consequences drawn from Darwin's *Origin of Species*, because the authors writing about the consequences of the Lisbon earthquake were trying to avoid as consequently as possible any naïve naturalistic 'short cut' conclusions.

Major parts of this discourse are illustrated in reflections on the earthquake by three well-known philosophers of the eighteenth century, namely Voltaire (1694–1778), Rousseau (1712–78) and Kant (1724–1804).

When I compared the arguments in the discourse about the Lisbon earthquake with the more recent discourse concerning the nature of nature and dealing with natural and *technical* catastrophes, I was astonished to realize that during the last three hundred years we have not advanced significantly in our treatment of these questions. In order to demonstrate this, I will give a short account of the earthquake and its philosophical evaluation, and discuss what we can learn from this in attempting to answer our leading question, namely the evaluation of 'nature's nature'.

The Lisbon earthquake – the incident

Contemporaries regarded Lisbon as a particularly beautiful and extremely *pious* town. It housed more than 90 convents and more than 40 churches. As a sign of great benevolence in 1749 Pope Benedict XIV (1740–58) gave the King of Portugal (Juan V, 1706–50) the title of 'the most pious majesty'.

On the morning of 1 November 1755, All Saints' Day, most of the Lisbon inhabitants went to church as usual. At 9.45 a.m. a disastrous earthquake struck the town. Contemporaries have reported that the houses looked as if they were riding on waves. Even solid buildings such as the cathedral collapsed. All those at church were buried within the ruins. Half of the King's palace was destroyed. The sky was darkened by dust from the ruins and smoke from the numerous fires that broke out (consequences of the many candles used on All Saints' Day and the open fires in private houses). People fled to the harbour in order to escape from the falling debris and suffocating dust and smoke. The drama was completed by the appearance of a tsunami, a tidal wave more than 30 feet high, which destroyed the harbour completely. Thousands of people who had hoped to find shelter at the harbour were drowned. Thereafter, new shocks hit the town region, producing gigantic landslides, and more dust blackened the sky.

It has been reported that the Lisbon earthquake destroyed nearly two-thirds of the town. Of Lisbon's 275,000 inhabitants, 10–15,000 lost their lives. Other sources even estimate this number to be as high as 30–60,000 (Seibold 1995).

The Catholic Church proclaimed the earthquake to be an act of God, inflicted on Lisbon's inhabitants to punish them for their sins. The surviving victims were encouraged to pray for the forgiveness of their sins and told not to commit further sins by speculating about the 'natural causes' of earthquakes.

The King's prime minister, the Marquee de Pombal (1699–1782), was not convinced that such pronouncements were promising strategies for helping the surviving victims. When the King consulted his prime minister about what could be done for the surviving inhabitants, De Pombal suggested taking the following action: removing the deceased (including dead animals) from the town to prevent epidemics; organizing medical care for the wounded victims; the provision of drinking water and food; the building of storehouses; and acting as effectively as possible against plunderers. The King was convinced. All actions were realized with the help of the military (the Red Cross and other aid organizations did not yet exist). In addition, the King gave his prime minister leadership in the planning and organization of the rebuilding of the town. In order to prevent a second disaster of such enormous impact, the new Lisbon town was equipped with broader streets in order to provide better emergency exits for the inhabitants in case of a new earthquake. Lastly, Pombal organized an earthquake research project. Many questionnaires were sent out to the parishes within the country region around the town. In these questionnaires the priests were asked to collect all reports about earth slides and other geographical disasters suspected to have been caused by the earthquake.

If one reads literary sources about the Lisbon earthquake, it becomes evident that all 'enlightened' contemporaries were deeply shocked by it. I have already mentioned how the evaluations of this specific incident were transformed into a broader philosophical discourse about the different faces of nature. If one studies the contributions of three prominent philosophers, Voltaire, Rousseau and Kant (original sources reprinted in Breidert 1994), the focus of that discourse can be established more precisely. In a nutshell, the discourse dealt with the question of whether the two leading doctrines about nature within the early Enlightenment period had been put at stake by the Lisbon earthquake or not. These doctrines were that (a) *Everything is right* (defended in the 'Essay on Man' by Alexander Pope, 1688–1744), and (b) We live *in the best of all possible worlds* (according to Leibniz, 1646–1716). These doctrines are often subsumed under the title of 'physico-theology'.

Voltaire

In a long poem about the Lisbon earthquake, Voltaire rejected radically these two theses on the nature of nature. He subsequently developed his reflections into his well-known novel *Candide*. The incident made him dwell on the *enormous suffering of mankind* in general. It is clear from his poem that he was actually deeply disturbed by the enormous suffering which had taken place in this beautiful town. Driven by his compassion with the victims, as well as by his sorrow at the loss of the architectural beauty of the town, he rejected rigorously the moralizing thesis of the Church that the town of Lisbon had been condemned by God for sins and vanity. Lisbon, as Voltaire argued, had been no more full of sins and vanity than many other towns. Furthermore, he regarded any attempt to declare the earthquake to be an incident of 'right', in the sense of the Pope's philosophy, as purely cynical. Finally, in contrast to Leibniz, Voltaire claimed that it is perfectly possible to conceive of a world better than the existing one. He regarded the rationalism of Pope and Leibniz as cold. According to him, their doctrines lacked sensitivity for the human potential of suffering. According to Voltaire, a portrait of God who had been not able to create a world better than the existing one characterizes God as a Being lacking any capability of creativity and fantasy. Voltaire's radical conclusions are driven by a deeply pessimistic attitude: neither science nor any philosophical system would be able to solve the problem of the theodicy.

Rousseau

Voltaire corresponded with his friend Rousseau on the subject of the earthquake; Rousseau, however, considered Voltaire's poem *disgusting*. He judged the view elaborated in the poem to be a pessimistic and depressing one. In Rousseau's view, it left suffering humanity without any positive perspective. Against Voltaire, Rousseau defended the system of Pope and Leibniz. He was convinced that their theses on nature would furnish humans with confidence, if they reflected on their own suffering. Rousseau, however, shared with Voltaire a vivid interest in adding new aspects to the discussion about the causes of the theodicy. From Rousseau's point of view humans were themselves responsible for the origin of evil and therefore for most (!) of their suffering. Concerning the Lisbon earthquake, Rousseau declared that it was not nature that had built up 20,000 houses, each equipped with seven floors, but humans. Furthermore, he argued that nobody would have been crushed to death in the earthquake, if the houses in Lisbon had been built in a less dense manner and/or of a lighter material than stone. Rousseau argued that many people would not have lost their lives, if they had not been driven by their passion to save their possessions before trying to escape. Finally, Rousseau criticized Voltaire's reflection that it would had been better, if the earthquake had taken place in a desert instead of in Lisbon, because then nobody would have died or suffered. Rousseau asked Voltaire, ironically, if he (Voltaire) actually thought that the order of nature was obliged to follow humans' capriciousness, and how he (Voltaire) was honestly able to defend the position that we humans should and could always be able to forbid nature to cause an earthquake at a particular place, just because we wanted to build a town there.

Kant

Immanuel Kant (the *younger* Kant of his so-called 'precritical' works) shared with Rousseau two convictions. (a) He had confidence in the system of Pope and Leibniz. (b) Humans should not build towns in areas endangered by earthquakes. If humans were constrained to settle within regions regularly subject to earthquakes, unsuitable building materials for houses should be avoided. Kant exemplified this point by means of the inhabitants of Peru and Chile. He judged them to be wiser than the inhabitants of Lisbon in the construction of their buildings: their houses were (according to Kant) equipped with just two floors. Furthermore, only the first floor was constructed of stone, the second one being of light material such as wood.

On the other hand, Kant agreed with Voltaire in rejecting the moral evaluation of the earthquake defended by the Church. However, in contrast to Voltaire, Kant's motivation to argue against the moral position of the Church was not driven by the aspect of suffering humankind, but by a *scientific* point of view. Kant had collected very many reports about earthquakes. He concluded that it could be proven that in the Lisbon area earthquakes happened regularly. Therefore, Kant declared the fact that Lisbon had been built within an earthquake-endangered area as a completely sufficient explanation for the catastrophe. In consequence, he was convinced that the moral or religions speculations invented by the Church were not necessary to explain the earthquake.

If we consider all these reactions, we are able to identiy the following characteristics:

(1) All of the statements primarily seek to deal with suggestions or reflections about how to improve human life. All the authors and institutions at least initiate their reflections about nature from an *anthropological* point of view. In other words, in terms of philosophical methodology their analyses and their judgements about the character of nature do not begin with the question of what the essential character of nature is. In contrast, they all start with aspects of the abilities and limitations of human conduct.

(2) The reasoning about how to improve human life is supported by two different models or metaphors for nature. One is 'fallen (evil) nature', the metaphor adopted in the statement of the Church. The three philosophers (even Voltaire, at least implicitly) defend the metaphor of '(well-balanced) economic nature'.

(3) The participants in the philosophical and practical discourse who defended explicitly the economic model for nature (Kant and Rousseau) came to very different conclusions about what has to be done for the sake of humans.

(4) Even if the perspective of all positions is anthropological, philosophers and politicians were not able to agree conclusively on how to deal with a central aspect of human nature, namely the ability to suffer (emphasized by Voltaire). However, the metaphor of 'fallen nature'

(chosen by the Church to explain the Lisbon earthquake and its consequences) was played down or completely neglected by the members of the 'economic nature' camp.

I will argue in the following section that the central goal of the system of Pope and Leibniz ('the system' in the following text) was humanity's moral improvement, and that the four characteristics outlined above were a consequence of ideas about how to achieve that purpose.

Analysis of the historical and philosophical context

It is very important to emphasize the *anthropological* perspective, because many historians and philosophers still identify the early Enlightenment period with the rise of the natural sciences (and therefore with naturalism), as if the sciences were the only or at least the most important novelty of that period. However, this view reflects our modern bias towards scientism. The primary focus of almost all the philosophical texts of the early Enlightenment period (beginning with Hobbes and Descartes) is actually an anthropological one. The issues discussed were questions like: what is humans' nature? How can humans' nature be improved to help them live a good life? What are the successful strategies for living a good life? And finally, what *is* a good life?

Two convictions were absolutely basic in almost all treatises about human nature since the time of the early Enlightenment. First, humans *are* able to develop their moral abilities by their own activities. Second, to live a good life humans are obliged to live 'according to nature', a doctrine adopted from the stoic philosophy – including all its advice – which meant in particular controlling their passions and tolerating by 'imperturbability' all kinds of suffering, no matter how severe. Hence, the aspect of human suffering had to be played down, and was played down, in many treatises of the early Enlightenment.

Both convictions claim that a human is responsible for his/her own destiny. In order to make humans able to live a good life, education became a central issue. The genre of the 'education novel' ('Bildungsroman') became fashionable, along with treatises about nature, or a mixture of both (like Pope's 'Essay on Man'). People were advised to be gentle, to develop benevolence and 'sentimentality' (which means 'sensitivity' in modern terms), and to study or at least to admire the wonderful 'economy of nature' to convince themselves that everything had its proper place in it. However, the pragmatic aspect as part of the programme should not be underestimated. There was a belief that raising people's living standards was necessary to support human improvement. Therefore, 'Science' became crucial. It was defended as a useful profession, useful in a twofold way: contemplation of nature's economy should help to raise the moral standard of humanity; and studying the structure of nature's economy should support efforts to raise people's living standards.

The model for nature as an economical construct was circumscribed so vaguely that under the concept of 'utility' moralizing contemplations about nature's providential order, scientific investigations of nature and pragmatic welfare projects could all be subsumed. This is true of Kant, who focused mainly on 'scientific' explanations of earthquakes, of Rousseau, who critiqued the cultural and moral behaviour of humans, and of the King, who was concerned to help the survivors of the earthquake.

On the other hand, it is quite evident that the 'fallen nature' metaphor was totally unsuitable for dealing with the 'utility' aspects of nature. The model of nature as a well-balanced 'economy' was much better adapted to support all the different goals of improvement. As a result, not only 'suffering' (see above) but also the idea of 'fallen nature' had to be played down and was (for the spectrum of goals and perspectives of the Enlightenment see historical studies such as Barth 1971; Gay 1967; Hirsch 1949; Philipp 1957; Shapin 1996; Sieferle 1989; 1990; Worster 1977).

Consequences of the Lisbon earthquake revisited

I have already remarked that the system of Pope and Leibniz came under attack after the Lisbon earthquake. Historians agree about that point. However, what exactly was challenged? One common view is that the validity of the doctrine of 'nature's economy' as a well-balanced system created by God's Providence was challenged.

However, the earthquake had of course been used to attempt to reinvent the 'fallen world' metaphor. On the other hand, the construction of the Pope/Leibniz system offered enough potential to develop pragmatic and/or scientific arguments that were strong enough to brush off such an attempt. It is clear from the pragmatically driven actions of the King as well as from the philosophical statements of Kant and Rousseau that the pragmatic and moral constructions of the system were quite immune against a reinvention of 'fallen nature'. Therefore, it is too superficial to regard the Lisbon earthquake as an incident that was able to break down the arguments of 'nature's economy' completely.

Voltaire came much closer to hitting the anthropological Achilles' heel of the system than any of his contemporaries. He detected a very important gap within the moral reasoning of the system. Within the system the moral human is obliged to be able to be sensitive to the suffering of others. However, if people were to be capable of this, they had to be allowed to experience suffering themselves and live through their own suffering with all its consequences. It is not sufficient to live a life according to the principle of playing down one's own suffering. Self-suffering and reflections about self-suffering, however, were, as already mentioned, either missing, played down or even forbidden within the Pope/Leibniz system.

The Lisbon earthquake showed that the question of whether nature is beautiful and well organized or, alternatively, evil, cannot be answered so simply as in the Pope/Leibniz system. The catastrophe demonstrated that it is extremely difficult to encompass the subjective aspect (how a human is *obliged* to live a good life) and the aspect which was regarded as an (objective) fact (namely, that nature *is* well ordered and good) in the *same* concept of nature. In serious cases of doubt (and the Lisbon earthquake was such a case) the line of reasoning that disposed of human suffering by means of 'economical' arguments as an object of 'right' ran the risk of becoming absolutely relativistic or even cynical, as Voltaire had complained.

It was one important consequence of the discourse about the Lisbon earthquake that it became evident that the aspect of 'evil' or 'fallen' nature cannot be exterminated from human life by rationalism. It should not be denied that humans are often self-responsible when they try to manage nature. They are responsible and guilty, if they have sufficient knowledge and the potential to avoid errors. However, not only our knowledge, but also our potential is limited. Humans are not able to prevent earthquakes. In addition, even if human conduct is driven by established knowledge, it is always limited, although it is difficult to evaluate and foresee these limitations. In other words, it is too simple-minded to condemn humans as guilty according to their cultural activities, as Rousseau had tried to argue. It is too simple-minded to assume that the avoidance of all disasters is a matter of sufficient knowledge about 'natural causes' and about 'technical management', as Kant had been inclined to argue. For instance, if humans were able to choose to settle within an area where earthquakes do not occur, are these areas really better alternatives (I mean 'better' in terms of complete protection)? I think such utopian visions are very naïve, at least from a contemporary point of view. They can only be excused as optimistic elaborations of the scientific aspect of the Pope/Leibniz reasoning of the eighteenth century.

A second and almost certainly more important consequence is the *pluralistic* picture of nature. If we analyse these debates about the characterization of nature, it becomes obvious that although all the arguments are indebted to the Enlightenment programme of rationalism, and although the status of all the arguments has at least some plausibility according to rational standards, the arguments led not to a consensus, nor even to complementary pictures, but to *incommensurable* portraits concerning the character of nature. In fact, although driven by rationalistic standards, they led not to a definite answer about the 'essential' character of nature but to *pluralistic* views. However, since all these different characterizations of nature are bound to rational arguments, none of the alternatives can be brushed aside or stigmatized as superstition, as anthropomorphism, as non-rational, as non-scientific, as too scientistic, or the like. In addition, the pluralistic 'list' of 'natures' comprises *descriptive* and *normative* portraits of nature. If we call nature 'evil' or, alternatively, 'good', these ascriptions are normative. On the other hand, if we refer to nature as 'balanced', this is a descriptive statement. But descriptive statements cannot be transformed into normative statements. The step from 'is' to 'ought' is logically impossible and therefore termed (and philosophically condemned) as the 'naturalistic fallacy'. Descriptive portraits of nature cannot be transformed into normative ones and, vice versa, normative ones cannot be reduced to descriptive ones.

How to deal with the question of nature's nature today?

The philosophical discourse about the Lisbon earthquake led to a pluralistic picture of nature. We still discuss these different pictures of nature as alternatives of the 'essential' character of nature today. I think our primary task is to deal with this pluralism as effectively as possible. In contemporary discussions pluralism is often identified with relativism. As a result, people who are still searching for the 'essential' character of nature feel themselves very uncomfortable, if they become confronted with such different and incommensurable pictures of nature. However, I would argue that this pluralistic picture must not be condemned as sheer relativism. First of all, it is not relativistic, because all these portraits of nature are bound to or follow from our rationalistic tradition (as I have demonstrated in my historical case study). Secondly, it is possible to reconstruct all the different conclusions about the character of nature from the *life–world* perspective. In this perspective they assume their proper (that means rationally justified) place. To adopt the life–world perspective, and therefore an anthropological or culturalistic perspective, to reconstruct our different views on nature is not to go against the intentions of the philosophical authors I have discussed. Furthermore, I would argue that such a perspective is rationally justified. If we do not want to lose our way by focusing on a wide variety of excessively speculative questions about the character of nature, we have to start from ourselves, with our own abilities and an analysis of how we deal with nature. This is necessary simply because we humans are not able to step back behind our own efforts, experiences and feelings. If we analyse and reflect on our *methods* of dealing with nature, we will find that our methods as well as our reflections about nature shape and determine our discussions and pictures of nature. That does not mean that nature is 'only a sheer construct' of our language praxis. Of course nature exists independently of human conduct. But as long as this nature is left untouched by human conduct, this untouched nature is so 'neutral' that it has no meaning *to us humans*. We achieve only a meaning, or even more than one meaning of nature, if we humans *interact* with nature or if we *experience* nature. Whether we experience in our interaction with nature ourselves, nature, or ourselves as part of nature, I will leave open for further thought and discussion. However, independently of such a discussion, it seems quite clear to me that our human talk about experiences with untouched nature leads to portraits of nature which are very different from such untouched nature. These portraits should be classified as *models* and/or as *metaphors* for nature. Models and metaphors are not 'just' models or metaphors, insofar as they could be brushed aside or reduced to an 'essential' meaning of nature. In contrast, we humans would not be able to communicate without such metaphors. They represent our experiences with nature (for necessary metaphors and models of nature see Weingarten 1999).

I would like to give at the end of my chapter an overview of how basic metaphors and/or models for nature can be reconstructed from a cultural-istic life–world perspective.

The basic meaning of nature – 'the self-(re)producer'

In accordance with the life–world perspective, I would first like to intro-duce, or remind 'the reader' of, a very *basic* meaning of 'nature'. This is *nature in contrast to culture*, or, in other words, everything which has not been produced/constructed/influenced by human (cultural) activities, namely animals, plants, earth, water, weather etc., in contrast to human products such as houses, furniture, pictures etc. This basic distinction (between the natural and the artificial) can be traced back to Aristotle (see, for example, his paragraph about 'physis' in his *Metaphysics*, Book Δ 1014^b 16–1015^a 19). However, even this very basic distinction between nature and culture represents a human cultural experience. We humans have learned that nature reproduces itself, because we have learned to manage this kind of self-reproduction by our agricultural (and other tech-nical) activities. Our experiences of and efforts to manage self-reproducing nature led to the distinction between nature and culture (Janich 1997, in which there is also an overview of fundamental arguments on the cultural-istic philosophy of science).

'Nature' (as a self-reproducer) we have to manage for our own survival, whether we like or not. How to do this successfully is a matter of negotia-tion, in other words, of proper methods. In order to manage nature (the self-reproducer) we humans have to invent and have indeed invented metaphors and models. Terms like 'evil nature' or 'good (economic) nature' are such metaphors.

'Evil nature' and 'good economic nature'

We can learn from Voltaire's emphasis on human suffering that 'fallen (or evil) nature' is a basic metaphor that covers all aspects of that part of the anthropological discourse which comprises our consciousness that our human actions are extremely endangered, and that our personal existence is vulnerable as long as we live; in other words, existential dread.

'Good or economic nature', on the other hand, is another basic metaphor. It deals with our confidence that we are able to manage nature (the self-reproducer) successfully. Even if we pretend to have very pessimistic world-views, we should be honest enough to confess that this confidence has been and still is very often justified. In my view, it would be a very distorted understanding of 'rationality' that would deny this optimistic perspective on our human conduct.

Both terms, evil and economic nature, are 'necessary' within the context of their practical issues. We need these two metaphors in order to be able to decide *if* we want to leave pieces of nature (the self-reproducer) untouched or to change them for our own (cultural) purposes. Without these metaphors we would not be able to manage anything – we would not be humans.

The non-normative picture of nature

Scientific talk (but also, it should be emphasized, technical talk) about nature is non-normative. We have a plethora of scientific models for pieces of nature (the self-reproducer) that seem to characterize nature as 'neutral', i.e. neither evil nor good. These models, however, are not identical (or more or less identical) copies of nature (the self-reproducer). They are copies of machines or logical thought processes invented by humans as instruments to manage their life–world and/or nature (the self-reproducer) more successfully. That does not mean that they are 'only' models, because the application of models is rationally justified if the quality of the original of the model is well known and if the application of the model works well – 'well' relative to its defined boundaries and expectations. The application of models is necessary to manage nature, but models cannot be identical with nature, because if natural processes are well known, scientific models to describe nature become superfluous.

That normative aspects do not occur within such models should not be too surprising. To make a 'model for ...', life–world questions have to be transformed. Typically, a scientific model for a life–world problem treats the problem in terms of a particular model, as if the world is as described in one particular set of hypotheses. The question 'assume as if it is ..., what will then happen?' is the typical question of scientific experiments. It is due to this methodological 'as if' transformation process that no evaluative aspects of the life–world occur within these models. Scientific models

117

for nature (the self-reproducer) have their origin within (advanced technical) human life–world practices for managing that nature. The transformation process is determined by itself to strip off all normative or evaluative aspects dealing with nature. So we should not be too astonished at being unable to find these aspects in scientific arguments about nature. This non-normativity is inherent to the scientific method. It is simply not the task of science to think about moral questions.

Summary and conclusions

All philosophers of the early Enlightenment were dedicated to making suggestions about how to improve human life and what constituted a good life. Within a discourse about the good life, I am convinced that necessary metaphors for nature, as well as models for nature, have their proper place. These metaphors and models are not 'just only' models and/or metaphors understood as constructs which may be brushed aside and replaced by something else. I would deny, however, that one of these metaphors or models should be discussed as an alternative representation of *the* ultimate real (in the sense of 'essential') nature. Depending on the human life–world context, 'fallen world' metaphors may be as useful as scientific models. The central issue of metaphors like 'fallen world' is the question of guilt. Scientific models, on the other hand, may help to invoke new technical aspects of how to manage successfully. I do not want to argue against science. However, scientific models are not able to cover all aspects of the human life–world – and, if properly understood, this is not their function. They are imprisoned by their own methods. Therefore, they can give answers only to a limited spectrum of human life–world problems.

In conclusion, I would argue that both metaphors for nature and (scientific) models for nature are *necessary* to organize human life. By *necessity* I mean that the prime mover of all human conduct is routed within the basic needs that humans have to survive, and that this survival management is guided by such metaphors and models. Therefore, these metaphors and models are not 'just only' models and/or metaphors understood as constructs without any 'realistic' impact. Metaphors of a 'fallen world' may be able to teach us why we have failed and why we should be motivated to do things better. Scientific models may help to discover new technical aspects of how to manage successfully to do things better.

References

Aristotle, *Metaphysics*, Book H, Δ and ε, translated with notes by C. Kirwan, Oxford: Clarendon Press, 1971.

Barth, H.- M. (1971) *Atheismus und Orthodoxie – Analysen und Modelle christlicher Apologetik im 17. Jahrhundert*, Göttingen: Vandenhoek & Ruprecht.

Breidert, W. (ed.) (1994) *Die Erschütterung der vollkommenen Welt – Die Wirkung des Erdbebens von Lissabon im Spiegel europäischer Zeitgenossen*, Darmstadt: Wissenschaftliche Buchgesellschaft.

Cosslett, T. (ed.) (1984) *Science and Religion in the Nineteenth Century*, Cambridge: Cambridge University Press.

Darwin, C. (1859) *On the Origin of Species*, London: Murray.

Dawkins, R. (1976) *The Selfish Gene*, Oxford: Oxford University Press.

—— (1995) *River out of Eden: A Darwinian View of Life*, New York: Basic Books.

—— (1996) *Climbing Mount Improbable*, London: Viking Books.

Desmond, A. and J. Moore (1991) *Darwin*, London: Penguin Books.

Gay, P. (1967) *Zeitalter der Aufklärung*, The Netherlands: Time Life.

Hirsch, E. (1949) *Geschichte der neueren evangelischen Theologie – im Zusammenhang mit den allgemeinen Bewegungen des europäischen Denkens* Band I, Gütersloh: Mohn.

Janich, P. (1997) 'Methodical Constructivism', in D. Ginev and R.S. Cohen (eds) *Issues and Images in the Philosophy of Science*, Dordrecht: Kluwer, 173–90.

Mayr, E. (1982) *The Growth of Biological Thought*, Cambridge, MA: Harvard University Press.

Philipp, W. (1957) 'Das Werden der Aufklärung in theologiegeschichtlicher Sicht', in *Forschungen zur Systematischen Theologie und Religionsphilosophie* Band III, Göttingen: Vandenhoek & Ruprecht.

Sedgwick, A. (1860) 'Objections to Mr. Darwin's Theory of the Origin of Species', in *The Spectator*, 24 March, 285–6.

Seibold, E. (1995) *Entfesselte Erde – Vom Umgang mit Naturkatastrophen*, Stuttgart: Deutsche Verlags-Anstalt.

Shapin, S. (1996) *The Scientific Revolution*, Chicago: University of Chicago Press.

Sieferle, R.-P. (1989) *Die Krise der menschlichen Natur – Zur Geschichte eines Konzepts*, Frankfurt a.M.: Suhrkamp.

—— (1990) *Bevölkerungswachstum und Naturhaushalt – Studien zur Naturtheorie der klassischen Ökonomie*, Frankfurt a.M.: Suhrkamp.

Weingarten, M. (1998) 'Darwinismus und mechanistisch-materialistisches Weltbild', in M. Weingarten, *Wissenschaftstheorie als Wissenschaftskritik*, Bonn: Pahl Rugenstein Nachfolger, 77–123.

—— (1999) 'Wahrnehmen', in M. Weingarten, *Bibliothek dialektischer Grundbegriffe* Band 3, Bielefeld: Aisthesis Verlag.

Wilberforce, S. (1860) 'On the Origin of Species, by means of Natural Selection; or the Preservation of Favoured Races in the Struggle for Life. By Charles Darwin, M.A., F.R.S', in *The Quarterly Review* (London) 108: 225–64.

Worster, D. (1977) *Nature's Economy: A History of Ecological Ideas*, Cambridge: Cambridge University Press.

15

TRAGEDY VERSUS HOPE

What future in an open universe?

Arnold Benz

Recent evidence from astronomical observations suggests that the universe will expand forever. Nevertheless, all cosmic structures from galaxies to planets and even the matter of the universe itself are bound for decay and destruction. Life cannot continue forever, as the planet Earth will become uninhabitable, the Sun will burn out, and the galaxy will contract to a black hole. The history of all things ends intrinsically in tragedy.

On the other hand, the past history of the universe is full of spontaneous appearances of new phenomena. Not only have new stars and living beings been formed, and still are, but new dimensions for development have also opened up that did not exist in the beginning.

Will this cosmic creativity continue in the decaying universe, and is there any hope for this universe? Hope for something new is an emotion based on existential sensations. Religious hope expects the new from beyond this space and time. Science and faith thus will and must remain in dispute concerning the future. The outlook into the future is a crucial test for the significance of propagated values and of the dialogue between science and religion, which so far has been constricted to the issues of past evolution.

Observations of distant supernovae have shown that their parent galaxies move more slowly than would be expected in a uniformly expanding universe (Riess *et al.* 1999; Perlmutter *et al.* 1999). As the light that reaches our telescopes today was emitted a long time ago, the result means that the universe used to be expanding more slowly than it is today. In other words, the expansion of the universe is accelerating and will probably continue forever. Does that mean that the universe will exist forever? Maybe, but certainly not in its present form.

Most ethical thinking and acting are oriented towards the future and based on certain expectations. The future is the primary nexus of ethics, science and religion (Benz 2000). The past development of the universe makes it clear that the evolution of the universe is very innovative and impossible to predict. We will have to distinguish between various forms of perception leading to different prognoses and expectations.

Thesis 1. All things in the universe decay.

Predictions have always played an important role in astronomy. Old Egyptian astronomers were able to predict the yearly flooding of the River Nile, and Babylonians could predict lunar and solar eclipses. The goal of today's astrophysics is the understanding of the formation of cosmic structures, and their evolution and decay.

The planet Earth is bombarded by meteorites, and occasionally such impacts have led to major catastrophes. Their influence on biological evolution has been profound, but life on Earth has continued. This will not be the case forever. The Sun has already fused a few per cent of its hydrogen fuel into helium. The pressure in the centre has increased and the fusion rate is increasing. Since its formation, the Sun's luminosity has grown by 40 per cent. Our star will enter the red giant phase in 5.5 billion (10^9) years. The surface temperature will sink to 3000 °C, and the diameter will increase by a factor of one hundred. For this reason the temperature on Earth will rise beyond a thousand degrees, too hot for any life. Our planet will no longer be habitable.

After the red giant phase, the Sun will contract to a white dwarf and will cool over 10^{15} years. Since the size of the Sun will then be only about that of the Earth, it will not be able to radiate enough heat to warm the Earth significantly. The temperature on Earth will approach the frigidity of space at minus 270 degrees.

Perhaps life will migrate to other stars and planetary systems. However, this is not possible for infinite time. New stars still form, but the hydrogen in our galaxy will last for only some 100 million future stars. The last stars will develop at the edge of the Milky Way, possibly triggered by a collision with another galaxy. Some time in 10^{13} years the epoch of star light will end. The last white dwarfs will cool and no star will shine any more.

Galaxies lose energy through the very rare encounters between stars. Gravitational waves carry off energy, and some stars may be slingshot out of the galaxy. The orbits of the remaining stars contract and the diameter of the galaxy shrinks. The remains of stars will eventually disappear in the central black hole of the Milky Way, where gravity is so large that even the emitted light falls back. The central black hole currently contains 2.7 million solar masses and is located 25,000 light years from here.

The matter outside black holes does not live infinitely, as even protons, the most stable nucleons, will decay radioactively. According to the prevalent but still speculative theories, protons (and with them all other matter) will decay in about 10^{33} years. Their decay produces positrons and photons.

Even black holes do not live forever. They probably emit a weak thermal radiation at their horizon and thus are losing energy. After some 10^{100} years the massive black holes in the centre of galaxies will evaporate in this way and disappear. The universe will finally consist only of photons, positrons and electrons. Although the very distant future is still speculative, due to uncertainties in the physical theories, it seems unavoidable that all cosmic objects and even the universe itself will decay.

Is the universe a tragedy, where innocent individuals are bound for destruction? Is the existence of heavenly bodies, animals and human beings an absurdity without purpose or meaning?

Thesis 2. The evolution of the universe has been extremely creative. The very possibilities for the formation of matter, galaxies, stars, planets and life have developed only in the course of time. Even today new things are forming.

In our Milky Way, a regular galaxy of a few hundred billion stars, about ten new stars are born every year. The formation of stars takes roughly ten million years. Some hundred million stars thus are forming today in our astronomical neighbourhood. The cosmos overflows with fertility.

Stars evolve from interstellar molecular clouds, well known for their beautiful, fluffy, dark structures. In places where the gas is denser, gravity attracts more gas. The fluctuation gets denser and attracts even more, so the process reinforces itself. The interstellar matter concentrates gradually into cloud cores until these collapse under their own gravity. The gas then falls freely towards the centre of the core, where the remaining angular momentum forms it to a rotating disk.

After ten million years the temperature and density in the centre become large enough to start the fusion of hydrogen to helium. Nuclear energy of stupendous proportions is unleashed and the additional gas pressure stops further contraction. In the innermost part of the vortice equilibrium between gravity and pressure forms: the star is born.

The cosmos as it appears today to the observer did not emerge in the Big Bang. Even the simple hydrogen atoms formed half a million years after the beginning. The Sun's age is only one third of that of the current universe, about 14 billion (10^9) years. Human consciousness has existed only for a few hundred thousand years, one hundred thousandth of the age of the universe, i.e. in the cosmological present.

When we look up at the starry sky on a clear night and believe that at least the stars are the same as always, this impression arises from the fact that our timescale is too small. In reality, the universe displays amazing dynamics; the origin of stars and formation of planets only represent one segment of processes that build upon earlier cosmic events such as the formation of matter out of elementary particles in the early universe or the origin of galaxies. Qualitative development is a fundamental characteristic of the cosmos, and time plays a crucial role.

The cosmos materialized not as in a theatre when the curtain rises, the stage is set, and the play begins. The universe formed much more dramatically, as if in the beginning there was only a glowing magma that solidified to stone, from which a building was made. Therein a workshop for stage design and an actors' school appeared, a stage and the auditorium were built, everything collapsed, was rebuilt etc., and finally our play started.

> *Thesis 3. The notion 'God' does not appear in astrophysics. When scientists communicate their observations and theories they do not use this term.*

Is a creator involved in this dynamic creativity? For more than two hundred years scientists have pointed out again and again that this hypothesis is not needed (e.g. Laplace 1799). Obviously, much remains unexplained scientifically, yet there are already models of how even the universe may have formed from a vacuum according to physical laws. In this sense there are no gaps in the rational understanding of the universe from the Big Bang to the evolution of humans that could be interpreted only as a result of the action of a supernatural being. Existing gaps are the working fields of scientists, who have the great goal to diminish or to close them.

For philosophers one essential question remains: why did something form and not nothing? The question addresses the fundamental issue of a principle behind the laws of nature. That all things have formed is indisputable, and considerations similar to those of the Greek philosophers in the fifth century BCE on the 'foundation of being' are appropriate. Its modern analogue in a dynamic universe would be a principle of structure formation. Appealing here to God's creative will, however, may introduce a mere metaphysical entity without direct relation to science or to the questioner.

> *Thesis 4. The new does not emerge from nothing, but is a new organization of existing or decaying entities.*

Physical theories describing the formation of the universe are still very speculative and unproven. Nevertheless, it is imaginable that the universe could have formed from a vacuum containing zero energy but obeying all physical laws known today. It could have 'borrowed' energy against gravitation during a fluctuation in the primary vacuum. It would follow from this vacuum hypothesis that the universe did not originate from nothing, but from a physical entity, the vacuum, and according to pre-existing rules.

Star formation is an example of how new structures are created even today. Nonetheless, it is not an eternal circle. When the energy is exhausted, stars shrink to white dwarf stars or explode as supernovae and heave a part of their matter and ashes into interstellar space. There, new stars form again and in addition completely new structures, planets, emerge from the cinders of previous generations of stars.

Similarly, the extreme order constituting living beings cannot last. Death is unavoidable for several reasons ranging from chemical decay to physiological deterioration. It is, on the other hand, a necessary ingredient of evolution. Animal species can persist only by selective adaptation in a sequence of generations. Through the death of individuals, a species survives when conditions for life change. In special circumstances, possibly produced by unusual environmental stress, extremely rapid evolution may lead to a new species.

Thesis 5. Within the frame given by the conservation laws, the future is open. The universe is not a clockwork mechanism.

Today's technology is based on conservation laws, such as the constant energy in a closed system. There are other physical parameters conserved in processes of nature. The conservation laws make it possible to predict the future of a system, as for example our solar system, including the nine planets, but only to a certain extent. The view into the future is limited for almost all natural systems because they are only weakly stable. This means that a small deviation from the initial orbit will bring the system into an orbit that deviates increasingly at an exponential rate. Such systems are called *chaotic*. Although the systems behave causally, their development cannot be predicted after a certain interval, called the Lyapunov time. This time horizon depends on the system and can be milliseconds in microscopic structures up to millions of years in planetary systems. The motion of the Earth, for example, cannot be predicted for more than 100 million years.

Chaos limits qualitatively the description of nature by mathematical precision, and thus the applications of science to technology. The chaotic character of nature also lowers certain expectations raised by the age of Enlightenment, when the cosmos was pictured as a machine in which individual parts fitted together like the gears of a clock, according to its given design. If a gear turns at a certain angle, another one rotates the predetermined amount. If the first gear turns at double the angle's size, the angle of rotation of the second gear doubles also. This view of the universe was, without a doubt, linear and does not describe the present world-view of science.

Another limit of the scientific knowing of the future is the uncertainty of quantum mechanical systems. As position and velocity cannot be known simultaneously and with infinite precision, the future development is given only by probabilities. In quantum mechanics, the very basis of today's physics, reality materializes when an irreversible interaction occurs, such as an observation. What lies ahead is not yet determined and will be decided only later.

The chaotic behaviour of most systems in the universe and quantum mechanical uncertainty limit the prognostic capabilities of science.

Whether this openness is intrinsic or follows necessarily from the ever-limited accuracy of measurement makes no difference in practice. The future is neither fully predictable nor determined. It is open.

Thesis 6. It is quite imaginable that something unexpected could arise in the future that would be as new as life on Earth was four billion years ago. This kind of newness certainly cannot be foretold, for such evolutions are chaotic.

The reliability of scientific predictions is very good concerning, for example, the exhaustion of an energy supply. The remaining lifetime of the Sun, some 6 billion years, is well known. Its decay is certain. All scientific prognoses of the future – whether for living creatures, planets, stars, galaxies or the universe itself – thus can only foresee decay at the last. The Sun will become cold, the Earth will lose itself in space, and even the matter in the universe will decay into radiation.

For systems with many interacting parts, like the planetary system or terrestrial weather, this is different. Their development is unpredictable after a certain time, and thus chaotic. Although the system may be in the process of decay, new structures can form spontaneously in a state of non-equilibrium at certain locations. There is an intriguing asymmetry between the decay of all objects in the universe, which we can predict quite accurately, and chaotic systems that cannot be predicted and that may even form new structures.

Most structures astronomy has detected in the universe have a touch of surprise. Most would not have been predicted if humans had been around at the time of formation. Afterwards causal laws and chance may explain them.

Thesis 7. The universe and its development appear to be optimal for human beings. However, there is no scientifically provable hope for new beneficial development.

The universe has properties that are necessary for the developments that have led finally to the evolution of living beings. The basic physical parameters are precisely such that life could arise. The properties of the carbon nucleus, for instance, are favourable for its easy forming in nucleosynthesis, but this is not so for oxygen, the element that would have depleted carbon otherwise. The evolution time to intelligent life is about half the lifetime of a solar-like star, but not orders of magnitude longer. There are many more such fine tunings of the universe that are necessary for our existence.

The anthropic principle states that the observed cosmic and biological developments are the a priori condition for the possibility of cognition:

'What we can expect to observe must be restricted by the conditions necessary for our presence as observers' (Carter 1974). To put it more simply, to make it possible that we can wonder at all why the universe is as it is, the universe must be exactly as it is, for otherwise we would not be there to wonder. This principle proceeds from the tenet that the human being is part of the universe and has originated according to natural laws. It reminds us that, as for any observation, the limits of the measurement apparatus (in this case the observer himself) must be taken into consideration.

Historically, the anthropic principle was formulated just at the time when it became clear to astrophysicists that the universe had a beginning and that evolution began with the Big Bang. The observed coincidences are a priori conditions for the possibility of biological evolution. They must have been given before we could perceive the world at all. Certain physical, chemical and biological characteristics are required. Yet the anthropic principle is no explanation of the cosmological coincidences. As established fact that must be fulfilled by any acceptable model of the universe, it is a triviality. The anthropic principle, however, makes one conscious of how strongly human existence is grounded in the whole of the cosmos and what consequences follow as a result of this participation for our theoretical cognition.

To explain coincidences on the level of the whole universe, there appear to be three possibilities:

1   There are physical reasons, which we still do not understand, why the universe must be exactly as it is (a causal explanation).
2   There are many universes. We inhabit one that has the correct characteristics for evolution and for life (a selective explanation).
3   The universe is given a direction, the goal of which is to create life (a teleological or purpose-oriented explanation).

The usual methodology of modern science proceeds from what is observed, and seeks a causal explanation. With the selective explanation, the anthropic principle becomes a selection criterion among many universes with random characteristics. Each of these universes would have other basic constants and other conditions at the beginning. Their totality would perhaps be an infinite ensemble of universes. According to the definition of the term 'universe', we could, however, observe no other except our own. The extension of the sciences beyond our reality into other, unobservable universes is therefore a step in the metaphysical direction, from which a number of experts turn away on principle.

The teleological explanation (*telos*, Greek for 'end, goal, purpose') introduces a structure of finality into science. It has been taken into serious consideration, even though it is largely rejected, and has unleashed much emotion in the camp of rationalistic scholarship. The new law would ascribe a tendency to the cosmos that enables life to come about, similar to the characteristic of constant energy. Unlike energy conservation, for which no scientifically proven exception is known apart from temporary quantum effects, this character of finality would only guarantee the necessary conditions for life and would not be compelling. It seems unlikely that this view will ever find the kind of consensus other natural laws enjoy in physics. Nevertheless, finality is not a stranger to the analytical structure of otherwise causal physics. The second law of thermodynamics contains finality with an assertion pointing to the future – the increase in entropy – without citing a causal basis. Self-organizing processes have an attractor or a goal towards which they independently set a course. It gives them a direction towards which the causal micro-processes line up. Finality does not contradict causality and does not exonerate science from the task of finding the individual causal events.

The anthropic principle explains at least partially why the universe appears 'good' for us and made to the benefit of humanity. To sustain a development that led to conscious beings in which the universe can think about itself, the universe must have certain conditions. The anthropic principle cannot explain why there is such a development at all.

From the above discussion it must be concluded that the anthropic principle cannot be applied to the future. Some developments are predictable from conservation laws with great certainty, but they may not be 'good' for us. Some new structures are conceivable, but newness remains speculation.

Thesis 8. Pattern recognition is an important way to perceive. We cannot mathematically predict the future, but recognize patterns in the 'signs of the times'.

Because there are these two counter-streaming, unpredictable developments of decay and formation, recognition of patterns plays an important role. Pattern recognition is a significant way of human apprehension and is distinct from pure measurement. Here we make an important step from the exact sciences to other sciences and finally in the direction of religion. Pattern recognition means that we can interpret perceptions and construct their meaning. Two steps are required.

First, out of countless perceptions and experiences human reason selects facts that are considered typical. This selection may occur unconsciously, without reflection or even by computer. Concerning the future, we search for and select the 'signs of the times'. The second step in construction is the recognition of a pattern. Patterns are derived from previous perceptions and experiences constituting mental prototypes. A pattern is recognized by its similarity to the new situation, if the probe and the example agree within a certain margin. Errors can occur when a pattern is not recognized or a pattern is erroneously found to fit. The two-step interpretation by selection and pattern recognition constitutes a successful method for solving certain problems and has important applications in technology, such as robotics.

The way we anticipate the future depends on how we interpret the present. There is a choice of various patterns: it is getting better; it remains as it has always been; it gets worse and worse; something new will appear. The fourth pattern is central for Christian hope, where the events of Good Friday and Easter are the archetype. The four patterns are diametrically different. Independent interpretations of the same present may thus contradict each other. Only later experiences will confirm or refute an interpretation.

Interpreting the present is important as the coming future may require preparation, initiative or defence. Human beings are masters of interpretation, very likely because reliable pattern recognition was a selective advantage in the evolution of the *Hominidae*. Those who interpreted well had more chances to survive and have descendants. The future punishes those who interpret wrongly.

Thesis 9. Hope is not a scientific term. It can only grow in a trusting relationship. Such trust involves a certain foreknowledge with which a person faces the future.

Scientific predictions can be objectively justified. Hope, however, is not independent of a subject. It touches on the relationship between the subject and the world. On the basis of this relationship, reality is perceived in a different way than on the basis of the scientific method. Hopes are based upon promises, ideals or the perception of the world as creation. Hope cannot be brought about by dogmas or metaphysical constructions but must accord with one's own perceptions.

The Christian tradition does not postulate the sort of optimism in which the development of the world is seen as a straightforward progression towards the good and the reasonable. Its hope lies not in protection from crisis, but rather in the formation of newness. The last book of the Bible, the Revelation of John, expresses this perspective in apocalyptic visions. Hope is established within a divine dimension of time, namely its creativity. The crisis will be overcome, though it is not specified how this will occur in concrete terms. It is not easy for scientifically minded people to accept a hope for which there is no causal justification. The scientific pattern for 'the formation of newness' cannot establish Christian hope, but can make hope understandable by supplying relevant metaphors. As with the concept of creation, the scientific 'how' must recede into the background, where hope for the future is concerned.

The apostle Paul expressly describes the resurrection of Christ as the basis for Christian hope (1 Corinthians 15: 12–19). What took place on

Good Friday followed by Easter, says hope, will occur again in some comparable fashion. The experience-pattern of crisis and redemption has this precedent by which hope can be gauged at any time. It is not surprising if Christians always come back to Good Friday and Easter. Moreover, the transcendent basis for hope becomes obvious in this proto-type, since the resurrection appeared as a part of the new to come from beyond space and time. Christians hope for nothing less than newness in the realm of death and in a world of merciless decay; in religious language, they hope for a new creation.

Thesis 10. Many of our perceptions, in particular relating to reli-gion and expectations of the future, cannot be objective as the human being participates in and is part of the process.

Scientific measurements and observations must be reproducible and objec-tive. The researcher is exchangeable and the result independent. In religious perceptions, on the other hand, a human being is always strongly involved. I would not say that such participating perceptions are purely subjective, as they are often reported as a relation to an outside entity. Such perceptions are universally human and change the life of many people in a visible and often very positive way. If 'reality' denotes what has a lasting effect in real life, these changes testify to the experienced reality. The human being directly takes part in the process of perception and is the observing instrument. Thus the observer is not interchangeable, as in the case of experiences of art. It follows that seminal perceptions are the very starting points of both science and religion. However, they are fundamen-tally different. The two fields of experiencing reality consequently span two different planes of methodology and language.

It leads to misunderstandings and false expectations in the present discourse between science and theology, when the two planes of percep-tions are not clearly separated. This difference is the reason why science can neither prove the existence of God nor deny it. It is as hopeless to find a compelling trace of God in scientific results as to find a palm tree in a Canadian forest. There is no direct path from scientific measurements to religious experience.

The path can only be indirect and through the human consciousness. For example, the apparent fine-tuning of the universe to the benefit of evolution is certainly amazing. If a person on the basis of other experiences believes in God, he or she can apprehend in cosmic evolution the work of God. Only then the fact that something has formed and not nothing (the Principle of Formation) becomes what is meant by the biblical concept of divine creation. Without participating perceptions it remains an abstract principle.

It is worth recalling that no objectively certain facts are available concerning the Easter event. The Good Friday–Easter pattern makes sense only on this other level of perception – the participatory level, where subject and object meet in an interactive relationship and form a whole. So neither the pattern nor the hope can be regarded as objectified facts. Christian hope does not follow from an interpretation of nature independent of the observing person and cannot be objectively confirmed. It cannot even be made plausible to scientific reason. Like love, hope is not compulsive, but is rather something like a gift that one can accept or not. Hope is no abstract idea, for ultimately hope becomes integral to one's humanity and changes nothing less than the condition of human life.

If we speak of 'hope contrary to all reason', we acknowledge that the factual appearances as observed in science do not define the whole of reality.

Thesis 11. Hope is based on participating perceptions.

How does one arrive at such hope? In hope, religious experience expresses itself on the level of faith. Such experience formed originally from elements of existential sensory perception, particularly in everyday life. It also includes relational, 'interior' perceptions of wholeness, dream-like visions, and sudden insights while completely conscious. The traditional pattern helps to identify and to integrate these perceptions. Living with hope, I do not perceive time only as a sequence of causal processes or chance occurrences, and as an infinitesimally brief present. Once the hoped-for future enters the picture, time embraces duration. It is the duration of waiting until newness forms. Through attentive waiting, we may occasionally discover foreshadowings and intimations of the future newness. But this kind of perception requires patience, and a willingness to develop a reciprocal relationship to reality.

The tension between science and religion concerning the expectation of the future cannot be fully harmonized and must remain. It is the tension between practical knowledge and visionary hope. This tension is within ourselves, not between fields of inquiry, and it is an important part of reality and of our life.

Thesis 12. Nature has always been a source of metaphors for experiences on the level of participating perceptions. Today science has partially and unconsciously taken over this role.

The two planes come into constructive contact when a pattern of one plane serves as an image in the other. This comes about when a religious experience is expressed by a metaphor (Greek for 'transfer') from science. A metaphor transfers a well-known pattern (e.g. 'formation of new structure') into the other plane of concepts. The notion of 'hope' could thus be communicated by the following metaphor:

130

Despite decay and death something new will arise out of this existence, just as our planet formed from cosmic dust, the ashes of former stars.

The hope that is expressed here cannot be deduced from the physics of planet formation, but must originate in the plane of religious perceptions where this boundless confidence is experienced.

Hope for new is one of several patterns for the interpretation of the signs of the times. If we live with this pattern, the past development of the universe may become a metaphor for the future of our existence. And more, by interpreting scientific results they are evaluated on the basis of other, additional experiences. The scientific facts then appear in another perspective and in a different light: the universe is revealed as a continuous creation not a horrible tragedy, and there is hope for creation also in the future.

References

Benz, A. (2000) *The Future of the Universe: Chance, Chaos, God?*, New York: Continuum.

Carter, B. (1974) 'Large Number Coincidences and the Anthropic Principle in Cosmology', in M.S. Longair (ed.), *Confrontation of Cosmological Theory with Observational Data*, Dordrecht: Reidel.

Laplace, P.S. (1799) *Traité de la mécanique céleste*.

Perlmutter, S. *et al.* (1999) 'Measurements of Omega and Lambda from 42 High-Redshift Supernovae', *Astrophysical Journal* 517: 565–86.

Riess A. *et al.* (1999) 'BVRI Light Curves for 22 Type I A Supernovae', *Astronomical Journal* 177: 707–24.

16

TRAGEDY VERSUS HOPE?

A theological response

Eduardo R. Cruz

Let us face the facts: whichever universe is available for us, we are still in an existential situation of estrangement from it. This also means that our consciousness is alienated from the possibility of a comprehensive and permanent understanding of the cosmos. It follows that some dissonance is to be expected, not only within scientific discourse itself, but especially when different disciplines are invoked. In other words, in the dialogue between science and religion we must acknowledge that discourses from different approaches may pass through each other, leading to misunderstanding perhaps, but also to opportunity for further inquiry.

The chapter by Arnold Benz, 'Tragedy versus hope: what future in an open universe?', is a good example, first, of an acknowledegment of the differences in approach, and, second, of such an unintended dissonance. In fact, while the scientific side of his theses is expounded with ease and precision, something to be expected from a leading expert in the field of cosmology, the exposition of crucial terms such as 'tragedy' and 'hope' is marred by some distortion of meaning.

The purpose of the present response is not so much to face the challenge of an open future in full-blown theological terms, but rather to give more precision to these two non-scientific terms, tragedy and hope. We will also show that the 'tragedy versus hope' framing of the situation is inadequate, pointing rather to a 'hope through tragedy' approach.

On tragedy and the tragic

It is a common phenomenon in any language that a word, with time and usage, may acquire a new, transposed meaning, alongside the original one. That is the case with 'tragedy.' In common usage, it means '2a: disastrous event: CALAMITY b: MISFORTUNE' (*Webster's Ninth New Collegiate Dictionary*), whereas the original meaning is closer to '1b: a serious drama typically describing a conflict between the protagonist and a superior force (as destiny) and having a sorrowful or disastrous conclusion that excites pity or terror' (*idem*). The stories of Prometheus and Sisyphus come readily to mind when we try to grasp the breadth of cosmic and biological evolution.

By reading Benz's essay we are led to the common usage meaning, which is likely to impoverish the argument. The Earth being burned by the sun in 10^9 years, and 'heat death' coming in 10^{100} years, are surely misfortunes, albeit only from our petty, anthropomorphic perspective. But any other scenario for the distant future would also be gloomy: 'big crunch,' eternal rearrangement of the universe, fleeing through worm holes, even the scientifically impossible eternal continuity of the present state of the universe. Steven Weinberg (1977: 154) is more precise at this point, speaking of 'the grace of tragedy.'[1] We have to take seriously the words of the psalmist about our lot:

> Thou turnest man back into dust; 'Turn back,' thou sayest, 'you sons of men'; for in thy sight a thousand years are as yesterday; a night-watch passes, and thou cast them off; they are like a dream at daybreak, they fade like grass which springs up with the morning but when evening comes is parched and withered. So we are brought to an end by thy anger and silenced by thy wrath. Thou dost lay bare our iniquities before thee and our lusts in the full light of thy presence. All our days go by under the shadow of thy wrath; our years die away like a murmur. Seventy years is the span of our life, eighty if our strength holds; the hurrying years are labour and sorrow, so quickly they pass and are forgotten.
>
> (Psalm 90:3 –10 in the *New English Bible*)

We are latecomers in the universe, and soon will pass away. We experience fate and indifference in the cosmos, and the absence and wrath of God. The Judaeo-Christian tradition, indeed, is filled with 'flirtations with the tragic' (to use the apt expression of Lee Humphreys – see Humphreys 1985: 73), and the message is harsh and straightforward: whatever hope we can expect from the universe that science is able to describe, it comes in a strange yet graceful manner. No Disney-like dream-come-true expectations here! To be fair, Benz does point out that for the Christian tradition 'hope lies not in protection from crisis, but rather in the formation of newness.' We will explore the nuances of his argument in the section on hope below.

Elsewhere we have explored in some detail the convergences and divergences between the form and spirit of the tragedies of ancient Greece and our religious heritage (Cruz 1996: 72–80, 94–7, 101–3, 143–6, 156–62). In doing so, we relied almost entirely on other sources, which means that using 'tragedy' without referring to sources such as these may introduce even more misunderstandings in academic discourse. To be fair to Benz, even sophisticated theologians and philosophers may think that it is not necessary to work out the meaning of 'tragedy' (e.g. Haught 2000: chapter 7; Rolston 2003). The tragic must be distinguished from the farcical, the unfortunate, the sorrowful, the pitiful, and the pathetic. Only where there is greatness and nobility is the tragic present. Is there any nobility in the universe?

'Hope contrary to all reason'

As opposed to 'tragedy,' Benz's essay has several references to 'hope,' all of them being beyond any serious questioning. As his starting point for religious experience is the Christian tradition, he rightly takes the paschal event as the pivotal element that grounds hope for the future (see also Benz 2000: 119–22). Hope is no wishful thinking, insofar as it is grounded on reliable witnesses. Moreover, Christian religious experience has as its main content the ever-presence of this unique event, the resurrection of Jesus Christ. But, within the conditions of existence, the cross is also ever present. As Jürgen Moltmann once said, 'the Cross of Christ modifies the resurrection of Christ under the conditions of the suffering world so that it changes from being a purely future event to being an event of liberating love' (Moltmann 1974: 185).

Because of the very nature of the paschal event, it is possible to say that tragedy is not opposed to (*versus*) hope, but there is an intimate relationship between them. Reinhold Niebuhr, for example, acknowledged this relationship long ago: 'The second Adam is crucified by the first Adam, particularly by the first Adam who is trying to be good and is seeking to build up government and churches and standards of conduct which will hold sin in check' (Niebuhr [1937] 1965: 182). He then continues in the same vein: 'The modern church ... has forgotten that the Kingdom of God enters the world in tragic terms. The "prince of glory" dies on the cross.' He combines the two assertions by saying: 'The Kingdom of God must still enter the world by the way of crucifixion.' The connection between tragedy and the cross, however, would not be fully established if God's plan and will were not in some way involved in it. Therefore, Niebuhr concludes by saying: 'In the very crucifixion God has absorbed the contradictions of historic existence into Himself. Thus Christianity transmutes the tragedy of history into something which is not tragedy' (*ibid.*, 184, 185, 193). This 'something which is not tragedy' is hope.

What is valid for human history is also valid, *mutatis mutandis*, for cosmic history. Benz himself hints at this dialectical process, indicating in the explication of his fourth thesis what it is possible to ascertain by the sciences. 'Similarly, the extreme order constituting living beings cannot last. Death is unavoidable for several reasons ranging from chemical decay to physiological deterioration. It is, on the other hand, a *necessary* ingredient of evolution' (Benz 2002; my emphasis). For the Christian this assertion, warranted by the sciences, has a clear resonance in John 12:24: 'In truth, in very truth I tell you, a grain of wheat remains a solitary grain unless it falls into the ground and dies; but if it dies, it bears a rich harvest.' Further exploration of this life-through-death theme may be found in several contemporary authors (e.g. Rolston 1987). The tricky point here, however, is how to understand the meaning of 'life *ever*lasting' in the scientific picture. But let us move first to some epistemological considerations.

Where is this opposition, tragedy versus hope, to be located in Benz's view? Perhaps we have to look for a possible double standard in his episte-mology. Indeed, when he works within his field, cosmology, he clearly adopts 'the present world-view of science.' This includes novelty within chaotic and quantum-mechanical systems, implying that: a) science seeks suitable explanations for unique events also, starting with the Big Bang itself; b) this explanation goes beyond the standard, causal form. For example, explanations for the increase in entropy and for self-organizing processes may take a teleological form; scientific explanations also involve pattern recognition (eighth thesis).

But when it comes to the foundations of Christian hope, Benz seems to retreat to a more strict, instrumentalist epistemology. He thus resorts to sober statements such as: 'Scientific measurements and observations must be reproducible and objective'; 'It is worth recalling that no objectively certain facts are available concerning the Easter event'; and 'It [hope] cannot even be made plausible to scientific reason'. By drawing such a sharp borderline between scientific measurement and religious experience or faith, the author seems to borrow from logical empiricism the dichotomy between the context of discovery and the context of justification, and to completely disregard theology as a cognitive enterprise.

Well, precisely because of the peculiar nature of this 'hope contrary to all reason,' the latter being understood as Niebuhr understood it (i.e. as the practical, commonsensical reason which seeks 'to build up government and churches'), this hope can be made plausible to scientific reason. It is true that the 'wisdom of the cross' is a 'stumbling-block to Jews and folly to Greeks' (1 Corinthians 1:23), but on the other hand it is true that science too bursts through commonsense (science has a 'heretical nature' – see Cromer 1993, Ridley 1996), robbing wishful thinking of its illusory hope. Theology, on the other hand, cannot stop short of any standards of rationality in its efforts to submit its arguments on the cross and resurrection to public scrutiny.

Does this mean that the future depicted by science matches the hope of Christians based on the paschal event? Not quite so, if we seriously take into account our own introductory remarks. Yet, the literal (and preferably mathematical) language of science, as Benz himself recognizes, does not rule out the symbolic language of religious experience. It is true that in the latter case there is some measure of circularity – we do not know the referent of the symbol outside of its own enacting in myth and ritual – but symbols such as 'eternal life' and the 'Kingdom of God' are not opposed to the tentative depiction of the ultimate fate of the universe in terms of 'photons, positrons and electrons.' Science does know the future of the universe (unavoidable decay), and at the same time does not know it (uncertainties in the physical theories). Likewise, the Christian symbol does know the future (reversal of decay into a qualitatively different stage called 'resurrection'), and at the same time does not know it – religious sensibility can only hope (*sperare*) for the future in faith and love, based on a unique event in the history of the cosmos and humankind alike, the death and resurrection of Jesus Christ.[2]

This unique event bestows meaning on the 'grace of tragedy' of Weinberg. Rolston also reminds us that Weinberg was not the first to be astonished by this ambivalent nature of the universe:

> Suffering through to something higher is always messianic. Transfigured sorrow is ever the divine glory. That was never more true than at Calvary, but it has always been true ever since the capacity for sorrow emerged in the primeval evolutionary process. The creatures 'were always carrying in the body the dying of Jesus' even before he came. J.B.S. Haldane found the marks of evolution to be 'beauty,' 'tragedy,' and 'inexhaustible queerness.' But beauty, tragedy, and unfathomable strangeness are equally the marks of the story of this Jesus of Nazareth. It is a fantastic story, but then, again, to recall the conclusion of a puzzled astronomer, Fred Hoyle, the universe itself is a fantastic story.
>
> (Rolston 1987: 328; see also Rolston 2003)

We are not sure, however, that it is possible to go along with Rolston all the way. Without a sustained treatment of God's freedom and transcendence, on the one hand, and the grounds for hope in christological and eschatological terms, on the other, it is difficult to assert the Goodness of Creation. Philip Hefner's position seems to be more consistent at this point (Hefner 2003).

Conclusion

Our earth is 'the third rock from the Sun,' a speck of dust in the immensity of the cosmos. Yet, in this tiny corner of ours the universe became self-conscious, was ennobled and gracefully vested with beauty, truth and love. It does not matter whether it has happened before, or will happen again in the future. We do not know, and perhaps never will know. What is important is that, in the long life of the universe, in our fleeting passage on earth, a flash of awareness is taking place. Dust has become 'vital,' capable of foresight and expectation. I agree entirely with Benz when he uses the following metaphor: 'Despite decay and death something new will arise out of this existence, just as our planet formed from cosmic dust, the ashes of former stars.' Dare we say something more, to avoid falling into wishful thinking? I think so: as hope is both a theological virtue and embodied in symbols, this 'something new' may be experienced now in fragmentary anticipation and confidence (see Cruz 2003). 'When I look up at thy heavens, the work of thy fingers, the moon and the stars set in their place by thee, what is man that thou shouldst remember him, mortal man that thou shouldst care for him? Yet thou hast made him little less than a god, crowning him with glory and honour' (Psalm 8:3–5). Only a being crowned with glory and honour can withstand tragedy and wait diligently for a new creation to be formed out of mere ashes, but also out of the side of the pierced one. Through this witness of ours, the universe itself becomes the 'ecological niche' of tragedy and hope, holding in check any assignment of the equally anthropomorphic idea of 'fate' to its everlasting future.

Notes

1 In his book Benz also mentions the often-cited phrase by Steven Weinberg: 'The more the universe seems comprehensible, the more it also seems pointless' (Benz 2000: 169, n.24). It is a pity that he, together with many other commentators, does not quote Weinberg to the very end: 'But if there is no solace in the fruits of our research, there is at least some consolation in the research itself. ... The effort to understand the universe is one of the very few things that lift human life a little above the level of farce, and gives it some of the grace of tragedy' (Weinberg 1977: 154). Granting that cosmology can be discussed at the crossroads of astrophysics, metaphysics and theology, to speak of 'the grace of tragedy' is a nice way to give much food for thought and amazement.

2 It may be argued that such sensibility leads to quietism. Our response, however, deliberately excludes the realm of human action – we are restricting ourselves to natural processes.

References

Benz, A. (2000) *The Future of the Universe: Chance, Chaos, God?* New York: Continuum.

—— (2003) 'Tragedy versus Hope: What Future in an Open Universe?', in W.B. Drees (ed.), *Is Nature Ever Evil? Religion, Science and Value*, London: Routledge.

Cromer, A. (1993) *Uncommon Sense: The Heretical Nature of Science*, Oxford: Oxford University Press.

Cruz, E.R. (1996) *A Theological Study Informed by the Thought of Paul Tillich and the Latin American Experience: The Ambivalence of Science*, Lewiston, NY: Mellen University Press.

—— (2003) 'The Quest for Perfection: Insights from Paul Tillich', in W.B. Drees (ed.) *Is Nature Ever Evil? Religion, Science and Value*, London: Routledge.

Haught, J.F. (2000) *God after Darwin: A Theology of Evolution*, Boulder, CO: Westview Press.

Hefner, P. (2003) 'Nature Good and Evil: A Theological Palette', in Willem B. Drees (ed.) *Is Nature Ever Evil? Religion, Science and Value*, London: Routledge.

Humphreys, W.L. (1985) *The Tragic Vision and the Hebrew Tradition*, Philadelphia: Fortress Press.

Moltmann, J. (1974) *The Crucified God: The Cross of Christ as the Foundation and Criticism of Christian Theology*, New York: Harper & Row.

Niebuhr, R. ([1937] 1965) *Beyond Tragedy: Essays on the Christian Interpretation of History*, New York: Charles Scribner's Sons.

Ridley, M. (1996) *The Origins of Virtue*, New York: Penguin.

Rolston, H., III (1987) *Science and Religion: A Critical Survey*, New York: Random House.

—— (2003) 'Naturalizing and Systematizing Evil', in Willem B. Drees (ed.), *Is Nature Ever Evil? Religion, Science and Value*, London: Routledge.

Weinberg, S. (1977) *The First Three Minutes*, New York: Basic Books.

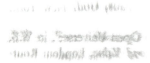

17

COSMIC FINE-TUNING, 'MANY UNIVERSE' THEORIES AND THE GOODNESS OF LIFE

Neil A. Manson

This volume addresses the role value judgements play in science. It is my contention that a particular research programme in modern physical cosmology rests crucially on a value judgement. Before making my case, let me introduce the following abbreviations for the following propositions.

K   The free cosmic parameters in standard Big Bang cosmology require fine-tuning in order for life to be possible in the universe.
E   Life is possible in the universe.
D   There exists an extra-cosmic designer.
M   There is a vast array of universes in which the laws are the same as in our universe but with varying values of the free parameters.

Here is the essence of my argument, with elaboration to follow.

(1) Most contemporary physical cosmologists think that, in light of K, an explanation is demanded for E. Many of them offer M as that explanation and they attempt to provide models whereby M is true.
(2) The best explanation of (1) is that these physical cosmologists think D is a 'tidy explanation' of E.
(3) If they think D is a 'tidy explanation' of E, they must judge that life is intrinsically valuable.

Why think fine-tuning for life needs explanation?

Many physicists and cosmologists today are attracted to theories whereby there are many universes rather than just one. Theorists such as Lee Smolin (1997) have constructed elaborate mechanisms for the production of these other universes. Their stated rationale for pursuing such models is that, without them, the fact that the universe permits life – a fact which is extremely surprising in light of the discovery that life requires exquisite 'fine-tuning' of the free parameters – would have to be judged a lucky coincidence. For example, Smolin – who argues that the 'existence of stars is the key to the problem of why the cosmos is hospitable to life' (p. 29) – maintains that 'any philosophy according to which the existence of stars and galaxies appears to be very unlikely, or rests on unexplained coincidence, cannot be satisfactory' (p. 35). Many physical cosmologists share Smolin's sentiment that, in light of K, there is something about E that demands explanation.

Why? Oftentimes we dismiss coincidences (e.g. the fact that two men are wearing the same tie) as the way things just happen to be. What is unsatisfactory about dismissing E as happenstance? There are plenty of thinkers who are more than happy to do just this. Consider, for example, Stephen Jay Gould:

> something has to happen, even if any particular 'something' must stun us by its improbability. We could look at any outcome and say, 'Ain't it amazing. If the laws of nature had been set up just a tad differently, we wouldn't have this kind of universe at all.'
>
> (Gould 1998: 189)

Gould and like-minded thinkers will grant that the fitness of the universe for life is fascinating, stunning, fortunate … but also something that it is perfectly appropriate to view as pure coincidence.

How should those surprised by E reply to Gould? Any successful response must meet the following condition: the fact that E must do some work in generating the demand for an explanation. That is, the account given should not be such that on it the existence of just any sort of universe would be surprising; nor should it be such that on it the values of the parameters would be just as surprising even if life didn't require that they be fine-tuned. Otherwise, those who think life-permittingness demands an explanation are confused.

Consider, as an analogy, the case of a securities regulator who asks a stockbroker to explain why she made 1,350,000 pounds last week from investing in British Petroleum. The stockbroker is right to ask the regulator what it is about making 1,350,000 pounds last week from investing in British Petroleum that demands explanation. Is it the fact that 1,350,000 pounds were made? Is it the fact that the money was made last week? Is it the fact that the money was made from investing in British Petroleum? Is it some combination of the three? What is it? If the regulator cannot answer these questions, any judge will surely agree with the stockbroker's lawyer that the regulator's demand for an explanation is unmotivated and so needn't be satisfied. If, by demanding an explanation, the regulator is going to occupy the stockbroker's valuable time, the regulator ought to be very clear about his justification for making this demand.

With this restriction in mind, it is clear that the demand for an explanation of E cannot be based solely on the Principle of Sufficient Reason (PSR). True, this principle has often been invoked by those who demand an explanation for the existence and nature of the universe. Consider the archetypical rationalist, Leibniz:

> Assuming this principle, the first question we have the right to ask will be, why is there something rather than nothing? For nothing is simpler and easier than something. Furthermore, assuming that things must exist, we must be able to give a reason for why they must exist in this way, and not otherwise.
>
> (Leibniz 1989: 209–210)

Plenty of philosophers think these are good questions. For example, regarding any one of the most general causal laws governing the universe, Peter Unger says we can ask of it the following question:

> Why is it that just that very general phenomenon, or law, should be so fundamental, or indeed obtain at all, in the world in which we have our being? Within the usual framework of explanation, law and causation, there seems no place for such curiosity to come to rest. There seems no way for us to deal adequately with the brute and ultimate specificity of the ways in which almost everything appears to happen. And what seems worse, the specific character of certain of these laws or ways, even of quite fundamental ones, often seems so quirky, the height of arbitrariness.
>
> (Unger 1984: 29)

In response to this question, Unger proposes a 'many-universe' theory of his own (though this theory is entirely philosophical and includes 'universes' which, unlike Smolin's, follow neither General Relativity nor Quantum Mechanics).

The reason the PSR cannot be the basis for the demand for an explanation of E is that the PSR generates a demand for explanation regardless of whether the universe permits life and regardless of the ease or difficulty with which it does so. 'Why is there anything at all, and why is it the way that it is?' and 'Why does the universe permit life when our physical models indicate that the parameters require extreme fine-tuning in order for life to be possible?' are very different questions. The former can remain unanswered even when the latter is answered.

To see the distinction between these two questions, imagine that the n free cosmic parameters are listed in a table and consider the decimal expression of pi out to the n-th decimal place. We can describe a different possible value for each of the n parameters simply by multiplying the actual value of the i-th parameter in the table by the i-th digit in the decimal expression of pi. Let us call the universe which results from performing this operation 'the pi universe'. For example, if the first three entries in the table describing our universe are for the masses of the proton, the neutron and the electron respectively, then in the pi universe (pi being 3.14...) the proton will be three times as massive, the neutron will have the same mass, and the electron will be four times as massive. If the literature on fine-tuning and the anthropic principle is correct, the pi universe would almost certainly forbid life.

Let us suppose (fancifully) that Leibniz, Unger and Smolin are disembodied souls endowed with awareness of the nature of physical reality, and let us also suppose that the pi universe rather than our universe is the actual universe. Would the questions and demands for explanation of Leibniz and Unger persist in this scenario? Yes. First, there would exist a universe rather than nothing, so that would demand explanation. Second, the universe would be some particular way rather than another, and that, too, would demand explanation. Leibniz and Unger would maintain these demands for explanation even though the pi universe is destined for lifelessness. Again, suppose that, in studying their models, contemporary physical cosmologists had discovered not that life requires fine-tuning of the parameters, but that life is extremely insensitive to the values taken by the parameters. (This is exactly the opposite of what contemporary physical cosmologists have discovered, but, as far as was known even just eighty years ago, they could have discovered it.) Would this discovery lead Leibniz and Unger to drop their demand for an explanation of the existence and nature of the universe? No. Smolin, on the other hand, would have his questions answered. In this hypothetical scenario, the existence of a universe with stars and galaxies – a universe that is conducive to the formation of life – would not be an unexplained coincidence. Rather, it would be a likely outcome. Based on what he has said, that should be enough for Smolin.

Leibnizian rationalism of the sort expressed in the PSR is a perfectly respectable basis for demanding an explanation of why the universe is the way it is, but the contingency of the universe is not what most contemporary cosmologists point to when they express dissatisfaction with the present state of cosmological theory. They point to fitness for life and the fact that such fitness requires fine-tuning. Why do these facts cry out for explanation?

'Tidy explanations' and the design hypothesis

Paul Horwich (1982), D.J. Bartholomew (1984), John Leslie (1989), and Peter van Inwagen (1993) are among a number of philosophers who point out that, when it comes to generating demands for explanation, there can be grounds for doing so weaker than the PSR. Leslie notes that: 'A chief (or the only?) reason ... for justifiable reluctance to dismiss [something] as how things just happen to be, is that one in fact glimpses some tidy way in which it might be explained' (p. 10). For example, we do not dismiss as mere happenstance phenomena such as the flipping of 1,000 heads in a row. The reason that we do not is not that those phenomena could have turned out differently. After all, any time we flip 1,000 coins, we will get a particular sequence of heads and tails, and it will be true of that sequence that it could have been different. No, the reason we would bother to explain the flipping of 1,000 heads in a row is that there is a better ('tidier') explanation of the event – better, that is, than the account according to which the coins by chance just all happened to turn up heads. The flipping of 1,000 heads in a row strongly suggests a double-headed coin or some other such trick. The 'trickery' hypothesis, while a priori improbable, is far more probable a posteriori (in light of the 1,000 heads flipped) than the 'lucky coincidence' hypothesis. And that's why getting 1,000 straight heads would cry out for an explanation: it is not what you would expect if pure chance were operating, but it is just the sort of thing you'd expect if there were trickery afoot. This account of explanation-demanding phenomena fits into a larger Bayesian framework of confirmation and scientific inference.

Remembering the abbreviations I supplied at the beginning of this chapter, let's apply the preceding insight to the case of fine-tuning. Those who argue from fine-tuning to a designer claim that

$$P(D|E \& K) \gg P(D|K)$$

because

$$P(E|D \& K) \gg P(E|{\sim}D \& K)$$

In other words, given that the universe permits life and that its parameters need to be fine-tuned in order for it to do so, it seems we're better off believing that there is a designer than that there isn't. Because of this, E demands explanation; after all, it is not what one would expect if the universe were the product of chance.

However, there seems to be an alternative explanation of E, namely M. Given a vast number of universes, it would be unsurprising if at least one of them permitted life (even though it would be very improbable that any particular universe selected at random from the array would permit life). Of course, we could only find ourselves in one of the life-permitting universes; this 'observational selection effect' lies at the heart of the anthropic principle. So according to advocates of M

$$P(M|E \ \& \ K) \gg P(M|K)$$

because

$$P(E|M \ \& \ K) \gg P(E|{\sim}M \ \& \ K)$$

Since M and D are both confirmed by E, it is wrong to say D is the only way to explain E.

There is something curious about this dialectical situation, however. The need for explanation of E is generated solely by D. E is surprising in light of D, but not in light of M. This is because M neither favours nor disfavours the existence of any particular sort of universe. While M makes E more probable, it also makes more probable the existence of the pi universe, the existence of the Fibonacci universe (constructed in the same way as the pi universe, but using instead the first n numbers in the Fibonacci sequence), and so on. M raises the probability of all of these universes indiscriminately; D, on the other hand, is selective. Consequently, in asking why, given K, we should not dismiss E as mere coincidence, we can't answer that M makes E much more probable, because in that case E does no work at all in generating the demand for an explanation.

So if cosmologists like Smolin think E is a special problem that demands an explanation, it has to be because they take seriously the design hypothesis D – seriously enough to warrant the construction of an alternative theory M that would thwart D. In saying this, I don't think I'm saying anything new or controversial. Lots of physicists and cosmologists are quite open in acknowledging that the universe looks to be, in Fred Hoyle's words, 'a put-up job,' and that it is this appearance which motivates them to develop the multiple-worlds theories which, if true, would explain away that appearance. But why? Why would any scientist think the universe looks like a put-up job?

The value of life

The obvious answer is that a universe that allows for life is a very good thing – just the sort of thing one would expect an extra-cosmic intelligent designer to create. And it is here we see the crucial role that a value judgement plays in the particular scientific research programme of generating multiple-universe models. If many-universe theorists didn't judge life to be good, they wouldn't think an intelligent designer would be any more likely to create our universe than some other sort of universe, in which case they wouldn't see our universe as surprising.

Now one might be tempted to argue that 'life is good' is too weak a judgement to bother with – so modest that it is hardly fair to deem the many universes research programme a value-laden enterprise simply in virtue of being motivated by it. But we shouldn't go too easy on the cosmologists. They are committed to an absolutely startling position. They are saying that, before we came on the scene, back before there were stars, back before there were even galaxies, right back to the Planck time, an ethical proposition ('Life is good') was true. Whatever else the many-universe research programme entails, it requires that at least one value judgement be true prior to the existence of any human beings.

Many people, not all of whom are philosophers, think that value judgements depend for their truth on facts about what rational agents believe, what their communities are like, and how they live – or, if not, that this is only because value judgements are not literally true at all, but rather express our emotions or indicate our (individual or group) preferences. Yet for the design hypothesis to explain the existence of a universe fine-tuned for life, the value judgement that life is good had to be true at a time when (or, if one prefers, in a situation where) there were no rational agents in the universe. Accepting this value judgement, moreover, requires a rejection of certain sorts of moral metaphysics (those variously described as 'anti-realist,' 'subjectivist,' or 'social constructivist') because on them it is incoherent to talk of true moral propositions in a universe with no moral agents in it.

Conclusion

Multiple-worlds theorists theorize so as to provide an alternative to the design hypothesis. In letting their theory construction be motivated by such a concern, however, they implicitly agree that the design hypothesis is explanatory. But for the design hypothesis to be explanatory, the value judgement 'life is good' must be true prior to the existence of human communities or any other communities. Whether or not multiple-worlds theorists recognize this implication – and whether or not they should abandon their research programme as a consequence – is a matter I will leave for discussion.

References

Bartholomew, D.J. (1984) *God of Chance*, London: SCM Press Ltd.

Gould, S.J. (1998) 'Mind and Supermind', in J. Leslie (ed.) *Physical Cosmology and Philosophy*, Amherst, NY: Prometheus Books.

Horwich, P. (1982) *Probability and Evidence*, New York: Cambridge University Press.

Leibniz, G.W. (1989) 'Principles of Nature and Grace, Based on Reason', in G.W. Leibniz *Philosophical Essays*, transl. by Roger Ariew and Daniel Garber, Indianapolis: Hackett.

Leslie, J. (1989) *Universes*, London: Routledge.

Manson, N.A. (2000) 'Anthropocentrism and the Design Argument', *Religious Studies* 36(3): 163–76.

Smolin, L. (1997) *The Life of the Cosmos*, New York: Oxford University Press.

Unger, P. (1984) 'Minimizing Arbitrariness: Toward a Metaphysics of Infinitely Many Isolated Concrete Worlds', in P.A. French, T.E. Uehling, H.K. Wettstein (eds) *Midwest Studies in Philosophy* IX, Minneapolis: University of Minnesota Press.

Van Inwagen, P. (1993) *Metaphysics*, Boulder, Colorado: Westview Press.

Part III

IMPROVING NATURE VIA CULTURE AND TECHNOLOGY?

Introduction to Part III

Willem B. Drees

The preceding essays were, by and large, about our understanding of reality. However, we as humans also act in reality. Science has an active side to it; we seek understanding in order to control reality, in order to make things better, to create useful machines and medicines. And religion, too, is not limited to the quest for understanding, a quest for answers to ultimate questions as to the origin of life or reality as such. Religion is about life; myths and rituals seek to transform people. Traditions such as the Christian one are not limited to thinking about God as Creator; there is also a vocabulary of redemption, of a different world, or of this world as different. In the first chapter of this part the historian John Brooke explores discourses on 'improving nature' as examples of interactions between science and religion in the United Kingdom in the last few centuries. The clinical geneticist Leo ten Kate challenges all those who take time to ponder whether we should improve nature. If we ask the victims of nature, the patients he sees in his professional work in the clinic, there is no question as to whether we should attempt to improve nature – even though there may be plenty of questions about the extent to which we can. The philosopher Geertsema offers quite a different commentary, challenging all who use the discourse of improvement to reflect on the standards by which one judges 'improvements' – are they merely human standards, or do they have a deeper foundation? The essay by Kris Dierickx on the concept of health brings such questions more down to earth; can 'health' be defined in neutral, scientific terms?

The theologian Philip Hefner, who advocated in earlier writings the designation of humans as 'created co-creators', explores further a theological understanding of nature which is not opposed to human activity as it shapes culture and technology, but inclusive of it. A commentary by the theologian Wessel Stoker deepens the debate on the implicit theodicy involved in such approaches. Further essays explore our human, technological activity as a quest for perfection (Eduardo Cruz), as raising issues about 'natural law' and normativity (Mathew Illathuparampil) and as resulting in new interpretations of the human as cyborg, a combination of nature and culture (Anne Kull).

18

IMPROVABLE NATURE?

John Hedley Brooke

Genetically altered food crops take mankind into realms that
belong to God, and to God alone.
(HRH Prince Charles, *The Times*, 7 June 2000, 4)

The application of science and technology to meeting human needs has
generated a rhetoric of amelioration with a long history. Advancing
knowledge through experimental methods was famously justified by
Francis Bacon in terms of bringing glory to God and relief to man's estate.
Keeping the two parts of that formula together has not always been easy.
To speak of 'improvement' at all seems to suggest that 'in Nature' things
are not as they should be. And this has immediate implications for how
one might answer the question that gives this book its title; for if Nature
were never flawed, what improvements would be necessary?

In this paper I offer a few reflections on how natural philosophers and
scientists have dealt with such questions, especially when drawn into theological debate. I shall use the perceptions of Charles Darwin as a way of
identifying what might be said to be imperfect in Nature. Divisions within
natural theology will be examined that reflect the tension between
presenting the world of Nature as good (even the 'best' of all possible
worlds) and presenting it as seriously flawed. I shall then explore some of
the many different ways in which the remedial promises of medicine,
science and technology have impinged on concepts of the 'natural'. The
sciences have sometimes been a medium through which Nature has been
declared less imperfect than appearances suggest, whilst interventionist
medicine has provided perhaps the most basic model for the sanctification
of remedial projects. It is instructive to examine the resources available
within theology itself for accommodating programmes of improvement. By
equating altruistic applications of science with the *redemption* or *restoration* of Nature a certain congruence has been possible, but the
open-endedness of modern biotechnology cannot easily be accommodated
through such language. There is in fact a good case for suggesting that
ambivalence in public reactions to genetic engineering is a legacy from an

earlier theological ambivalence towards the imitation, control and especially the improvement of Nature.

The unnaturalness of Nature

As other contributors have observed, to ask whether Nature is ever evil
would be a simplistic question if it implied a world of Nature 'out there'
that can be exhaustively described in objective terms and then measured
against agreed standards of goodness, rightness and beauty. As cultural
historians never cease to point out, what we mean by 'Nature' is not a
given; and the criteria for any kind of moral evaluation are unlikely to be
agreed. When Thomas Burnet, author of *Sacred Theory of the Earth*
(1684), wrote of mountains, he described them as symbols of a ruined
world – a world whose surface had once been smooth but which, since the
flood described in Genesis, was now cracked and crushed. Mountains were
gloomy, dismal reminders of human sin and a providentially synchronized
punishment. For Burnet's contemporary, Richard Bentley, the case was
very different. In his *Confutation of Atheism* (1692) Bentley argued that
the seemingly cracked and crumpled parts of creation had their uses: an
irregular coastline gave shelter to ships; hills and mountains had the
benefit that views were very fine from the top. There are elements of
subjectivity in the perception of 'Nature' that are difficult if not impossible
to eliminate.

Such perceptions also reflect changes in sensibility that can occur with
the passing of time. In a well-known study Marjorie Nicolson showed how
in the world of the Romantic poets mountains were transformed from
objects of fear and gloom to objects of majesty and awe (Nicolson 1959).
During the nineteenth century the English Lake District became a place of
pilgrimage and the Alps evoked a new sense of grandeur rather than terror.
There is no 'natural' way of reading the book of Nature. Even the
language in which it is deemed to be written has changed over time,
Galileo insisting early in the seventeenth century that the apposite
language was not that of teleological processes but of mathematics.

Galileo's remark reminds us of yet another complication. Nature is a
modelled object that has been captured in different world pictures and
world views. In some models Nature is subject, not object, as in the
'Mother Nature' who nurtures her offspring. In others, as in Cartesian
philosophy, Nature is reduced to a soulless machine. Among the chemists
of the nineteenth century Nature became a chemical laboratory, as, in large
measure, it had been for the alchemists. The most appropriate form of
modelling will often be a divisive issue within the sciences themselves.
Whether the workings of the brain and the correlates of consciousness
should be modelled electrochemically, pharmacologically or via computer
simulation would be a contemporary example.

The crucial point, however, is that different world pictures and world views may put different sets of constraints on what is desirable or possible when the issue of improvement is engaged. It is easy to overstate the case, but it seems reasonable to hold that sensitivity to the knock-on (and possibly deleterious) effects of technological change is likely to be greater where Nature is envisaged as an organism or an interconnected web of interlocking processes than when interpreted in atomistic terms. There is also a very deep question concerning the circumstances in which Nature is envisaged as a unity or as a plurality. In this context theological ideas have played their part in the modelling process. The secular drive for a unifying theory in physics had its equivalent in earlier times when Newton, Faraday and Einstein in their different ways looked for a unification on the strength (in part) of their monotheism (Gouk 1988; Cantor 1991; Jammer 1999).

To speak of Nature as many do who, in their defence of social policies, appeal to what is 'natural' can be simplistic for the additional reason that there have been centuries during which whatever might once have been 'natural' has already been changed by human intervention. This applies to landscape and to the production of new varieties of crops and domestic animals long before the modern techniques of genetic engineering arrived. In the exposition of his theory of evolution Charles Darwin appealed to the accumulation of variation under domestication through *human* selection as a model for explicating what he meant by *natural* selection. Hence yet another image of the natural in which Nature came to be personified, if only for heuristic purposes: 'Let us now suppose a Being with penetration sufficient to perceive differences in the outer and innermost organization quite imperceptible to man, and with forethought extending over future centuries to watch with unerring care and select for any object the offspring of an organism produced under the foregoing circumstances; I can see no conceivable reason why he could not form a new race ... adapted to new ends' (Darwin 1844: 114).

Such language stands in marked contrast to the mechanical philosophies of the seventeenth and eighteenth centuries, which not only implied a fixed clockwork universe but which had deliberately eliminated personal agencies from the workings of Nature. For Robert Boyle it had even been an anathema that 'Nature' should be capitalized because that implied autonomous powers of initiation, which belonged properly to God alone. To say, for example, that 'Nature abhorred a vacuum' was to be guilty of a category mistake. Nature, for theological as well as philosophical reasons, had to be purged of intelligences mediating between God and creation. Otherwise the Sovereignty of God was compromised. The consequence for Boyle was that 'nature' (without a capital) had to be understood as a set of rules under the jurisdiction of the deity. Nature, as it were, had to be de-natured in the interests of both science and theology (Boyle 1686). In stressing such points I do not wish to be understood as adopting extreme forms of social constructivism. It is simply that there has been no uniquely privileged or 'natural' construction of 'Nature'.

Nature and its discontents

Let us return to Darwin because, as one of the nineteenth century's most discriminating agnostics, he might help in identifying facets of Nature that could be considered defective. One could not expect Darwin to be a neutral witness. After all, he had done more than any other naturalist to change perceptions of Nature – from a harmonious system, even 'a happy world', as William Paley had described it, to a Nature so red in tooth and claw that it would often seem irreconcilable with belief in a beneficent deity. Darwin certainly recognized that when his contemporaries spoke of Nature they were deluding themselves if they thought they had access to a neutral reading that was not theory-laden. In a memorable aphorism he wrote that the contented face of Nature is but a mask. The unmasking was a staggering experience because one was brought face to face with the enormous extent of extinction. Once unmasked, what were Nature's imperfections?

For one thing, the sheer volume of pain and suffering, Darwin declaring that this had always seemed to him one of the strongest arguments against belief in a beneficent deity. Disease, too, especially when it took the life of a cherished daughter. The death of his innocent Annie, just 10 years old, was perhaps the most demoralizing experience of his life. It marked the 'crucifixion of his hopes' (Desmond and Moore 1991: 384). Nature could be repugnant as well as diseased. The revulsion Darwin experienced when thinking of the egg-laying habits of the Ichneumonidae is well known. Such behaviour meant a gruesome death for the caterpillar in whose body the eggs would hatch. This was one of the 'horridly cruel' works of Nature on which a 'devil's chaplain' might write (Desmond and Moore 1991: 449).

The instability of Nature was arguably another imperfection. During the *Beagle* voyage, Darwin witnessed the devastating effects of an earthquake. In Concepcion the cathedral collapsed in the most violent quake that could be remembered in the vicinity. Would Paley's natural theology have been quite so plausible if England had been ravaged by such disturbances? Darwin drew a dismal conclusion: 'If beneath England the now inert subterranean forces should exert those powers, which most assuredly in former geological ages they have exerted, how completely would the entire condition of the country be changed! In every large town famine would go forth, pestilence and death following in its train' (Brooke 1974: 63).

It has often been observed that belief in progress became a surrogate religion for Victorian intellectuals. By the time Darwin published his

Descent of Man (1871), it was possible to point to technological advances that had improved human communication beyond what Nature alone could offer. As one contemporary observed: 'Close and fruitful intercourse, through the railway, the steamboat, the electric telegraph, the penny post, the public meeting, and the cheap press' was now 'the notable feature of our modern civilisation' (Baldwin Brown 1871: 343). Emphatically human life was improvable through science and technology. Even human nature itself might be perfectible if, as in Darwin's theory, humans became part of Nature. The practice of slavery, which Darwin abhorred, was an evil in society if not in Nature itself. Looking to the future, he could be sanguine about prospects for change: 'as natural selection works solely by and for the good of each being, all corporeal and mental endowments will tend to progress towards perfection' (Passmore 1970: 239). Though Darwin had a keen sense of the imperfections of Nature, the very existence of a mechanism for perfectibility complicates the picture. The question as to whether Nature is flawed could be read as presupposing a static view of 'Nature' whereas it might need re-drafting if 'Nature' is to be construed as an ongoing evolutionary process. The picture is further complicated by the fact noted by John Passmore that, on Darwin's scenario, it does not follow that *man* must be perfected: the process might involve the evolution of man into a new species (Passmore 1970: 240).

At this point the obvious question arises as to whether it is necessary to the world's religions that Nature should be above criticism. In a recent interview, A.N. Wilson, author of *God's Funeral* (1999), reminded his questioner that 'religions – certainly the Judeo-Christian tradition – are not based on going with the flow or accepting the system. They are based on the idea that there is something *wrong* with the system.' And again, 'religion goes out to find the way the universe is constructed and then tries to explain to individuals why they do not feel at ease in it' (Wilson 2000: 45). Nature may once have looked good to its Creator; but the postulation of a primal 'fall', with its consequences for the natural world as well as for humanity, was clearly one way of asserting that all is not well with the world. In the conclusion to his book *Science, Religion and Naturalism* Willem Drees observes that in religious belief there is often a prophetic element, arising from precisely this contrast between what is the case and what is believed ought to be the case (Drees 1996: 281). It should not then be surprising that tensions have existed both within and between systems of natural theology according to the manner in which evil has been rationalized.

Natural theology and its divisions

In one well-known style of natural theology, Nature may not be represented as perfect but it is portrayed as the best of all *possible* worlds. In much of eighteenth-century natural theology the existence of repugnant forms of life was simply rationalized in terms of a principle of plenitude according to which the Creator had brought into being a maximum variety of creatures. With sufficient ingenuity a reason could usually be found for abhorrent facets of creation. The ugliness of the megatherium was dispelled by the Oxford geologist William Buckland, as he explained how the grotesque forelimbs had been perfectly designed for excavating roots (Rupke 1983: 242). Hemlock was poison to Socrates, remarked William Derham in his *Physico-Theology* (1713), but it provided food for goats. Noxious insects and poisonous snakes teach us watchfulness. The rattlesnake does at least issue a warning before it strikes!

By contrast, there were natural theologies in which the defects of Nature were not to be rationalized but redeemed. In his book *The Age of Atonement*, Boyd Hilton has shown how a more pessimistic form of natural theology took shape among evangelicals in early nineteenth-century Britain. The wretchedness of the human condition was reflected in various ways in the world of Nature. There was still evidence of a divine power to whom one was answerable; but Nature was replete with reminders of a depravity and degeneracy to which humans had succumbed (Hilton 1988). It is impossible to generalize about this because different evangelical thinkers struck their own balance between the beauty and the ugliness of creation. An instructive example is the Scottish evangelical Hugh Miller, who extolled the beauty of fossil forms, comparing them with the finer features of Gothic cathedrals. It was a way of showing that man and his Maker shared the same aesthetic sensibilities (Brooke 1996). By examining the species introduced at the beginning of each geological epoch, Miller could even see a pattern of progress as one ascended the fossil record. But Miller's world was also distorted and degenerate. Within each epoch there had been a degeneration of form and the effects of the 'fall' were to be seen on the human faces of the less favoured races. It seemed to Miller that 'the further we remove in any direction from the Adamic centre, the more animalized and sunk do we find the various tribes or races'. The importance of this observation lay in its refutation of theories of organic development, since Miller could argue that 'the course is not one of progression from the low to the high, but of descent from the high to the low'. In some of his least attractive writing he described the physiognomy of the Laps as 'squat and ungraceful'. He was clearly repelled by the 'sooty skins, broad noses, thick lips, projecting jaw-bones, and partially webbed fingers' of the negro tribes. The Hottentots were 'repulsively ugly'. At the southern extremity of South America were the 'hideous, small-eyed, small-limbed, flat-headed Fuegians, perhaps the most wretched of human creatures'. Then the punch line: 'they are all the descendants of man as God created him; but they do not exemplify man as God created him' (Miller 1857: 229–31). They were hideous caricatures, fallen, degraded.

This is shocking to modern sensibilities but it shows that a pious evangelical scientist had no difficulty in seeing ugliness in Nature. Such a fallen world was, however, improvable, and here we find Miller embracing a special role for humanity as a 'fellow-worker' with the Creator. This motif of our *collaboration* with the Creator has become prominent again in current theologizing about biotechnology. That it should be so explicit in an evangelical writer of the nineteenth century is fascinating. It shows there were resources even in conservative Christian theologies for presenting man as a 'mighty *improver* of creation'. What Miller meant by improvement was, however, thoroughly anthropocentric: 'We recognise that as improvement which adapts Nature more thoroughly to man's own necessities and wants, and renders it more pleasing both to his sense of the aesthetic and to his more material senses also' (Miller 1857: 200).

The presence of imperfection in the world has been rationalized by theologians in a multiplicity of ways, from references to the limitations of Plato's Demiurge to the consequences of the Fall, from notions of God's self-limitation in dealings with Nature to the poverty of human stewardship. A denial of imperfection would be a difficult tack. To minimize it has surely been a spur to human action.

Remedial medicine

At the most rudimentary level medical practice probably constitutes the most obvious model for the legitimation of ameliorative technologies. To refrain from intervening in the treatment of disease on the ground that this would be to interfere with Nature (or with God's will) would usually sound callous, and in the context of Christian theology deeply at odds with Christ's exemplary role as healer. In many theocentric communities, prayer and medication would be seen as complementary not mutually exclusive. Scholars have sometimes argued that clerical forces have opposed technological innovation because it presumes to interfere with Providence. In his *History of the Warfare of Science with Theology in Christendom* (1896), A.D. White lamented the obscurantism shown by Europe's clergy, who failed to fit Franklin's lightning conductor to their churches, so abetting the continuing deaths of bell ringers who were struck even as they superstitiously rang their bells. Recent research has suggested that there was relatively little resistance to the new device based on such a constrictive view of Providence. The fear was that a lightning rod might *attract* a strike and, if doubts were raised about technological intervention, medical practice was available for analogical justification. When the issue of presumption was debated in Philadelphia in 1760, in what became the American Philosophical Society, it was medicine that quelled any doubts: 'with what care we endeavour to guard against the bad effects of other elements, to prevent and remove disorders of the body plagues and sickness of every sort, and this without any imputation of presumption; why then should it be imagined more presumptuous in the present case?' (Cohen 1990: 142–3).

In recent discussions of biotechnology it is striking how much of the rhetoric in defence of manipulative techniques appeals to medical benefits. It is a disarming appeal because the mitigation of disease is an irresistible goal. In a report published in 1996 moral, legal, scientific and clinical issues raised by gene therapy and other genetic interventions were examined from a Roman Catholic perspective. The working party believed that the human genome, 'simply one highly influential part of our bodies', may *in principle* be altered, to cure some defect of the body'. In some cases this might be morally required (Catholic Bishops' Joint Committee Report on Bioethical Issues 1996).

Remedial science

With remedial medicine in mind as a theologically acceptable model, let us briefly consider some of the ways in which the sciences have offered prospects of improvement. Their cultivation has often been encouraged as a method of improving the mind, making the most wholesome use of the gift of reason and escaping the snare of sensual indulgence. For Robert Boyle the gratification of a pious curiosity far outweighed the delusory pleasures of fame, bags, bottles and mistresses. A similar point was made by Thomas Chalmers in the context of improving popular education. In his view there obtained a 'very close affinity between a taste for science, and a taste for sacredness'. Both were 'refined abstractions from the grossness of the familiar and ordinary world' (Brooke and Cantor 1998: 157). The plight of the poor, to which Chalmers was exposed in city slums, was not necessarily a defect of Nature. Nor did he favour institutionalized poor relief. But one reason for his opposition to the latter was that it deprived the altruistically inclined of the need to give and so denied them an opportunity of spiritual edification. In the individual life there was always the better nature to which, with God's grace, one might aspire.

If the practice of science can be construed as a form of self-improvement, it is the products of science that have so often been claimed to change the world. There is, however, an ulterior issue here. It can be thrown into relief by considering another statement attributed to the Prince of Wales: 'Humankind should be careful to use science to understand how nature works, not to change what nature is.' The difficulty is that to understand how Nature works has often involved changing what Nature is. The point is captured in Wordsworth's well-known line that 'we murder to dissect'.

Controlled experiments for Francis Bacon meant that Nature had to be put on the rack – questioned, as it were, through torture. And the torture could be real rather than metaphorical in experiments on animals. This is not an issue I wish to explore here but it is obvious that our efforts to improve the world have often extracted a high cost.

An issue which has attracted less discussion is the role of the sciences in permitting a re-evaluation of Nature. Might advances in scientific knowledge be used to show that Nature is not as wrong as it seems? Science-based natural theologies have often had this feature. The Copernican innovation eventually permitted a more elegant model of planetary motion than the Ptolemaic – to such an extent that John Ray could observe that if Alfonso the Wise were living in the seventeenth century he would no longer be so rash and profane as to suggest that he could have advised the deity on a better arrangement (Ray 1717: 63–4). In much the same spirit, Ray observed in his *Wisdom of God* (1691) that what might appear to be a disproportionate amount of water on Earth compared with dry land conformed to a formula that could not be improved once one understood how rainfall was produced and how much was required.

There are many variations on this theme in the history of science. Features of Nature *seemingly* defective would be given an upgrade in the light of new scientific understanding. We have already encountered William Buckland's rehabilitation of the megatherium, the giant sloth whose fossil bones suggested a grotesque monster. In Oxford in the early years of the nineteenth century Buckland reconstructed the diet and ecology of the beast, arguing that its limbs were *so* well adapted to its needs that one could not escape an inference to design.

Later in the nineteenth century the Darwinian theory was used by some Christian commentators not to highlight the problem of suffering but to assuage it. There were several moves that could be made. If the working of natural selection required struggle and competition for limited resources, then one might see animal and human pain not as features of Nature to be deplored but as the necessary concomitants of a creative process. That at least is how Darwin's correspondent Asa Gray argued the case (Brooke 1991: 317). A science of evolutionary biology might offer other prospects for a theodicy. Darwin himself had speculated that it might be one advantage of a theory in which the deity did not create each species separately but through secondary causes that the more devilish features of Nature might be seen as indirect by-products of historical accident rather than planned according to a (dubious) blueprint. An even more striking appropriation was made by Frederick Temple in his Bampton Lectures of 1884, when Darwinian science was used to underpin a comprehensive vision of progress. This included human progress in the subjugation of Nature. And remarkably, what Temple had in mind was a kind of improvement that would strike us as peculiar. He noted how beasts of prey were diminishing in their numbers, and how those that remained were becoming more easily tamed. Nature might be red in tooth and claw, but the Earth was becoming a more congenial place (Temple 1884: 118).

For a contemporary example one might point to the re-evaluation of stars with the realization that they can be construed as factories for the heavier elements necessary for the production and sustenance of human life (Polkinghorne 1996: 84). From the time of Galileo it had been a problem to rationalize the existence of so many stars invisible to the naked eye. For Thomas Hardy, shaking his fist at Providence in the nineteenth century, the fact that they had not been made for man meant that nothing had. The affirmation of a plurality of worlds was an enduring speculative solution. But for those bent on preserving a traditional natural theology, the once superfluous stars now have a welcome function in the economy of creation.

The problem of course is that it all depends on how one selects the examples. The re-evaluation of Nature through the sciences can easily go the other way, as when Laplace, for example, calculated that if the moon had been designed for the purpose of providing illumination at night, it could have been better placed (Hahn 1986). British natural theologians might rescue monsters from monstrosity but in another sense of monster (those deformed at birth) a sense of the wrongness of Nature could easily be sustained. Nature *maimed* was a familiar refrain in Enlightenment critiques of a beneficent deity (Buckley 1987: 220).

When considering the mediating role of the sciences in evaluating Nature, it is also important to remember that aesthetic criteria are often invoked in the evaluation of the science itself. The point was made in extreme form by Einstein when he said that, on being presented with a new physical theory, he would always ask himself whether, had he been God, he would have made the world that way (Chandrasekhar 1987: 68). A sense of the rightness or wrongness of a representation of Nature has often been a criterion rather than a conclusion. Think of Leibniz's objection to the 'reformations' Newton required for his solar system. On Newton's view, a divine initiative was necessary to prevent the solar system from collapse, given such destabilizing tendencies as the slowing of the planets through friction or the loss of matter from the sun. Newton had the deity rectifying the problems through natural causes; but this did not prevent Leibniz's taunt that Newton could not be right because that would make God's creation wrong – a second-rate piece of clockwork (Alexander 1956). With the privilege of hindsight this example takes on other meanings. It is tempting to say that both Newton's science and Leibniz's philosophy were wrong but that Nature (through Laplace's demonstration of a self-stabilizing system) for a while turned out to be right!

In the above examples it is the redescription of Nature through *theoretical* science that changes perceptions. The more radical issue is whether through the *applied* sciences the components of Nature itself might be said to be improved. If the chemist makes a product artificially that has additional useful properties not found in natural analogues, does this not amount to an improvement? An example might be a faster-acting insulin for those with diabetes. The chemical sciences are particularly interesting in this respect because, as Marcellin Berthelot once observed, chemistry is distinctive in creating its own objects of study. Indeed, the simulation of natural processes and products by artificial means has had the deeper consequence of eroding distinctions between the natural and artificial, or at the very least problematizing our conception of the natural (Brooke and Cantor 1998: 314–46).

Remedial technology

It would be a mistake to suppose that the applied sciences and technology have only been geared to material improvements. The technologies that permitted the construction of Gothic cathedrals were subservient to the expression of transcendent values (Pacey 1976: 45–9). New technologies have sometimes facilitated religious observance. But there is no denying that a rhetoric of 'improvement' has often been associated with secular priorities. It might be possible to say that an improvable world is in certain respects better than one needing no improvement – in that it gives us something to work for. Yet this will sound like sophistry to those who see in the promotion and promises of technology an emancipation from what David Hume disparaged as the whole train of monkish virtues.

The applications of chemistry to agricultural improvement would be a classic case, Peter Burke observing that chemical fertilizers contributed to a new social cosmology among French peasants in the closing decades of the nineteenth century: 'The social cosmology was becoming scientific, in the sense that peasants drove tractors, spread fertilizers, practised family planning and generally lived their lives as if the world were subject to scientific laws rather than subject to supernatural forces which needed to be propitiated.' And he then adds the crux of the matter: 'They no longer felt helpless in the face of nature' (Burke 1979: 309). To improve control of Nature may not be the same as improving Nature itself. Claims for a 100 per cent safe male contraceptive pill would illustrate that point. But such common phrases as the taming of Nature may carry such connotations. The issue was baldly expressed by the nineteenth-century atheist Richard Carlile in a critique of natural theology: 'With the doctrine of intelligent deity, it is presumption to attempt anything toward human improvement. Without the doctrine, it is not any presumption' (Topham 1993: 210–17). As I have glossed this elsewhere, it is as if arguments for divine wisdom require this to be the best of all possible worlds, with the corollary that attempts at improvement would be both sacrilegious and ineffective (Brooke and Cantor 1998: 314).

Theologies of improvement

What resources have there been in Christian theology to de-rail that train of thought? We have already seen in Hugh Miller an understanding of man as co-worker with God, a model in which human labour can be sanctified when directed towards altruistic ends. Where the improvement of Nature was construed as a *redemption* of Nature, the taint of the sacrilegious might be suppressed. This was the language of Paracelsus, the controversial medical reformer of the Renaissance, for whom the chemist had a redemptive mission. There were echoes of the Fall narrative in the chemists' toil and sweat. 'They devote themselves diligently to their labours', Paracelsus observed, 'they put their fingers to the coals, the lute, and the dung, not into gold rings.' In seeking pharmacological cures, the pure had to be separated from the impure, permitting a technology of intervention. When Paracelsus spoke of the last stage of the alchemical process, the tincturing of a substance to change its colour, he stated that it 'makes all imperfect things perfect, transmutes them into their noblest essence'. To speak of the perfecting of things may have been contentious but for the followers of Paracelsus it was theologically admissible because it echoed spiritual motifs of purification and redemption (Hannaway 1975; Brooke and Cantor 1998: 321–2).

A discourse of redemption did not of course disappear with the Renaissance. It remained a source of hope when contemplating the fortuitousness of Nature. Responding to the challenge of an expanding scientific naturalism in the nineteenth century, Ernst Troeltsch insisted that: 'No physics and no biology, no psychology and no theory of evolution can take from us our belief in the living creative purpose of God, and … no anti-teleology, no brutality and no fortuitousness of nature … can take from us our belief in redemption as the destination of the whole world' (Sykes 1976, 157–8).

An alternative, though not dissimilar, resource lay in the concept of a *restored* world. Technologies offering improvement were construed by Francis Bacon in terms of a *restoration* of Nature. The Fall narrative could again be a point of reference. For Bacon, the applied sciences when directed altruistically could help to restore a dominion over Nature that had been intended for humankind but which had been lost through the Fall. In more overtly millenarian terms one could interpret the improvement of Nature (even the planting of fruit trees) as an appropriate way of preparing for Christ's return (Webster 1975). As with the motif of redemption, a rhetoric of restoration was to prove enduring even when shorn of its millenarian connotations. The scientists of the nineteenth century who first seriously applied chemistry to agriculture would argue, as did Liebig, that artifice was being employed not to subvert but to restore Nature's fertility (Sonntag 1977). Even today the meanings of stewardship often include a responsibility to restore a pristine Nature damaged or endangered by technologies that have backfired.

A quite different resource has been the doctrine of *imago dei*, interpreted to mean that human creativity may imitate that of the Creator. There was space then for the imitation, even the rivalling, of Nature, which might afford a glimpse of heaven. Here is William of Malmesbury celebrating improvements to Nature at the hands of the monks of Thorney:

> In the middle of wild swampland where the trees are intertwined in an inextricable thicket, there is a plain with very green vegetation which attracts the eye by reason of its fertility; no obstacle impedes the walker. Not a particle of the soil is left to lie fallow .... In this place cultivation rivals nature; what the latter has forgotten the former brings forth. What can I say of the beauty of the buildings whose unshakeable foundations have been built into the marshes .... This is an image of Paradise; it makes one think already of heaven.
>
> (Harrison 1999: 94)

As Peter Harrison points out, the motifs of dominion or material gain are absent here: 'Control of nature was exercised in this attenuated fashion to promote the concerns of the other world and thus, paradoxically, to further a detachment from material nature' (Harrison 1999: 94). In legitimating the imitation of Nature the doctrine of *imago dei* could spawn any number of anthropomorphisms. Where God's creative work was construed as the work of a Chemist, so the earthly chemist found justification, as Newton did, for the imitation of a subtle spirit at work in organic processes. Where divine creativity was understood as the work of an Artist or Artisan, the scholastic distinction between Nature and art was undermined, allowing both the modelling and manipulation of Nature in mechanical terms. As a devotee of the 'mechanical philosophy', Robert Boyle had no qualms about interventionist science. He simply interpreted the applied sciences as *assisting* Nature (Brooke and Cantor 1998: 323–6).

Yet another theological resource was the doctrine of Providence, which could easily be adapted to accommodate a doctrine of progress. This had already happened in England in the early years of the seventeenth century, when George Hakewill saw no reason why God should not have reserved opportunities for fresh discoveries and their application to be enjoyed by a later generation. Particularly among religious dissenters, concepts of scientific and technological progress would often be subsumed under a doctrine of Providence. This was emphatically true for Joseph Priestley, who looked forward to a time when the 'arbitrary power' of the Anglican Church would be dissolved and when science in association with a true, rational religion would triumph over superstition. A rational religion was a religion without the doctrines of the Fall and the Atonement, which meant that Priestley could not invoke Nature *redeemed* or Nature *restored* as Paracelsus and Bacon had. But he could invoke a Providence that had allowed the corruption of Christianity in order that a greater good would be effected through its subsequent purification. Improving on Nature could be part of this process. The 'dephlogisticated air' (our oxygen) that Priestley identified supported combustion and respiration *better* than ordinary air. A solution of 'fixed air' (our carbonated water) he thought might offer a cure for scurvy. In short, scientific and technological innovation promised a better world within a beneficently designed system (Brooke 1990). As one commentator has so nicely put it, England's industrial revolution for Priestley was taking place not behind God's back but at his express command (Orange 1974).

This list of theological resources is by no means exhaustive. It is sufficient to show, however, that notions of collaboration with the deity in improving the world did not have to be sacrilegious. References to the sanctification of labour, to the redemption or restoration of Nature, or in their weakest form to simply assisting Nature, to human creativity envisaged as part of what it meant to be made in the image of God, to a conception of Providence that not only accommodated technological progress but was in some measure substantiated by it – each could provide a frame of meaning conducive rather than obstructive to innovation. I am not suggesting that Christian theology failed to supply a critique of the unbridled exploitation of Nature. In fact on closer analysis one becomes more aware of an ambivalence in theologies of improvement, which may partly explain the inarticulacy often heard in public attitudes today. It is an inarticulacy that in some cases reflects a secular legacy from the theologies of the past. Concern that scientists, in their genetic engineering, are 'playing God' would be a crude but obvious example.

A legacy of ambivalence

Recent empirical research has uncovered latent theological concerns in the language used by the public when asked for their views on biotechnology. I have argued elsewhere that, in seeking to understand their concerns and their theological inarticulacy, it is helpful to recognize the ambivalence that has accompanied each of the models we have just examined (Brooke 2003). I deliberately placed a quotation from the Prince of Wales at the head of this chapter because the British press recently made a song and dance about divisions within the Royal family in their attitudes towards genetically modified crops. For the Prince 'it is wrong that nature has come to be regarded as a system that can be engineered for our own convenience and in which anything that happens can be fixed by technology and human ingenuity'. For the Princess Royal 'it is a huge oversimplification to say all farming ought to be organic, or that there should be no GM foods. Man has been tinkering with food production for such a long time that it's a bit cheeky to suddenly get nervous about it when, fundamentally, you are doing much the same thing.' And to complete the trio, the Duke of Edinburgh: 'The introduction of exotic species like the grey squirrel into this country has done far more damage than a genetically modified potato' (*The Times*, 7 June 2000). Such divisions probably reflect those in the public at large. In the case of the Prince of Wales the objection is explicitly theological: we are being led into 'realms that belong to God, and to God alone'. No explicit theology underpins the other two statements, but from the preceding section we can see how it might have been done.

I emphasize ambivalence in the theological legacy because in models of redemption or restoration there was always a divide between contemplative and activist modes. To speak of human initiatives in the redemption of Nature, as Paracelsus had, was anathema to the Calvinist Oswald Croll, who insisted that the necessary powers resided in God alone (Hannaway 1975: 52). From such a standpoint, it *would* be presumptuous to imagine that human enterprise could hasten the millennium. A tension within the Baconian programme introduces a further ambivalence that has often recurred in the appraisal of new technologies. There was a sense in which Bacon was caught between two different readings of the Fall narrative. On one reading it was presumptuous to seek forbidden knowledge; on the other, there was a moral obligation to work for the restoration of a fallen world. Bacon resolved the tension by conceding that knowledge sought for self-gratification was indeed suspect, but that knowledge sought for its beneficial applications could not be. The problem is that with the commercialization of ostensibly beneficial products the interests cannot be as cleanly segregated as Bacon might have wished. There have been recent references to a terrifying commercialization already in place in England by 1700 – a trade in imported flora, for example, that not only changed the English landscape beyond recognition but presumably involved denuding many places of their indigenous species (Jardine 2000: 35–6).

Another way of articulating the ambivalence would be to emphasize the blurring of the sacred and secular in so many revisionist philosophies of Nature. At its inception Bacon's vision of power over Nature through disciplined research could be couched within a biblical frame of reference. Bacon himself appealed to prophecies in Daniel, which seemed to say that an increase in knowledge and trade was one sign of the last things (Webster 1975: 21–5). Improving the human condition could be subsumed under a Providential reading of history. As historians have observed, however, a prospective millennium could easily be secularized into a science-based Utopia. Bacon might suggest that an empirical approach to Nature would promote the Christian virtue of humility, but at the same time he relished the prospect of 'effecting all things possible'. The history of natural theology affords examples of ambivalence in the more contemplative mode. Many were the arguments for design formulated originally with pious intentions but subsequently desacralized in the promotion and popularization of the sciences (Topham 1992, 1998).

In this respect the seventeenth-century mechanical philosophies, to which I have referred, throw the ambivalence into even sharper relief. Often they placed divine and human craftsmanship on the same level. But the implications might run in opposite directions. Was the effect to elevate humanity or to diminish the deity? It was the seventeenth century that gave us mechanical and engineering models for our relationship to Nature, but with further ambivalence as a consequence. Deep ambiguities arose concerning the theological interpretation of mechanism. These were sometimes explicit, as when John Ray interpreted the clockwork universe of Robert Boyle to mean that Boyle was a deist rather than a Christian theist, only to apologize later when he realized his mistake (McAdoo 1965: 283). Redefining the natural in mechanistic terms could be a vehicle, according to predisposition, both for eliminating the supernatural and for reaffirming it. This was because the mechanization of Nature conceivably helped to sharpen the boundaries between natural and supernatural, as it did for that nerve centre of the scientific revolution Marin Mersenne. For a Catholic apologist, a mechanized Nature made it easier to discriminate between miracle and marvel, assisting the authentication of genuine miracles (Lenoble 1971; Dear 1988).

For a radical Protestant such as Isaac Newton, that was not a priority. Given his chemical interests, however, Newton needed a model of our relationship to Nature that would allow the natural philosopher to take on the mantle of co-creator or at least co-producer. In a remarkable passage Newton justified the presumption by constructing an argument that conferred greater power on the original Creator, not less:

> If any think it possible that God may produce some intellectual creature so perfect that he could, by divine accord, in turn produce creatures of a lower order, this so far from detracting from the divine power enhances it; for that power which can bring forth creatures not only directly but through the mediation of other creatures is exceedingly, not to say infinitely greater.
>
> (Dobbs 1991: 36)

That Newton had to argue the case at all suggests a more general ambivalence on this point. If the deity needed a fellow worker might this not imply a depletion of divine power? Quite apart from fears of Pelagianism, the invocation of co-creator could be a high-risk strategy. As an exercise in natural theology Newton's argument foreshadows the kind of move made in the Darwinian debates when Charles Kingsley, for example, extolled the greater wisdom of a god who could make all things make themselves. The difficulty for the religious apologist is that without the eye of faith one simply sees things making themselves or oneself as a creator not co-creator. From where then come the controls?

If one thought in terms of collaborating with the deity as Hugh Miller did when describing improvements to cows and goats, there was the obvious question as to how one knew one was working *with* God rather than against. I have used Miller as an example because he was perceptive enough to realize that the issue was not merely how Nature was being improved but what Nature was becoming. The habits which man imparts to the parents 'become nature, in his behalf, in their offspring .... The udders of the cow and goat distend beneath his care far beyond the size necessary in the wild state' (Miller 1857: 201). To refer back to Miller is not to dwell in the past because this very example has been seized by contemporary critics of the hubris with which we have moulded Nature to our specification. The cow's udder is now 'large and pendulous, often hanging so low that new-born calves have difficulty locating the teats. As her hind legs have to change position to accommodate the bulging, swinging udder, she frequently develops gait problems which result in lameness' (D'Silva 1998: 93). On this view Nature is wrong now because she has been wronged; and for this critic lame cows and crippled chickens are the result not of innocent co-creation but of a thinly veiled profit motive. It is difficult to deny a deep tension between the aspiration of the alchemist, architect, animal breeder or engineer to come closer to God through the undertaking of God-like activity, and the more Augustinian suspicion of that assimilation, given the flaws in human nature.

Lisa Jardine has recently observed that the idea of 'scientific responsibility' was scotched at a very early stage in modern scientific experimentation because it was not clear to whom scientists were responsible (Jardine 2000: 36). Some, including Robert Hooke, did feel uncomfortable about the vivisection practised by early fellows of the Royal Society. Dogs would have all their blood replaced by beer to test the Cartesian mechanism for the workings of the heart. In the Christian virtuoso Robert Boyle one catches sight of a real ambivalence on such matters. For Boyle it was legitimate for animals to suffer in the production of knowledge that would improve human life; and yet the knife also pricked his conscience because once an animal had done its duty and survived, it would be replaced by another rather than be allowed to suffer again (Oster 1989).

To ask the question whether Nature is ever evil invites the riposte: 'for whom?' There is a final ambivalence lurking here because certainly within the Christian tradition there has been a tension between the more and the less anthropocentric readings of Nature. The Oxford historian Keith

Thomas found a significant shift in sensibility towards the end of the seventeenth century, when the notion that everything had been made for man was dismissed as untenable (Thomas 1984: 165–72). As one of his many witnesses he elicited the testimony of the naturalist John Ray, who observed:

> it is a generally received opinion that all this visible world was created for Man [and] that Man is the end of creation, as if there were no other end of any creature but some way or other to be serviceable to man .... But though this be vulgarly received, yet wise men nowadays think otherwise.
>
> (Thomas 1984: 167)

But what exactly did wise men think? Ray was emphatic, as was Boyle, that there were many things not made for us *alone*. But that did not exclude the view that everything had *some* human use, even if, as Ray surmised, the discovery of such a use belonged to the future. In the very renunciation of anthropocentrism a new anthropocentrism took hold and one that we have assuredly not renounced (Brooke 2000).

In this paper I have not answered the question whether Nature is evil. This particular question might be said to make sense only if Nature is conceived in personal terms, in some supra-holistic sense (in which personality emerges from the whole) or in a pantheistic sense in which Nature is identified with a personal Being. If the question were whether Nature *contains* evil, the answer would be a resounding 'yes' on any model that makes us part of Nature, as we surely are. If, however, dreams of a science-based Utopia were historically grounded in millenarian ideas, we can see how even in religious terms this Earth could be seen as a poor shadow of a new Earth, in the building of which we might expect to take a share of the responsibility. I have suggested that programmes for the improvement of Nature, even in the minimal sense of improving creature comforts, would seem to presuppose that Nature is less right, even less beautiful, than it might be. But I have also tried to expose a legacy of ambivalence in the theologizing about co-production, or co-creation, with a supposed Creator. As we know only too well, as soon as we turn to specific programmes of amelioration and manipulation, ethical issues of enormous complexity can arise. In their appraisal the theological ambivalence is often visible, even if articulated in dilute and secular forms. The role of religious values in such appraisal is clearly not a thing of the past. Religious views concerning the unique value of all human life continue to shape answers to such questions as whether human parts taken from a subject in a vegetative state should ever be preferred to animal parts in an organ transplantation. A revulsion to the patenting of onco-species may be the inarticulate expression of the conviction that God alone deserves the patent; for we act only as a demi-urge (not strictly a creator or inventor) in modifying the pre-existing substrate. Francis Bacon's appeal to humility over hubris, however weak as a constraint, still finds expression in concerns over animal exploitation. David Cooper has recently argued that 'a person abandons humility not *because* animal life has an integrity which he or she dishonours. Rather, integrity is said to be dishonoured when proper humility has been abandoned.' And where humility is absent, he reminds us, there is likely to be what Carl Jung, remembering the vivisections he had unwillingly performed as a student, experienced as 'alienation ... from God's world' (Cooper 1998: 144–5).

References

Alexander, H.G. (ed.) (1956) *The Leibniz–Clarke Correspondence*, Manchester: Manchester University Press.

Baldwin Brown, J. (1871) *First Principles of Ecclesiastical Truth*, London.

Boyle, Robert (1686) 'Free Enquiry into the Vulgarly Receiv'd Notion of Nature', in Michael Hunter and Edward Davis (eds) (2000) *The Works of Robert Boyle*, vol.10, London: Pickering.

Brooke, John Hedley (1974) 'Darwin', in J.H. Brooke and A. Richardson (eds) *The Crisis of Evolution*, Milton Keynes: Open University Press.

Brooke, John Hedley (1990) ' "A Sower Went Forth": Joseph Priestley and the Ministry of Reform', in A. Truman Schwartz and John McEvoy (eds) *Motion Toward Perfection: The Achievement of Joseph Priestley*, Boston: Skinner, 21–56.

Brooke, John Hedley (1991) *Science and Religion: Some Historical Perspectives*, Cambridge: Cambridge University Press.

Brooke, John Hedley (1996) 'Like Minds: the God of Hugh Miller', in Michael Shortland (ed.) *Hugh Miller and the Controversies of Victorian Science*, Oxford: Oxford University Press, 171–86.

Brooke, John Hedley (2000) ' "Wise Men Nowadays Think Otherwise": John Ray, Natural Theology and the Meanings of Anthropocentrism', *Notes and Records of the Royal Society of London* 54, 199–213.

Brooke, John Hedley (2003) 'Detracting from the Divine Power? Religious Belief and the Appraisal of New Technologies', in Celia Deane-Drummond (ed.) *Reordering Nature*, Edinburgh: T & T Clark (Continuum).

Brooke, John Hedley and Cantor, Geoffrey (1998) *Reconstructing Nature: The Engagement of Science and Religion*, Edinburgh: T & T Clark (Continuum); New York: Oxford University Press.

Buckley, Michael (1987) *At the Origins of Modern Atheism*, New Haven: Yale University Press.

Burke, Peter (1979) 'Religion and Secularisation', in Peter Burke (ed.) *The New Cambridge Modern History*, vol. 13 (Companion Volume), 293–317.

Cantor, Geoffrey (1991) *Michael Faraday: Sandemanian and Scientist*, London: Macmillan.

Catholic Bishop's Joint Committee Report on Bioethical Issues (1996), London: Linacre Centre.

Chandrasekhar, S. (1987) *Truth and Beauty: Aesthetics and Motivations in Science*, Chicago: University of Chicago Press.

Cohen, Bernard (1990) *Benjamin Franklin's Science*, Cambridge, MA: Harvard University Press.

Cooper, David (1998) 'Intervention, Humility and Animal Integrity', in Alan Holland and Andrew Johnson (eds) *Animal Biotechnology and Ethics*, London: Chapman and Hall, 145–55.

Darwin, Charles (1844) 'Essay', in Gavin de Beer (ed.) (1958) *Evolution by Natural Selection*, Cambridge: Cambridge University Press.

Dear, Peter (1988) *Mersenne and the Learning of the Schools*, Ithaca, NY: Cornell University Press.

Desmond, Adrian and Moore, James (1991) *Darwin*, London: Michael Joseph.

Dobbs, Betty Jo (1991) *The Janus Faces of Genius*, Cambridge: Cambridge University Press.

Drees, Willem B. (1996) *Religion, Science and Naturalism*, Cambridge: Cambridge University Press.

D'Silva, Joyce (1998) 'Campaigning against Transgenic Technology', in Alan Holland and Andrew Johnson (eds) *Animal Biotechnology and Ethics*, London: Chapman and Hall, 92–102.

Gouk, Penelope (1988) 'The Harmonic Roots of Newtonian Science', in John Fauvel (ed.) *Let Newton Be!*, Oxford: Oxford University Press, 101–25.

Hahn, Roger (1986) 'Laplace and the Mechanistic Universe', in David Lindberg and Ronald Numbers (eds) *God and Nature: Historical Essays on the Encounter between Science and Christianity*, Berkeley and Los Angeles: University of California Press, 256–76.

Hannaway, Owen (1975) *The Chemists and the Word: The Didactic Origins of Modern Chemistry*, Baltimore: Johns Hopkins University Press.

Harrison, Peter (1999) 'Subduing the Earth: Genesis 1, Early Modern Science, and the Exploitation of Nature', *The Journal of Religion* 79: 86–109.

Hilton, Boyd (1988) *The Age of Atonement: The Influence of Evangelicalism on Social and Economic Thought 1785–1865*, Oxford: Oxford University Press.

Jammer, Max (1999) *Einstein and Religion*, Princeton, NJ: Princeton University Press.

Jardine, Lisa (2000) 'Interview', *Science and Spirit* 12: 35–6.

Lenoble, Robert (1971) *Mersenne ou la Naissance du Mécanisme*, Paris: Vrin.

McAdoo, H.R. (1965) *The Spirit of Anglicanism*, London: A. and C. Black.

Miller, Hugh (1857) *The Testimony of the Rocks*, 1869 edition, Edinburgh: Nimmo.

Nicolson, Marjorie (1959) *Mountain Gloom and Mountain Glory: The Aesthetics of the Development of the Infinite*, Ithaca, NY: Cornell University Press.

Orange, Derek (1974) 'Oxygen and One God', *History Today* 24: 773–81.

Oster, Malcolm (1989) 'The "Beame of Divinity": Animal Suffering in the Early Thought of Robert Boyle', *British Journal for the History of Science* 22: 151–79.

Pacey, Arnold (1976) *The Maze of Ingenuity: Ideas and Idealism in the Development of Technology*, Cambridge, MA: MIT Press.

Passmore, John (1970) *The Perfectibility of Man*, London: Duckworth.

Polkinghorne, John (1996) *Beyond Science*, Cambridge: Cambridge University Press.

Ray, John (1717) *The Wisdom of God Manifested in the Works of Creation*, London.

Rupke, Nicolaas (1983) *The Great Chain of History: William Buckland and the English School of Geology 1814–1849*, Oxford: Oxford University Press.

Sonntag, Otto (1977) 'Religion and Science in the Thought of Liebig', *Ambix* 24: 159–69.

Sykes, S.W. (1976) 'Ernst Troeltsch and Christianity's Essence', in John Clayton (ed.) *Ernst Troeltsch and the Future of Theology*, Cambridge: Cambridge University Press, 139–71.

Temple, Frederick (1884) *The Relations between Religion and Science*, London: Lower Tower.

Thomas, Keith (1984) *Man and the Natural World*, Harmondsworth: Penguin.

Topham, Jonathan (1992) 'Science and Popular Education in the 1830s: the Role of the *Bridgewater Treatises*', *British Journal for the History of Science* 25: 397–430.

Topham, Jonathan (1993) ' "An Infinite Variety of Arguments": the *Bridgewater Treatises* and British Natural Theology in the 1830s', PhD diss., University of Lancaster.

Topham, Jonathan (1998) 'Beyond the "Common Context": The Production and Reading of the Bridgewater Treatises', *Isis* 89: 233–62.

Webster, Charles (1975) *The Great Instauration: Science, Medicine and Reform 1626–1660*, London: Duckworth.

Wilson, A.N. (2000) 'Interview', *Science and Spirit* 11: 45.

19

VICTIMS OF NATURE CRY OUT

Leo P. ten Kate

There is among the contributors to this book no consensus on the definition of nature. Some have argued that nature is everything that can be
observed, distinguishing nature only from the supernatural world. Others
have taken the view that nature is defined by life, in contrast to the inorganic world. Still others have set nature against culture. I will not take a
position in this debate, but concentrate on the indisputable parts of all
definitions of nature: living nature, human nature and our genetic constitution in particular. Our DNA is a necessary condition for our mere
existence, and is seen as an integral part of one's personality and self by
many people. As a clinical geneticist I come across this aspect of nature in
daily practice all the time.

Is nature ever evil?

I regard this question as intellectually superfluous and morally objectionable.
Intellectually superfluous because the mere observation of what man has done
and dreamed so far tells us that man is basically discontent about nature.
Morally objectionable because asking this question betrays a lack of attention
towards people who are more fit to answer the question than a learned
meeting in an ivory tower. Where have we been to ask such a question?

Man is basically discontent about nature in general and human nature
in particular. Like other animals, we have our physiological limitations,
but we have always tried and will try to overcome these. So we are able to
live in very cold climates thanks to our clothes, buildings and heating.
Writing and printing compensate for the limitations of our memory. We
use sound equipment because of our weakness of voice and hearing. We
use all kinds of transportation to make up for our limited mobility. Some
of us even come to conferences like birds, by air. And so on, and so on.
Would we ever have developed science and technology if we were satisfied
with nature?

Not only reality shows our lack of trust in nature, but also our dreams
betray our opinion. Many of us believe in eternal life, and in a new world

in which there is no pain and sorrow. And what about that vision of a peaceful kingdom where the wolf will be a friend of the sheep, where the lion will eat straw, and where an infant will safely play near the hole of a snake? Humans have the feeling that there is a better kind of nature than the one in which we live.

Like most people, I think nature is beautiful. I like to go outdoors, out of the city. I enjoy the scenery of hills and mountains, watching the sun set over the sea and observing living beings in their habitat. I also admire many aspects of the way nature functions. The intricate machinery of the cell and the elegant rules that govern nature command respect. But the way nature looks and how nature functions are not what nature is. We must not confine ourselves to observing the surface, but find the only really relevant point of view from where nature's real face can be seen.

What then is the only really relevant point of view from where nature's real face can be seen? As with many other things in life, the only morally acceptable view is through the eyes of the victims. This was and is true for warfare, for slavery, for apartheid, for dictatorship, for discrimination based on race, sex or sexual preference, and for many, many, many other things. For me, as a clinical geneticist, the victims of nature are the infants who are born severely malformed or seemingly healthy but with a genetic constitution that manifests itself in death, disease and handicap within weeks, months, years. The victims are these children, but also their parents, who could not know that they were at risk, and the other family members who now fear that they will be at risk too. Ask them whether nature is ever evil. They will tell you. It is not the point of view of the philosopher, the scientist, the historian, or the conservationist that is relevant.

Genetic disorders are caused by unfavourable mutations in our genes. These mutations may be recent ones, but may also be very old, passed on from generation to generation for thousands of years. Mutations are, however, not only the basis of diseases, but also the way in which variation within a species is achieved on which natural selection can act. Without mutations evolution would not be possible and man would not exist. So the patients and families with genetic diseases pay the price for their own and our existence as human beings. Cynically enough, both we and the victims of mutations have to blame nature for a flaw in design without which we would not be here.

Improvable nature?

In my inaugural lecture (Ten Kate 1994) I introduced the idea of co-creation in connection with genetic modification. I applied the co-creation concept, which I borrowed from contemporary authors of popular theological books, out of irritation with the uncritical lip service paid to the integrity-of-creation concept and to counterbalance the emphasis placed on stewardship by one of our political parties. At the same time, I recognized the danger of man as a co-creator. But I felt that creation is too merciless not to act as co-creator.

As John Brooke shows in his paper, the notion of co-creation has a longer history than modern discussions on biotechnology. The question, however, is not only whether nature should be improved but also whether it can be improved. This is a much more difficult question to answer. It is true that we already have at our disposal the tool of reproductive selection, and that, technically speaking, germ-line gene modification will become a possibility, but the objections to a systematic policy in these matters are overwhelming. There are not only many human-rights issues; there is also complete uncertainty about what would be an ideal genotype for now or for the future. Many mutations, for instance, being unfavourable in a double dose, may have had selective advantage in the past (and may still have) when present in a single dose. Who tells us that we will not need them in the future? Will mankind be able to maintain enough variability to adapt to new circumstances? Or will we cause our own extinction by tinkering with our genes?

It is clear that these are questions that cannot be answered easily, if at all. Nevertheless, it is our duty to help patients and families with genetic diseases as far as possible to live and reproduce according to their own values. There is only a very tiny little bit of co-creation involved.

Even when we agree that nature frequently is evil, and that it should be improved, our abilities to do so are extremely limited and humility should keep us away from irresponsible interventions.

Reference

Ten Kate, L.P. (1994) *Genen, grenzen en co-creatie*, Amsterdam: VU Uitgeverij.

20

'IMPROVABLE NATURE?'

Some meta-historical reflections

Henk G. Geertsema

Reading the paper by John Brooke, two things come to mind: 1) the complexity of the historical material; 2) the importance of keeping this complexity in mind when assessing the contemporary debate because it reminds us of the complexity of the issue itself. As I am not a historian of science, I will not discuss the historical material as such. My field is philosophy proper. Therefore, in my response I will reflect on some implications that the historical material might have for our understanding of the relationship between scientific argument and theological or religious conviction in general.

First, I will give some background to my comments by sketching the dominant approach concerning the relationship between science and theology and the alternative view I want to propose. Thereafter, I will highlight possible historical discontinuities in the discussion besides the continuities John Brooke has pointed out, and suggest some implications for our theme. Finally, I want to relate the theme of my response to the general question 'Is nature ever evil?' and ask in what way science itself is involved in this question and the possible answers to it.

Science and religion: some preliminary remarks

In my view, the dominant position concerning the relationship between science and theology is to see both in terms of their own nature and then proceed in such a way that science determines the limits within which theology can operate or within which religious convictions are still acceptable. In other words, the scientific understanding of the world determines the space that is left for religion and theology. Theology should integrate the results of science. On the other hand, science itself should pursue its search for truth independently of any religion or theology.

I am not defending the opposite, as if science should integrate the results of theology before starting its research and as if theology should ignore the results of the scientific pursuit of truth. Yet I do believe that science is not as independent of religious convictions or theology as the dominant position would have it. Certainly, science proceeds according to its own rules. But the interpretation of its results cannot do without some kind of what is usually called a metaphysical position. In this 'metaphysical position' some answers are implied to questions that are central to religious conviction or theology. Three questions seem to be crucial in this respect:

1   *How do we understand ourselves as human beings?* This question includes issues such as the meaning of life, our human destiny, how to deal with guilt and suffering. It is a basic question about our human existence and is at the heart of any religious conviction. The importance of this question for the interpretation of science becomes clear when we relate scientific results to our self-understanding. Is it the scientific method itself that decides how we understand ourselves or is it the concrete experience of life in all its diversity, including suffering, moral and human satisfaction, and guilt? Scientific research can certainly correct pre-scientific ideas, but is science as such able to replace our integral experience of life and the world? The answer to this question cannot be given by science itself. It depends on how we see the possibilities and the limitations of the scientific method in relation to our knowledge of the world. In fact, it depends on how we understand ourselves as human beings. Should all knowledge be measurable, including our knowing ourselves? Would this kind of knowledge do justice to our being human?

2   *What is the ultimate horizon from which we understand the world?* Does that horizon transcend our scientific or even our 'natural' experience or should we limit ourselves to what can be verified by means that exclude the experience of God? The statement 'Every part of me, even the most precious, is a product of natural processes', made by the theologian Philip Hefner during the symposium behind this book, will mean something different within a physicalist or naturalistic context from what it will mean for someone who believes in God as the Creator. In the first case, it will be meant in an absolute sense. Made by someone who believes in God as the Creator, it will have a limited meaning that leaves room for the involvement of God. Thus, even our view about the ultimate horizon for understanding our world will precede the interpretation of the results of science.

3   *How do the different fields of the sciences relate to one another?* Are they ultimately reducible to physical reality or do their respective properties and lawful regularities require the recognition of some independence, even if all non-physical realms presuppose the physical and in that respect are dependent upon them? In this respect, it is interesting that while epistemological non-reductionism is gaining ground because the attempt to reduce theories of a higher level to theories of a

less complex level most of the time appears to be unsuccessful, this does not seem to affect the defence of ontological reductionism. The latter must therefore be more than just a consequence of scientific research.

My point is that these three questions seem to be a necessary part of the framework through which the results of scientific research are interpreted. The answers to them will therefore somehow influence the interpretation that is given. To call this a metaphysical framework, as is often done, is misleading, insofar as the position which is taken is not necessarily theoretically reflected. As such, it is rather of a religious nature – if religion is taken in the general sense of a basic conviction – than a theoretical one. In fact, metaphysical positions in the strict sense are themselves to a large extent directed by these pre-theoretical basic convictions.

A legacy of ambivalence and historical discontinuity

The final part of Brooke's paper is called 'A legacy of ambivalence'. Under this heading he shows how the different positions of the past continue in the discussions of the present. The issue is: is it legitimate to intervene in nature as created by God? On the one hand, theology provides a positive answer: the intervention of science and technology in nature is understood in terms of redemption or restoration, or even co-production or co-creation with the divine Creator. On the other hand, there is also the fear of overstepping our human boundaries in relation to the constraints set for us by God as the Creator. In this context human greed and pride, as expressions of our sinful nature, are warned against. So the legacy is ambivalent. The same ambivalence can be seen in the contemporary discussion. In relation to the appraisal of ethical issues that arise with respect to specific programmes of amelioration and manipulation, 'the theological ambivalence is often visible, even if articulated in dilute or secular forms. The role of religious values in such appraisal is clearly not a thing of the past.'

My question concerns the nature of this legacy. What exactly is the place of religious values in the contemporary discussion? Is there only continuity or also discontinuity? Does the theological legacy influence the present-day discussion because for better or for worse we are still not free from theology and religion in spite of all the efforts to approach at least public affairs and scientific discussions in a completely secular way? Or is it because the questions that are raised by theology and religion as such do not depend on a theological or religious perspective but are an intrinsic part of the issue at hand and will present themselves whenever there is a serious discussion about the subject? In other words, are the different theological positions and arguments that are mentioned in the chapter indeed reflected in a secular form, even if a theological approach is explicitly rejected? Or is there a significant shift in the arguments and positions as a result of the secularization of Western culture?

Let me approach the question in a more systematic way. If there are normative questions to be raised in relation to human intervention in nature, we need criteria to distinguish between interventions that are permissible and interventions that are not. Where do these criteria come from? We can at least distinguish three possible answers:

1   The standards come from human subjectivity because it is only human subjectivity that can be the source of meaning and normativity. The question then is if it will not ultimately be our human interest that will decide about what we take to be acceptable.
2   The second possibility is that we think we can find these criteria within nature itself. The question then will be how it is possible to make a distinction between an intervention in nature that is acceptable and those that are not. Does nature in itself present us with a distinction between what is and what ought or is allowed to be?
3   The third possibility is that the standards are set by a divine Creator who put humankind in His creation at a special place and with a special responsibility. The question then is how do we know God's intentions for humankind and for creation as a whole?

I am not trying to argue for a specific answer. The point I want to raise is that the second and third positions imply the possibility of an intrinsic constraint on human intervention in nature because there is more to meaning and normativity than human interest. These positions can lead to an awareness that we should show humility towards what is given. But what about the first position? Would this position in principle have room for ambivalence, as indicated by Brooke in his paper? Or would there be no place for a theological legacy, let alone an ambivalent one?

It could be interesting to put the question of continuity and discontinuity in a wider historical perspective. In his selection of the historical material Brooke has limited himself basically to the modern period in Western culture. Would the picture be different if the medieval period in Western Christianity were also discussed and even more so if Eastern Orthodox, classical Greek, Babylonian and east Asian, especially Chinese, views were taken into account? Are the same questions asked in those different historical and cultural contexts (and similar answers given) or are they characteristic of our modern times? And if there are significant differences, what could be the explanation for that?

The reason for raising these issues is to make us aware of the fact that, in order to understand the way questions are asked and answers given, we have to take into account the possible influence of the cultural and historical context. If this applies to situations in the past and in other cultures, would it not hold for our own situation as well? And if basic convictions play an important role within these cultural and historical contexts, would this not also apply to us in our own context?

Basic convictions and the nature of nature

'Is nature ever evil?' Brooke responds to this question at the end of his chapter with a 'resounding "yes"', after having qualified it in two ways: first, by rephrasing it as 'whether Nature *contains* evil'; and, second, by adding 'on any model that makes us part of Nature'. Even without the second qualification my response to the question would be positive also. My concern at this point is different, though. My interest here is twofold: 1. Is this a scientific question? Can it be answered by means of scientific method, or is it of a different nature? 2. If so, does it affect science at all? Can science steer clear of it in all its pursuits?

Brooke's paper is certainly relevant in relation to the first question. In his paper he refers to different models of nature, such as the Cartesian soulless machine, the chemical laboratory of the nineteenth century or the mother who nurtures her offspring. He points out that with these different pictures and views of the world might be associated different sets of constraints on what is desirable or possible in relation to improving nature. Historical evidence suggests that the question 'Is nature ever evil?' cannot be answered by scientific means alone. The question as such might not even be a scientific one, even though it was of concern for many scientists.

The importance of this answer lies in the fact that it implies that history is an argument against the view that there is only one scientific answer to the question 'Is nature ever evil?', namely that nature as such is neutral to the question of evil. And hence value is only subjective human interpretation, which projects questions of good and bad on to nature. This answer affirming the neutrality of nature in relation to questions of good and bad is itself as subjective, as much part of a pre-scientific picture or view of the world, as the idea that there is evil within nature, even apart from human suffering and wrongdoing.

In other words, those who tried to defend the view that in other cultural and historical contexts or in theological settings the understanding of nature and the approach to questions of good and evil in relation to nature are to a large extent influenced by religious views and therefore subjective, while today our scientific worldview has left all this behind and can claim objectivity and universal validity, would have the historical evidence against them. Scientists themselves appear to have different models that they use when speaking about nature. That applies also to those that lay claim to the objective scientific view in which there is no place for good and evil. It is not only in the past that basic convictions of a pre-scientific nature have affected our understanding of nature; the same is true of the present. A scientific view in these matters that is neutral to basic convictions is just not possible. If it is defended, it itself is of a pre-scientific nature, 'metaphysical' or 'religious'.

The second question I could also phrase in this way: is it incidental that scientists have a view about nature in which their position about the possibility of improving nature is reflected, or is it a necessary aspect of scientific activity, either of the scientist as an individual or as part of the overall cultural framework, that it is pursued within the context of a view about nature in which questions about good and evil are implied? In other words, is it an incidental or a structural element of science that for the interpretation of its results a view of nature is required that cannot avoid implications concerning good and evil? Do the people that are discussed in the chapter just happen to be interested in this kind of question, while there are others for whom this kind of question has no interest at all and whose work cannot be related in any sense to this kind of question? Or, on the other hand, does at least the cultural setting of scientific activity require an implicit or explicit answer to the questions discussed, if only because science is part of human endeavour and questions of good and evil cannot be avoided in human life?

If the answer to this part of the question is positive too, this would be an argument for the view that scientific activity necessarily presupposes some pre-scientific view of the world at least as far as questions of good and bad are concerned. This would confirm the position I sketched at the beginning. The interpretation of scientific results necessarily presupposes some basic conviction concerning central questions about ourselves and the world. Questions concerning good and evil in nature clearly relate both to our understanding of ourselves and to the ultimate horizon from which we understand the world.

21

IS NATURE NEUTRAL?

The concept of health

Kris Dierickx

In classical reflection on medical matters health is conceived of as a bodily state which is in accordance with nature. It is a state of natural balance in the mixture of the primary qualities of the human body. Although few of the details of ancient natural philosophy and the Galenic philosophy of health have survived, it is important to note that two ancient ideas still influence our thought: the idea of a balance between opposing elements or forces, and, in particular, the idea of a natural or normal state of the living organism. In contemporary reflection there is a forceful attempt to formulate a conception of health and disease in terms of biological norms, where the interpretation is unambiguous. According to this conception, the biological norms are related to certain natural goals (for instance, survival). These goals are not attributed to the body from outside, but belong to the internal constitution of the body (Nordenfelt 1995).

In this chapter we present the essential tenets and main merits of such a theory, more precisely the bio-statistical theory of the American philosopher Christopher Boorse. Thereafter, we give a critical assessment of this perspective, mainly focusing on the claims of a value-free scientific approach and of neutrality.

The analytic objective approach

In several of his publications the American philosopher Christopher Boorse has developed an analytic theory, which has given rise to heated debate. This theory is known by many names: functionalist (Daniels 1985), mechanist (Hesslow 1993), reductionist (Lennox 1995) or biostatistical (Mordacci 1995). Boorse criticizes the idea that health and disease are evaluative concepts. In his view, this relativizing of the concepts leads to absurd consequences. Assume, for instance, that one defines disease in terms of unwanted things which are candidates for medical treatment (Boorse 1977). He claims that many recognized diseases are not really treatable. On the other hand, practices such as circumcision, termination of pregnancy or plastic surgery are not good reasons for considering the possession of foreskin, being pregnant or having ears that stick out to be diseases. Another possibility is that one invokes pain or suffering as a criterion for calling something a disease. But, according to Boorse, medical textbooks often describe cases where the absence of subjective discomfort is accompanied by serious internal injury. Conversely, people experience pain and discomfort in normal processes such as menstruation, teething and childbirth. Boorse's theory attempts to show that health and disease are neutral concepts. Disease and health can be objectively established and exhaustively characterized with the help of empirical science.

In introducing his theory, Boorse places himself explicitly within the Galenic medical tradition. To clarify what he means by this, he quotes Temkin, an expert in the history of medicine: 'Such a concept of health and disease rests on a teleologically conceived biology. All parts of the body are built and function so as to allow man to lead a good life and to preserve his kind. Health is a state according to Nature; disease is contrary to Nature' (Temkin 1973: 400). Boorse thus recognizes from the outset that his descriptions of health and disease are in a teleological framework. The idea of a directed function is one of the central elements of his theory. Nevertheless, he also preserves some distance from the Galenic medical tradition on an important point. In Galenism two meanings of a normal or natural function are linked to each other: (1) in the sense of normative normality, the norm indicates how the body or certain parts of it ought to function; (2) in the sense of natural normality, the norm is what is found in the majority of a population. Normal functioning, then, is not only the actual functioning of the average member of a group, but also the functioning that is desirable and good for all members of that group. Boorse, however, separates these two meanings. His idea of a normal or natural biological function implies no positive evaluation of the function: 'In my view the basic notion of a function is of a contribution to a goal. Organisms are goal-directed in a sense that ... they are disposed to adjust their behavior to environmental change in ways appropriate to a constant result, the goal' (Boorse 1977: 555). Correlated with the hierarchy of levels in an organism is a hierarchy of aims – which can be rather vague at the highest level. At the same time, the behaviour of organisms seems to contribute to various independent aims, for instance individual survival, the ability to reproduce, the survival of the species, the survival of the genes and ecological equilibrium. 'But,' he states, 'it is only the subfield of physiology whose functions seem relevant to health. On the basis of what appears in physiology texts, I suggest that these functions are, contributions to individual survival and reproduction' (Boorse 1977: 556). When Boorse speaks of physiological functions, he means the standard contribution within a reference group, i.e. a species. The notion of 'standard' or 'species design' is of crucial importance for Boorse. He describes it as 'the typical hierarchy of interlocking functional systems that supports the life of organisms of that type' (Boorse 1977: 557). This typical hierarchy is determined with the aid of statistical analysis. Such an analysis produces a species design, differentiated according to sex and age. The idea of a normal function, then, is that of a statistically normal function. The species design can be empirically established without ascribing value to the aims. It can serve as a basis for judgements about health in all species, not just the human species.

From this point of view, diseases are internal states that interfere with functions in the species design. Normal functioning in a member of the reference class is the performance by each internal part of all its statistically typical functions with at least statistically typical efficiency, i.e. at efficiency levels within or above some chosen central region of their population contribution. In other words, what normal functioning means can be statistically established for a reference class within a species, for instance an age group of a certain sex. Within the reference class, what contributes from a statistical viewpoint to individual survival and reproduction must be seen as a normal function. Boorse also argues that an organ which is unable to carry out a certain function (e.g. cases of blindness) must be considered diseased, even though there is no occasion to use the function (if the subject is asleep, or it is dark). A sick person can live and function normally in a specific environment, but what distinguishes him from a healthy person is that he is unable to function in every standard situation. So a person with diabetes who takes insulin every day still has a disease even though he or she functions 'normally'.

A significant feature of Boorse's theory is that it applies to both somatic and mental health. Boorse rejects any fundamental difference between these two kinds of health. For him, the idea of mental health is no more value-laden than the idea of somatic health. 'Mental health must be a constellation of qualities displayed in the standard functional organization of members of our species. Only empirical enquiry can show whether normal human beings have an even temper' (Boorse 1976: 70). Boorse states that there are a number of species-uniform mental aims, and it is the task of the various mental agencies to serve these aims. Intelligence and memory provide information for the effective guidance of action; drives serve to motivate such action; pain and anxiety function as signs of danger; linguistic behaviour is a method that makes intercultural cooperation possible, etc. If these faculties all function normally, then their bearer is healthy. If, however, some of them prevent a person from functioning normally, then that person is mentally ill.

We can summarize the central theses of Boorse's philosophy of health in the following manner (Nordenfelt 1995). (1) Health in a member of a reference group is the normal functional capacity, while disease is the internal state which reduces this capacity to a level that is lower than the typical efficiency levels. (2) The normal functional capacity is calculated statistically by comparison with an age group or sex of a species. It forms a statistically typical contribution by the members of the group to certain factual aims. In the case of somatic health, these aims are reproduction and individual survival. However, Boorse is well aware that this view of health and disease includes certain 'faults', which would, in ordinary language, be called diseases. He is thinking here of structural diseases (e.g. the congenital absence of an appendix, minor aberrations in the ears or nose which do not affect their functioning) and widespread or even universal diseases (e.g. tooth cavities, hardened arteries, prostate enlargement and common genetic mutations).

Boorse's ideas about medical concepts are not, however, restricted to his explanation of the theoretical notions of health and disease. In his view, there exists a concept of disease which contains meanings that reach much further than the idea of normal (or abnormal) biological functioning. Disease refers to an experiential aspect of the person, which is highly evaluative. For Boorse, saying that someone is ill, or has a disease, explicitly implies that the person is in a situation that they should not be in. To clarify the relation between the idea of 'having a disease' and the notion 'being ill', he makes the following comparison: 'Disease and illness are related somewhat as are low intelligence and stupidity. Sometimes the presumption that intelligence is desirable will fail, as in a discussion of qualifications for a menial job such as washing dishes or assembling auto parts. In such a context a person of low intelligence is unlikely to be described as stupid. ... And sometimes the presumption that diseases are undesirable will fail as with alcoholic intoxication or mild rubella intentionally contracted. Here the term 'illness' is unlikely to appear despite the presence of disease. One concept of each pair is descriptive; the other adds to the first evaluative content, and so may be withheld where the first applies' (Boorse 1981: 554). For Boorse, 'having a disease' also implies 'being ill' when it is serious enough to disable the person and, hence, is (1) unwanted by the subject, (2) gives them the right to special treatment and (3) is an acceptable excuse for negligent behaviour in normal circumstances. So one can have a disease without being ill, but one is never ill without having a disease.

Benefits and criticisms of the value-free concept of disease

For many, including his critics, Boorse's theory of health and disease describes a concept of disease (and hence of health) that is held by many scientists and physicians. 'It is a good reflection of what medical scientists and physicians actually mean by the term "disease"' (Hesslow 1993: 3; for the same idea see also Khushf 1997). It is, despite the theoretical approach, a useful practical concept. Boorse himself points out some of the benefits of his theory in comparison with other approaches (Boorse 1977). First of all, his theory draws a distinction between statements about disease and statements related to desirability and treatability. Colour-blindness probably claims fewer victims than not being able to smell carbon monoxide, but the former is a disease and the latter is not, since recognizing colours is a function that is typical for humans. In addition, statements about disease and health can be made independently of the disease's external manifestation. One can distinguish whether a single visible or felt effect is or is not the result of a disease. Another advantage, according to Boorse, is that his theory can explain how biologists can apply his concept of disease to animals and plants. The theory, moreover, is applicable to both somatic and mental health. Finally, Boorse's theory gives a clear explanation for the 'scientific' status of concepts of health. By defining the basic concepts of health and disease in a purely theoretical (not evaluative) fashion, it becomes possible in this theory to utilize these concepts directly in science. Whether someone has a disease can be established totally objectively. What is needed is to find out the specific aims of the organs and mental capacities, to calculate the average contribution of these organs or capacities to attaining the aims, and to see whether a certain organ reaches that average or not. It would seem that, in principle, all these things could be carried out by an empirical science, medicine for example.

For all its ingenuity, Boorse's theory has been received critically by many. It is not my intention to subject every term or expression to a detailed critique, as some have done. Rather, I will survey the most important trends of the various criticisms. In the first place, according to Khushf there are internal contradictions in Boorse (Khushf 1997). He observes a distinction between 'speaking and acting according to a concept' and the definition that has been chosen. For Boorse, the intention is to analyse the concepts of health and disease as they are understood by traditional physiological medicine. He is not interested in showing how the inductive processes of the basic sciences lead to a concept of disease. Instead, he begins with clinical medicine – especially the American Medical Association's 'Standard Nomenclature of Diseases and Operations' – as well as medical textbooks and publications. He subsequently states that an analysis of disease must be conceived as an explanatory theory of the use of these sources, and must be judged according to this standard. At the end of his exposition, he criticizes the normative approach because it does little to explain the actual inventory of disease. He believes such approaches cannot explain this inventory because they cannot predict it. Yet if the concept of disease is a theoretical judgement that does not lead to, or cannot be led by, a therapeutic judgement related to medical treatment, why does he link the concept so closely to its use in the literature, where it is mostly a matter of therapeutic judgements?

A further crucial question is how, and by whom, the distinction is made between the typical and the atypical in normal functional capacities. On this point, Boorse himself refers to the convention: 'Abnormal functioning occurs when some functions' efficiency falls more than a certain distance below the population mean. ... This distance can only be conventionally chosen, as in any application of statistical abnormality. The precise line between health and disease is usually academic, since most diseases involve functional deficits that are unusual by any reasonable standard' (Boorse 1977: 595). In a value-free objective theory, agreement and convention are rather uncommon. An additional criticism is that new 'features' which might be able to provide new benefits but which do not possess the ordinary benefits of an established feature are initially classified as a disease, despite there being members of the species that might consider them to be beneficial changes. Boorse's theory would seem then to depend on the history of the species and its evolution – a dependency that appears to be irrelevant for concepts of disease that are oriented to the individual (Goosens 1980). Making reference to this, Engelhardt claims that Boorse is only interested in the species, and directs no attention to the enormous variation within the species or to the individual person (Engelhardt 1982).

An additional objection is that by appealing to species-specific normal functioning, certain diseases can be interpreted as signs of health. In the case of an infectious disease, germs attack, say, the throat and produce toxins which immediately destroy a large number of the cells in the mucous membranes. The body reacts quickly to this attack, generating a higher concentration of blood in the infected areas, increasing body temperature, and producing antibodies to counter the viruses and pathogenic toxins. As a result of this, the toxins are gradually neutralized and the microbes are killed. This description of the process of infection is at the same time a description of a species-typical reaction to a serious attack on the body. Paradoxically, then, a typical disease can be considered as a species-typical reaction to an environmental threat. Such a disease is therefore the prototype of health, according to Boorse (Ten Have 1988).

This example leads to another form of criticism. The theory is viewed against a fixed background; the influence of the context is ignored. But in the case of human organisms one of the problems is precisely the lack of a standard environment or fixed context. One posits a shortcoming (genetic, for instance) and an environmental influence as two independent entities, overlooking the fact that hereditary factors can only be determined in specific life situations; environmental influences have been at work since conception. Nor is there any mention of the fact that scientific research methods, and their results in the area of disease recognition and definition, can change dramatically through history and are culture-related phenomena. In itself, a physical state cannot be considered healthy or unhealthy. One must also take into account the social and cultural context. For instance, colour-blindness by itself is not a sign of disease or health. It depends on the context: is it considered important to be able to distinguish colours or to recognize camouflage?

A similar criticism can be made of Boorse's analysis of the aims to which species-specific functioning is directed. First, there is a question of methodology: how and by whom is the highest aim determined? Second, one could question his choice of survival and reproduction as the highest aims. Is mere survival one of the highest aims? What happens in the event of a conflict between the two highest aims, individual survival and the survival of the species (Agich 1983)? Something that is beneficial for an individual's descendants can be detrimental to the interests of that individual. Boorse assumes that illness must be caused by some kind of subnormal function, and also that the subnormal function that is responsible for the disease is subnormal in relation to the highest aims: survival and reproduction. But what if the incapacity itself determines the subnormal functional capacity to attain the aims? There is no place for this. The overall state of inability of the entire person is not a subnormal functional inability or incapacity within the analytic theory. Illness in the ordinary sense of the word (with pain and discomfort) can, under certain circumstances, be the result of species-typical reactions when carrying out normal functional ability. Hence, illness can result from things other than disease. This means that other aims are involved in health, for instance the aim to have certain abilities or capacities (Nordenfelt 1995). Paradigmatic cases such as infectious diseases show that these can only be discovered if their relation to illness and inability is taken into account. These concepts, however, belong to an evaluative discourse, and the place for this is not in a neutral objective theory, but in a more holistic approach to disease and health.

The role of values in a philosophical determination of health

There are several accepted models of explanation in the philosophical thinking about disease and health. We can distinguish two representative tendencies: (1) the biological model, which I have presented and criticized, that explains disease in terms of structural changes and diminution of bodily and mental functioning; (2) a more holistic model, in which cultural and social factors are taken up in addition to somatic factors. Common to the holistic approach is that health always has to do with the functioning of a person as a whole. The emphasis is on the person as a social being, part of a network of relations in which a range of activity is carried out. According to this view, the concept of health refers both to an empirical reality and to whatever people in a specific situation want to attain. At the centre is the idea that health lies partially or entirely in the ability to execute a certain set of actions or to attain or preserve a certain set of goals. If a person can execute all the actions in that set (or can attain all the goals), then he or she is completely healthy; otherwise he or she is to a greater or lesser degree unhealthy. This ability does not stand alone, but must be specified in relation to a specific person, a specific project or goal, and the circumstances. The success of an action thus depends on three things: the person with a particular biological and psychological constitution, the nature of the goal and the nature of the circumstances under which the action takes place. Using this as a background, Nordenfelt, whose theory of well-being has health as a fundamental concept, defines health as the ability of a person to attain their vital goals under standard circumstances (Nordenfelt 1995).

Both of these approaches offer a different answer to the problem of normativity. The problem of normativity deals with the question of whether or not the use of the concept of health (or disease) includes a normative claim (Beauchamp 1982). In other words, does labelling someone as healthy or ill merely imply a description of a feature, or is one (also) pronouncing a value judgement? From the analytic objective point of view, statements about health and disease do not imply any value judgements, so a value-free standpoint is possible.

However, the presentation and critical analysis of this descriptive position has shown that the neutrality claim is untenable. In theology and philosophy there is an on-going discussion about what the highest goal might be for human life and for the human species. Defining it as 'individual survival and reproduction' is not a neutral matter. Boorse's preference is understandable, but it also implies a value judgement. In addition to the question of whether the determination of a biological reference group or 'standard person' is possible on purely objective grounds, there is also the problem of measuring against this reference group. The comparison of factual data contains an evaluative moment: discrepancies from the standard norm are either acceptable or unacceptable. This boundary between typical and atypical is a matter of convention; it cannot be drawn in isolation from 'prudential interests which make up part of a particular ideology and the ultimate goals of a society' (Margolis 1981: 252). The limit between an acceptable and an unacceptable deviation from the norm could be determined, for example, on the basis of practical or economic ends. In clinical practice, the results of diagnostic tests are called objective and value free when no errors have been committed. But this information by itself is not always sufficient to determine if someone is healthy or sick. It presupposes interpretation, which, in turn, is influenced by certain presuppositions related to a specific medical model, image of human nature, conception of society, etc.

Taken together, these factors constitute one of the most significant objections to the analytic objective point of view. Disease and health are not simply derived from the body's biological makeup; they also contain a value judgement. One could even go so far as to say that Boorse, despite claims to the contrary, is himself a proponent of normativism: 'Boorse defines health by appealing to the natural structure of the species as ultimate norm. In this, Boorse differs not at all from other normativists with their idea that health is a normative concept' (Ten Have 1988: 116).

In the holistic perspective, the evaluative factor is explicitly recognized and included as an integral part. The biological order, according to this view, is indeed a necessary precondition for health, but health does not coincide with the biological order. Outlining the limits of what we consider health to be is not an exclusively biomedical matter. It is also a judgement, with a social, cultural and even a political character (Nordenfelt 1995). The social and physical environment, as well as the dominant values, influence the concept of health. The lower limits of human happiness are set by the members of society, and this decision is partly based on an evaluation of what a minimal human life must presuppose in terms of happiness. Since this perspective starts with the entire person, its conception of what a human being is will also contribute to determining what disease and health are.

This analysis allows us to conclude that discussion of disease and health is never merely a scientific matter, but always includes a value judgement as well. This is the reason why De Clercq states that 'every concept of disease and health is at least implicitly an ethically laden concept' (De Clercq 1981: 128). According to this view, a crucial role is played by the tradition in which one is placed and the society in which one lives. This normativism has a moderate and an extreme version. The extreme version claims that a judgement about disease and health is exclusively an evaluation without any descriptive content (Szasz 1981; Ingleby 1982). Our discussion has shown, however, that this position is untenable. As for the moderate normativists, they believe that statements about health contain both a descriptive and an evaluative aspect. In order to determine what health is, a reference to norms is a necessary but not a sufficient condition.

References

Agich, G.J. (1983) 'Disease and value: a rejection of the value-neutrality thesis', *Theoretical Medicine* 4: 27–41.

Beauchamp, T.L. (1982) 'Concepts of health and disease', in T.L. Beauchamp and L. Walters (eds) *Contemporary Issues in Bioethics*, 2nd edn, Belmont, California: Wadsworth, 44–7.

Boorse, C. (1976) 'What a theory of health should be', *Journal for the Theory of Social Behavior* 6: 61–84.

—— (1977) 'Health as a theoretical concept', *Philosophy of Science* 44: 542–73.

—— (1981) 'On the distinction between disease and illness', in A.L. Caplan, H.T. Engelhardt, Jr and J.J. McCartney (eds) *Concepts of Health and Disease: Interdisciplinary Perspectives*, London: Addison-Wesley, 545–60.

Daniels, N. (1985) *Just Health Care*, Cambridge: Cambridge University Press.

De Clercq, B.J. (1981) *Politiek en het 'goede leven': Zeven hoofdstukken uit een politieke en sociale ethiek*, Leuven: Acco.

Engelhardt, H.T., Jr (1982) 'The roles of values in the discovery of illnesses, diseases and disorders', in T.L. Beauchamp and L. Walters (eds) *Contemporary Issues in Bioethics*, Belmont, California: Wadsworth, 59–63.

Goosens, W.K. (1980) 'Values, health, and medicine', *Philosophy of Science* 47: 100–15.

Hesslow, G. (1993) 'Do we need a concept of disease?', *Theoretical medicine* 14: 1–14.

Ingleby, D. (1982) 'The social construction of mental illness', in P. Wright and A. Treacher (eds) *The Problem of Medical Knowledge: Examining the Social Construction of Medicine*, Edinburgh: Edinburgh University Press, 123–43.

Khushf, G. (1997) 'Why bioethics needs the philosophy of medicine: some implications of reflection on concepts of health and disease', *Theoretical Medicine* 18: 145–63.

Lennox, J.G. (1995) 'Health as an objective value', *Journal of Medicine and Philosophy* 20: 499–511.

Margolis, J. (1981) 'The concept of disease', in A.L. Caplan, H.T. Engelhardt, Jr and J.J. McCartney (eds) *Concepts of Health and Disease: Interdisciplinary Perspectives*, London: Addison-Wesley, 561–77.

Mordacci, R. (1995) 'Health as an analogical concept', *Journal of Medicine and Philosophy* 20: 475–97.

Nordenfelt, L. (1995) *On the Nature of Health: An Action-theoretic Approach*, Dordrecht: Kluwer Academic Publishers.

Szasz, T. (1981) 'The concept of mental illness: explanation or justification?', in A.L. Caplan, H.T. Engelhardt, Jr and J.J. McCartney (eds) *Concepts of Health and Disease: Interdisciplinary Perspectives*, London: Addison-Wesley, 459–74.

Temkin, O. (1973) 'Health and disease', in P.P. Wiener (ed.) *Dictionary of the History of Ideas: Studies of Selected Pivotal Ideas*, New York: Scribner, 395–407.

Ten Have, H. (1988) 'Gezondheid tussen beschrijving en waardering', in J. Rolies (ed.) *De gezonde burger: gezondheid als norm*, Nijmegen: SUN, 107–23.

22

NATURE GOOD AND EVIL
A theological palette

Philip Hefner

The questions posed by our theme – whether nature is good or evil, friendly or unfriendly – are among the most important that we could discuss, and they are also among the most complex and difficult imaginable. I do not claim to take the measure of what the theme requires, if it is to be discussed in a comprehensive and conclusive manner. Rather, I sketch four areas of reflection that must be considered if we are to respond adequately to our theme. I think of these as four colours on an artist's palette, or four kinds of stone to be included in a mosaic. To present a full and coherent picture remains the task for future reflection, but that picture will of necessity include the four elements discussed here.

Human ideas of nature

Twentieth-century philosophers like Collingwood and Whitehead reminded us of what Immanuel Kant had already pointed out in the early eighteenth century: that the word 'nature' refers to all that is 'out there' and also to our concepts and definitions of what is out there. Nature is unknowable apart from our ideas or concepts of nature. The idea of wilderness is a good example. Wilderness is a human concept. Wilderness areas have precise boundaries, and are governed by human laws and practices. In the United States, for example, we hear contrasting ideas about areas of Alaska: whether they are wilderness or not and whether wilderness areas can be tapped for petroleum. Proponents say that our technology will permit us to drill for oil, pump it out of the ground, transport it to refineries, without compromising the wilderness. This discussion is an example of how nature is a human construction – just as much as it is an objective reality independent of humans.

Our theme raises questions that are totally dependent on humanly constructed ideas about nature – whether it is evil or good. It is hard to imagine that any other creature in nature except for humans has such ideas of nature. Ideas that interpret the relationship of humans to nature are particularly important for this discussion. Are we 'over against' nature, or are we part of nature? Are we some kind of animal, or do we stand outside the class called 'animal'? Do we speak of humans and nature, or humans and the *rest* of nature?

Collingwood traced the history of Western interpretations of nature through three normative ideas: nature as living organism (ancient Greek philosophy), nature as machine (later Middle Ages, Renaissance, Enlightenment), and nature as historical process (late nineteenth and twentieth centuries, as exemplified in Darwin's theory of evolution and quantum physics).

There is a great deal of scholarship in our own time that analyzes how our ideas of nature govern our attitudes and behaviors with respect to nature. Among the ideas of nature that have received special attention are: nature as machine, as a domain to be conquered and manipulated by humans, as a resource for enhancing human life, as a realm of sacrality, as our sibling, as a realm that we must protect and care for (Haraway 1997, Swimme 1996, Sittler 2000, etc.). There is a consensus that our experience of nature is inseparable from our ideas of nature. Obviously, there are important reasons for saying that nature is prior to and independent from humans. Nevertheless, it also seems to be true that we have no conscious experience of nature that is not significantly under the impact of our human ideas.

I have previously suggested that 'good' and 'friendly' are two key issues in our consideration of nature and our relationships to it (Hefner 1992, 1994, 2000). Of course, both of these are human ideas, and they overlap. They are not identical ideas, however. To say that nature is good is to acknowledge that, whatever nature is, it possesses an intrinsic value and character that can be called 'good.' Friendship is a term of relationship. Thomas Aquinas made the point that friendship is a medium of communion. He included God as the ultimate dimension of communion, but his thinking is useful even if we do not bring God into the discussion. Friendship with nature brings communion with it. Drawing from Thomas, we may say that there are three kinds of relationship between humans and nature: understanding, which is attained through the natural sciences; intrinsic valuation, or aesthetic and moral appreciation of nature's intrinsic dignity and worth; love (*caritas*), which knows that nature is friend, in that we are joined with it in whatever course it takes or purpose it may have. Friendship speaks of our complex relationships of belonging, to ourselves and also to nature. Love is the action of friendship.

These gleanings from Thomas are consistent with my assertion that nature's friendship means that the reality system of nature in which we live is itself an ambience in which we truly belong, an ambience that brought us into being and enables us to fulfil the purposes for which we were brought into being. For Christians, this reality system is grounded in God and the purposes of God (Hefner 1994: 508). Thomas himself asserted that friendship with nature is a medium of friendship with God and with God's purposes for nature.

The contribution of Christian faith to the theme, like all religious world-views, lies in the ideas that it proposes for apprehending and responding to nature. Since the ideas of traditional Christian theology grow out of the very logic of the Christian faith, the theologian will bring them to bear on any reflection upon nature. Today theologians are challenged, on the one hand, to clarify how these traditional assertions illuminate the topic at hand, while, on the other hand, they must demonstrate how these assertions continue to be viable for our contemporary interpretation of nature.

The nature of God: God as one creative source without mediation

The Christian tradition sets the stage for understanding and conceptualizing God's relation to nature in its assertions about God and God's work as Creator. These assertions include, at the most basic level, the idea that God is sovereign and free in creating. In contrast to certain other creation myths, the Hebrew–Christian stories do not set God over against foes or any other inhibiting forces in the act of creation. God simply wills the creation, and it comes into existence. These assertions are articulated doctrinally in the concepts of creation-out-of-nothing (*creatio ex nihilo*) and continuing creation (*creatio continua*) (Hefner 1984).

Although the concept of creation-out-of-nothing emerged in the late second century in response to misunderstandings and attacks on Christian faith by Hellenistic thinkers, its meaning cannot be reduced to the polemical situation in which it took shape. Rather, it grew out of Christian awareness that the faith expressed in the Bible required this conceptual development, if it were to be articulated in the Hellenistic situation (see Wilken 1984: 91).

The Christian creation doctrines also put forward two additional assertions. First, that there is but one ultimate grounding for the natural world: the God that is affirmed by the Christian tradition (which we can describe as a God of love, freedom, and intentionality). Second, these primal affirmations say something about the conditions under which this grounding exists. These two assertions are the foundation for everything that the Christian religion asserts about nature.

The out-of-nothing affirmation establishes that the one and only source of the natural world is, as I have already said, the God of the Hebrew–Christian tradition. This is the core of the presentations in the two Genesis creation stories, as well as the traditions that are embedded in the book of Job, the nature Psalms, and the New Testament traditions that we find in the Gospels and the writings of Paul, the Epistle to the Hebrews, and the Book of Revelation.

We grasp the significance of this motif of a single grounding for the natural world when we compare it with the creation story that most Hellenistic intellectuals accepted, the story reported in Plato's *Timaeus*. Plato reports that God, the demiurge, was constrained by a second grounding element of nature, pre-existent chaos. Consequently, God could not create the world that was most desirable but had to work within the possibilities that chaos would allow. The end result was a natural world that was defective, capable only of partially conforming to the creator's intention. If perfection were to be attained, it would require separation from the world; the soul would have to be liberated from the prison-house of the body.

In addition to the motif of a single ground of the natural world, the creation-out-of-nothing doctrine also eliminates all mediation between the creator God and the natural world. As Gerardus van der Leeuw (1957: 346) points out, the Hebrew story of creation is a very simple equation, comprised of three factors: God, what God creates, and the future that God brings about for the creation. The interface of God and the natural world is one of immediacy. The significance of this immediacy comes to the fore when we compare the Hebrew story with myths that require some sort of testing or ordeal before God's creation work can be completed. Such myths include those that depict creation as the conquest of chaos. The Babylonian *Enuma elish* is an example of such a story. Marduk must struggle in a violent contest with chaos, killing the primordial mother, before the natural world can emerge (see Ricoeur 1967: 175–83).

There are Christian traditions of theological reflection that insist that God's mode of creation has itself distanced God's work of creation from the world – in the classical ideas of first and second creation, primary and secondary matter. In this way of thinking, God created being itself, perhaps (as Luther writes in his commentary on Genesis, *Lectures on Genesis*, chapter 1, verse 6) prior to the first day of creation recounted in Genesis 1. From this primary creation, the creation of determinate things followed. Thomas Aquinas employed these ideas, as Luther and the Lutheran dogmaticians did. Stephen Pope (1997) argues that the consequence for Aquinas was that, when Aquinas spoke of creation, he referred to the mode by which all things 'emanate' from the First Principle. Creation is the production of being as such, not the production of one or another particular being. Thus the evolution of a particular species, or even the emergence of life itself, would not be regarded as creation in this sense. By creation in the proper sense, Aquinas referred not to particular acts of creation, but rather to the emanation of 'all being from the universal cause' and 'First Principle,' which is God. This is the sense in which he claims that 'to create belongs to the action of God alone' (Pope 1997: 222–3).

Luther and Lutheran theologians have placed God in more intimate relation to secondary causation, in what Quenstedt called God's 'concurrence' with the needs and requirements of each natural thing. God permits natural agents to act freely and naturally (Schmid 1875: 185).

In any case, this distinction between primary and secondary causation does not stand as a barrier or mediator between God and the act of creation, because if this distinction is indeed valid, its basis lies in the decision and action of God, and not in any agent or force external to God.

The nature of nature: nature conditioned by the nature of God

The logic that comes into play from this theological base is of great significance for understanding nature and the fundamental stance of Christian theology toward nature. This significance is not often perceived, even by Western theologians. By means of this affirmation, that God is the sole ground of nature and that God stands in an unmediated relation to the creation, these theological traditions assert *that the character of God conditions the nature of nature, in a fundamental way.* This view is expressed in the Augustinian tradition of comparing the creation to the song of God, the *carmina dei*. Zachary Hayes describes the Franciscan elaboration of this tradition:

> Centuries later the great medieval theologian and mystic, St. Bonaventure, compared the world of creation to a splendid stained glass window. The light of divine truth, goodness, and beauty is refracted through the fabric of the universe as physical light is refracted in a rich fabric of shapes and colors by the window of the great Gothic cathedrals .... Or again, for Bonaventure as for Augustine, the world may be seen as a book containing the very revelation of the mystery of God.
>
> (Hayes 1997: xii)

An analogy may help us understand this point, even though it is finally inadequate. Think of a person who wishes to give a special gift to a beloved friend or lover or family member, perhaps for a special occasion or as special sign of love and respect. If the person buys a gift, we recognize immediately that the giver is dependent upon what is available, and must accept the fact that what is available was not made especially with the beloved, the occasion, or the special relationship between the giver and recipient in mind. The giver must make do, in other words, in the context of a formidable array of constraints that are in fact obstacles to the intention of the giver. Consider, however, the difference if the giver makes the gift personally – designing it with particular reference to the relationships involved, the occasion and the beloved. We also assume that the giver can acquire whatever materials and tools are desired; here the analogy breaks down, because the giver must accept the inherent properties of the available materials. Given these factors, when the gift is bestowed, we know that it is exactly what the giver desired, and that it is precisely what the giver believes is appropriate to convey the giver's intentions on this specific occasion, for this particular beloved person. We know that the nature of the gift is conditioned by the character and intentions of the giver. This example is but a poor restatement of what Augustine wrote in his *Confessions*:

> But *how* didst thou make the heaven and the earth, and what was the tool of such a mighty work as thine? For it was not like a human worker fashioning body from body, according to the fancy of his mind, able somehow or other to impose upon it a form which the mind perceived. ... thou didst speak and they were made, and by thy Word thou dost make them all .... Whatever it was out of which such a voice was made simply did not exist at all until it was made by thee.
>
> (Book 11, chapters 5 and 6)

The upshot of this double affirmation of God, both as sole ground of nature and also maintaining an unmediated relationship to the creation, is to place God in the position of the giver who designs and makes the gift, with the exception, as Augustine elaborates it, that God could create whatever materials were desired. God, therefore, worked under no constraints except those of God's own character and choosing. The end result, according to the logic of the Christian system of belief, is that nature, when perceived from within the Christian frame of vision, is not only the creation of God but it is also the creation that God intended.

The argument that the nature of nature is conditioned by the nature of God, that it is in some sense the song of God, is grounded in traditions that are even more primary to the Christian faith than those we have mentioned here: the New Testament and the theology of the Trinity. In the New Testament we note several key loci. There is the Fourth Gospel's opening reflection on the *logos* – 'In the beginning was the Word, and the Word was with God, and the Word was God. He was in the beginning with God; all things were made through him, and without him was not anything made that was made' (John 1:1–3). In an intense manner, this type of thinking links the creation with God's revelation in Jesus Christ, thus suggesting a Christological understanding of nature. Perhaps the earliest text in this line of thinking is I Corinthians 8:6, which may have an early liturgical origin: 'there is one God, the Father, from whom are all things and for whom we exist, and one Lord, Jesus Christ, through whom are all things and through whom we exist.' The so-called 'cosmic Christology' traditions of Ephesians 1, Colossians 1:15–20, and Hebrews 1:1–3 carry this tradition further in the New Testament. Colossians explicitly includes the natural world within the Christological framework: 'for in him all things were created, in heaven and on earth, visible and invisible – all things were created through him and for him.' We must conclude that the revelation set forth in Jesus Christ is the *content* of God's conditioning of nature.

Trinitarian theology provides doctrinal elaboration of these New Testament witnesses, in that it not only insists that all of the three persons are present in each, but also that Christ, the *logos*, is the divine agent of creation. This thinking is widespread in the theological tradition, from at least the time of Origen, through Augustine, the Cappadocians, and medieval theologians (Pannenberg 1994: 20–35).

The conclusion to be drawn from this survey of Christian theological ideas of nature is that nature is a medium that is consonant with the nature of God, which means, first of all, that nature expresses God's goodness and love. This proposal is not accepted in much of traditional theology, for two reasons. First, nature was experienced oftentimes as raw, cruel, and without purpose, and second, the most important dimensions of human being were not dependent on nature, but were supernatural.

Today it is untenable to separate humans from the rest of nature, as I will argue in more detail later. Our most intimate character is shaped by nature, specifically our genetic composition and our neurobiology, which enable what we call the spirit, and which are intrinsically related to our abilities to think, conceive of God, and understand ourselves as children of God. If the nature of nature is conditioned by the nature of God, then nature must be a medium or means for the goodness, love, and redemption that God intends. If that proposal proves to be untenable, then the theological parameters that I have set forth from the tradition are also untenable.

In this chapter I elaborate some of the ways in which I intend to allow the parameters of the tradition to direct my reflection. It is beyond the scope of my effort here to argue conclusively whether those parameters are tenable or untenable. That is the task of another work.

Human efforts to make nature friendly

The chief point I wish to make in this section, and perhaps the major contention of this chapter, is that the questions of whether nature is good, friendly, or evil cannot be understood properly if we do not consider them within the context of human efforts to make nature friendly. Our interventions in natural processes, efforts to improve nature, are at bottom aimed at making nature friendly, and the larger aim is thereby to enable communion with the rest of nature and with God.

For most of their history, but especially in the last three centuries, humans have attempted to change the natural world and improve it. Most of the time, we have focused our efforts on changing the nature outside us, but in the past century, particularly with the advent of genetic engineering, we have turned to improving human nature. Since our work of improving ourselves employs many of the same means and concepts that we apply to non-human nature, it is accurate to say that agricultural plants, animals, and human beings now stand together as objects of our efforts to improve nature. Of course, we have always tried to improve ourselves through our culture, aiming to influence our minds and spirits, but now we are turning to our physical nature, including our genes, neurobiology.

Our activities for improving nature are generally absorbed into two opposing ideologies: on the one hand, the ideology of progress, allied to the view that we are destined by God or history to be nature's conqueror, and, on the other hand, the opposing opinion enunciated by Rousseau, that nature is pure and only man is vile. The one position is premised on the assumption that all of nature is a resource for human development, and improvements are for the most part defined by whatever enhances human beings. The other perspective considers humans to be intruders into nature, despoilers, and at best temporary tenants of the planet. Mastery of nature is the core of the one perspective, while supporting nature, even to the point of leaving it untouched altogether, is central to the other.

I will present a view that differs from these, while recognizing what is valid in each of them. They each possess a kernel of truth, but their elaborations pervert that truth. Let me lay the groundwork for this assessment. First, we recognize that the natural world, including humans, is a dynamic realm. Change, often dramatic, is intrinsic to nature in all its aspects: its molecules and biochemistry, its flora and fauna. Continuity is also inherent in nature, but change is just as prominent. In the history of planet Earth, for example, it is not possible to describe a single preferred state that can be norm for the entire history of the planet. Only by freezing the movement of evolutionary history into a single frame or set of processes can an ideal state of the planet be held up as normative.

Second, the capability to imagine that the world can be different, together with the capacity to design and enact changes in the world, is a fundamental dimension of human nature and therefore of nature itself. Working to change the world around us is not a perversion of human nature, but an expression of it. I have offered the concept of humans as created co-creators as a way of interpreting this aspect of human nature. One of the problems with the view that humans ought not to intervene in nature's processes is that it flies in the face of this fundamental and primordial element of human nature. Nature itself has engendered such creatures as humans.

Third, humans have emerged within the processes of nature. Humans belong to nature in that the overarching narrative of human life is the history of nature. The ideology of progress is flawed for its inability to acknowledge this fact. Indeed, one of the great challenges of our recent history is that of placing human history within the domain of natural history. We have for the most part done just the opposite, insisting that nature's history be subsumed within our human story. Our relationship to nature can be characterized as that of *belonging*, but it is constituted by an asymmetry: we belong to nature in a way that is more primordial and enduring than the sense in which nature belongs to us.

The *cantus firma*: communion within nature with God

Within the framework of Christian theology, the dynamic of nature is to be explained as its trajectory toward communion with God, according to God's intentions. Remembering what I said earlier, this is the dynamic of love and friendship. This is also fundamental and primordial to nature, both human and non-human – the trajectory of communion. Nature is a realm of becoming, and its underlying thrust, its *cantus firma*, if you will, is communion of its parts with each other and with God.

Theology has spoken of these things in the technical vocabulary of *eschatology*. The fundamental nature of nature is to become what God intends. The coherence of the creation, the meaning of its processes and components, can be known only by reference to what God intends for the world. Our work of intervening in nature, improving it, and making it friendly should be placed within this concept of eschatological communion of nature with God.

The dimensions of communion require some elaboration – communion of humans with the rest of nature, and the communion of nature with God. Our attempts to improve nature need the backdrop of the idea of communion if they are to be fully understood.

The dimension of kinship

I spoke earlier about the idea of nature which encompasses humans. The communion of humans and nature is communion within nature, between entities, all of which are nature. The model of kinship is appropriate for representing our intense interrelationship with the rest of nature. The concept of kinship points not so much to our sibling relationship with the ecosphere, but rather to our primary continuity with nature's processes, and our origin and future within nature. The pertinent metaphors here are not so much drawn from ecology as from genetic kinship. The elements that comprise the periodic table we all learned in high school, and which also form the building blocks of our own bodies, were produced in

197

previous epochs of the universe's history, many of them in the monster furnaces of the galaxies. The concreteness that defines us bears the marks of life's pilgrimage on our planet. *Bricolage* – constructing new things from the materials at hand – is evident throughout the biosphere. Whether we note the formation of jawbones from antecedent gill slits or the triune structure of the human brain that contains within itself the neurological ancestry of reptiles and ancient mammals, it is stunningly clear that the human being is a segment of a process that can be related reasonably, on the basis of empirical observation, to the whole of nature. When we add the testimony of genetics and the results of nucleotide sequence comparisons, including those that deal with mitochondrial DNA, the sense of our kinship within one human community and with the higher primates is rendered very intense indeed.

The ecological model also depicts our intense belonging to the rest of nature. In some ways, this is a simpler and more graspable model than that of kinship, particularly since the delicate balance and interweaving of the many factors that make our continued existence possible on the planet become more vivid to us every day.

The models of kinship and ecology help us to understand communion with nature and God. We perceive the other citizens of nature with brains that natural processes have brought into being, and we interpret those others and ourselves with those same brains. Increasingly, we are aware that these others are not only fellow roomers with us in the hotel that is planet Earth, but also enablers of our lives, even though they also at times threaten our lives.

We come to know God also through our natural bodies, our senses and our brains. We know how faulty and fragile our sense of God can be, and how perverted our ideas of God often are. We become even more aware that when God seeks our worship and obedience, it is the worship and obedience offered by the creation that is at issue, not some otherworldly offerings.

The dimension of nondualist wholism

The human being who relates to the rest of nature is also fully nature, which means that our culture, including its technology, is part and parcel of our natural involvement in this relationship. Of course, other animals also bring culture to the relationship, and even some examples of technology. Because human culture and technology are so much more elaborate and sophisticated than those of other animals, we often consider these aspects of human nature to lie outside of nature. There are certainly distinctive problems posed by human culture and technology, but they are no less natural than the culture that the chimps or the honeybees bring to their communion with the rest of nature.

It is sometimes difficult to speak of the interrelationship of nature, humanity, culture, and technology. Donna Haraway speaks of technonature and technomen and -women. If we consider the impact of human culture and technology on the entire planet, we are driven to say that on our planet there is no other nature except technonature, and there are virtually no human persons who are not technopersons (Haraway 1991, 1997; see also Kull in this volume). The human being who enters into communion with the rest of nature is cyborg, and so also, one could argue, is the entire commonwealth of nature with which the communion is acted out.

A model of interaction

It is not enough to content ourselves with a view of human efforts to improve nature, to make nature friendly, that takes into account only the raw, brute bending of nature to our will. Such a view guarantees superficiality of insight on the one hand and brutal practice on the other. I offer here a model of interaction that may bring 'improvement' into the realm of communion with nature and God. I draw this model from medical practice, both what I observe and what I have experienced. I believe, however, that this model applies outside the medical sphere as well.

This model is marked by four activities: listening, cooperating, learning, and teaching.

Listening Physicist William Klink has suggested that our scientific-technological activities ought to be considered as the medium for communicating with nature so that a dialogue can emerge, which in turn provides a reinterpretation of what science and technology are about. He writes: 'If technology is used as a means of communication, as a new possibility for carrying on a dialogue with nature, the very notion of technology changes, from a means of more control and power, to a means for listening, responding, being open to new possibilities in the life of the earth' (Klink 1992: 208). Klink speaks of the sciences associated with ecology, but certainly the same can be said about science and technology associated with medicine. We first of all listen to the body and its processes, and their placement within the structures of personal life, hoping to hear how things work, what they are for, what heals and hurts them.

Cooperating Even if motives of control and power lie behind medical interventions, their success depends on the underlying ability to cooperate with the processes of nature as they pertain to the body. A transplant, for example, cannot succeed if it must contravene the body's processes, including those of the complex immune system and its rejection mechanisms. The healing process requires cooperation between the patient and her body. Diet, physical rehabilitation, medication – and the continual adjustments that must be made – are examples of this cooperation. The same can be said of implanting prostheses. Genetic intervention require enormous listening, understanding, and cooperating between the one who intervenes and the nature of the patient.

Learning and teaching In this medical realm, nature and the human agent continually learn from and teach each other. The patient and care-givers often teach the body to behave in new ways, sometimes ways that seem quite 'unnatural,' but if they do not let the body teach them its ways, if they are poor learners, their teaching will be in vain, even counterpro-ductive. Heart attack victims and recipients of by-pass surgery know this very well.

This model of interaction within the commonwealth of nature, including listening, cooperating, learning, and teaching, illuminates what is funda-mental to all human relations with the rest of nature. It describes patterns that are present in every human interaction with nature, even if some or all of those patterns are vestigial and perverted. This model, as Klink intended, is a proposal to govern human relationships with the rest of nature, especially those that are driven by science and technology.

(1) Proceeding from the human effort to make nature friendly

What is the significance of considering whether nature is good, friendly, or evil in the context of human efforts to make nature friendly? Just this, that since nature, on the one hand, is an unfinished process, dynamic and changing, and human nature, on the other hand, inherently imagines how nature can be re-fashioned, goodness, friendship, and evil are not static givens posited initially in the process of nature, only to be worked out in the history of nature. Rather, the entities of nature must learn what good, evil, friendship, and love mean. And what they mean is something to be worked out in the actual unfolding of natural life, in which creatures, particularly humans, will try to teach the rest of nature to be friendly, according to criteria that are worked out from moment to moment. To speak in terms of ecology, specifically the air we breathe, humans, the atmosphere, and perhaps other entities, must learn from each other and also teach each other what good, evil, and friendship can mean in ways that are relevant to atmosphere. This was not even an issue five hundred years ago, but today it is a field of discovery and action. To speak in terms of medicine, humans and their bodies must learn together and teach each other about what it means to be good, friendly, or evil to another in contemporary life. No doubt we can learn from previous eras, but the situation is distinctive in each generation, and so the terms of the dialogue and the goals of the action also change dynamically.

This conclusion could be interpreted in a number of ways. It could be understood as a praxis-oriented approach, insisting that only in the actual attempt to make nature good do we gain knowledge of what nature's goodness or evil is. Or it could be construed as an expression of American pragmatic or neo-pragmatic philosophy, which argues that ideas can be understood only in their actual working out in the processes of life. Finally, it could be an example of evolutionary epistemology, that the evolution of nature itself carries knowledge that is intended for the further-ance of the evolutionary process.

All of these possibilities for interpretation make the point that the theme of this volume is finally accessible most significantly in the actual dynamic process of nature itself.

The most important point is that humans, because they are created co-creators, devote themselves to making nature friendly. In those efforts they reveal, explicitly and implicitly, their deepest beliefs about nature.

(2) Love, friendship, communion

The aim of medical intervention is to improve nature in some manner. This improvement is also, perhaps more profoundly, the effort to make nature friendly, rather than hostile. Without by-pass surgery, the arteries will be the agents of death, rather than life. The intervention may also be inter-preted as an attempt to enable the natural body to love its inhabitant.

Communion is not an inappropriate term to describe what happens in the interactions I have sketched, between the persons involved and the nature that is their body. The theological framework I proposed earlier interprets this communion. This communion ought to take place, because God wills it; it is an expression of God's love for the creation. The commu-nion among the natural creatures can also become a medium of their communion with God.

The idea of communion, with nature and with God, is that grand idea in which Christian theology frames our theme. Now the task remains to determine whether that is a viable idea for interpreting nature in contem-porary human experience.

References

Haraway, D.J. (1991) *Simians, Cyborgs, and Women: The Reinvention of Nature*, New York: Routledge.
—— (1997) *Modest_Witness@Second Millennium. FemaleMan_Meets_Onco-Mouse: Feminism and Technoscience*, New York: Routledge.
Hayes, Z. (1997) *A Window to the Divine: A Study of Christian Creation Theology*, Quincy, IL: Franciscan Press.

Hefner, P. (1984) 'Fourth Locus: the Creation', in C.E. Braaten and R. Jenson (eds.) *Christian Dogmatics*, Volume 1, Minneapolis: Fortress Press, 265–358.

—— (1992) 'Nature, God's Great Project', *Zygon: Journal of Religion and Science* 27: 327–43.

—— (1994) 'Can Nature Truly Be Our Friend?', *Zygon: Journal of Religion and Science* 29: 507–28.

—— (2000) 'Natural Evil: the Continuing Theological Challenge', in T. Fretheim and C. Thompson (eds.) *God, Evil, and Suffering: Essays in Honor of Paul R. Sponheim*, St. Paul, Minnesota: Word & World, Luther Seminary, 108–19.

Klink, W. (1992) 'Nature, Technology, and Theology', *Zygon: Journal of Religion and Science* 27: 203–10.

Kull, A. (2002) 'The Cyborg as an Interpretation of Culture-Nature', *Zygon: Journal of Religion and Science* 36 (March 2001): 49–56.

Pannenberg, W. (1994) *Systematic Theology*, Volume 2, Grand Rapids, MI: William B. Eerdmans.

Plato (1937) *Timaeus*, transl. by Benjamin Jowett, New York: Random House.

Pope, S. (1997) 'Neither Enemy nor Friend: Nature as Creation in the Theology of Saint Thomas', *Zygon: Journal of Religion and Science* 32: 219–30.

Ricoeur, P. (1967) *The Symbolism of Evil*, Boston: Beacon Press.

Schmid, H. (1875) *The Doctrinal Theology of the Evangelical Lutheran Church*, Minneapolis: Augsburg.

Sittler, J. (2000) 'Called to Unity', in S. Bouma-Prediger and P. Bakken (eds.) *Evocations of Grace: The Writings of Joseph Sittler on Ecology, Theology, and Ethics*, Grand Rapids, MI: William B. Eerdmans, 38–50.

Swimme, B. (1996) *The Hidden Heart of the Cosmos: Humanity and the New Story*, New York: Orbis Books.

van der Leeuw, G. (1957) 'Primordial Time and Final Time', in J. Campbell (ed.) *Man and Time*, vol. 3 of *Papers from the Eranos Yearbooks*, New York: Pantheon Books.

Wilken, R. (1984) *Christians as the Romans Saw Them*, New Haven: Yale University Press.

23

NATURE GOOD AND EVIL
A theological evaluation

Wessel Stoker

In general I agree with Hefner's theological view of nature. The framework of his approach to nature is *praxis-oriented*. This is in line with his main work *The Human Factor*, the thesis of which is that human beings are created co-creators. Moreover, he regards the relation between human beings and nature as a *communion*. In spite of my agreement in general with Hefner's view, however, I have some comments on its elaboration. My main objection is that his view of nature is *too optimistic*. The title of his paper is 'Nature good and evil: a theological palette', but he speaks of evil only in passing. In his book *The Human Factor* he calls natural evil the falsifier of his theory of human beings as created co-creators. In the introduction to his conference paper he refered to his article on natural evil and stated 'that God is not yet finished with nature, and that divine providence will unravel the contradictions that are noted'. Is this statement to be explained in line with Hick's theodicy, which he endorses in *The Human Factor* (1993: 44) and his article on natural evil (2000)?

I will discuss three issues: first, the issue of nature as creation; second, the problem of natural evil; and third, nature as a communion.

Nature as creation: the counter-world

How can we view nature as God's creation? This issue is important with regard to the question of whether the Christian idea of nature as conditioned by the nature of God, as Hefner puts it, 'can continue to interpret our experience of nature today adequately'. Hefner speaks of nature as a gift. He is right to distinguish between the Christian idea of creation out of nothing and Plato's second grounding element of nature, pre-existent chaos, but I miss in his theological view of nature as a gift the element of the dark counter-world. Creation out of nothing means only that creation is an act of God alone. The question 'is creation out of nothing or from something?' is not raised in the creation story of Genesis itself. The dilemma for P, the author of Genesis 1, is creation or formlessness: 'The earth was formless [*tohu*] and empty [*bohu*], darkness was over the surface of the deep, and the Spirit of God was hovering over the waters' (Genesis 1:1). In Hefner I miss the distinction between creation and nature. In the Genesis story (and in other parts of the Bible) there is always an awareness of an opposing world. In God's good creation the counter-world is a constant threat, present in drought, earthquakes, floods, miscarriages and disease. The threatening chaos appears when in creation God separates the light from darkness. Only the light is called good (Gen. 1:4). The night is a reminder of the darkness of chaos that has been eliminated. God imposes a limit upon the threatening power of chaos, of primeval flood and darkness. Thus the Genesis story articulates the experience of many of the ambiguity of nature and God's limiting of the counter-world. If it is right to acknowledge the element of chaos in God's good creation, then in my opinion Hefner's speaking of creation as a gift is too strong. This image misses the ambiguity of the world and nature, which is becoming God's creation. Do all events, all things refer to God? I do not believe that everything in nature speaks of the goodness of God. There is a counter-world and therefore we must distinguish between nature and creation.

I will present two ways of viewing nature other than as a gift. The first is Tillich's proposal of viewing nature in God ('Natur in Gott'). As far as the counter-world is concerned, Tillich holds that this cannot be seen apart from God. He points to the Protestant mysticism of Boehme and Schelling, who pose the question of how God as pure spirit can bring forth nature. The answer of Protestant mysticism is: He can do it only *if He has nature within Himself*. This mysticism thus speaks of a mysterious presence of nature in God: God is not an abstract spirit without nature but a spirit that stands in a vital, tension-filled union with nature in Himself. This expresses, according to Tillich, the divinity of the ground of nature ('Naturgrund'). The divine ground of nature is not only the creative but also the destructive principle, not only divine but also demonic. In all places where nature does not achieve union with the Spirit, it is demonic. Thus this mysticism also sees nature as terrifying, dark, melancholy, as a place of fear and torment (Tillich 1930; Jahr 1994).

Tillich elaborated on this *doctrine of nature in God* in his dissertation in connection with Schelling and retained it as a basis for his own doctrine of God. He views God as a unity of being and contradiction. Thus he writes in his *Systematic Theology* (1986: vol. 1, 210): 'If God is called the living God, if he is the ground of the creative processes of life, if history has significance for him, if there is no negative principle in addition to him which could account for evil and sin, how can one avoid positing a dialectical negativity in God himself?' Greek philosophy held that nothing originates from nothing (*de nihilo nihil fit*). There must have been something like eternal matter out of which God made the world. Plato called this the principle of indeterminacy. But can monotheism recognize two principles? Early Christian theology held to a creation *ex nihilo* and thus rejected the second principle. Nevertheless, the second principle of matter (*me on*) continued to survive, viewed as the nidus of evil in the Christian tradition. Tillich places, as indicated by the quotation, the negative dialectical principle in God. It concerns a dialectical negativity in which negativity or non-being is a *negative dialectical principle* that we encounter as an abyss, as the ontological shock and as the stigma of our own finitude (Stoker 1999). Thus God is both the abyss as well as the loving God who overcomes evil. There is a contradiction that has been overcome in the being of God. That is the difference between God and the world of human beings and nature in which evil has not (yet) been overcome. Tillich holds that the positive side of the mystery 'that includes the negative' is revealed in Christ and the work of the Spirit. God thus works as the Power of (New) Being, conquering natural evil.

With his view of nature in God, Tillich provides a view of the relation of God the Creator and the world that differs from the view of nature as a gift. Is it convincing? Tillich's approach raises objections. According to Tillich, the divine life *is* creative and realizes itself in an exhaustible fullness. God's being is creative and shows itself to us as a negative and positive mystery. Evil is thus very directly linked to God. If one shares Tillich's view of nature in God, then one receives the impression of natural evil in creation as an emanation, a coming forth from God. Evil as chaos is, after all, both a (conquered) part of God as well as destructively present in the world of human beings and nature. Although Tillich would want to deny that – 'God reveals himself primarily as a power for salvation', according to Tillich –, it seems difficult to avoid the notion of God as a split being.

Yet another view that differs from that of nature as a gift can be found in Kierkegaard. Kierkegaard comments on God's omnipotence and evil as follows. Characteristic of omnipotence is that it recognizes true freedom and therefore tolerates something independent alongside itself. It is precisely this that is strange for human practices of power, which always include the element of the other as dependent. God in His omnipotence does indeed tolerate something independent alongside Himself and therefore it is His goodness, for goodness means: 'to give absolutely, yet in such a way that by taking oneself back one makes the recipient independent' (1958: 113). God creates, in a free decision, a world that is independent of Him. That obtains for both nature as well as human beings. This means that the existence of natural evil is logically implied in God's choice for a creation that is independent of Him. This view concurs with the view of the natural sciences of an 'emergent universe' that includes probabilistic processes that lay the basis for free and creative acting. It also concurs with Hefner's stress on freedom as arising from nature. However, it differs from Hefner's view on nature as a gift, because it also gives room for our experiences of the world of nature as ambiguous. According to this view, nature can possibly develop into a direction contrary to the intentions of God.

Teleology and natural evil

In *The Human Factor* Hefner gives a teleological interpretation of evolution. The human being is created by God to be a co-creator in creation for which God establishes goals. The process of evolution is God's process of birthing forth a creature which represents a more complex phase of the zone of freedom and which is therefore crucial for the origination of a free creation. There is thus a teleology with respect to the bringing forth of human beings in the process of evolution. But there is also a problem: does natural selection not contradict this? Empirical observation does not reveal an end in any direct way. And, further, this process is full of injustice and pain, without respect of persons. It is this that poses the problem for theodicy.

Hefner attempts to respond to the first objection with his theory of the human co-creator: the freedom that characterizes the created co-creator and his culture is an instrument God uses to have creation participate in the intentional fulfilment of God's purposes (1993: 265). God's purposes are not only that the creation will freely acknowledge its creator and fulfil the will of the creator in freedom, but also that the human being as co-creator will help build a future that is wholesome for all of nature (43f., 264).

How does Hefner deal with the problem of natural evil? Given his accent on human freedom that has arisen through the process of evolution, he justifies evil by means of an elaboration on the 'free will defence'. If humans are to choose freely, it is logically inevitable that they also have the possibility of choosing evil. The free will defence is primarily concerned with moral evil but not with natural evil, which is the issue here. Therefore it must be developed further into a theodicy in which natural evil is justified. This has been done by Hick as well as by others. Hefner endorses Hick's theodicy in his *The Human Factor* (1993: 44). He holds with Hick that evil is inevitable in the evolutionary process in connection with the origination of human freedom and personhood (1993: 271). To understand his argument, we need to take a closer look at Hick's theodicy of evil.

A creation with free human beings implies not only the possibility of moral evil, according to Hick, but God also allows natural evil precisely in connection with human freedom. Hick (1981) proposes the following:

1   It is the divine intention to create perfect, finite beings in a personal relation with their creator.

2   Because we can enter *freely* into a relation with God and can freely choose between good and evil, it is logically impossible for human beings to be created immediately into this perfect state of a personal relationship with God.

3   Therefore the human being is created via the process of evolution as a spiritually and morally immature being as a part of a world that is

both religiously ambiguous as well as ethically challenging for good moral acts.

4 Moral and natural evil are necessary aspects for the current stage of the process in which God creates perfect finite persons via a gradual development.

5 The process of 'person-making' is completed only when all people have a perfect relationship with their creator.

Without discussing these points extensively, I raise the following objections:

1 The justification of natural evil lies in that it occurs for the greater good (human freedom). Natural evil is defended here on the basis of its service to an end. Natural evil exists for the sake of something else: the human choice between good and evil and its consequences. But does every evil have such a reason to exist? Does this answer to the question of why truly explain the reality of evil? Questions like these strengthen the following objection.

2 Does an *excess* of natural evil not outweigh the good (human free choice) that it serves? The following objection coheres closely with this.

3 Is evil not discussed *in an abstract way*? Someone who has been affected by serious natural evil will not be convinced by Hick's argument for the inevitability of the reality of natural evil.

In short, God places us in a dangerous world with natural evil in which mutual care and love can arise. Within such a world we are on the way to the Realm of God in which all people live in a loving relationship with God. Hick emphasizes the *eschatological* dimension. The process of evolution and natural evil are assessed from the perspective of an alleged perfect end. Hefner (1993: 43) considers this eschatological dimension indispensable for the justification of natural evil: 'The conditioning matrix that is constituted by evolutionary processes is understood by Christian faith, however, not simply in terms of what it has been and is now, but in terms of what it can become, and what it can become in the light of God's intentions.' Hick and Hefner thus provide a *theistic teleology* in which insight into the whole from the beginning to the completion of the world is given.

The teleological argument is used here in two ways: as the argument of natural evil as a means for serving the greater good of freedom and of the 'person-making' of the human being and also from the perspective of the whole of creation, and the final state of the Realm of God. It would require too much space to go into the issue of how this final situation is represented. I will limit myself to the question of the validity of the use of a theistic teleology concerning the justification of natural evil. This use of teleology is, in my view, problematic.

I will first say something about teleology in general. As is well known, since the modern period a teleological view of nature has been both disputed as well as defended (Spaemann and Löw 1985). If a causal explanation of nature is the only one that has any validity, the question as to the purpose of our knowledge of nature would vanish. Empirical facts could no longer be connected to the ultimate meaning of the facts in the way in which Hefner does that in *The Human Factor*. Mental processes ask for an explanation of values, according to Keith Ward (2003). That is why they defend a teleological view of nature: a teleological explanation of nature as a complement to the causal explanation of nature.

A teleological view of human beings and nature can be defended on the following grounds:

1   The human being does not live by scientific knowledge alone but also by 'successful contact with values that transcend him' (De Dijn 1993: 40). In addition to science there is also religion, the attribution of meaning and world-views. A religion such as the Christian religion claims to state how things truly are. I will show below that teleology must be more closely specified, if it is intended to provide answers to questions of meaning and the attribution of meaning.

2   A causal explanation always stands in the context of the action of the researcher in question. Causality cannot be conceived, according to the thesis of the so-called interventionist theory of causality, without a teleological moment. This entails that every causal interpretation of an event presumes that we actively 'whether in fact or mentally' influence event A, change it and then establish (or consider) what happens with B (Spaemann and Löw 1985: 245f.).

3   The ecological crisis requires a different approach from a one-sided causal explanation of nature which has given rise to much violence against nature. Hefner provides such an approach in his *The Human Factor*.

4   A theological reason is that speaking of God's purpose for the creation is given in the Christian view of creation.

We should understand that the teleological view of nature is of a different order from the causal view. It does not entail prediction and is given *a posteriori* or as a draft of a future development. It rests on the interest of reason. That can be a theoretical interest, as we see in Ward; Ward provides us with a teleological metaphysics. It can also be of practical interest. That is the case with Hefner's theory of the created co-creator.

To acknowledge the justification of a teleological view of nature, as Hefner proposes in *The Human Factor*, does not, in my view, imply that natural evil needs to be justified within this scheme. I consider that to be problematic.

The question of (natural) evil is a question that belongs to the area of the attribution of meaning. The attribution of meaning is the interpretation of existence as such, successful contact with values that transcend us. Insights into fundamental questions such as that of natural evil play a role in this. Evil can, after all, so overwhelm us that the contact with transcendent values fails. We then bid God and perhaps life farewell. I wish to state that questions of meaning, such as that of natural evil, are *existential questions*, questions that have to do with an interest in *attributing meaning*. That is an interest, as I have defended elsewhere, that must be distinguished from the theoretical and the practical interest, even if it is connected to them (Stoker 1996: 11f.). With regard to ascription of meaning, purposes are often spoken of, but one must ask what is meant by purposes? A distinction can be made between *external teleology*, something that is a means for something else, something that is good or of value for something else, and *internal teleology*, something as an end in itself, something (relatively) unconditional, something good or of value in itself. In the interest of the attribution of meaning the concern is primarily internal teleology: something is good or of value in itself. If such contact with something good in itself succeeds, then one can speak of an experience of meaning. It concerns matters that are ends in themselves, values such as love, justice, the enjoyment of art, of striving to be God's co-creator. Where the attribution of meaning is spoken of in terms of means and ends, it often concerns the pseudo attribution of meaning. A relation is not a true relation in which the other is seen only as a means to an end, for example entering into marriage in order to acquire the other's inheritance after their death. We can actively position ourselves over against something of value outside ourselves, but whenever we use that as a means to an end, then we do not recognize that in an experience of meaning we have to do with something that is (relatively) unconditional.

In short, the attribution of meaning concerns successful contact with values or ends in themselves that transcend us and not an external teleology, a means/end relation. I will show this by considering the question why there is natural evil. Such a question can in my view not be answered by external teleology.

Let us look, for example, at Hick's theodicy. He portrays the development in the world of humans and nature as a road that leads to the perfect end. The adversities experienced while underway are responded to by the remark that they are means to an end. Natural evil is ascribed value (*sic*) in connection with our soul-making and with the final end of our journey. Thus the meaning of life is discussed in terms of means and ends. The attribution of meaning is viewed in terms of a chain of reference (Stoker 1996: 170–4). The final whole, the perfect state is the ultimate justification for the reality of natural evil under which people now suffer. Thus insights into the questions of life overshoot their goal in connection with the meaning of life.

Let me give another explanation of the image of the road. This certainly leads somewhere for the Christian, but the stages along the road are not only a means to the end. Each stage on the road has its end in itself, its meaning in itself. A mountain path reveals panoramas at every step that are worthwhile in themselves, regardless of the fact of whether the path leads to the top. The issue is that natural evil affects people precisely in their experience of meaning at a certain stage of the journey of life, and then insights about evil as a means to an end do not suffice. The reason is that the attribution of meaning has to do with internal teleology and not external teleology. The present stage of the road can be its meaning, its value can be in losing itself because of an excess of natural evil. Hefner's example of natural evil uses the means/end relation, and for that reason I consider it less convincing. I will add two more objections to this.

From a shocking experience with (natural) evil questions emerge that have more the character of a protest than that of a search for insight. Job came to a renewed contact with values that transcended him not through a teleological rationalization but through the recognition of the character of mystery that evil has. The reality of natural evil is recognized in Scripture. Sometimes Scripture makes a connection between moral evil and natural evil (Genesis 3) and sometimes provides no reason for the reality of natural evil, as in the wisdom of Ecclesiastes and Job. Dys-teleological natural evil and suffering also exist. This view stands perpendicular to any function-alist reasoning regarding evil such as: if we do not understand unruly reality, then we need to understand that it is a stage on the road to an all comprehensive whole, the perfect end. But there are seeds that die and do not bear any fruit. There is something that does not square in this reality. The absurd is a category of life.

Finally, by referring as Hick does to creation as a whole, to the supposed perfect end of morally perfect people in a personal relation with God, one claims to have *insight into the whole*. This theodicy posits the acceptance of natural evil *for the sake* of an end that is hoped for. Natural evil is viewed as a means for soul-making, a process that is only completed at the end. As far as this insight into the whole is concerned, God poses the following questions to Job:

> Where were you when I laid the earth's foundation?
> Tell me, if you understand. (38:4)
> Have you comprehended the vast expanses of the earth?
> Tell me, if you know all this. (38:18)

'God's design,' remarks Ricoeur about Job's newly acquired insights into evil, 'is removed from any transcription in terms of a plan or a program; in short, of finality and teleology. What is revealed is the possibility of hope in spite of ... This possibility may still be expressed in terms of a design, but of an unassignable design, a design which is God's secret' (Ricoeur 1980: 87).

In short, insights into questions of meaning such as that of natural evil are not adequately answered by means of the means/end response. The attribution and experience of meaning concern primarily internal teleology rather than external teleology. In addition, with such an answer we ignore the fact that there is also pointless natural evil. Moreover, human knowledge is limited and we do not have insight into the details of God's plan for this world.

God, human beings and nature as a communion

Serious experiences of natural evil invoke questions that do not have the character of a search for insight in which teleology can be of help. The why question concerning evil has the character of a protest. The adequate answer is the struggle against evil. Therefore I will argue for a practical theodicy, in which I will indicate how God is involved in the process of evolution and natural evil without *wanting and being able to answer the why question of natural evil*. Kierkegaard's remark on omnipotence and evil (see above) requires supplementation. A God who only tolerates something independent alongside Himself could also be a deistic God who withdraws Himself from the world after a creation in the beginning. Hence this supplement with respect to the way in which God, according to a Christian theology, is involved in the evolutionary process with its natural evil.

Prigogine, in connection with the 'thermodynamics of life', points to dissipative structures (Van der Veken 1990: 40f; see also De Boer 1989 88–94). According to the second law of thermodynamics we live in a universe in which differences in energy are increasingly being levelled. Everything tends towards entropy, the loss of order. Nevertheless, evolution goes in precisely the other direction: not towards chaos but towards order. There are phenomena which appear in open systems, of a physical, chemical or biological nature, which remain far removed from the state of balance. Evolution chooses the way of the improbable. The local vulnerable increase in order is possible only if use is made of the all-ruling entropy. It concerns a dissipative structure. The continuing existence of that structure goes together with dissipation or with increasing disorder elsewhere in the system. Plants make use of the increasing entropy in their environment, and in their own existence suppress entropy. Every state of order appears to have to be fought for: hence the title of the English translation of Prigogines' book, *Order out of Chaos*.

If I interpret these scientific facts theologically, then I see nature in its ambiguity as an order that goes against the stream of disorder. There is an opposite side to order. Only if I see the shadow side, can I, with De Boer, see a reflection in the evolutionary process of a divine strategy that, as Paul says, 'makes its strength perfect in weakness' (De Boer 1989: 94). The human being is a fellow-sufferer with nature. With plants and animals we experience a fleeting victory over the powers of disintegration. Like Hefner and Tillich, I would also emphasize the communion of nature and human beings. Tillich comes to this communion of human beings and nature on the basis of an idealistic philosophy of identity and Hefner on the basis of the facts of the natural sciences.

Therefore, redemption is not only a matter of the human being alone but of the human being and nature. Human beings and nature are each other's fellow-sufferers. Tillich (1964: 89) states in a sermon that the tragedy of nature is bound to the tragedy of man, as the salvation of nature is dependent on the salvation of man: 'man and nature belong together in their created glory, in their tragedy and in their salvation'. Because the human being is a creature of nature, the redemption through Christ, the true man, obtains also for nature: 'Therefore, Jesus is called the Son of Man, the man from above, the true man in whom the forces of separation and tragedy are overcome, not only in mankind but also in the universe. For there is no salvation of nature, for man is in nature and nature is in man.'

References

De Boer, T. (1989) *De God van de filosofen*, 's-Gravenhage: Meinema.

De Dijn, H. (1993) *Hoe overleven wij de vrijheid?*, Kapellen/Kampen: Pelckmans/Kok Agora.

Hefner, P. (1993) *The Human Factor: Evolution, Culture, and Religion*, Minneapolis: Fortress Press.

—— (2000) 'Natural Evil: the Continuing Theological Challenge', *Word & World*, Supplement Series 4, 119.

Hick, J. (1981) 'An Irenaean Theodicy', in S.T. Davis (ed.) *Encountering Evil*, Atlanta: Westminster/John Knox Press.

Jahr, H. (1994) 'Tillichs Theologie der Natur als Theologie der Versöhnung von Geist und Natur', in G. Hummel (ed.) *Natural Theology versus Theology of Nature?*, Berlin/New York: De Gruyter, 156–83.

Kierkegaard, S. (1958) *The Journals of Kierkegaard*, edited with an introduction by Alexander Dru, New York: Harper Torchbooks.

Ricoeur, P. (1980) 'Towards a Hermeneutic of the Idea of Revelation', in P. Ricoeur, *Essays of Biblical Interpretation*, ed. A.S. Mudge, Philadelphia: Fortress Press.

Spaemann, R. and Löw, R. (1985) *Die Frage wozu? Geschichte und Wiederentdeckung des teleologischen Denkens*, Munich/ Zurich: Piper.

Stoker, W. (1996) *Is the Quest for Meaning the Quest for God?*, Amsterdam/Atlanta: Rodopi.

—— (1999) 'Can the God of the Philosophers and the God of Abraham be Reconciled?', in G. Hummel and D. Lax (eds) *Being versus Word in Paul Tillich's Theology*, Berlin/New York: De Gruyter, 206–24.

Tillich, P. (1930) 'Natur und Geist im Protestantismus', in P. Albrecht (ed.) *Gesammelte Werke*, vol. XIII, Stuttgart: Evangelisches Verlagswerk, 95–102.

—— (1964) *The Shaking of the Foundations*, Harmondsworth: Penguin Books.

—— (1986) *Systematic Theology*, Volume 1, London: J. Nisbet & Co.

Van der Veken, J. (1990) *Een kosmos om in te leven*, Kapellen/Kampen: DNB/Kok Agora.

Ward, K. (2003) 'Two forms of explanation', in Willem B. Drees (ed.) *Is Nature Ever Evil? Religion, Science and Value*, London: Routledge, 247–64.

24

THE QUEST FOR PERFECTION
Insights from Paul Tillich

Eduardo R. Cruz

> People are religious to the extent that they believe themselves
> to be not so much *imperfect*, as ill. Any man who is halfway
> decent will think himself extremely imperfect, but a religious
> man thinks himself *wretched*.
>
> Ludwig Wittgenstein, *Culture and Value* (45e)[1]

That there is a drive for human perfection is an undeniable fact of
everyday life. The Olympic games are there to confirm this, especially for
those activities that involve a score. Who does not recall Nadia
Comanecci, the perfect ten in 1976? But this drive is especially visible
today in areas where, until a few years ago, ideals of perfection were only
a dream. Among them, we may cite plastic surgery, gene correction, artificial life, and the like. The turn to the year 2000 also brought some
interesting reports in the media concerning the future to be yielded by
science and technology, where some present yearnings for perfection
would be fulfilled. So what we see at the brink of the twenty-first century
is an increase not only of the drive for perfection, but also in the means to
accomplish it.

Yet, some of the fears that we are repeating errors of the past, and that
part of this renewed fascination with perfection may be related to busi-
ness-oriented interests, are also present in contemporary authors. The
increase in the desire for perfection may foster new Utopias, and new
'perfect systems,' as we have seen in the recent past, may enslave more
than liberate human beings.

Important as these social concerns may be, they are almost harmless
when compared to our existential situation as being the outcome of an
evolutionary history. First, there is the danger recognized by scientists that
'fooling around' with our genome or our acquired traits as an organism
may be deleterious for individuals and the species as a whole. More importantly, however, at least from a philosophical and a theological perspective,
is the clash between the intrinsically goal-oriented drive for perfection and
the purposelessness of the evolutionary process. Apart from the scientific

214

question of whether (and how) we may speak about a *telos* in nature at all (for a good assessment of the question see Ruse 2000), there is the question of the mismatch between natural processes and our dreams of perfection and their metaphysical, anthropological, and ethical overtones – a mismatch that many twentieth-century authors have called our 'estrangement' from nature.

The purpose of this paper is to comment on a few philosophical and theological aspects of these questions, resorting to some ill-explored (in recent times) facets of the doctrine of original sin. Then I am going to suggest that Paul Tillich's notion of the 'ambiguity of perfection' is a good way to bridge the perception that the processes of nature are blind and the conviction that the quest for perfection is purposeful.

Taking seriously the purposelessness of nature

In a previous paper of mine (Cruz 2001), I have argued against deducing univocally any purpose or benevolence in nature, supposedly ascertained by the sciences, from the Goodness of Creation. The message that we receive from nature, both in daily experience and in scientific knowledge, is ambiguous: we may turn our attention either to its bounty and aptitude for life, or to its ruthlessness. Traditional theology has had special difficulty with the latter aspect. It spoke of 'natural disasters', occasional events that have a particular impact on nature, but almost ignored the bare fact of 'life living on life'. In doing so, it left aside the perception enhanced by modern evolutionary studies that nature is 'cruel' in its ordinary processes. Both for ontogenetic and phylogenetic purposes, killing other living beings is the rule, not the exception. The quotation marks around the cruel have a purpose: from an evolutionary perspective, nature could not care less about the fate of individuals and species. Richard Dawkins (e.g., Dawkins 1986) likes to put his finger on this particular trait of evolution, and we had better pay attention to it.

As is well known, traditional theology has followed the Augustinian synthesis on original sin. So, whatever cruelty is found in nature, it is always ascribed to Adam's disobedience. Nature (indistinguishable from Creation) was good and purposeful, because God could not create anything less than perfect, and will be re-established to its pristine state only in the Parousia. Incredible as this view has become in the face of contemporary knowledge, it still takes sin and evil quite seriously, rejecting by the same token any law of progressivism.

Augustine, moreover, keeps his relevance by reminding us of human self-deception. In the past century or so theologians have devised ingenious ways to account for the continuity of creation, 'fall,' and redemption. They have done so by uncovering and expanding on the Christological, Trinitarian, and eschatological layers of the Doctrine of

Creation and Providence. This is surely the right move, and this new path is certainly yielding its fruits. Yet, it may be asked whether it has not been done at a price, namely, giving up the universal neoplatonic framework in which the Doctrine was originally formulated, and by the same token 'covering up' the unfathomable depths and amount of suffering and 'evil' in nature. Indeed, after removing the guilt of Adam, and nonetheless exempting God from any responsibility for this state of affairs, it is hard to develop a credible 'theology of cruelty,' in accordance with data and explanations from evolutionary theory, and then match it with a 'theology of perfection.' After all, specifically Christian doctrines are good at accounting for the grace of God and His/Her benevolence toward nature and human beings alike, leaving natural evil in a certain cloud of mystery.

It seems to be desirable, therefore, to retrieve from obscurity certain aspects of the old account that have been embarrassing to modern theology, and to try to give an adequate interpretation to them. Take, for example, the 'state of original justice', its relationship to perfection, and how suffering and 'cruelty' entered into the world. What follows below are but a few indications of the issues at stake.

Perfection as a theme for scientific and theological reflection

Contemporary science has a dubious stance regarding human perfectibility. On the one hand, scientists gladly provide popularizers and journalists with stuff that lead us to think that science and technology are the only venue for perfection in the future. On the other hand, based on past experiences (as hinted at in my introduction), they are the first to disavow any attempt to base perfectibilistic Utopias on the findings of science. Grounded on the most recent of the latter, they can be very explicit in this respect (e.g., Ridley 1996: ch. 14). Yet, it is precisely in this kind of finding, through evolutionary psychology, neurosciences, and the like, that a nexus can be found from what has blindly come from the past to the future-oriented pursuit of perfection, so as to eventually produce a single scientific account of both seemingly contradictory histories. As an interpretation of these findings would take us well beyond the limits of this chapter, we will turn our attention to the theological underpinnings of these counter-movements of blindness and purpose.

It is at least curious to notice that, considering the importance that words such as 'perfect' and 'perfection' have played in the history of theology, how little has been said on the subject in contemporary developments. It seems that Adolf von Harnack was right after all, when he said that Christian doctrines had been overburdened with Greek categories in patristic times. Charles Hartshorne, a renowned process philosopher, does give an extensive discussion on 'perfection' (Hartshorne 1962). Yet, alas, he also thinks that Greek classical views have impaired the Semitic tradition in this respect. Wittgenstein's epigraph at the beginning is a sort of anticipation (as much of contemporary theology is influenced by him) of this state of mind. We have reason to believe, however, that the Judaeo-Christian tradition does provide bridges between a 'religious man' and a 'man who is halfway decent'!

Anyhow, the scriptures do not have many references to perfection (*teleios* [perfect] occurs about twenty times in the Septuagint, the Greek translation of the Hebrew Bible, and twenty more in the New Testament), the most famous of them occurring in Matthew 5:48: 'Be ye therefore perfect, even as your Father which is in heaven is perfect.' The embarrassment about perfection is so great that some versions of the Bible prefer other renderings, sometimes awkward, of this passage. The New English Bible, for example, has: 'There must be no limits to your goodness, as your heavenly Father's goodness knows no bounds.' But the limited number of references to perfection does not mean that the notion is unimportant to a biblical outlook – see the Qumranic usage of *t_mîn*, 'to be complete.' In any case, meeting with the Greco-Roman civilization meant to the Fathers the adoption not only of standards of perfection, but also of a long tradition of reflection on what 'being perfect' means. This tradition will not be retraced here (see Passmore 1972; Rogers 2000). Suffice it to say that in the first centuries of Christianity people had to expand on assertions such as 'God is perfect,' 'Jesus Christ is perfect,' 'human beings were created perfect,' and the like. This new reflection entailed many of the controversies and heresies of those times, which circled around how these perfections were to be understood. Pelagianism was one of the most important heresies, having to do with the capacity of human beings to perfect themselves without a special grace from God.

To preserve God's sovereignty, goodness, and perfection, the theological tradition from Augustine onward had then to postulate (following many Fathers in this respect; for a somewhat different, Eastern reading see Hefner 1993: 123–38) that Adam had been created in a state of Original Justice, having preternatural gifts that would be his special marks in his being the image and likeness of God, vis-à-vis the merely natural gifts with which the rest of the natural world had been endowed when created. These are infused knowledge, integrity, and immortality. However, it is certainly incredible, from our vantage point, to picture that in a remote past a first couple represented the Greek ideal: unambiguous, rational knowledge of whatever needed to be known; perfect, rational control over their sensuous nature; and absence of the suffering and bodily decay that leads to human death.[2] Even more incredible, from a Christological perspective, is to imagine that, in a way, the wrong doing of Adam was stronger than the redemption accomplished by Christ: Adam's sin immediately led to distortion and imperfection of the entire human race, whereas

Christ's death left us on probation, as it were, so that we would have to wait until the Parousia to have the preternatural gifts back!

Incredible as it is, however, this doctrine deserves perhaps more than ostracism: there is implied in it the confidence in human reason to unveil essential traits of the human being in the midst of contradictory phenomena (especially in Thomas Aquinas); it reminds us that we are the products of lawful, ordered structures; it is likely to provide us with some standards of perfection, to help us to understand why we engage so earnestly in the pursuit of perfection, and to challenge us to seek a better bridge between the apparent lack of concern for perfectibility in natural processes, and our own drive for perfection. So suffused as it is with Greek thought, the notion of 'preternatural gifts' is perhaps more adequate to provide for this bridge than the more parochial renderings of the doctrine of Creation in Christological, Trinitarian, and eschatological terms.

I am not denying that the doctrine of original sin must be understood against the yardstick of these other doctrines. As a Christian, I fully agree with a commentator on Karl Barth who says that: 'The fathomless depth of sin can only be glimpsed under the tutelage of the redeemer' (Anderson 2000: 39). Yet, if we come for a dialogue with other religions and the sciences only with these doctrines in hand, we will not only be misunderstood, but also leave behind other aspects of Judaeo-Christian philosophical and theological resources that could work better in the way of a dialogue, if appropriately interpreted.

Paul Tillich on perfection and perfectibilism

As a good modern theologian, Paul Tillich has little to say on the 'preternatural gifts' of Adam, and treats them solely in a negative manner. The main passage is this:

> It [a state of dreaming innocence] is not perfection. Orthodox theologians have heaped perfection after perfection upon Adam before the Fall, making him equal with the picture of the Christ. This procedure is not only absurd; it makes the Fall completely unintelligible. Mere potentiality or dreaming innocence is not perfection. Only the conscious union of existence and essence is perfection, as God is perfect because he transcends essence and existence.
>
> (Tillich 1957: 34)

In a positive manner, we may draw from this short passage three aspects of Tillich's thought. First, he retains the idea of perfection in his conceptual scheme: God is perfect and so is Jesus Christ, making human perfection a possibility and a vocation. Second, he provides us, here and in other parts of his works, with a coherent picture of human essence 'from the past' (see the reference to 'the ontological elements' below). Third, and more important, there is how he regards human beings in the stream of natural processes. Humans are placed in continuity with the rest of nature, in a specific dimension that emerges in evolutionary history:

> Man is the creature in which the ontological elements are complete. They are incomplete in all creatures, which (for this very reason) are called 'subhuman.' Subhuman does not imply less perfection than in the case of the human. On the contrary, man as the essentially threatened creature cannot compare with the natural perfection of the subhuman creatures.
>
> (Tillich 1951: 260)

By 'natural perfection' is not meant that the natural world is flawless and nice. He has in mind the teleological perfection of Aristotle and Aquinas, that is, the actualization of potentialities, from natural entities to humans. In another passage Tillich is more specific about what he has in mind:

> One distinguishes between lower and higher forms of life in the realm of the organic. Something must be said about this distinction from the theological point of view, because of the wide symbolic use to which all forms of organic life, especially the higher ones, are subject and because of the fact that man – against the protest of many naturalists – is often called the highest living being. First of all, one should not confuse the 'highest' with the 'most perfect.' Perfection means actualization of one's potentialities; therefore, a lower being can be more perfect than a higher one if it is actually what is potentially – at least in a high approximation. And the highest being – man – can become less perfect than any other, because he not only can fail to actualize his essential being but can deny and distort it.
>
> (Tillich 1963a: 35–6)

Is there a place in this scheme for suffering, cruelty, and evil in nature? Yes, for as we have argued elsewhere (Cruz 1997), nature is not 'innocent' (it is important to emphasize this point in an age of ecological romanticism), and participates in whatever evil inclinations humans display. How can we reconcile the assertion made before, endorsed by most biologists, that nature is neither 'cruel' nor 'nice', with this more anthropomorphic view of Tillich? By recognizing that its perfection is ambivalent. In fact, one of the most original contributions of this author to contemporary thought is his extensive discussion of the 'ambiguity of perfection,' both at the natural and the social levels. As Tillich suggests:

Theology should not take the consequences of these insights [even the most sublime functions of the spirit are rooted in the vital trends of human nature] too lightly; they are, indeed, most serious in their effect on the image of perfection .... He who admits the vital dynamics in man as a necessary element in all his self expressions (his passions or his *eros*) must know that he has accepted life in its divine–demonic ambiguity and that it is the triumph of the Spiritual Presence to draw these depths of human nature into its sphere .... There is no nicety in the images of perfection in the saints of the Catholic Church or in representatives of the new piety of the Reformation. He who tries to avoid the demonic side of the holy also misses its divine side and gains but a deceptive security between them. The image of perfection is the man who, in the battlefield between the divine and the demonic, prevails against the demonic, though fragmentarily and in anticipation. This is the experience in which the image of perfection under the impact of the Spiritual Presence transcends the humanistic ideal of perfection. It is not a negative attitude to human potentialities that produces the contrast but the awareness of the undecided struggle between the divine and the demonic in every man, which in humanism is replaced by the ideal of harmonious self-actualization.

(Tillich 1963a: 241)

Tillich goes beyond, therefore, the tradition of teleological perfection, which in modern times has taken the shape of progressivistic theories.[3] He places the drive for perfection (most clearly seen in the human realm, enhanced by our quest for freedom) within the framework of a philosophy of religion, which is itself less parochial than specific Christian doctrines. It is true that at this point he is dealing with Spiritual Presence, which is little more than a rationalization of the doctrine of the Holy Spirit, leading us to the realm of redemption, which is beyond the scope of our concerns here. Most important is that this philosophy of religion (as presented, for example, in Tillich [1925] 1969) may function as one of the bridges between a 'theology of cruelty' and a 'theology of perfection.' This philosophy has drawn from Augustine an important insight: as finite and fallen creatures we are bound to deception: what we take for perfection may as well be demonic distortion (the dialectical tension should be kept: perfect it still is, but in a destructive and enslaving manner). On the other hand, what we regard as imperfect may reveal itself to be perfect. One is reminded of 1 Corinthians. Rolston has developed this point in an insightful and poignant manner when, in seeing nature as 'cruciform,' he interprets the presence of suffering and the simultaneity of good and evil in kenotic terms. In the language of perfection, he asserts the following: 'It is the imperfection that drives the world toward perfection, the disvalue that is necessary in the search for more value' (Rolston 2003: 71; see also Rolston 1987: 286–93; 1994). However, we may question his kenotic outlook: it seems to us that God's positive attributes are threatened on this view. Moreover, the way of the cross is not paved by suffering only. It is a paradoxical way, revealing to us a two-storied world, as Hegel pointed out in some of his writings.

This ordered yet paradoxical character of reality, coupled with human self-deception (ontological and epistemological traits being discussed by contemporary science), places an important proviso on our ideas of perfection, including those arising from the realm of science. However excellent and thorough scientific findings may be, this fundamental ambiguity will not be removed from our consciousness.

Conclusion

Toward the end of his life Paul Tillich faced a very select audience, on the occasion of the fortieth anniversary of *Time* magazine (May 6, 1963). The title of his address was 'The Ambiguity of Perfection,' from which we quote one of its most significant excerpts (on ambiguity see also Cruz 1996):

> It is my conviction that the character of the human condition, like the character of all life, is 'ambiguity': the inseparable mixture of good and evil, of true and false, of creative and destructive forces – both individual and social.
>
> (Tillich 1963b: 69)

There was certainly a note of irony in his choice, for before him was the best of what American perfection could offer in terms of human resources. He also meant perfection – which he did not deny was achievable (even though 'fragmentarily and in anticipation') – in the Platonic trinitarian scheme: the True, the Good, and the Beautiful. 'Life,' on the other hand, is not restricted to the organic realm, but includes all that is subject to the evolutionary process (starting from the 'Big Bang') and involves creativity and destructivity, order and chaos, life and death (see Cruz 1995 for a more thorough explanation).

Ambiguity (or ambivalence) does not deny that perfection is there – it simply asserts that it is also 'not there.' Tragedies of old Greece help us to understand one of the crucial aspects of this ambiguity: the nobler and more god-like the being or the action, the more it is liable to a fall (see also Cruz 2003). There is no intrinsic conflict therefore (even though I agree it is hard to conceptualize it) between a nature that does not care for our ideals of truth, goodness, and beauty – yet displays many impressive examples of perfection – and our quest for perfection, beyond and even against any immediate need for survival. The notion of the 'preternatural gifts' accounts for what, within nature and without any immediate appeal to Christological mediation, makes the difference between humans and the rest of creation. In a fallen state they are not immediately accessible to us, so we have to strive and long for them. Purposelessness – in nature and in human existence – is not at odds with this drive for perfection: if it is a reflection of the state of estrangement from God's purpose, it is also an opportunity to exercise freedom, both on our behalf and on behalf of nature, as well as to hope for the coming of God's Redeemer.

Notes

1   I am borrowing this epigraph from Stanley Hauerwas's excellent essay 'Sinsick' (Hauerwas 2000: 7). This aphorism by Wittgenstein is enigmatic enough to allow for more than one interpretation, and I think Hauerwas's interpretation is the opposite of mine: religious thinking, as can be drawn from what follows, does account for both imperfection and wretchedness.

2   Yet, the writers of the new *Catechism of the Catholic Church* decided to stay on the conservative side at this point. The relevant paragraphs deserve to be quoted in their entirety, as they give us a nice summary of the doctrine of the 'state of original justice':

374. The first man was not only created good, but was also established in friendship with his Creator and in harmony with himself and with the creation around him, in a state that would be surpassed only by the glory of the new creation in Christ.

375. The Church, interpreting the symbolism of biblical language in an authentic way, in the light of the New Testament and Tradition, teaches that our first parents, Adam and Eve, were constituted in an original 'state of holiness and justice'. [DS 1511.] This grace of original holiness was 'to share in divine life'.

376. By the radiance of this grace all dimensions of man's life were confirmed. As long as he remained in the divine intimacy, man would not have to suffer or die. The inner harmony of the human person, the harmony between man and woman, and finally the harmony between the first couple and all creation, comprised the state called 'original justice'.

377. The 'mastery' over the world that God offered man from the beginning was realized above all within man himself: mastery of self. The first man was unimpaired and ordered in his whole being because he was free from the triple concupiscence that subjugates him to the pleasures of the senses, covetousness for earthly goods, and self-assertion, contrary to the dictates of reason.

378. The sign of man's familiarity with God is that God places him in the garden. There he lives 'to till it and keep it'. Work is not yet a burden, but rather the collaboration of man and woman with God in perfecting the visible creation.

379. This entire harmony of original justice, foreseen for man in God's plan, will be lost by the sin of our first parents.

As the text refers to 'creation', not to 'nature', it is still vested in symbolic language, in need of interpretation. Note the reference to perfectibility, in para. 378.

3   Perhaps the major difference between the humanistic outlook (if we are allowed this degree of generalization) and the Augustinian one is the role of human will. A 'bound will' is also bound to deception concerning our capabilities and accomplishments. Rolston here offers a kenotic alternative: 'The Creator is present, perfecting his creation through suffering. "For it was fitting that he, for whom and by whom all things exist, in bringing many sons to glory, should make the pioneer of their salvation perfect through suffering" [Hebr. 2, 10]' (1987: 327). We are not arguing for an either/or view of perfection, but rather sorting out the basic differences between them. For a criticism of the 'humanistic outlook,' see also Shattuck (1996).

References

Anderson, G.A. (2000) 'Necessarium Adae Peccatum: the Problem of Original Sin', in C.E. Braaten and R.W. Jenson (eds.) *Sin, Death, and the Devil*, Grand Rapids, MI: W.B. Eerdmans, 22–44.

Cruz, E.R. (1995) 'On the Relevance of Paul Tillich's Concept of Ontological Life and Its Ambiguity', in F.J. Parrella (ed.) *Paul Tillich's Theological Legacy: Spirit and Community*, Berlin/New York: Walter de Gruyter, 118–24.

—— (1996) *A Theological Study Informed by the Thought of Paul Tillich and the Latin American Experience: the Ambivalence of Science*, Lewiston, NY: Mellen University Press.

—— (1997) 'Is Nature Innocent? Reflections on Niebuhr and Tillich', in N.H. Gregersen, M.W. Parsons, and C. Wassermann (eds.) *The Concept of Nature in Science and Theology (part I)*, Geneva: Labor et Fides, 215–24.

—— (2001) 'Paul Tillich's Realistic Stance Toward the Vital Trends of Nature', *Zygon: Journal of Religion and Science* 36 (2 June): 327–34.

—— (2003) 'Tragedy versus Hope?', Chapter 16 in this volume.

Dawkins, R. (1986) *The Blind Watchmaker*, Harlow: Longman.

Hartshorne, C. (1962) *The Logic of Perfection*, LaSalle, IL: Open Court.

Hauerwas, S. (2000) 'Sinsick', in C.E. Braaten and R.W. Jenson (eds.) *Sin, Death, and the Devil*, Grand Rapids, MI: W.B. Eerdmans, 7–21.

Hefner, P. (1993) *The Human Factor: Evolution, Culture, and Religion*, Minneapolis: Fortress Press.

—— (2003) 'Nature Good and Evil: A Theological Palette', Chapter 22 in this volume.

Passmore, J. (1972) *The Perfectibility of Man*, London: Gerald Duckworth.

Ridley, M. (1996) *The Origins of Virtue*, New York: Penguin.

Rogers, K.A. (2000) *Perfect Being Theology*, Edinburgh: Edinburgh University Press.

Rolston III, H. (1987) *Science and Religion: A Critical Survey*, New York: Random House.

—— (1994) 'Does Nature Need to be Redeemed?', *Zygon: Journal of Religion and Science* 29: 206–229.

—— (2003) 'Naturalizing and Systematizing Evil', Chapter 8 in this volume.

Ruse, M. (2000) 'Teleology: Yesterday, Today, and Tomorrow?', *Studies in History and Philosophy of Biological and Biomedical Sciences* 31: 213–32.

Shattuck, R. (1996) *Forbidden Knowledge: From Prometheus to Pornography*, New York: St. Martin's Press.

Tillich, P. (1951) *Systematic Theology*, Vol. I, Chicago: The University of Chicago Press.

—— (1957) *Systematic Theology*, Vol. II, Chicago: The University of Chicago Press.

—— (1963a) *Systematic Theology*, Vol. III, Chicago: The University of Chicago Press.

—— (1963b) 'The Ambiguity of Perfection', *Time*, 17 May 1963: 69.

—— ([1925] 1969) *What is Religion?*, edited with an introduction by J.L. Adams, New York: Harper & Row.

Wittgenstein, L. (1984) *Culture and Value*, edited by G.H. von Wright, translated by Peter Winch, Chicago: University of Chicago Press.

25

NORMATIVITY OF NATURE
Natural law in a technological life-world

Mathew Illathuparampil

Keeping in view the presumption that science views nature as neutral and the humanities tend to view it evaluatively, this chapter tries to answer the question whether the progress of science and technology weakens the purported evaluative properties of nature. To address this issue, proposing natural law as an instance which presumes the normative properties of (human) nature, we examine whether the current technological life-world affects or even debunks the presumed foundations of natural law. Prior to addressing this question, we give a sketch of the classical contours of natural law in the first part of this chapter, and in the second part we examine how nature assumes a normative stance in natural law. In the third part of this chapter we propose that the foundations of natural law are weakened in a technological 'life-world' (an expression to be explained later) in two ways: first, the technological life-world seems to have undermined the classical consciousness of primitive culture(s) that assumed nature to be inviolable, which was fundamental to the formulation of natural law; second, the growth of science and technology diffuses the distinction between the natural and the artificial which has been a key presumption behind the developed versions of natural law.

It is almost a commonplace to grant that 'science' views nature as neutral and the humanities tend to view it in an evaluative way. Within the humanities there is an 'instance' in which nature is given not only an evaluative status, but is even accorded a *normative* stance, namely, in the natural law tradition. Natural law has found its place in the political, juridical and ethical realms, inviting both total acceptance and scathing criticism. From an historical point of view, the appeal to natural law has been decisive in the West during three distinct periods. First, natural law justified the codification of Roman law by distinguishing the civil law of a particular society from international law. In this process the Romans distinguished law enforced by power from law recognized by reason and grounded in nature. Second, natural law provided an outline for medieval ethical development and synthesizing pagan reason with Judeo-Christian revelation. Third, Thomas Hobbes and John Locke used it as a foundation for their discourse on the liberal theory of the state, which eventually led to the American and French revolutions. Though the natural law tradition had its low ebb with the rise of utilitarianism and purely rational (Kantian) theories of obligation, many have shown renewed interest in it at different times in a number of contexts. However, the question remains whether nature can claim a normative status, as has been presumed in natural law, in a predominantly technological culture which has relocated human–nature relations in many ways. Keeping this broader issue in view, this chapter seeks to address two distinct questions. First, how does nature assume a normative status in natural law? Second, does the current technological life-world affect or even debunk the presumed foundations of natural law? We would propose this inquiry as an attempt to verify whether the progress of science and technology weakens the purported evaluative properties of nature. To initiate a meaningful discussion, we begin with a brief summary of the momentous phases of the classical description of natural law.

Classical contours of natural law

Broadly speaking, from an ethical perspective, natural law refers to the view that morality derives from the nature of human beings (Hughes 1998: 47–56; Watson 1966: 65–74). This apparently simple proposition, which is in fact a conclusion drawn out of a number of differently described premises, has had many historical ramifications. In this section we try to outline the conceptual limits of natural law, restricting ourselves to the contributions of a few representative classical authors.

The early version(s) of natural law seems to start with Heraclitus (Diels 1951: 176). One of the extant fragments from Heraclitus says that 'all human laws are fed by the one divine law.' The distinction which he makes between the laws of the city and 'something superior, universal and enduring' (fragment 114) seems to represent a prefiguring of natural law. However, the *locus classicus* of natural law which has been cited by many, including Aristotle (*Rhetoric* I, 13, 1373b12; I, 15, 1375b5), is found in Sophocles' tragedy *Antigone*. The tragedy reaches its climax in Antigone's defiance of the edict forbidding burial honors to her brother. She justifies herself by invoking 'the unwritten and unfailing statutes of gods ... (whose) life is not of today or yesterday but for ever; and no one knows when they first appeared' (*Antigone* 454–60).

Plato prefers to use the expression 'law of nature,' a choice that seems to convey a paradoxical sense. In Plato's *Gorgias*, law of nature, there is meant to be a deliberate challenge and a paradox (*Gorgias*, 483e). For in antiquity there was an opposition not only between what was brought about by 'nature' (*physis*) and what was produced by human art (*techne*), but also between nature and law or custom. So natural law in itself would appear a misnomer. To divest this phrase of its paradoxical character, it was necessary for Plato to invest it with qualities taken from the domain of *nomos* or law, from the domain that is ruled by moral considerations, arrayed according to what is right and wrong. This Platonic stance had its historical antecedents. Some of the Sophists argued that the model of nature justified what instinct induced one to do; and by this argument they sought to question the ultimate validity of political laws and ethical codes (Close 1969: 468). In response to the threat of a probable moral relativism implied in this position, Plato specified the normative quality of *physis* according to the nature of each being. That means that nature prescribes a different conduct to beings animated by a spiritual soul, as distinct from other beings in nature.

Aristotle attempted no formulation of an explicit theory of natural law, nor a detailed application of it (*Rhetoric* I, 12, 1373b5). However, Aristotle's concept of nature in its medieval versions was used remarkably by Thomas Aquinas in his formulation of natural law. Thus, after considering the Thomistic idea of natural law, we will return to Aristotelian insights on nature to examine the question of how natural law theorists make a transition from nature to human nature and try to derive ethical norms from the norms of nature, which will be dealt with in the next section.

There is a general agreement that the Stoics were the first to systematize the concept of natural law. But the questions of which Stoics and what concept of natural law are not easy to answer. For the Stoic school stretches over half a millennium and includes thinkers who differ even on essential matters. Hence, we have to be satisfied with certain characteristic ideas of Stoic ethics in delineating natural law. The Stoics shared the Aristotelian vision that the universe was a rational system. Aristotle considered each individual as a self-suffient unit, operating with its own laws of development. He thought that an all-pervasive cosmic finality ordered individuals. But for the Stoics, the universe as a whole was the ultimate unit of intelligibility. With their pantheistic bent of mind, identifying God with the universe, they maintained that the universe was rational, as God was the principle of reason or *logos*. Hence, it followed that the end of man consisted in having the right relation with the universe. This would produce virtue and ensure happiness. So natural law for them was natural conformability of human nature to the rational order of the universe as a whole (Russell 1965: 438–9). Nonetheless, the Stoics do not explain the inner dynamism that drives human beings toward conformity to the universe.

St. Paul seems to have used natural law as a means to esteem the supreme value of (even 'gentile') conscience (Romans 2:14–15). Although Paul's words are suggestive of a moral law accessible to reason, it is debatable whether he had a clear conception of natural law itself. However, there is an intriguing reminder of Aristotle in the Pauline phrase about the law written in the hearts of the gentiles: 'being a law to themselves' (*heautois eisin nomos*). However, 'it is impossible to state apodictically that he [Paul] had or had not been somehow influenced by the teachings of Aristotle, but his choice of phraseology is undeniably close to that of the Stagyrite in the *Nicomachean Ethics* 1128a: "The cultivated and free minded man will behave as being a law to himself"' (Greenwood 1971: 264). In any case, the Pauline text was interpreted by early Christian authors as the textual basis of the natural law doctrine (Chroust 1946: 26–71).

Natural law got its most impressive medieval formulation from Thomas Aquinas (*ST* I–II, qq. 90–7). We can summarize the core of Thomistic natural law in four propositions: all those things to which humans have a natural inclination are good and their opposites are bad; there is a hierarchy among these inclinations, such as those for self-preservation, living in society, knowing truth about God, etc.; the most general natural law precepts are spontaneously recognized and shared by all humans; the most general precepts are unchanging and if they change at all, it would be at the lower levels of generality (Durbin 1984: 212–13). The Thomistic idea of natural law would be inadequate unless it is placed in its theological context, elucidated in terms of God's eternal law and in the context of his overriding ethical concern for the virtues. But due to the constraints of space, we will limit ourselves to this truncated version of Thomistic natural law.

From cosmos to ethos

Having given a (too) concise account of the momentous phases of the classical description of natural law, we will now address the crucial question, while referring to nature: (how) did these authors refer to human nature? Or, how did they make a transition from the natural order of things (*cosmos*) to ethical norms (*ethos*)? In other words, as we mentioned in the introduction to this chapter, how does nature assume a normative property in natural law?

To answer this question, we need to examine how (the term) nature is used by the natural law theorists; and for that purpose, we will limit our inquiry to some of the authors we have already considered. It must be remarked that nature is an ambiguous philosophical term. Michael B. Crowe holds that the word nature has been attributed dozens of meanings in different contexts (Crowe 1977: 255–6). By 'nature' we usually mean the totality of all existing things around us. The original word *phýsis* was never used as 'nature' (*natura*) in the common sense of the term, as we use it today. On the contrary, it meant a process of coming-to-be or originating (Schadewaldt 1983: 160–1).

Though Plato preferred to use the expression 'law of nature,' it is not clear how nature is attributed a normative value. However, he held that one became more *kosmois* (ordered) through a correct understanding of the *cosmos*. This would be effective only in the case of people who have a combination of philosophical knowledge and a virtuously harmonized character (Plato, *Timaeus* 47b–d, 90a–d; Gill 1995: 74). Hence, apparently Plato is unable to help us to address the question at stake.

Before Aristotle the idea of nature remained rather flexible. Aristotle identified seven meanings for the word 'nature', arguably adding to the complexity of the situation (*Metaphysics* IV. 1014b, 16ff.). But we might reduce them to three closely related but distinctive strands of meanings. For Aristotle nature broadly meant, first, the coming-to-be of beings which contain within themselves the source of motion and the power of growth (*Metaphysics* IV. 4, 1015a7); second, the essence of a developing thing or the archaic, as yet undifferentiated material ground of all coming-to-be, out of which genesis and growth come about (*Metaphysics* III. 4, 1030a3); third, the permanent, essential form of an individual thing which has reached its final form, *entelechy* (*Politics* I. 2, 1252b).

But how exactly Aristotle derived ethical conclusions from the natural order of things is much more difficult to answer. For, as Aristotle was the first Greek philosopher to distinguish ethics from physics, metaphysics and psychology, the question arises of how closely an ethical conception of human nature is integrated with those of other branches of knowledge. However, there is an overarching conception of a teleology (being for the sake of) in his metaphysics. He comes to the point of explaining organic development as 'for the sake of something' (*Physics* II. 8, 198b34–199a7). Aristotelian ethics seems to be dominated by a reference to happiness as a 'human function,' as found in *Nicomachean Ethics* 1.7. Nonetheless, it is difficult to establish a clear relation between these two aspects. Aristotle seems to have understood the idea of nature as a transcendent realm in which humans could partake, and which constituted a normative standard. This realm was both intelligible and intelligent. The apex of this intelligible/intelligent nature is God, who is thinking (*noésis*) who thinks (*noéseós*) thinking (*noésis*) (*Metaphysics*, 1074b30). Being intelligible, human beings can know nature; being intelligent, human intelligence can imitate it. It transcends human consciousness as both subject and object. That could be a reason why nature was given a normative standard.

However, it seems that how ethical ideas can be derived from the norms of nature was not a big concern for Aristotle. For according to the Aristotelian account, nature is a comprehensive term including both matter and form, nature and spirit, nature and freedom. By *cosmos* the classical Greeks understood the moral, aesthetic and, of course, the physical processes. 'Taken together, the three characteristics of Aristotle's concept of nature constituted a teleological conception that none of the later developments of each of them taken singularly ever attained. Only being simultaneously potential and norm is nature able to achieve the goal it pursues' (Dupré 1993: 27). Later generations, however, came to interpret and elaborate these meanings without keeping them in unison or their inner coherence. For instance, the idea of nature as a perfective norm came to dominate Stoic philosophy and thus the Scholastic theory of natural law as well. As Aristotle's idea of nature seems to have included theological, anthropic and physical meanings, to insist on getting a clear answer for the question of how he derived ethical norms from the norms of nature would be going beyond the intent of the Aristotelian perspective.

As a representative of Stoicism, we could consider Cicero. The crucial element in Cicero's version of natural law is that he saw a link between the standard of conduct present in nature and the use of human reason. It is good to recall that the Stoics perceived nature as a rational system. However, Cicero did not address the epistemological question of how to link these two 'reasons' found in nature and human being, and to ascertain the content of the standard found in nature. Hence, we might hold that in Cicero the link between 'natural reason' and human reason is fairly rhetorical (Weinreb 1987: 40–2).

A link between the order of nature and ethical order seems to have been suggested by Thomas. He proposed a teleological understanding of human nature which is a set of dispositional properties divided into three generic sets – living, sensitive and rational (*ST* I–II, q. 94). Perhaps the only bridge between nature and human nature seems to be that both are teleological; that means, (human) nature acts for an end. That end could be discerned by human reason, with the help of revealed truths. The rational character of human nature has a significant role in the promulgation of natural law according to Thomas. Similarly, Thomas's philosophical account of natural law presupposes the role of a supernatural ultimate end, God, in explaining natural law. Thomas seems to have discerned teleology in nature in its pre-rational inclinations. From a reflection on natural inclinations Thomas argued we could establish the inclinations characteristic of the human species: 'the natural inclination in those things devoid of reason indicates the natural inclination belonging to the will of an intellectual nature' (*ST* I 60. 5). Having made this subtle link between the pre-rational inclinations of nature which he deemed worthy of imitation by rational beings, Thomas made extensive use of this point in his ethics. For example, in his discussion of showing preference to one's kith and kin in acting out of charity, he defends it on the ground of natural inclination, arguing that the disposition of charity is both an inclination of grace and a natural appetite (*ST* II–II 26.6). He condemned suicide and self-mutilation on the grounds of going against the natural inclination of all creatures to stay alive and to keep bodily integrity (*ST* II–II 64.5; 65.1). Finally, Thomas' consideration of human sexual behavior was grounded on the natural purpose of it, understood in relation to the purpose of 'sexual' inclination in the rest of the creation. It seems that these pithy references clarify that Thomas held that nature and human nature share in a teleology – a purposive existence, out of which he drew ethical conclusions.

To arrive at a conclusive answer to the question of upon what grounds natural law theorists made a link between nature and human nature is difficult. For the content of law, of nature and of human nature (hence, of natural law too) is not identical in these authors. But what we can deduce from a joint reading of the Aristotelian and Thomistic idea of nature is that both nature and human nature have a purposive existence. This purposive existence presupposes a dynamic character, both for nature and human nature. They have a tendency to develop, to a large extent determined by their nature. But this dynamism is not blind, it is teleological. It is not an arbitrary movement. It aims at a goal – greater perfection. Any creature in nature grows, assumes its natural perfection, acquires greater powers such as strength, mobility, etc. Aristotle paid less attention to the perfection of the individual than to the perfection of the species. And the whole rational nature sees to it that all species co-exist harmoniously. There is also a consequent feature of this teleology: nature is specific. The goal toward which nature and human nature tend is specific to their characteristic nature. For instance, a human embryo cannot develop into any other organism than a human being. It is to be remarked here that while a teleology supported by internal dynamism and specificity characterize (human) nature, the absence of these features distinguishes an artefact from nature. And this aspect was relevant in the (Scholastic) formulation of natural law. For, as Jean Porter says, the Scholastic concept of natural law was grounded in the traditional distinction between the natural, the ground of human actions, and those practices and institutions that build on nature (Porter 1999: 98).

The conclusion that the recognition of a teleology in nature and in human nature is the justification for deriving ethical norms from nature does not mean that the claims of Aristotle and Thomas are intact in all respects. For instance, Aristotle could not explain why human nature does not always tend toward intellectual and moral perfection. He identified the ultimate goal of moral perfection in happiness or total flourishing (*eudaimonia*). He proposed two ways to bring happiness: first, contemplation of God as the highest possible object of intellectual activity; second, a virtuous life in which one's feelings or actions do not err either by excess or by defect. But the relation between these two are not clear in Aristotle (Russell 1965: 438–9). Later, Thomas tried to fill the lacuna left by Aristotle with his theological propositions, such as the idea that the impact of original sin distracts human beings from the perfection to which they have to strive, etc.

Status of natural law in a technological life-world

Having concluded that it is the aspect of a proposed teleology that links nature and human nature in natural law, we address the second question: whether such a conception of nature, presupposed in the (developed form of) the natural law tradition, is affected in any way in a technological life-world. Drawing on the insights of Husserl (1962: 123–38), we mean by technological life-world the world of our experience, including nature mediated by technology. This understanding is based on the conviction that what we know of nature would be little unless humanity had been aided by technological instruments. A concomitant feature of a technological life-world, irrespective of the question of whether it is desirable, is that by viewing technology as an instrument for using (and dominating) nature, our perception of nature has become that of a pliable object of human intervention.

The question to be addressed is: what is the status of natural law in a technological life-world? The proposed answer to this question is that in a technological life-world, in which nature is predominantly viewed as an instrument of human use, the foundations of natural law are weakened in two ways.

First, it seems that classical consciousness of primitive culture(s), which justified natural law, is undermined by the technological life-world. Primitive people esteemed the process of nature as inviolable. For the ancient people, it was simply foolish to fight against the formidable powers of nature. A more primitive and less technological society found happiness in conforming to the patterns of nature. But in a technological life-world conformity to nature is not the measure of happiness (Curran 1991: 259–60). Thus, in a technological life-world it is unlikely that the rule of nature becomes the measure of happiness as an ethical principle. Moreover, if we follow strict logic it could be argued, as Blumenberg does, that

> once morality has been defined as dependent on the given reality – that is, as the *human conduct that is fully appropriate to the situation*, that guarantees man a peaceful conduct of life thanks to the absence of conflicts with reality – then this conception already contains the conclusion that not only the adaptation of man to reality but also the adaptation of reality to man can bring the same effect (even though this may no longer be aptly described as 'morality').
>
> (Blumenberg 1983: 209, italics added)

We do not wish to argue that respect toward nature as an inviolable process was the sole principle equally effective in all stages of the development of the natural law tradition. Rather, we argue that it was at least one of the decisive elements that remained operative behind the formulation of natural law. Broadly speaking, what we want to underscore is only that technological advancements have greatly changed the non-technological attitude toward nature as an inviolable principle, which was the cultural background of the classical natural law tradition. Two comments are due here. First, this does not mean ancient people were simply succumbing to the forces of nature. They had indeed been making constant attempts to make nature 'inhabitable.' In a technological life-world, however, humans have reached a stage in which our world is simply mediated by technology; we do not evaluate other implicative consequences of the change of attitude, such as the ecological risks.

Second, there is another way in which the foundations of natural law are weakened: the modern idea of nature has radically relocated the traditional distinction (or even opposition) between nature and the artificial which seems to have been presupposed by the natural law theorists in their adoption of a teleology for nature. But according to modern scientific knowledge, all natural things are *constructs* of some basic elements, called atoms, if you will. Such constructs are not different from one another, whether they were constructed with human intervention or not. Even prior to the technological boom and the consequent changes in our views about nature, philosophers had begun to think along these lines. For instance, Descartes offered a telling example: 'when a clock marks the hours by means of the wheels of which it is made, it is no less natural for it to do so than it is for a tree to produce its fruits' (Descartes 1984: part IV, art. 203) Recasting this example in Thomistic categories, one might say that just as a tree has a natural inclination to produce fruits, a clock has a 'natural' inclination to mark the hours! John S. Mill seems to question tight distinctions between the natural and the artificial. So, indirectly, he questions the teleology attributed specifically to nature and which was thought lacking in human constructs. 'Everything which is artificial also is natural. Art is but the employment of the powers of Nature for an end. ... we only take advantage of what is found (hidden) in nature. A ship floats by the same laws of gravity and equilibrium, as a tree uprooted and blown into the water by wind. The corn which men raise for food, grows and produces its grain by the same laws of vegetation by which the wild rose and mountain strawberry bring forth their fruits and flowers' (Mill 1969: 7). This provides us with a radically expanded view of artefacts and, conversely, a shrunken view of nature. Accordingly, we might conclude that the natural–artificial distinction has to do with cultural and historical elements. As Joseph Selling puts it, '[i]f one reasons from a position that is unaware of being immersed in a relatively specific culture at a particular time in history, it is easy to overlook that the vast majority of so-called interpretations of what is "natural," and hence somehow proper or fitting for the natural law, are little more than the expressions of a particular ethos or even a political ideology' (Selling 1998: 62). What is to be remarked is that, in an overwhelmingly technological life-world, the sharp distinction between the natural and artificial does not look as strong as it used to in a less technological culture. Hence, a teleology exclusively attributed to nature, on the strength of which the link between cosmos and ethos is built, seems to be weakened in a technological life-world.

More than the cogency of the conclusions we have drawn, we want to highlight that the theme of the normativity of nature is a matter to be discussed. In this respect, we mean the discussion on natural law in the context of the technological life-world only as an example. Moreover, the foregone discussion brings in the 'postmodern' wisdom that nature, reason, etc. are not simply the given constants of normativity, rather they have to be viewed also as cultural constructs, lest, for instance, a patriarchal culture (continue to) 'perpetrate' the 'natural' subordination of women to men. Nonetheless, if we hold strictly to the conclusions that we have arrived at, they would raise a number of critical issues in all areas in which an appeal is made to natural law. In addition, another issue would be reopened, namely, what is the 'measure of things,' if it is not human beings and/or nature? This chapter, despite its apparent gravitational pull toward theoretical issues, leaves many practical questions unresolved which call for separate treatment. For example, according to natural law, is it right to alter the nature of animals, plants and bacteria at a genetic level? Can we ever think of the nature of animals and plants, etc. without an anthropic reference? We may surmise that the significations of natural law change in a technological life-world for the primary reason that it emerged in a world which was not so technological. By way of analogy (and recognizing its manifold limitations) let us say that the assertion that 'the earth is round' meant different things before and after Copernicus.

References

Aquinas, T. (1973) *Summa theologiae*, vol. 47, trans. J. Aumann, London: Blackfriars.

Aristotle (1966) *Metaphysics*, trans. H. G. Apostle, Grinnell, Iowa: The Peripatetic Press.

—— (1992) *Physics: Books I and II*, ed. W. Charlton, Oxford: Clarendon Press.

—— (1981) *Politics*, trans. T.A. Sinclair, London: Penguin.

—— (1960) *The Rhetoric of Aristotle*, trans. L. Cooper, New Jersey: Prentice-Hall.

Blumenberg, H. (1983) *The Legitimacy of the Modern Age*, trans. R.M. Wallace, Cambridge, MA: MIT Press.

Chroust, A.-H. (1946) 'The Philosophy of Law from St. Augustine to St. Thomas Aquinas', *The New Scholasticism* 20: 26–71.

Close, A.J. (1969) 'Commonplace Theories of Art and Nature in Classical Antiquity and in the Renaissance', *Journal of the History of Ideas* 30: 467–86.

Crowe, M.B. (1977) *The Changing Profile of the Natural Law*, The Hague: Martinus Nijhoff.

Curran, C.E. (1991) 'Natural Law in Moral Theology', in C.E. Curran and R.A. McCormick (eds.) *Readings in Moral Theology, no. 7: Natural Law and Theology*, New York: Paulist Press, 247–95.

Descartes, R. (1984) *Principles of Philosophy*, part IV, art. 203, trans. V.R. Miller, Dordrecht: Reidel.

Diels, H. (1951) *Die Fragmente der Vorsokratiker*, 6th edn., vol. I, Berlin: Weidmannsche Verlagsbuchhandlung.

Dupré, L. (1993) *Passage to Modernity: An Essay in the Hermeneutics of Nature and Culture*, London: Yale University Press.

Durbin, P.T. (1984) 'Thomism and Technology: Natural Law Theory and Problems of a Technological Society', in C. Mitcham and J. Grote (eds.) *Theology and Technology: Essays in Christian Analysis and Exegesis*, New York: University Press of America, 209–25.

Gill, C. (1995) *Greek Thought*, Oxford: Oxford University Press.

Greenwood, D. (1971) 'Saint Paul and the Natural Law', *Biblical Theology Bulletin* 1: 262–79.

Hughes, G.J. (1998) 'Natural Law', in B. Hoose (ed.) *Christian Ethics: An Introduction*, London: Cassell, 47–56.

Husserl, E. (1962) *Die Krisis der europäischen Wissenschaften und die transzendentale Phänomenologie*, III 33–4, Vol. I, ed. W. Biemel, Den Haag: Nijhof.

Lalande, A. (1926) *Vocabulaire technique et critique de la philosophie*, Paris: Presses Universitaires de France.

Lisska, A.J. (1996) *Aquinas's Theory of Natural Law: An Analytic Reconstruction*, Oxford: Clarendon Press.

Mill, J.S. (1969) 'Nature', in *Three Essays on Religion*, New York: Greenwood Press, originally published in 1874.

Plato (1985) *Gorgias*, trans. W. Hamilton, London: Penguin.

—— (1971) *Timaeus*, trans. D. Lee, London: Penguin.

Porter, J. (1999) *Natural and Divine Law: Reclaiming the Tradition for Christian Ethics*, Cambridge: W.B. Eerdmans.

Russell, J.L. (1965) 'The Concept of Natural Law', *The Heythrop Journal* 6: 434–5.

Schadewaldt, W. (1983) 'The Concepts of *Nature* and *Technique* according to the Greeks', in P.T. Durbin (ed.) *Research in Philosophy and Technology*, Vol. II, Greenwich: JAI Press, 159–71.

Selling, J. (1998) 'Authority and Moral Teaching in a Catholic Christian Context', in B. Hoose (ed.) *Christian Ethics: An Introduction*, London: Cassell, 57–71.

Sophocles (1987) *Antigone*, trans., ed., and notes by A. Brown, Warnminster: Aris & Phillips.

Watson, G. (1966) 'The Early History of "Natural Law"', *The Irish Theological Quarterly* 33: 65–74.

Weinreb, L.L. (1987) *Natural Law and Justice*, London: Harvard University Press.

26

EXPLORING TECHNONATURE
WITH CYBORGS

Anne Kull

The idea of nature, its construction and reproduction, performs an important cultural work. It is an idea that reverberates across all conceptual fields, and is modified as it passes through and by the elements and concepts of that field. The content of the idea of nature, however, is disputed, mobile, and relative to ethnic position. Culture–nature interplay became, and has remained, a constant and outstandingly important aspect of all human situations, including the situation in which we find ourselves now. In one sense this is a common-sense statement, almost trivial – it is what human history is all about: take the biological components out of human situations, and we, i.e. humans, cease to exist. But the fact that the world exists for us as 'nature' is an achievement among many actors. It is a kind of relationship; nature emerges as co-construction among humans and nonhumans, machines and our other partners. Nature is artifactual, at every level; that is, made – but not just by us.

While environmental crises have brought nature to the foreground in public consciousness, a novel kind of nature has emerged almost overnight and imperceptibly – nature as a product of technosciences. This technonature, the nature of no nature, has not received much attention in religious and theological studies. That is, an important part of our experience of nature is not congruent with our thinking about nature. Following people's constructions of nature, science and technology could provide access to our situation today, to emerging power relations, and to the sources in fantasy and imagination, fiction and scientific fact for discourses in everyday life, among other things.

Theologians as such do not have a privileged knowledge of culture–nature, our only natural environment today. Therefore we have to look for reliable guides. Donna Haraway locates us in the New World Order, Inc., in the 'informatics of domination,' within constructions of nature which follow closely capitalist economic relations. In this transnational enterprise culture species (human and nonhuman) are technically and literally brought into being by interdisciplinary, long-term, multi-billion projects. It is quite obvious that Donna Haraway's works extend the scope of environmentalism, feminism, and the history of science. It is less obvious how her works are a serious challenge to contemporary theology. Yet our location in technoculture and technonature seems to require a theological response. Taking her seriously, it is hard to justify having a world without participating people, i.e. a creation without created and creative co-creators, or people without world and artifacts, as a subject for theology. A theology which does not remain immune to cultural studies à la Haraway may have to remember its constructions outside the premises of the Enlightenment (i.e. the binary pairs of culture and nature, science and society, the technical and the social, etc.), and reconsider cultures–natures without oppositional quality, without using one to explain the other. Also, this theology must demonstrate that it has understood the concerns that gave rise to its theological response. And simultaneously it should be in continuity with Christian tradition.

Both the human and the artifactual have specific histories. Cyborg anthropology allows us a glimpse into production of the human through, by, and along with machines – and other organisms. Cyborg anthropology deals with those who are in the realm of technoscience. While all cultures are technological, not all are technoscientific. Technoscience is a form of life, a practice, a culture, a generative matrix. Haraway defines techno-science as 'dense nodes of human and nonhuman actors that are brought into alliance by the material, social, and semiotic technologies through which what will count as nature and as matters of fact gets constituted for – and by – many millions of people' (Haraway 1997: 210). Technoscience is about the implosion of science and technology; it designates a condensa-tion in space and time, a speeding up and concentrating of effects in the webs of knowledge and power. This accelerated production of natural knowledge structures commerce, industry, healing, community, war, sex, literacy, entertainment, and worship. The implosion of culture and nature, technological and organic, issues in the cyborg – the hybrid of cybernetic machine and organism. The cyborg is also an intense form of reflection on the world and world-making, what it means to be human in technoscien-tific society, self-construction and self-loss. It explores the borders and frontiers of imagination and lived reality. Haraway's goal is not a mastery of ultimate boundaries but rather an acknowledgment that 'we are not in charge of the world' but that we are still 'searching for fidelity, knowing all the while we will be hoodwinked' (Haraway 1991: 199).

The cyborg nature (also referred to as postvital, posthuman, technona-ture, nature of no nature) is an attempt to understand nature in a way that challenges the features of the culturally authorized concepts of nature; it is an attempt to free ourselves from conventional ideas of nature. The problem with conventional ideas is that they tend to become oppressive and normative – especially when the situation is perceived to be one of crisis. Then the nature of nature is denied change. Donna Haraway defines cyborg as 'a cybernetic organism, a hybrid of machine and organism, a creature of social reality as well as a creature of fiction' (Haraway 1991: 149). The conceptual boundaries of what it means to be human or what we humans mean by nature have never been less secure. Cyborgs appear where boundaries are transgressed: between human/animal, organism/machine, physical/nonphysical (Haraway 1991: 152). The figure of cyborg has become the focus for debates around human nature, with important questions being raised about embodied and disembodied identities. If we find it impossible to have a persuasive definition of what it means to be human or what is nature, we might follow Haraway and find new figurations. Cyborgs are aware that boundary construction is never innocent, and that it is crucial to ask: did anybody take responsibility for constructing those boundaries? *Cui bono*?

The cyborg in Haraway's terms is a feminist figuration. Certainly there are also macho-figurations in the current scene: the Terminators who appear as our technologically enhanced saviors prefigure one kind of possible future. Haraway's method is to be very specific, and thus one can claim that her vision of cyborgs offers new metaphors to both academic and popular theorizing for comprehending the different ways that sciences and technologies work in our lives – metaphors that start with our complicity in many of the processes we may wish were otherwise. Metaphor is not a fantasy, or rhetorical embellishment. Like animals and machines, metaphor is co-constructive and co-creative in the relationship between humans and nonhumans. Likewise, metaphor resists, enables, engages, disrupts, constrains, and displays. No narrative construction (including theological ones) is an innocent pastime; our stories may have world-changing consequences.

The cyborg renews talk of a (morally) ordered universe, a cosmos, which is made up of things modern Westerners formerly would have classified either as natural or cultural. Now this taxonomy does not work any more, if it ever did – nature for us is made but not all agents are human. Inherited as a gapped reality, nature and culture are better expressed hyphenated, or perhaps even better – to preserve the momentum and energy – non-hyphenated, as one word. The cyborg position is a lived historical position; it describes humanness or, more generally, the culture–nature relationship in a particular time, namely ours.

Choice is not over-abundant in this matter: we inhabit the world of technoscience whether we acknowledge it or not, asserts Haraway, and this world is constituted as a mixture of transgressions, mutations, and boundary violations, rather than as something akin to nature corrupted by culture. Contemporary technoscience challenges the distinction between science and technology, as well as between nature and culture, subjects and objects, natural and artifactual, physical and nonphysical, real and simulated.

Cyborg is also a useful tool to discuss human nature – cyborg anthropology poses a serious challenge to the (only) human-centered foundations of anthropological discourse. It explores an alternative, as the autonomy of individuals has already been called into question by post-structuralist and post-humanist critiques, by examining the argument that human subjects and subjectivity are crucially as much a function of machines, machine relations, and information transfers as they are machine producers and operators. Haraway asks: 'Why should our bodies end at the skin or include at best other beings encapsulated by skin?' (Haraway 1991: 178).

Commonly, both theology and ethics were assuming the concept of human to be given and unchanging (even while there were significant differences between different schools of thought). Since human nature was a constant, the categories of good and evil could be relatively easily determined. The nonhuman world, including organic nature and technology, was assumed to be morally neutral, as well as a given and a constant that could be little affected or changed by any human action. Thus, humans had little responsibility for nature or technology. The decentered, fragmented focus of 'cyborg' anthropology and/or theology must be on the mechanical/cybernetic-organic system (on the cyborg, in other words).

Haraway's creative mythic matrix seems to be distant enough from domination patterns of modernism to be a resource for a theology of culture–nature, but it does not take into account that religion may be our most intense and comprehensive way of valuing, and underplays a possible critical contribution of religious thinking to our knowledge projects. From a critical perspective one should not avoid the theological wisdom that warns the knowing subject to be mistrustful of our self-knowledge – that it is essentially correct reflection, a mimesis, of our real and true selves (even if these selves are multiple or fragmented). The self has endless resources to occupy itself with self-deception. On the other hand, the specifically Christian theology has always regarded the human and the rest of nature (to use Philip Hefner's wording) under the common rubric 'creation.' This affirmation has been preserved despite the widespread tendency in actuality to separate humans from the rest of nature as a part of nature with supernatural additions, or as endowed with reason or freedom, in contrast to the rest of nature, or as the sole object of salvation, and other possible qualifications. Haraway's reminder that the idea of nature is our (human) construction does not contradict the Christian intuition that nature as we know it is somehow a manifestation of God's intentions for the creation, which is recognized as 'good,' and which is comprised of both humans and the rest of nature. Nature as we know it in its full constructivist glory and misery can be good, evil, ugly or something else because the idea of nature is our construction. Nature as a good creation expresses potentiality destined by its Creator, and actualized in the process of co-creating by the human and nonhuman others. We know also from our Christian framework that this Creator-God has a particular weakness toward freedom, which means that the outcome of the co-creating process will be ambiguous: a 'mixed bag' of the disastrous and beneficial.

Paul Tillich was a theologian who reflected earlier and more deeply than most of his contemporaries on what nature means to us and to itself in the great drama of creation and salvation. Nature participates in humanity and humanity in nature, united in a shared destiny (Tillich 1957: 42). Both Haraway and Tillich intend to establish a public place, a common ground for culture and nature – Haraway achieves it by debunking the supposedly sacred in science and society by her satiric and ironic writings, Tillich by placing humans and nonhumans into the same framework of tragedy and greatness.

And while much of what is wrong in our world has been laid at the door of that which distinguishes the modern world, namely its reliance on science and technology, this is not true of Tillich. For Tillich, culture does not refer only to ways in which we express ourselves in religion, narrative myths, arts, but it also includes characteristic ways in which people organize their society, and make and use tools. Tillich did not revert to escapism or utopianism in face of the negativities of the modern situation. He did not bracket nature, culture, religion and technology as pure 'objects' or 'closed systems' so that one would cancel the other out.

Paul Tillich has noted that:

> With a suddenness and violence comparable to a natural catastrophe, modern technology came upon Western nations. And they bowed themselves before it without understanding what had happened .... To comprehend the logos of technology, its essence, its characteristic forms of being, its relation to other forms of being, that is thus our first and most important task.
>
> (Tillich 1988: 51)

He attempts to understand technology in two steps: first, through an analysis of the essence of the technical structure; second, through the systematic location of technology within other functions of culture/realms of meaning. The technical function is itself one of the functions through which life creates itself under the dimension of spirit. Paul Tillich wrote in 1927, concerning the place of the mythos of technology in the ultimate meaning of our life:

> We no longer have a mythos that expresses itself in symbols as past times had. We cannot determine a place for technology as they did. We can only contemplate the matter itself and interpret it and hope that in the interpretation something resonates from the

hidden, symbol-less mythos that sustains our time and gives it meaning.

(Tillich 1988: 59)

The following year, 1928, he presented his 'The Technical City as Symbol' for his age. Here he claimed that behind the technological 'ordering of things according to laws and relationships that is calculable in every one of its parts,' there is to be found a 'feeling of uncanniness,' a feeling of threatening strangeness and incomprehensibility, that hovers on the edges of all technical constructions (Tillich 1988: 180). The technical city is the symbol of pure autonomy; its structures are strictly rational and highly organized but are lacking spiritual depth. The technical city as symbol 'unites the thought of the domination of being with that of making a home within being' (Tillich 1988: 182). While the technical city symbolizes the age of the fulfilment of the technical utopia of the Renaissance, it has also become

> the symbol for the uncertainty that hangs over our age .... As the technical structures develop an independent existence, a new element of uncanniness emerges in the midst of what is most well known. And this uncanny shadow of technology will grow to the same extent that the whole earth becomes the 'technical city' and the technical house .... [The technical city] has become lifeless, and it induces lifelessness in us .... [This new uncanniness], a kind of dread of the lifeless world, which serves us but which cannot speak as life speaks to life.
>
> (Tillich 1988: 182–3)

The technical city is redeemed through the creation of a theonomous unity of form and meaning.

It seems to me that in the cyborg figure a symbol has been found to interpret our time and our technologies and ourselves. Our technical things have acquired uncanny liveliness of their own. As Haraway writes: 'Our machines are disturbingly lively, and we ourselves frighteningly inert' (Haraway 1991: 152). Paul Tillich wrote about the genesis of symbols, especially symbols of nonconformism in the midst of surroundings that try to compel adjustment to models and patterns. He agreed that we are made by our environment, and we make it at the same time. But on some happy occasion a symbol for the time is born. His description could be a birth certificate to Haraway's cyborg:

> We should not imagine that we can change our cultural trend, either as architects or as theologians or as educators .... Symbols cannot be produced intentionally. They are born and grow and

die. But one can tell how they are conceived and born: out of the
personal passion of individuals who in total honesty and total seriousness penetrate into the demands of the material with which
they work, who have a vision of the form that is adequate to their
aim, and who know that in the depth of every material, every
form and every aim, something ultimate is hidden that becomes
manifest in the style of a building, of a poem, of a philosophy. Out
of this depth, symbols can and will be born that, by their very
character, say no to present conformity and that point to an environment in which the individual can find symbols of his encounter
with ultimate reality.

(Tillich 1988: 143)

The disruption of boundaries that the cyborg myth foregrounds is always
and necessarily ambiguous with respect to its promise. And this signals a
kind of playful daring of the cyborg. Haraway's cyborg signals not a
collapse into some variant of a return, but an advance into the zone of
greatest danger. Haraway's wager is that the cyborg can find the weak
points, the points that offer political possibilities for more pleasurable
modes of life from within the planetary grid of technological dominations.
Yet, story telling and myth-making are not opposed to materiality. But
materiality itself is tropic; it is a knot of the textual, technical, mythic,
political, and economic. Perhaps cracking open possibilities for belief in
more livable worlds would be the most incisive kind of theory, indeed,
even the most scientific kind of undertaking in the midst of permanently
dangerous times. 'Who cyborgs will be is a radical question; the answers
are a matter of survival' (Haraway 1991: 153).

Contemporary practices are unfinished, ongoing, continuously maintained, and something in which one's own practices can potentially
intervene. While indifference or opposition are more common options, the
ongoing critical participation allows more creative responses. There are no
neutral positions. The cyborg as a figure of contemporary identity might
encourage a responsible awareness of and interaction with the material
world. It is worthwhile to remember that significant experiences, knowl-
edge-producing experiences, come to us through interaction not only with
humans but also with nonhuman others. Nature, however defined,
constructed, or invented, is beyond any comprehensive conceptual grasp
yet wholly within the domain of our social, political, and moral responsibility. Environmental problems are human problems but not merely
human moral problems. There are many ways and places where nature is
produced, and there is a wide variety of people whose experience of
nature, uses of nature, ideas about nature never come to the foreground.
The culturally particular way of creating nature is an enterprise that
combines science, technology, politics and free market capitalism. Even if

the image of cyborg may make us nervous, we will have to learn to speak as cyborgs, to express the qualitatively and quantitatively different experiences of technology and nature. Cyborgian nightmare could be a vision that they could not only be patented, sold, and possessed but fundamentally reconstituted in response purely and simply to market pressures, thus making cyborg society the terminal and purest form of capitalism. Further, any science or technology is an explication of a fundamental view of existence, of human being and of nature. In Tillich's interpretation of culture–nature, however, there are extra-scientific and extra-technological elements of cultural life without which an autonomous, namely our, technoscientific culture is not sustainable. A merely instrumental knowledge of nature, and so a merely manipulative use of it, fails in the end to understand it and culminates in destroying it – and in destroying nature, it destroys us. Nature is misunderstood as merely an object over against us, as are we, its knowers, if we understand ourselves as merely objective knowers and manipulators of its forces. Christian understanding of nature as the creation is an alternative available to us in our culture.

Acknowledgments

The present essay continues earlier reflections on this theme, published in *Zygon: Journal of Religion and Science* 35 (March 2002): 49–56.

References

Haraway, D.J. (1991) *Simians, Cyborgs, and Women: The Reinvention of Nature*, New York: Routledge.

—— (1997) 'Mice Into Wormholes: A Comment on the Nature of No Nature', in G.L. Downey and J. Dumit (eds.) *Cyborgs & Citadels: Anthropological Interventions in Emerging Sciences and Technologies*, Santa Fe, NM: School of American Research Press, 209–43.

Tillich, P. ([1927] 1988) 'The Logos and Mythos of Technology', in J.M. Thomas (ed.) *The Spiritual Situation in Our Technical Society*, Macon, Georgia: Mercer University Press, 51–60.

—— ([1928] 1988) 'The Technical City as Symbol', in *The Spiritual Situation in Our Technical Society*, 179–84.

—— ([1957] 1988) 'Environment and the Individual', in *The Spiritual Situation in Our Technical Society*, 139–43.

—— (1957) *Systematic Theology*, Volume II, Chicago: The University of Chicago Press.

Part IV

VALUES AS EXPLANATION OR VALUES EXPLAINED?

Introduction to Part IV

Willem B. Drees

Religion is not limited to understanding reality, the way science is. Religions openly acknowledge their normative intentions. The first essay in this final section, by the theologian and philosopher Keith Ward, is about the way these two aspects of theology might be understood. Upon a theistic view, as he argues, reality is explained not only along the lines followed by science (causal, laws of nature), but in terms of intention and valuation – the world is the way the world is, because God intended the world to be so, and God intended the world to be so because God valued the world positively. Thus, theology offers more than any scientific explanation can offer. A partner, or rather opponent, in this argument is the scientist who argues that we can do without any such further explanations – and Ward takes E.O. Wilson, author of the book *Consilience*, as his prime opponent in this respect. Comments by the theologian Martien Brinkman and the mathematician Ronald Meester nicely challenge Ward on various essential aspects, without, however, totally abandoning this view of theology as a richer form of understanding reality. Similarly, Edwin Koster's essay can be understood as an exemplification of Ward's argument for the co-existence of multiple explanations.

The other central essay in this section, by the geneticist and Anglican priest Lindon Eaves, is more firmly rooted in the scientific study of the world. Twin research, he argues, reveals the richness and power of scientific understanding of human behavioural characteristics, including human morality and religiosity. Within that context, Eaves seeks to understand the way we nonetheless continue to use – and need to use – a richer vocabulary than science offers – a vocabulary which has valuational language ('ought') in it. The philosopher Angela Roothaan offers some comments, questioning the relevance of genetic factors when we justify views and

245

judgements. Besides, she wonders about the role of one's own moral preferences in evaluating the data, an issue that is exemplified in a different context by the essay of Tatjana Visak on scientific disputes in primatology. A 'so what' argument about the relevance of genetic factors is also advocated by the biologists Van Straalen and Stein, who discuss the evolutionary origins of religion, with emphasis on the distinction between heritability (as a population concept) and genetic determination (at the level of individuals). The theologian Mladen Turk offers some additional reflections on the impact of an evolutionary understanding of religion on religious faith by considering a parallel, the impact of an evolutionary understanding of mathematics on the epistemic standing of mathematics.

27

TWO FORMS OF EXPLANATION

Keith Ward

The simple theme of this paper is that there is more than one type of explanation which is needed if human beings are to understand the universe in an adequate way. Broadly speaking, the natural sciences and the social sciences contain disciplines which practise two very different ways of explaining, neither of which can be reduced to the other, and which use different concepts and patterns of explanation. One way of stating the major difference between them is to say that one is primarily descriptive and the other is primarily normative. What I shall call 'physical explanation' is descriptive, in that it says what regular patterns there are in nature, in accordance with which objects in fact behave. What I shall call 'personal explanation', or more usually 'value explanation', is normative, in that it essentially contains a reference to what ought to happen, or at least to what some conscious beings think ought to happen. Moreover, it is very difficult if not impossible to exclude personal valuations from value explanations, that is, to avoid value judgements about the sorts of behaviour one is seeking to explain. Whereas in physical explanations, there is little need to appeal to one's personal desires in recording what happens in a laboratory. It is for this reason that historical forms of explanation, for example, are usually imbued with implicit and explicit comments on the rationality or stupidity of the people one is writing about. But laws of physics or chemistry do not speak about the rationality or stupidity of electrons. The old distinction between fact and value, between 'is' and 'ought', is well expressed in a broad distinction between two very different types of explanation, the physical and the valuational.

I am not claiming that there are only two types of explanation. But this broad distinction is one which obviously marks contemporary intellectual life, being enshrined in our Universities and institutes of higher learning, and it does, I think, point to an important feature of what explanation is.

Total consilience and the scientific world-view

It may seem quite obvious that when students set out to explain a historical or political event they are doing something very different from their friends who are trying to explain why subatomic particles decay in particular ways. But in his recent book *Consilience*, Edward Wilson says bluntly: 'There is intrinsically only one class of explanation' (1998: 297). What is this favoured class? Well, says Wilson: 'All tangible phenomena ... are based on material processes that are ultimately reducible ... to the laws of physics' (297). So the view that he calls 'total consilience' holds that 'nature is organised by simple universal laws of physics to which all other laws and principles can eventually be reduced' (59). One could hardly wish for a clearer statement of the thesis I am opposing. I do not have to invent a man of straw, since a real human being has offered himself to be aimed at.

Are there any laws and principles which play a role in the organization of nature that are not reducible to simple universal laws of physics? I suppose that the first thing one would like to draw attention to, in the formulation of the principle of total consilience, is the almost wholly speculative nature of the proposal. It is not a modest generalization from careful experimental observation. It is a completely universal statement which sets out an ideal for the scientific enterprise, the ideal of simple and total reductionism. It is not the case that even all scientific laws have been successfully reduced to laws of physics. So it is a speculative hypothesis which is intended to guide research programmes. It says something like: 'Try as hard as you can to reduce all explanations to simple laws of physics. To do so will be very illuminating, and I bet that you will be able to do it in every case'.

As a methodological proposal it may sound worth pursuing. But it is a fairly good working principle for assessing the force of such proposals that one should be able to specify situations in which they would fail. This is an innocuous form of the verification principle – if you can imagine no circumstances in which a hypothesis would be shown to be false, it is suspect, at least as a scientific hypothesis. So what would cause this proposal to fail? Obviously, the existence of some event or state of affairs, some 'material process', which does not fall under some simple universal law.

The requirement that laws of physics should be simple is difficult to specify. Most of the laws of quantum mechanics cannot be understood by non-mathematicians at all, but does that make them non-simple? Perhaps they are simple in some other sense, like being elegant or symmetrical. Of course one would like to reduce the complexity of what is often called the particle zoo to something more easy to handle, but there is no guarantee that one can do so. Are superstrings simple? Maybe in the sense that one could say the ultimate constituents of matter are all of the same type. But certainly not in the sense that anyone can easily frame a conception of what they are. One of the lessons of quantum mechanics, as it is currently understood, is that we do not have a simple theory as the basis of explanations in physics. We need an extremely complex mathematical apparatus even to state the theory.

But even if the basic laws of physics are mathematically complex, it is easy to think of possible exceptions to them. All one has to think of is some process which does not conform to the law of the conservation of mass, for example. There could be such a process, which occurs so rarely that there is no useful law which could be formulated under which it falls. So the rule that every physical event falls under some statable universal law has definite content. It is a contingent truth, which could be either true or false, as far as we know. Whether it is true or not is very hard to establish. I suppose the most we should claim is that we have formulated some universal laws – those of mechanics, for example – and we have not found any measurable events under controlled experimental conditions which break them. In addition, using them enables us to predict the behaviour of many objects in fairly normal and undisturbed situations with a great deal of reliability – though such prediction is often inexact because of factors of which we may not have taken account. The laws of mechanics do, however, seem to be principles in accordance with which physical objects always act, other things being equal. So perhaps all objects will always act in accordance with those principles. This generates the hypothesis that there is a finite statable set of principles which states how physical objects always act. These are the 'simple universal laws of physics'.

We should be aware of the limits of justified assertions in this area. We can justifiably only say that all objects so far observed by us have acted in these ways. But there may be many objects not observed by us, or there may even be objects that fall within our ordinary experience but have not been precisely measured by us, which do not act in those ways. Where physical movements are fairly simple and relatively isolated, like the movements of the planets around the sun, we might expect objects to act in regular and predictable ways. If they did not, life would be much more arbitrary and unpredictable than it is, and we would have much more difficulty in understanding and explaining the universe. So it is highly desirable, if we are to explain how physical processes occur, that physical objects should act in regular and predictable ways.

The natural sciences have made spectacular advances by not remaining content to speak of regularities in a general way. They have explained physical changes by discovering the small physical particles of which physical things are made, by measuring some of their properties precisely, and by framing laws which capture the relation of these properties in closed and controlled systems. But in this process scientists have also discovered that none of their laws gives a complete explanation of physical processes in general. Newton's laws fail to explain the behaviour of sub-atomic particles, and quantum mechanical laws fail to explain exactly when particular particles will decay. What has been established is that there are general regular ways in which physical objects act, and these are mathematically statable in very useful ways. But it has not been established that any set of known laws captures all physical changes exactly. One might say that there are laws yet to be discovered. Or one might say that there are some occurrences which simply are not explained by laws alone.

A good example is the present state of quantum field theory. Some theorists, like David Bohm, believe there is a deterministic account yet to be found – an account which would explain every occurrence as following inevitably from some prior state in accordance with a statable principle. But there are others, the majority, who accept the Copenhagen interpretation of indeterminacy. They would hold that, even though the Schrödinger equation is deterministic, the actual collapse of the wave function is such that alternative states, within closely definable limits, are possible, and neither collapsed state follows inevitably from its prior wave-function state. Whether or not Schrödinger's cat is superposed in both states prior to its collapse, I do not pretend to know. But when it collapses, it is in one state or another, and which it is in is not precisely predictable from the wave function.

Would this be an occurrence not explicable by a universal law of physics? At this point ambiguity enters. Of course the Schrödinger equations are laws of physics, and they do explain what happens. Yet they do not determine precisely what happens. The explanation is indeterministic; it leaves open alternatives. So the question is raised: does a law of physics have to be such that every state is sufficiently determined (such that no other alternative state is possible)? Or does it only have to be such that one can discover patterns of regularity and predictability in physical processes, even though one cannot (perhaps in principle) predict everything in precise detail?

I do not want to base my argument on disputed interpretations of quantum theory, but I do wish to point out that there is widespread disagreement among physicists about the extent to which laws of physics explain physical occurrences. Only some would offer a deterministic account. Many would be happy with a looser claim that there are many discoverable regularities in physical processes, enough for us to predict controlled processes with a high degree of accuracy. But there may be events which happen that do not inevitably follow from an initial state in accordance with some universal law alone.

This issue is further complicated by the fact that it now seems that we can never in principle measure the initial state of a system accurately enough to get exact deterministic predictions out of it. There is good reason to think that we can never accurately predict everything that is going to happen – though that, of course, does not decide the issue of whether things are in fact sufficiently determined or not. That issue is empirically undecidable.

The consequence is that we cannot decide whether every physical event falls under some universal law, in the sense of a sufficiently determining law. The methodological principle might be: 'Look for determining laws, but do not necessarily expect to explain everything. That may be beyond our powers.' Laws of physics might be sufficiently determining, other things being equal – that is, if no other factors enter the situation. But there may well be other factors. Suppose, for example, that there are new or emergent states of affairs in the history of the universe. It is necessarily true that there are some such states. The cosmos itself began to exist. Stable atomic structures were formed at a particular time. Self-replicating molecules were fairly late developers in cosmic history. Organic bodies, brains and consciousness are even more recent. The thoughts that inhabited the brain of Einstein had possibly never occurred before in the whole history of the universe. Some of these states are new in the sense of being more complex integrated structures which behave in accordance with principles applying specifically to such structures as a whole (as the principle of natural selection applies to self-replicating organic molecular structures). Some, like consciousness, are new in introducing what seem to be quite different properties into the universe for the first time.

If universal laws connect some states with others according to a general rule, the genesis of new states will have to generate new causal laws. Even if the new law is a fairly unfruitful one, like 'Whenever brain state x occurs, a sensation of blue enters some consciousness', it will be a putative new universal law (though it is hardly a law of physics). So some states do not follow deterministically from preceding states by established laws of physics alone. There is always the possibility of new laws arising. These laws will seek to express new deterministic relations which arise between states of affairs. This raises the question of whether such new relations need always be deterministic. In the case of brain states, for example, it seems that there is not a one-to-one correlation between specific brain states and phenomenal experiences, so one has to seek a broader sort of correlation, expressive of a looser causal relation. And in the case of very complex integrated physical systems, it is plausible to say that they seem to introduce non-deterministic yet still broadly regular and predictable relations between states of affairs. Human beings are very complex integrated physical systems, and so it is a reasonable hypothesis, fully consistent with scientific practice, to suppose that there are non-deterministic causal relations between many of the states which go to make up the history of a human person.

This first part of my chapter has been devoted to asking whether total consilience is part of, or even identical with, the 'scientific world-view'. Is total consilience a necessary foundation for good scientific practice? Is it even the most reasonable formulation of the 'Ionian enchantment', the belief that the world is orderly and can be explained by a small number of natural laws? My suggestion is that it is not, even at the physical level, since the discovery that there are principles of regular predictable physical action does not entail that everything that occurs is sufficiently determined by such principles plus some physical initial state alone.

Theism and the priority of personal or value explanation

Of course one might not care for a situation in which there are universal laws of physics, but events happen which simply do not fall under them, for no reason. One might dislike the ideal of total consilience, which is meant to be reductionist and materialist, but like a rather more flexible ideal of intelligibility, regularity and predictability in nature. One might prefer the Platonic enchantment to the Ionian, namely the idea that there is a reason for everything, but that not all reasons are sufficiently determining explanations. In fact, there is some tension between saying that there is a reason for some process to happen, and saying that it is sufficiently determined. I can say that the reason a stone falls to the ground is that it obeys the law of gravity. But I might also say that, just because it acts in accordance with that law, it does not fall for any particular reason. Its motion has a cause, but not a reason.

This tension arises from the fact that the term 'reason' can be used in at least two senses in these contexts. It can mean the citation of a causal principle in accordance with which it changes. Or it can mean the reason for which it changes. The former sense is broadly backward-looking – it looks to a past state and an existent law which together compel the change. The latter sense is broadly forward-looking – it looks to a future state which a process is aimed at actualizing. Aristotle included both sorts of reasons or causes in his account of explanation. Post seventeenth-century natural science has usually excluded the latter sort of explanation from its consideration. That is because the area of its success has been in the realm of the non-personal, a realm in which things do not seem to have aims and intentions, and in which it has come to seem misleading to suppose that they do. The great success of empirical science has been the depersonalization of nature, and the replacement of talk of purposes and goals by talk of material properties and the laws of their interaction.

Persons, however, undoubtedly exist as part of the natural order. When persons are explicitly considered, as they are in the social sciences, some things that happen are explained not by saying that they inevitably follow by some general principle from a preceding state, but by saying that they realize a desire or goal which is itself more or less intelligible. Such a form of personal explanation is commonplace, and different in kind from causal law explanation. It is different in kind because it uses quite different concepts. Physics makes no mention of desires, goals, intentions, or in general of mental states. That vocabulary simply is not part of physics. The only hope for total consilience in the area of the social sciences is that all such concepts can be translated into concepts of physics (brain-states, most probably), or at least, if they cannot be translated, that their applicability makes no difference at all to the processes of nature, which are determined solely by physical laws. Either mental concepts have to be translatable into physical concepts, or mental events have to be wholly epiphenomenal to physical states, without having any independent causal role.

At this point the ideological commitment is clear. A materialist has good reason for saying that there are only physical principles of explanation. But someone who believes that mental events and processes exist has good reason for saying that there are types of explanation which do not reduce to the physical. These types of explanation will apply to persons and at least some animals. For anyone who believes in a creator God such personal explanations will ultimately have priority over all physical explanations.

Most religious believers think that there is a God, a supreme being who created the universe, and whose existence does not depend upon that of the universe. Furthermore, in being a creator, God is thought of, however analogously, as free, conscious and active, as intentionally bringing about the universe for some consciously entertained reason. It would be absurd to think that the universe follows from God in accordance with some pre-existing universal law. God is not a physical state, and there cannot be a law of physics for the unique case of the relation between God and the whole physical cosmos. God brings about the universe by a unique act, and presumably for some reason.

Since God is not a material being, and has no physical body, believers are committed against hard-line materialism. They are committed to the coherence of the idea of a non-embodied consciousness, which can formulate a purpose and implement it by creating a material universe. Theists do not think that the universe somehow has a purpose inherent in itself. They think that there is a creator God, who exists independently of the universe, and who can create it for a purpose.

God, for most believers, has knowledge of everything that is possible and actual. God is able to bring about, to make actual, sets of possible states. So God has knowledge and will. The primary object of God's knowledge and will is said by most classical theologians to be the divine being itself – as Aristotle put it, God's being consists in a 'thinking upon thinking'. God is aware of and wills or affirms the divine being as it exists in its own proper perfection. So knowledge and will do not, as such, depend upon some material substratum for their existence. Indeed, they are ontologically prior to all material existences. The primary form of being is something like what we know as non-material conscious agency. That is a basic postulate of theism, and it seems a perfectly intelligible one.

If God is already perfect in self-knowing and self-willing, why should God create any universe at all? For most theists God has the ability to actualize states which are not states of the divine being itself, and indeed to actualize beings like God, made in the divine image, insofar as they have knowledge and creative will, naturally to a limited degree. The reason God should actualize such beings is normally thought to be that it is good to do so. Such created beings can enjoy something of the enjoyment that God derives from knowing and willing, and so they increase the number of beings who enjoy, which is good. Perhaps, too, God can enjoy different sorts of actualities by co-operating and sharing experiences with such created personal beings. On some Christian interpretations, it is part of the divine nature to be essentially loving, which involves some form of relationship to other persons, and therefore some creation of such persons. Whether or not that is so, created persons are in the Jewish and Christian traditions said to be like God in having knowledge and will, though their knowing and willing is limited in a way that God's is not.

The theist is thus committed to saying that consciousness, knowing and willing can exist without a material substratum. It follows that for a theist the primary sense of 'identity' is not of continuous existence in space or time – a sense which does normally apply to physical objects in general. In God identity seems to be given by two main factors, a unity of experience by which all objects of knowledge are members of the same consciousness, and a continuous agency by which many things are brought about by the same causal agent. God is a being such that everything that can possibly be known by one being is a conscious element of the divine experience, and everything that exists is an effect of the divine agency, either directly or indirectly. One might say that divine identity is given by an all-encompassing unity of experience and an equally all-encompassing conscious agency. God is whatever it is which experiences and causes everything other than itself. The unity of co-conscious experience and the continuity of intentional agency are, for a theist, more fundamental aspects of reality than the sort of spatio-temporal continuity which is often taken as the criterion of identity for physical objects.

This means that a fundamental and ontologically prior type of explanation, for theists, is explanation in terms of the purposes of a conscious agent – personal explanation. God's purposes cannot be translated into any physical terms, and they have a causal role, bringing about the whole of the physical cosmos. It does not deductively follow from this that human purposes are not physically translatable or that they have an independent causal role in nature. But since, for Christians and Jews at least, humans are made 'in the image of God', it does seem probable that there will be some non-material elements in human beings which are associated with knowing and willing, with intentions and the causation of physical processes which realize them. There is good reason for a theist to expect that personal explanations will not be reducible to physical explanations.

In the case of God, purposes will not be given by the constraints of physical nature, like getting food or defending territory. Since God is omnipotent, God can realize any purpose God wants. Since God is omniscient, God knows all the purposes that could possibly be realized. If we think of God conceiving all possible states, and deciding which ones to actualize, can we think of any reason why God should actualize some rather than others? It is at this point that a notion must be introduced which has no place in physical explanations, the notion of 'value'. The notions of purpose and of value are closely related. If I freely intend to do something, then by definition what I intend to do is of value to me. I choose it over alternatives because I place some value on it.

There can be little doubt that some conscious states are of more value than others. A state of great happiness is of greater value than a state of great pain. Appreciation of beauty is of greater value than indifference to it. Knowing and delighting in many things is of greater value than knowing few. States of pleasant consciousness are of greater value than unconscious states. So in general value lies in the realization of conscious states of taking happiness in various objects of consciousness. We might say, then, that God creates because God takes delight in what is created, and perhaps in the act of creation itself. If God creates this universe, then it is by definition of value to God. If the universe contains, in the form of personal agents, conscious states of taking happiness in creating and appreciating various objects and activities, then it realizes things and states of value in themselves as well as to God. This implies that the universe can be explained as purposively chosen by God for the sake of the values it realizes. The answer to the question 'Why does the universe exist, and exist as it does?' is that it is intended by God, and is of value to God because of the intrinsically good things it contains.

To some, to Edward Wilson perhaps, such an explanation is vacuous. It does not yield any precise predictions, and God's choice seems to be veiled in mystery anyway. It does not enable us to understand any better how the universe works. That is true. This is not a scientific or physical explanation. But, since you are part of the universe, the most general form of personal cosmic explanation may suggest to you that you are intended by God, and are of value to God, and that God has some purpose for your life, which can – since God is powerful – be realized. Does this explain anything? It is admittedly a rather incomplete sort of explanation, which leaves you largely in the dark about what that purpose is exactly, and about why particular things happen to you that do not seem very purposive. Yet even if it does not explain everything about your life, it does explain why you exist. You exist because someone wanted you to exist, and loves you, and will bring your life to some sort of fulfilment if you do not resist.

Compare this with the neo-Darwinian thesis that you exist because you are the result of millions of accidental mutations which have been selected through struggle and competition over millions of years. This tells you how you got here and what sort of being you are. It explains the nature of human existence by putting your life in the context of a long, largely random evolutionary process. The theistic postulate in an exactly similar way explains the nature of human existence by putting it in the context of a universe intentionally brought about by a wise and loving personal being. It answers the age-old questions 'Who am I?' and 'Why am I here?' Admittedly it answers them in a very general way – you are a child of God, created to help realize some purpose of God. But that is still an answer, an explanation, however general and however incomplete.

If the theistic hypothesis is true, any explanation of the universe which fails to mention the purposes of God is incomplete, for that is the most general and basic explanation there is. Physics fails to mention God's purposes and is careful to exclude them from consideration. In that sense, all physical explanations must be incomplete, if theism is true. It is clear, then, that Edward Wilson is ruling out the truth of theism by definition. Anyone who believes in a creator God is bound to think that personal explanation is the primary form of explanation.

One can see how this is so in a general way. Physical explanation explains changes in terms of universal laws, but assigns no reason why those laws should be as they are. It thus leaves the universe as ultimately inexplicable. Even quantum cosmological theories that see the universe as arising out of quantum fluctuations in a vacuum must posit the laws of quantum mechanics and the basic fluctuating 'stuff' of the actual cosmos as simply given. There are, it is true, quantum cosmologists who might argue that there is a necessity or self-evidence about the ultimate laws of nature, if they are mathematically necessary in some way. But it is still hard to see how the selection of a particular set of quantum laws from all the possible array of mathematical truths is necessary, or why it should issue in physical embodiments. Mathematics may be necessary, but it is an unrestricted realm of pure possibility, and some explanation is needed of why some sub-section should be actualized in a physical universe. The best that can be done is to posit a necessary realm of possibility, with the cosmos arising by chance.

Personal explanation assigns reasons for things and processes in terms of purposes which are achieved. If one again posits a necessary realm of possibility, the selection of an actual cosmos can be explained as chosen by a personal agent for the sake of the value it realizes. Of course one still has the existence of a personal agent to explain. But now comes the basic theological axiom. A supreme personal agent exists because it is the supreme form of value. If a value is a conscious state of taking happiness in creating and appreciating various states and activities, then the highest possible, the supreme, value lies in a conscious agent which takes happiness in creating and appreciating all the actual states and activities which exist – that is, in a creative personal agent who actualizes states from the realm of possibility for the sake of their value. God exists in order that the supreme value should be realized.

There can be an ultimate value explanation for existence. The best reason why anything should exist is that it is a good thing that it does, that it is of value. The reason why God exists is that God realizes the highest possible value. The reason why the universe exists is that God chooses to realize a set of distinctive values by creating it. The reason why the laws of nature are as they are is that they are necessary means to realizing the values God chooses.

An obvious reply is that just because something is very good, that does not entail that it exists. But suppose one does accept the Platonic postulate, that there is a reason for everything. Then there are only two possible ultimately explanatory reasons why there should be anything at all. One is that something exists by necessity, that it cannot fail to exist. The other is that something is of supreme goodness. Edward Wilson tries to accept the first reason but not the second. But in fact necessity does not explain either contingent existence or goodness. One cannot infer the contingent from the necessary, and one cannot infer goodness or value from necessity.

Necessity cannot be inferred from goodness either. From the fact that something is good, one cannot infer that it is necessary or even that it is existent. This suggests that for a complete explanation one requires some being or state which combines both necessity and value. One would require something which could not fail to exist and which was of supreme value, and whose value in turn explained the existence of contingent values. That is what is classically meant by God.

In support of such a hypothesis, one might say that if actuality is prior to possibility, then if there is necessarily an array of possible states, there must be an actuality in which they inhere. This actuality might be analogously conceived as mental in nature, since it underlies possibilities insofar as it conceives them as possible. It is the ultimate power of being, since, as the substratum of a necessary set of possible, it is itself necessarily actual. That is, it is self-existent, not deriving its existence from another, but having the power of existence in itself. As such, it has, if anything has, the power of actualizing sets of possibles that it conceives. It would naturally choose the best possible set of actualities, states and processes which it can enjoy. Or if, as seems likely, there is no best possible set, it would at least choose some set which realizes a set of values which would not otherwise exist, and whose goodness far outweighs the evils that may be necessary in any such creation of that sort.

If value consists in personal agents finding happiness in creating and appreciating objects, states and processes, it may well be a necessary condition of the possibility of such agents emerging in an evolutionary universe that they might also be able to destroy and despise such objects and one another. The possibility of evil might be necessarily implied in the existence of any such universe. If such persons are to emerge from a universe which is in part indeterminate in ways necessary to make the later emergence of freedom possible, then some actual evil might be necessary. At any rate, if there is evil in nature, in the form of suffering or the frustration of creative endeavour, the theist will have to account for it as a necessary condition or consequence of the sorts of values that a universe of a specific sort makes possible. The cosmos itself will have to be such that it does realize very great and not otherwise obtainable values, and all disvalues within it will be explicable as necessary parts (or as necessarily possible parts) of the general structure it must have to fulfil this purpose. In this way the fundamental explanatory concepts of necessity and value are linked. The necessarily existent substratum of all possibles, in being supremely knowing and the source of all actuality, is itself of supreme value, and generates states and processes for the sake of their intrinsic value.

This is not a proof of God. It is more like saying: 'If there were a self-existent actuality, the necessary substratum of all possibilities and the source of all actualities by free choice of values, then there would be a complete explanation of reality.' That explanation would be fundamentally in terms of two basic concepts, necessity and value. Only then would the Platonic ideal be fully satisfied.

In this section of the chapter I have argued that, for those who believe in a creator God, value explanation must be the most fundamental form of explanation, and that a complete explanation of reality is only possible if both value and necessity explanations are forthcoming in principle. It must be remembered, however, that part of the theistic postulate is that only God can comprehend these necessities and values as they objectively are, so the most we could do would be to point towards their possibility, and to show how they are implicit in reflective theism.

The complementarity of physical and value explanations

In the final section I will draw back from the heady realms of rational theism, and concentrate on personal explanations at the ordinary human level. The necessity with which physical explanations deal is the necessity of acting in accordance with universal principles which are usually not themselves necessary. Such explanations do not deal in preferences or values at all. Preferences and values are rooted in desires, which are internally related to choices of states of value, states which a rational agent has a good reason to choose. It is possible to state certain rather general conditions of value, and to state in a formal way what a value would be – a conscious personal agent taking happiness in creating and appreciating a number of complex and diverse states and processes. Value explanations try to set out what intrinsic values there are, and the values which are instrumental to obtaining them, and to explain personal conduct in terms of attempts to discover what they are or to attain them. All value explanations terminate in the specification of states which are of intrinsic value. They explain sequences of human acts in terms of their intention to realize some such values. The reason such statements could never be translated into laws of physics is that neither intentions nor values are mentioned in physics.

The forms of physical and value explanations are quite different. In the former, one has an algorithmic process of applying rules to transform physical states. The outcome is simply what results from the application of the algorithm, and there is no sense in which the result is foreseen at the beginning of the process. In the latter, the process begins with an intentional state – a conscious state of having as an object of thought some future state. Such an internal representation of the future is not a physical state at all, since the very idea of a 'representation' of something absent is not a physical property. Similarly, the idea of a future state as a value, as something worth choosing, ascribes a non-physical property to a state. Then in reflecting on how to realize the desired state, one aims to think validly or invalidly, truthfully and untruthfully, appropriately or inappropriately. Considerations which are normative enter into this process essentially, whereas physical processes cannot as such be assessed as correct or incorrect. Finally, in the realization of the desired state there is the enjoyment of value, which is the final explanation of the whole process. But enjoyment is again a mental, not a physical property. In short, in value explanations, there are elements of representation, normative assessment, value and enjoyment which are not parts of any physical process, and the process itself is non-algorithmic in that it follows no statable, predictable universal law. The two sorts of explanation are epistemically quite distinct.

The only hope for the naturalist is somehow to translate the mental into the physical, to map mental states on to physical states of the brain. But that is impossible. To map mental on to physical states one would need translation rules by which one state could be mapped on to another, or at least on to a range of other states. The problem is that very many thoughts are new and original, and so there cannot be an existent translation for them. Also, they are never repeated exactly, since even qualitatively identical thoughts differ in specific mental content because of their differing locations in psychological history. So one can never set up the required translation rules. The mental cannot be mapped on to the physical.

I have connected the disjunction of physical and mental with the disjunction of descriptive and normative. Mental events are normative, in that they essentially relate to such things as intentions – what I think it is worth bringing about – desires – what I would choose to bring about – and criteria of truth or rationality. Edward Wilson would like to collapse the normative into the descriptive. He writes: 'If the empiricist world view is correct, *ought* is just shorthand for one kind of factual statement, a word that denotes what society first chose (or was coerced) to do, and then codified' (Wilson 1998: 280). This is a very odd statement. In the first place, society does not choose to do anything. It is individuals who choose to do things, and if they choose they make a decision about what to do. The language of decision implies that there are alternatives, between which a choice can be made. Choices can be rational or irrational, sensible or silly, moral or immoral. But these possibilities are not explored by Wilson. What we want to know, when considering the term 'ought', is what makes a choice a rational or moral choice. We can say 'you ought to do something, if you are a rational egoist', or 'you ought to do something, if you want to take the moral point of view'. These are different, and often conflicting, recommendations. We can often make a choice between them. The reason we cannot explain 'ought' in terms simply of what someone chose to do is that what we want to know is precisely what sort of choice a moral choice is.

On this question there is perhaps no general agreement, though it would be widely held that a moral choice is one that takes the interests of all relevantly affected people into roughly equal consideration. It contrasts with an egoistic choice of what is for my own good, and it asks, roughly, what is for the good of all. Many choices made in society are not moral choices in this sense. It may be the case that most people choose to do what is in their own interests – Adam Smith thought one could take that as axiomatic. This can readily be codified into such principles as 'Always look out for yourself', and 'Invest for your old age'. These will be rational principles, but will they be moral principles? For some people they may be, but that will be strongly contested by others, who might rather say, 'Put others before yourself', or 'Take no thought for tomorrow'.

If moral principles are rational recommendations for action, they will be contested, since people might rationally decide on different general courses of action – egoistic and altruistic principles being the most obvious competitors in this area. If that is so, it makes sense to ask, 'Which set of principles are really moral?' That is, 'What ought I to do, which set of principles ought I to act on?' Wilson, in trying to reduce the normative question to a descriptive question, suggests that what I ought to do is whatever someone, or some group of people, has chosen to do in the past, which has somehow got codified within a society. But that is no help, since all these competing principles have been so formulated and codified. If I say, 'Do whatever is in the law', or 'Do whatever the majority say', many people (including, oddly, Wilson himself) will raise the questions 'But is it right to do so?', 'Is the law just?', 'Is the majority right?'

The point is a simple one: the question of what one ought to do can never be resolved just by giving a description of what people are predisposed genetically or otherwise to do, even less by informing us that people really have no choice. To raise the moral question at all is to presuppose that we have a choice of how to act, and that we suspect there may be a way in which it is right to act. In other words, the word 'ought' is logically inexponable; it cannot be translated into any other term, and it is not analysable into simpler components which do not possess the same moral import as it does. What is that moral import? Simply that there may be ways in which people ought to act, whether or not they tend to do so, or want to do so, or perceive that everyone else ('society') does so.

One consequence of reducing value explanations to physical explanations is that moral sensibility is thereby eliminated. The possibility that there may be ways in which people ought to act can no longer be raised, and so the moral question itself becomes subsumed in some other sort of question, like 'What sort of behaviour is most conducive to survival?' That is the evolutionary psychologists' favoured sort of subsumption, since all moral principles are explained as genetic predispositions which have been formed and have endured because they turned out (by accident) to have survival value (in that they favoured the replication of genetic codes which produced these beliefs and forms of behaviour in animals).

But suppose it is true that we act in certain ways, and have beliefs about how we ought to act (e.g. we ought to obey our superiors), because such acts and beliefs have been selected in a long evolutionary process. That gives a causal account of how we come to have moral beliefs. I cannot help believing these things, because they are genetically programmed by my genes. But now, if the question 'How should I act?' arises, the only answer obtainable is: 'Act in the way you cannot help acting, because it is programmed into you'. In other words, the rational thing is not even to raise the question, since it has no possible answer. You will act in the way you are going to act anyway. Moral questions are simply not raised, except as the playing out of certain mental scenarios – 'rational choice is the casting about among alternative mental scenarios to hit upon the ones which, in a given context, satisfy the strongest epigenetic rules' (Wilson 1998: 199). The epigenetic rules are genetically coded rules, built up over millennia of selection for survival. Rational choice becomes a belated conscious recognition of a process which in fact takes place at a largely unconscious level, by which some of these programmed rules win out over others and determine our actual behaviour. Again, personal choice is eliminated in favour of a passive recognition of activities taking place at a physical level in our brains. Personal agency disappears, and with it all talk of real decision and moral choice.

It is not even that I can take as a conscious moral principle 'Do whatever conduces to the survival of me, my tribe, the species, or my genetic code'. It is rather that, whatever principles I act upon, ultimately the principles which are selected to govern future human behaviour are those that will in fact be conducive to survival (that is, to their own replication). That, of course, is an analytic truth: whatever survives, survives. It is supremely uninformative about what principles I ought now to adopt. Yet that practical question cannot be avoided. Nor do writers like Wilson avoid it. He says: 'It should be possible to adapt the ancient moral sentiments more wisely to the swiftly changing conditions of modern life' (285). So we can adapt our genetically programmed rules, in view of changing conditions. We could have a more rational morality. But then the question 'What is a more rational morality?' is unavoidable. And we have to ask what the goals of morality are.

What is envisaged is a two-stage process – first, evolution has programmed into us certain rules of behaviour and feelings of obligation, which are there because they had survival value. But second, we can take rational control at least to some extent of these predispositions and feelings, to make them more efficient at obtaining the goals we want. Value explanations have not after all been reduced to physical explanations, because we have to ask what rational goals of conduct we should have, what values we should aim at, and the best physical explanations can do is tell us how we are in fact predisposed to act and feel. The dilemma the evolutionary psychologist faces is this: if morality is what is laid down in our genes and culture, then no questions about what is right arise. If the question does arise of what goals we should follow, then the story of evolution cannot resolve them for us, since it only tells us what we would do if we did not think about it and decide rationally.

On either account, survival itself is not a value worth pursuing for its own sake; it is only an accidental consequence of past struggles for survival. Of course, in order to make a rational decision we should know ourselves, our predispositions and basic feelings, as well as we can. We might well be predisposed, as evolutionary psychologists tend to tell us, to protect our kinship groups against all others, and give up all for their welfare. But we can now ask if that is a rational thing to do. Or is it an irrational relic of past struggles for survival, programmed into us by genes, selfish or otherwise?

Is there any way of answering that question, in general? All I want to say here is that many humans think there is. A rational decision is one that selects efficient means to its chosen goals, and a moral decision is one that selects goals which realize the flourishing of all persons in a roughly equitable way. The moral decision is one that generalizes rationality, in view of the fact that what is good for one person is good for anyone relevantly like that person. So the moral point of view is one of generalized rationality, of discovering goals which all can select and work for. The Golden Rule is for most people the basic ethical rule, that one should do to others what one would like them to do to oneself. How does one decide that? By realizing the principle that similar rules should apply in similar situations, which is a basic rational principle. Aquinas formulated the first axiom of ethics as that one should pursue good and avoid evil. Having discovered what is good by seeing what humans can rationally choose as objects of desire, one pursues what can be rationally desired by all, and that becomes a basic moral principle of action.

To explain a person's moral views is to explain how individual humans apply, or fail to apply, reason to the task of discovering what is good for human beings as such, what makes for the good life. It is to uncover what their basic values are. It is not to try to describe what they do, somehow without mentioning values, reasons, desires or intentions. Such an attempt would depersonalize human beings, turning them into physical machines which only think they decide, reflect and evaluate. So what is at stake here is the extent to which humans are truly responsible and rational agents, centres of active causality of a distinctively purposive sort, in a world of regular and largely predictable physical, non-purposive processes. If they are rational agents, then value explanations, which consider rational reflection by humans, the insights that humans feel themselves to have and the principled decisions they make, are a basic and inexponable part of the explanation of the nature of things.

The exact relation of personal to physical cannot be a concern of this chapter, though my general view is that the personal, in the case of finite beings, is constituted largely by a set of emergent properties from the physical, a fuller realization of properties of internalization and response which characterize all objects to some degree. What I have tried to bring out is the way in which value explanations are irreducible to physical explanations, and have a substantial explanatory role to play. They point to aspects of reality which are not physical, in the ordinary sense of possessing mass and volume, or at least momentum and position.

Science itself is committed to pursuing such values as elegance, simplicity and constancy in its quest to understand the universe. Such values turn out to be well exemplified in reality. But there are other values, of creative freedom, patterned complexity and holistic unity, which also have a place in reality, and can only be understood by the more participative forms of personal knowing which are largely found in the humanities. If explanation is what increases understanding and appreciation, then to explain a piece of music is to show the values which it expresses, the skills involved in imaginatively writing it, the pattern and form it has. To explain a successful play is to show how it captures aspects of human life in a distinctive way, how the words are chosen to evoke profound feelings, and how the plot achieves a satisfying formal shape.

It is not hard to show that such value explanations are irreducible to physical explanations. It is perhaps harder to show that they reflect objective features of reality, and that they point to a personal dimension to the world with which the natural sciences are not concerned. It is apparently contentious, in this secular age, to claim that such a personal dimension can be found at the cosmic level as well as in the experience of human beings. Such however is the claim of theism, and if the cosmos shows intelligibility and elegance, and has a propensity to generate emergent beings capable of creative freedom and intelligent understanding, that claim might be said to be supported by the scientific enterprise. Scientific understanding can perhaps show that there is beauty and elegance in the natural order, that there is a propensity in cosmic emergence towards life and consciousness, and that those elements of nature which seem harsh or indifferent towards human life are in fact necessary to the highly integrated structure of physical laws which makes emergent human life possible.

There can and should be consilience between physical and value explanations. But it will not be a reduction of one to the other. Science is, after all, an activity of intelligent and creative personal agents. The physical explanations which constitute the study of nature may aim to be value free in their expression, but their pursuit embodies the values of intelligibility and understanding, of intellectual beauty and elegance, which arise from the intrinsic nature of the human intellect. On the other hand, the goals which humans articulate and express in the exercise of their free agency require a regular, ordered and largely (but not wholly) predictable world as their context. So true consilience will show how both physical and evaluational forms of explanation are oriented to each other, and how each requires the other for a full understanding even of its own proper character.

Reference

Wilson, E.O. (1998) *Consilience*, London: Little, Brown and Co.

28

TWO FORMS OF
EXPLANATION
A response to Ward

Martien E. Brinkman

In my response to Keith Ward's contribution on 'Two Forms of Explanation' I shall concentrate on the second section of his presentation, 'Theism and the priority of personal or value explanation'. The point Ward is dealing with in the first section seems convincing. Indeed, there is widespread disagreement among physicists about the extent to which laws of physics explain physical occurrences.

In a certain sense, Ward's remarks with regard to the question of whether total consilience is part of, or even identical with, the 'scientific world-view' deal with the preconditions for theology. If there would be total consilience between universal laws of physics and all other imaginable laws and principles of human life, the theologians could be silent furthermore.

Ward's line of thought

I would like to address especially Ward's concept of God. My main question concerns the proposed relation between God, supreme value and intrinsic goodness.

First I shall give a sketch of Ward's line of argument by means of some literal quotations which I place in a certain order presenting the logic of Ward's concept of God. I quote four short sentences from Ward's chapter in this volume:

1   'If I freely intend to do something, then by definition what I intend to do is of value to me.'
2   'If God creates this universe, then it is by definition of value to God.'
3   'This implies that the universe can be explained as purposively chosen by God for the sake of the values it realizes'
4   'The answer to the question "Why does the universe exist, and exist as it does?" is that it is intended by God, and is of value to God because of the intrinsically good things it contains.'

This line of thought explains a lot of important aspects of God. It says to the believer: you are intended by God, you are of value to God and God has a purpose for your life. Ward gives here a good example of one of the main tasks of adequate theology, namely to explain who we are, why we exist, etc. The way Ward answers these questions, however, has some implications for our concept of God and I will try to make some of them more explicit.

Ward's line of thought finds its climax at the point at which he relates God, supreme value and intrinsic goodness. His basic theological axiom is that a supreme personal agent exists because it is the supreme form of value. Or in other words, God exists in order that the supreme value should be realized. Then a next and last step follows: something is of value to God because it is intrinsically good. Put in the same personal, pastoral terms as those just quoted, that would mean: you are of value to God, because you are intrinsically good.

Every continental Calvinist, however, brought up with the Heidelberg Catechism, will – upon reading this sentence – furrow his or her brow and refer to the words of Sunday 2, question 5 of this Catechism, which talks about our distorted nature 'prone to hate God and my neighbour'. 'Where could I find intrinsic goodness?' every Calvinist would ask. That same question seems to be the background to this volume, *Is Nature Ever Evil?* That sounds like an extremely Calvinistic question and suggests that in any case nature is certainly not good, as many Roman Catholics would assume.

Of course, I am fully aware of the fact that Ward's concept of God is primarily a philosophical concept of God. It states: if there is to be a reasonable concept of God as hypothesis, the theologian has as a philosopher to show that it could be rational to choose this God. Even such a God as hypothesis, however, has to stand the test of consistency with any given religious tradition. Ward's own work is a good indication of the preparedness to stand such a test. In *Religion and Human Nature*, for example, he deals with substantial themes of classical Christian theology (original sin, atonement, salvation, eschatology, etc.) in order to compare them with similar themes in other religions and to integrate them into his philosophical concept of God. Therefore, philosophical talk about God as hypothesis on the basis of a certain logic is for Ward not completely at odds with dealing with the classical substantial themes of Christian dogmatics. Hence, I consider my reference to this example of Calvinistic thinking as justified by his own procedure. I referred, in a certain sense at random, to a Calvinistic approach. I could have referred to a Baptist, Lutheran, Methodist or even Buddhist or Hindu approach as well.

Ward on original sin

The point to which I referred is the observation in many Christian traditions of a lack of visible goodness among people, in nature, etc. This observation is historically articulated in the doctrine of original sin. In a chapter on 'Original Sin' in *Religion and Human Nature* Ward dedicates many thought-provoking pages to this doctrine. He underscores that to live by faith is to accept the inevitable disorder of this world and to accept the power of divine love to open up a positive relationship to God. The doctrine of original sin prevents us – so Ward states – from being utopian about human dreams of a perfect society. It counsels total reliance on divine forgiveness and mercy for healing human incapacities and granting fulfilment in a life of perfected relationships beyond the ambiguities of this earthly life (Ward 1998: 185).

If we try to relate this paragraph on the ambiguities of earthly life to the above-mentioned emphasis on the strict relation between God, supreme value and intrinsic goodness, I could imagine two solutions to cope with this tension. Either we relate every kind of evil and all the ambiguities of life to sinful human decisions and keep them far away from God, or we accept that the concept of supreme value and intrinsic goodness is a concept that differs in relation to God from how it relates to us.

The first solution was the solution of the Heidelberg Catechism and virtually the whole of Western Christianity. It states that all kinds of evil, moral and natural, point to the so-called 'Fall' of Adam and Eve. I would not like to defend this position. I have criticized it elsewhere and shall not repeat myself here (Brinkman 1999: 11–56).

The second solution – emphasizing that the use of the concept of supreme value and intrinsic goodness is a concept that differs in relation to God from how it applies to us – seems to be the option or at least the implication of the choice of Ward.

If this interpretation is correct, we are confronted with a serious problem, because the origin of Ward's concept of supreme value and intrinsic goodness is theism and therefore God. Without God no supreme value and no intrinsic goodness was the line of his argument. If we have to accept, however, that our values are different from God's, and if we have to admit that our goodness is of a different kind from God's goodness, we have to account for the gap between supreme value and intrinsic goodness in relation to God and to us. In the history of Christianity this is the point at which the doctrines of original sin and of redemption have to be brought out.

Some suggestions

It might be that a concept in which the distance between God and us is more explicitly digested could be of help in overcoming this dilemma. In order to discover such an approach I would suggest reflecting upon five more or less intertwined aspects of the relation creator–creature.

1   Belief in God the creator implies a certain degree of independence of the Earth from God, like the work of an artist has a certain independence from the artist. The Earth is not alien to God, but different from God.

2   The Earth, however, is not completely different from God. Nicholas of Cusa spoke of the *aliud* (the other) and the non-*aliud* (non-other) character of creation in relation to its creator. In this sense dependence and independence are not completely opposite concepts. The non-divine Earth and the divine creator remain interrelated, as a result of God's continuous action in sustaining the earth by means of his Spirit.

3   In the creative work of God's Spirit we can recognize the integration of the experience of creative contingency and preserving providence. Such a dual unity between contingency (freedom) and determination creates some order out of our earthly chaos of moral and natural good and evil.

4   The experience of 'goodness' with regard to the Earth could, because of all its ambiguities, be described as 'good enough to live with'. Is that intrinsic goodness? In any case, I would like to call the Earth a 'good enough mother', not a perfect one, but good enough for us.

5   To relate God to supreme value and intrinsic goodness means always that we compare God with humans according to the rule of the *via eminentiae*. There is nothing wrong with that procedure. The biblical idea of humans as the image of God implies that God is our perfection. Is God, however, also something other than that?

That's my main question: is this concept of God not too much developed according to the rules of a model of growth, of progress in which God is always the one who transcends our highest stage of development? This line of thought has a long and eminent history in Christian thought (Augustine, Anselm, Aquinas, etc.), but other, more *apophatic* or dialectical lines of thought have such long and eminent histories as well. Hence, my plea to look for other approaches which might be more adequate to account for the ambiguities of earthly life.

I am stressing this issue especially in the context of the discussion in this volume, because not only too much consilience between physics and the humanities makes theologians silent, but too much consilience between God and us could have the same effect.

References

Brinkman, M.E. (1999) *Sacraments of Freedom*, Zoetermeer: Meinema.

Ward, K. (1998) *Religion and Human Nature*, Oxford: Clarendon Press.

Ward, K. (2003) 'Two forms of explanation', in W.B. Drees (ed.) *Is Nature Ever Evil? Religion, Science and Value*, London: Routledge.

29

TWO FORMS OF EXPLANATION

A response to Ward

Ronald Meester

Although not explicitly stated, I interpret Ward's very interesting chapter as dealing with the relation between science and religion. Its goal is to convince the reader that a so-called physical explanation is not the whole story, and that in order to understand the universe in an adequate way one should also refer to so-called value explanation, which is normative in nature. This is an extremely important and fundamental issue.

An interesting phenomenon now occurs: I agree completely and unconditionally with the theme and the final conclusion of the chapter, but at the same time I have serious problems with the route followed and with the flow of the argument. Let me try to make this clear, taking the last sentence of Ward's paper as a starting point. 'So true consilience will show how both physical and evaluational forms of explanation are oriented to each other, and how each requires the other for a full understanding even of its own proper character.' How true this is! But when I talk about these matters with my scientific colleagues, the very first thing that needs to be done is to convince them that there is anything to talk about at all. Most people in the scientific community would argue (perhaps like Edward Wilson) that there is no need to talk about irrational beliefs and other explanations apart from the physical, for the simple reason that they think that there is nothing there. I do not think one can logically, by reason alone, convince Edward Wilson that not all processes can be reduced to physics. And, I have to admit, I will not be convinced by reason either. In that light it is extremely dangerous to build up an argument which apparently uses rational and logical steps which are amenable to logical counterarguments. Let me illustrate this with two examples.

1   According to Ward, the genesis of new states in the universe will have to generate new causal laws. Why so? These new states could simply be new input states into already existing laws. One could conceivably imagine a law that tells us how any state x is transformed into some state y, even if state x has never occurred in the universe so far. Also, it

is clear from Ward's paper that it is not obvious what we exactly mean by a physical law. In that light, a claim that new laws have to be generated is what we mathematicians call 'fishy'.

2   Ward claims that it is impossible to map the mental on to the physical. His argument is that many thoughts are new so there cannot be an existing translation for them. So one can never set up the required translation rules. Well, I agree that we human beings would never be able to set up these rules but, again, such rules could conceivably exist. And in the same way as before, new thoughts could serve as new input for these rules. A scientific sceptic will not be convinced by Ward's argument, and neither am I. As a side remark I want to point out that any mental process necessarily has a physical substratum, and it seems pointless to me to try to reduce one to the other.

The situation does not improve when Ward claims that most religious believers think or believe that there is a God who created the universe for some consciously entertained reason. Building up an argument with a notion of such an anthropomorphic God means losing many religious believers from the start, and among them there will be many Christians, including myself. I am a professional mathematician, and, at the very best, an amateur theologian, but I do have the impression that Ward's notion of an omnipotent, omniscient and good God is not really supported by modern theology. I completely agree with Ward when he says that if the theistic hypothesis is true, any explanation of the universe which fails to mention the purpose of God is incomplete. The problem is that I think that an argument for various forms of explanation should not be based on the theistic hypothesis. I do not believe in the theistic hypothesis as set out in Ward's paper, but I do believe in his final conclusion. It seems to me, there-fore, that the argument better be based on religious and spiritual claims which are, to some extent at least, independent of the religious tradition. Theism does not fall into this category. Let me illustrate this point with two examples from Ward's paper.

1   Ward claims that for anyone who believes in a creator God, value explanation must be the most fundamental form of explanation. Maybe so, but this point of view will frustrate the dialogue with the scientific community. Actually, by insisting on the theistic point of view, the theist does not really differ from the scientist who claims that all knowledge and all explanation is physical. Both statements cannot be verified, so both are statements of belief. The theistic claim is clearly speculative. Just as speculative as the reported claim of Edward Wilson that all processes can be reduced to simple physical laws.

2   Ward compares the neo-Darwinian thesis that we exist by accident to the theistic hypothesis that we exist because God wants us to exist.

Again, I do not see the point of this dualism, and I think the dilemma is a false dilemma, caused by the theistic hypothesis. John Haught (2000) has argued that the Darwinian thesis is a gift to theology and religion, rather than a danger or an enemy. He reaches this remarkable conclusion by distancing himself from the notion of an anthropomorphic God, and by interpreting creation as something that takes place here, everywhere and now.

The approach of Ward in this paper leads to a 'it does, it doesn't' discussion without any chance of agreement. As mentioned before, the reason for this is that both parties base their arguments on unverifiable claims. This is a rather sad state of affairs, which should, and perhaps can, be avoided. To this end, religion should perhaps try to argue from spiritual experience, since spiritual experience is part of every religious tradition. (Of course, spiritual experience is always interpreted in the actual religious tradition. I do not mean that spiritual experience is similar in all traditions, but they seem to share many important features.)

The most difficult task here, as I have already anticipated above, is to convince the scientific community that there is anything to talk about at all. A possible route was described by Ken Wilber (1998), who argued that religious experience is amenable to study by the scientific method. According to Wilber, just as taking up a microscope leads to a confirmation that cells exist, so does meditation lead to a confirmation that the divine exists as a phenomenon, not less real than cells are. Wilber doesn't reduce religion to science. He argues that science cannot ignore religion without giving up the method that is used by science itself.

I do not claim that Wilber has the last word in this discussion. One of his claims is that if religion is to survive in the modern world, it has to get rid of all statements that contradict science. I think that this demand is simply too big (in particular for many Christians). I also do not pretend to have the final answer, but I do have one more remark on the issue which I think is important.

As clearly explained by Ward in his paper, maybe the most important question here is: what does it mean to explain something? Maybe an explanation is nothing more than a reformulation in terms that we feel more familiar with. ('Familiar' does not mean 'simple'. A superstring can be quite familiar for a physicist, even though the very description of such an object requires very involved mathematics. A mathematician can be very familiar with the most abstract concepts.) For a physicist, these terms are perhaps physical laws. For a theist, an explanation in terms of God might serve the purpose. Sometimes I think that there is nothing more to say. As a contemporary Dutch mystic, Jan van den Oever, stated in a conversation: 'I have been searching for the answers to these questions for twenty years. Finally, the questions dissolved.'

References

Haught, J. (2000) *God after Darwin*, New York: Westview.

Ward, K. (2003) 'Two forms of explanation', in W.B. Drees (ed.) *Is Nature Ever Evil? Religion, Science and Value*, London: Routledge.

Wilber, K. (1998) *The Marriage of Sense and Soul: Integrating Science and Religion*, London: Random House.

30

THE EVALUATION OF
NATURAL REALITY

A watertight case?

Edwin Koster

Double vision is the fate of creatures with a glimpse of the view
sub specie eternitatis
(Nagel 1986: 88)

In (natural) reality all kinds of processes and events take place. Plants grow, flower and perish. The seasons come and go. Living creatures look for a place to live and a place to die. Sometimes the world seems to be a perfect, harmonious whole, at other moments it seems to drift from one catastrophe to the next.

There are different perspectives from which one can view (natural) reality. One approach, which can be identified as the way natural scientists observe the world, concentrates on processes in nature. Causes and effects are central to this approach and every effort is made to describe them in terms which are independent of human perception. From this point of view, nature is seen as a set of impersonal processes and frequently it is claimed that this approach proceeds from a neutral stance. An evaluation of nature based on such a description seems to be a pure subjective judgement. Another approach stresses the role of human actions. In this view reality is first of all the world in which we live, the world which is given in human experience. Events, among others determined by human reasons and motives, are seen as central in the process of understanding human and natural reality. From this point of view, the evaluation of reality takes place against a background of contextual practices and discussions.

In this paper I consider the evaluation of natural reality where human beings are involved. I will deal with a case in the field of environmental studies, where evaluation plays an important role. The main questions will be whether it is possible to describe natural reality from a 'neutral stance' and whether the evaluation of natural reality is just a matter of personal preferences. I shall argue that an evaluation of nature where human beings are involved needs scientific explanations as well as the interpretation of human actions.

Natural reality and human actions: a case study

In Western Europe the rain can be heavy and prolonged. Normally there are no far-reaching consequences. Nature knows how to manage excessive rainfall. Big rivers transport the surplus water to the sea. However, sometimes the water level in rivers such as the Rhine and the Meuse rises dangerously. In December 1993, for instance, heavy and constant rainfall in the Meuse basin in France and Belgium caused high water levels and floods in the south of the Netherlands. These floods led to the evacuation of 8,000 people and total damage of $120 million. A year later problems with the water level happened again. Heavy rainfall in Germany caused extremely high water volumes in the Rhine, the Meuse and their tributaries. As no measures had been taken since the previous year's floods, the threat of a dyke burst was quite serious in several places in the Netherlands. Approximately 250,000 people were evacuated and total damage of more than $500 million has been estimated (Schuurman 1995: 1–7).

The role played by climate change and human activities in all of this is interesting. During the past two centuries the climate has changed significantly. In a period of 130 years the average temperature of the surface of the Earth has risen by between 0.3 and 0.6 degrees Celsius. From systematic observations it can be inferred that this growth is not wholly caused by natural influences. Over the past three decades the scientific evidence for human-induced climate change has become steadily stronger. Human activities such as the combustion of fossil fuels, agricultural policy and industrial processes have led to an increase in the greenhouse effect, which has indirectly caused a rise in temperature. The Intergovernmental Panel on Climate Change concluded that 'the balance of evidence suggests that there is a discernible human influence on the climate' (Vellinga and Verseveld 1999: 2; Burton *et al.* 1998: xxi). Global warming brings about several kinds of climate change: a rise in the average amount of rainfall, heavier showers, a rise in the sea level, the melting of glaciers, etc. (Vellinga and Verseveld 1999: 3–5). These climate changes have consequences for the increasing risk of riverine flooding in the Netherlands. Many studies suggest that the rise in the water level and the peak amount of water transport are mainly caused by rainfall in the preceding period (Schuurman 1995: 36).

As has been noted, climate change – as a cause of riverine flooding – is not just the result of natural processes, but is also influenced by human behaviour. Other human activities such as deforestation, urbanization and changing the course of a river also raise the risk of riverine floods (Schuurman 1995: 36). Over a long period of time it can be said that in the Netherlands 'the root cause of riverine flooding lies in the expansion of human populace and activity' (Downing *et al.* 1996: 138).

Naturally we want to avoid disasters caused by river floods. What kind of policy can be developed to manage this? In *An Evaluation Tool for*

Natural Disaster Management (Tol *et al.* 1995) the method of cost–benefit analysis is used to reduce this risk. The cost–benefit ratio is considered to be a conceptually simple and elegant tool for project evaluation. It summarizes the desirability of disaster management. If the benefits of the policy exceed the cost, the ratio is greater than one and the policy is worthwhile. If the ratio is smaller than one, the cost exceeds the benefits and the policy should not be or have been implemented (1–4). Thus far the method seems to be transparent and simple. However, there are a number of problems and drawbacks. Benefits and costs cannot be compared directly. 'An evaluation of disaster management compares dissimilar entities, and not only apples and oranges, but also eggs and cows and motorboats. ... Ten lives saved and a million dollar of damage avoided are not easily compared to ten families forced to move and two million dollar invested. In addition, not only comparison, also measurement of costs and benefits appears to be hard' (5). Originally, the cost–benefit ratio was designed to evaluate projects which only had monetary costs and benefits. To use this method in cases like riverine flooding, a monetization approach has been developed. Each impact is valued in monetary terms. The monetary value reflects a hypothetical transfer of money equivalent to the impact. The obligation to move, for instance, can be estimated at $100,000 and the monetary value of accepting a riskier job may require an increase of at least $10 in the daily wage (5). Although some reject monetization on ethical grounds, according to the authors the alternative may be less attractive: 'Without an explicit valuation, valuation is either arbitrary or implicit. In case valuation is arbitrary, decisions are arbitrary. In case valuation is implicit, the values of the decision maker are imposed and cannot be checked' (6).

In (Tol *et al.* 1995) a general tool was developed to evaluate natural disaster management. Given that 'explicit valuation' seems to be highly dependent on the context and people involved, it would be very difficult to implement this tool in real situations, however.

Two different approaches to (natural) reality

In environmental cases all kinds of natural processes, human actions, evaluations and scientific disciplines are connected. This complex reality can be approached from several different points of view. The humanities, for instance, consider humans as the originators and organizers of the world in which we live. Our surrounding world – including political, social, historical, cultural, natural and religious aspects – is seen as constructed by individuals, groups and societies (Strasser 1985: 66). Explanations are given by citing reasons and motives for human actions. These explanations are interpretations of the meaning of the surrounding world: they articulate the meaning these actions have in certain local settings and historical contexts. In such contexts people also evaluate the world in terms of good and evil, right or wrong. This represents an aspect of explanation which can be called 'understanding'.

Natural science does not interpret the meaning of the surrounding world. It tries to describe and explain reality without considering social and historical contexts. Even if human actions play an important role in these contexts, natural scientific explanations are formulated in general terms and impersonal causal relations. Natural science is supposed to study a reality which is to a large extent independent of human beings (Drees 1996: 6–10). Although there are some interpretations of natural science and its practice which seem to challenge this view (an influential interpretation of quantum physics tells us that the observer plays an irreducible role in the description of micro-reality, and since Thomas Kuhn it is widely accepted that social and historical influences cannot be denied), many natural scientists still speak about an objective, univocal reality, which can be described and explained by impersonal instruments and methodologies (Bulhof 1988: 240–3). According to these scientists, explanations that cite reasons and motives can be substituted by the 'real' causes, which are described by the 'pure' sciences (Tuomela 1976: 190, 201). This approach of the natural sciences might be called 'a neutral stance' or 'View from Nowhere'. The View from Nowhere is the opposite of a personal, subjective view. The distinction between more subjective and more objective views can be regarded as a matter of degree: 'a view or form of thought is more objective than another if it relies less on the specifics of the individual's makeup and position in the world, or on the character of the particular type of creature he is' (Nagel 1986: 5). The View from Nowhere is the most objective view possible: it is without a centre and does not rely on any specific subjective capacity. Do the sciences have such a View from Nowhere, and, if so, how do they manage to achieve this view? Can this approach be substituted for the inquiry into human reasons and motives? And, last but not least, can the View from Nowhere be applied in environmental studies where evaluations play such an important role?

Natural sciences and the View from Nowhere

To deal with these questions, we will first have a look at 'the' method of the sciences. According to the Dutch philosopher C.A. van Peursen, the scientific method is, roughly speaking, characterized by a process of limiting and restricting ordinary language, perception and description. Ordinary language and perception are open systems: the meaning of words, sentences and texts are never fixed and ordinary perception is characterized by emotional and subjective interpretations which allow differentiations and uncertainties. The scientific method confines ordinary language to a closed system, regulated by logical rules, univocal definitions and generally accepted agreements. Furthermore, it transforms ordinary perception into scientific observation: from the unrestricted, open view of ordinary perception to a regulated observation of data belonging to prede-lineated phenomena (Van Peursen 1980: 27–43).

This process of transformation can be considered as an important step to the View from Nowhere. However, a few questions can be raised: is this image of 'the' scientific method, as a way to arrive at the View from Nowhere, a realistic one? Does it link up well with insights of philosophers of science in the tradition of Kuhn? Does it match, for instance, the ideas of certain scholars (in particular from the 'Starnberg school') who state that social needs and interests form the external guidelines for theory-formation (Krohn and Schäfer 1983: 46; cf. Rip 1989)? So had we not better deny any difference between ordinary language, perception and description on the one hand and scientific language, observation and description on the other? After all, both domains seem to be influenced by social and historical conditions. Furthermore, can we not say that there is a common or shared dimension in all human rationality present in both ordinary and scientific knowledge: the performance of critical discernment, the giving of the best possible reasons, the aims of optimal understanding and effective problem-solving, etc. (Van Huyssteen 1999: 118, 131–7)?

In my opinion, these questions and the notion of 'the' scientific method can be reconciled. Let us consider two concepts: 'local knowledge' and 'standardization'. According to J. Rouse (natural) scientific knowledge is local knowledge. A research project cannot be usefully disentangled from the scientist's skilful 'craft knowledge' of a field of objects and practices. The understanding of a particular scientific research project is always locally situated: crucial to such understanding is the reference to a partic-ular configuration of people, skills, equipment and concerns. Such skills, for example, can only be transferred outside their original physical setting and local community after one has gained a certain knowledge about the way the skills are dependent on their context and learned how to apply one's skills in the new context. What can count as a justified scientific claim is in part determined by local, practical understanding (Rouse 1987: 88–93, 108–11). But, as Rouse noticed, 'scientific knowledge does often appear shorn of contextual reference, and the ability to extend scientific capabilities outside the laboratory has been a hallmark of modern science and has been especially prominent in shaping its cultural image' (Rouse 1987: 112). Since scientific results are exchanged all over the world, the theory of scientific knowledge as local knowledge must be questioned. According to Rouse, this exchange is made possible because scientific knowledge can be standardized or delocalized.

The standardization of scientific knowledge means that local knowledge is transformed to make it applicable outside its original setting. This process can be compared to the transformation of a tool originally designed for a specific task within a particular context into a 'more general-purpose item of equipment'. From wrench to adjustable spanner, so to speak. The process of transforming local scientific knowledge into universal scientific knowledge succeeds, but not without some loss of context and clarity (Rouse 1987: 113–19). An example of the standardization of local knowledge can be found in water management in the Netherlands. As a nation born from the winning of land against water, the higher water levels are not the only threat the Netherlands have to deal with. Land drainage lowers water levels in much of Holland and causes soil subsidence. To keep our feet dry it is paradoxically necessary to allow higher water levels, and to restore wetland ecosystems in select areas. Already a number of local, relatively small (100–200 hectares) restoration projects have been implemented. To derive 'a regional performance indicator for spatial equity', and thus implement larger projects with a regional scope, a process of standardization (with the loss of specific, local conditions) is applied (Van Drunen *et al.* 2000: 9–11).

In my view local scientific knowledge is a phase in the development from ordinary knowledge to standardized scientific knowledge. Local scientific knowledge is related to the local setting of practices, skills, criteria, etc. It is connected with social and historical contexts. But it has also incorporated standardized knowledge which already is commonly accepted, and Rouse seems to neglect this. This may be one of the reasons why 'local' scientific knowledge has the capacity to be standardized. Another reason might be the transformation Van Peursen mentioned. To conclude, I think it is possible to describe the transformation from ordinary knowledge to standardized scientific knowledge in two steps. First is the step from an open system of ordinary language (with emotional, subjective and ethical dimensions) to a fixed system of local scientific knowledge. These forms of knowledge are both related to their social and cultural contexts. Second is the step from local scientific knowledge to standardized scientific knowledge. The latter is a general, applicable form of knowledge which loses some precision and contextual diversity. In this way the sciences increase their power over nature. The present level of science and technology would not have been possible without such methodologies. However, (natural) science abstracts from ordinary reality.

The View from Nowhere and the evaluation of natural reality

Now the process of standardization, as a way to realize the View from Nowhere, seems to be a fundamental process in the development of human knowledge, and it can be regarded as the main tool to control natural reality. But what may happen in the pursuit of objectivity is that the view without a centre – which is also in a sense featureless – escapes from the specific contingencies of one's personal and social context and is allowed to predominate (Nagel 1986: 9–17). Here, two remarks on the scope of the View from Nowhere and the possibility of the application of the process of standardization must be made.

The first remark concerns the relation between values and the View from Nowhere. From my analysis of the transformation from ordinary knowledge to standardized scientific knowledge, I propose that there is no guarantee that the whole of reality coincides with what we would arrive at if we carried the pursuit of objectivity to the limit. We are in need of different approaches to reality. Where values and the meaning of life are involved, we should look for a way between an 'inner' and an 'outer' perspective. On the one hand, from the inner perspective the most important values and conditions that determine whether life makes sense seem given. They are part of the human condition and are determined more specifically by a particular person and his or her social and historical setting. On the other hand, from the outer perspective every person hopes to arrive at normative judgements and at formulations of values which are to a large extent independent of a specific context. We do this with the intention of making such judgements more acceptable from an external standpoint. We want to share our values with other people (Nagel 1986: 138–43, 215). However, there is one fatal danger: 'the pursuit of objectivity with respect to value runs the risk of leaving value behind altogether' (Nagel 1986: 209; cf. Strasser 1985: 27). It can be concluded that the View from Nowhere may increase our power to control natural reality, but in contexts where values play an important role the process of standardization as a means of conceiving objectivity seems to eliminate these values.

The second remark is on the acceptability of the loss of local knowledge. Thus far we have seen that the View from Nowhere cannot be achieved without some loss of local knowledge. Rouse developed his thoughts mainly through the natural sciences, especially physics. Now it cannot be denied that physics contains theories with general features and universal scope. But can these results be achieved in other sciences as well? Biology, for instance, seems to have little or no general theories. For example, there are many specific and local theories of evolution which together give an image of evolutionary processes. The standardization of these theories would give a vague and inapplicable result, for the complexity of organisms does not allow for the construction of a practical, standardized theory such as can be found in physics (Van der Steen and Kamminga 1991: 445–67; Van der Steen 1994: 128–32). Academic disciplines studying objects with a similar or even higher degree of complexity (such as psychology, social sciences and history) should perhaps not be expected to contain theories that can be standardized. In the case of environmental studies, several scientific disciplines are involved and theories seem to be fundamentally dependent on contextual conditions (cf. Cheney 1989: 120). With reference to the history of river flooding and flood management in the Netherlands, links between economic and technological developments, and climate and political change, must be considered. It is hard to expect standardization to be a productive strategy here. Values and ethical evaluations would have to be filtered out.

Neutral stance or subjective evaluation?

Environmental studies can be characterized by a multidisciplinary approach. Researchers in this area have diverse backgrounds, ranging from chemistry and ecology to economics and other social sciences. Some of these disciplines can use the View from Nowhere. However, to evaluate natural reality and to determine effective disaster management this will not suffice. Reality is a complex combination of all kinds of factors, and human reasons and motives play an important role. The intelligibility and rationality of human actions are not taken into consideration if the View from Nowhere predominates. A second approach is necessary in order to complete the approach of the natural sciences (Widdershoven 1987: 157–61; Von Wright 1976). Cost–benefit analysis is a good example of the evaluation of natural reality using a combination of both approaches. To some extent, standardization is necessary to develop this method. Otherwise no calculations can be made to compare costs and benefits in advance. However, its 'evaluation tool' can only be employed by making subjective valuations which are highly dependent on local settings and conditions: the monetization of all kinds of human values. Paradoxically however, the tool is only possible if the analysis abstracts (at least to a certain degree) from individual preferences.

To conclude, culture seems to be the indispensable context of values. Human behaviour has an ethical dimension only from being seen in a wider perspective, from being set in a context of aims and cognitions. As MacIntyre puts it: 'I can only answer the question "What am I to do?" if I can answer the prior question "Of what story or stories do I find myself a part?"' (MacIntyre 1981: 216) Ethical questions can only be answered against the backdrop of a cultural and moral context, although the answers and values are not determined by these contexts. An evaluation of (natural) reality begins with our own moral experience. But in interpreting this experience we use our capacity to transcend our own situation and reflect on it as if we were outsiders. Here scientific results may play an important role. The end of this is not the elimination of human reasons and motives, but an evaluation which does justice to the contextual, human experience.

Both approaches are needed in the evaluation of natural reality. A neutral stance alone – if at all possible – is not sufficient. Through a prudent evaluation that uses both points of view, our glimpse of the view *sub specie aeternitatis* may no longer dazzle us by illusions.

References

Bulhof, I.N. (1988) 'Hermeneutiek en natuurwetenschappen', in T. de Boer *et al.* *Hermeneutiek: Filosofische grondslagen van mens- en cultuurwetenschappen*, Meppel: Boom.

Burton, I., Feenstra, J.F., Smith, J.B. and Tol, R.S.J. (eds) (1998) *Handbook on Methods for Climate Change Impact Assessment and Adaptation Strategies*, Amsterdam: UNEP/Instituut voor Milieuvraagstukken (IVM).

Cheney, J. (1989) 'Postmodern Environmental Ethics: Ethics as Bioregional Narrative', *Environmental Ethics* 11: 117–34.

Downing, T.E., Olsthoorn, A.A. and Tol, R.S.J. (eds) (1996) *Climate Change and Extreme Events*, Amsterdam: IVM.

Drees, W.B. (1996) *Religion, Science and Naturalism*, Cambridge: Cambridge University Press.

Krohn, W. and Schäfer, W. (1983) 'Agricultural Chemistry: the Origin and Structure of a Finalized Science', in W. Schäfer (ed.) *Finalization in Science: The Social Orientation of Scientific Progress*, Dordrecht: Reidel, 17–52.

MacIntyre, A.C. (1981) *After Virtue: A Study in Moral Theory*, London: Duckworth.

Nagel, T. (1986) *The View from Nowhere*, New York: Oxford University Press.

Rip, A. (1989) 'Sturing en stuurbaarheid van de wetenschappen. Het model van de Starnbergers', in M. Korthals (ed.) *Wetenschapsleer. Filosofisch en maatschappelijk perspectief op de natuur- en sociaal-culturele wetenschappen*, Meppel: Boom, 187–200.

Rouse, J. (1987) *Knowledge and Power: Toward a Political Philosophy of Science*, New York: Cornell University Press.

Schuurman, A. (1995) *Een verzekering voor een veilige Maas?*, Amsterdam: IVM.

Strasser, S. (1985) *Understanding and Explanation: Basic Ideas Concerning the Humanity of the Human Sciences*, Pittsburg: Duquesne University Press.

Tol, R.S.J., van der Werff, P.E. and Misson, C. (1995) *An Evaluation Tool for Natural Disaster Management*, Amsterdam: IVM.

Tuomela, R. (1976) 'Explanation and Understanding of Human Behavior', in J. Manninen and R. Tuomela (eds) *Essays on Explanation and Understanding: Studies in the Foundations of Humanities and Social Sciences*, Dordrecht: Reidel, 183–205.

Van der Steen, W.J. (1994) 'Theologie, ook een gewone wetenschap?', in W.B. Drees (ed.) *Denken over God en wereld: theologie, natuurwetenschap en filosofie in wisselwerking*, Kampen: Kok, 125–38.

Van der Steen, W.J. and Kamminga, H. (1991) 'Laws and Natural History in Biology', *British Journal for the Philosophy of Science* 42: 445–67.

Van Drunen, M., Gilbert, A., Mulder, P. and Wulfse, S. (eds) (2000) *Annual Report 1999, Institute for Environmental Studies*, Amsterdam: IVM.

Van Huyssteen, J.W. (1999) *The Shaping of Rationality: Toward Interdisciplinarity in Theology and Science*, Grand Rapids, MI: Eerdmans.

Van Peursen, C.A. (1980) *De opbouw van de wetenschap: een inleiding in de wetenschapsleer*, Meppel: Boom.

Vellinga, P. and Verseveld, W.J. (1999) *Broeikaseffect, Klimaatverandering en het Weer*, Amsterdam: IVM.

Von Wright, G.H. (1976) 'Replies', in J. Manninen and R. Tuomela (eds) *Essays on Explanation and Understanding: Studies in the Foundations of Humanities and Social Sciences*, Dordrecht: Reidel, 371–413.

Widdershoven, G.A.M. (1987) *Handelen en rationaliteit: een systematisch overzicht van het denken van Wittgenstein, Merleau-Ponty, Gadamer en Habermas*, Meppel: Boom.

31

'OUGHT' IN A WORLD
THAT JUST 'IS'

Lindon B. Eaves

Studies of religion and values have revealed the complex genetic and social factors that shape many aspects of humanity that were once regarded as outside the scope of scientific study. Some of the recent data concerning the genetic and environmental causes of individual differences are presented. Although these studies by themselves do not address some of the most profound human qualities, they establish a *prima facie* case for a unified theory in which human religious values might ultimately be understood in the same material terms as any other aspect of human behaviour. There is a temptation for the significance of such studies to be overstated and exploited against the overall human interest. While such research does not necessarily undermine the continuing adaptive significance of religious belief and practice, it certainly calls for a more nuanced understanding of the divine in the context of evolutionary materialism and requires a careful restatement of traditional human themes such as justice and freedom in a new intellectual environment.

Recent genetic studies of behaviour have begun to dissolve the distinction between matter and spirit in ways that open up new horizons for our understanding of those characteristics that were once thought to be quintessentially 'human' and to separate us from the rest of the plant and animal world. Population studies are shedding new light on how genetic and social factors contribute to differences in behaviours that are at the core of human life, including our attitudes, religious consciousness and values. The emerging picture shows that the influences of genes reach many aspects of human behaviour that have traditionally been viewed as purely social in origin.

The current paper outlines some of the research in the genetics of behaviour, and tries to delineate what conclusions may and may not follow from these findings and to speculate about their implications for how we will construe our humanity in the future.

Genetic and social factors in religion and values

Attempts to quantify the roles of genes in the genesis of human differences are as old as the modern science of genetics itself. While Mendel was working on his classic experiments in plant hybridization and Darwin was detailing the empirical foundation for his theory of evolution by natural selection, Francis Galton was conducting his crude but classic studies of hereditary genius and the histories of twins (Galton 1883). These three intellectual trajectories were largely independent, and sometimes even in conflict until the classical work of Ronald Fisher reconciled, on the one hand, many of the empirical findings of Galton and his successors on family resemblance with the particulate models of Mendelian inheritance (1918) and, on the other hand, Mendelian inheritance and evolution by natural selection (1958). To the trajectories empowered by Darwin, Mendel and Galton we must add a fourth, namely the progressive analysis of the molecular basis of inheritance ranging from the early demonstration of inborn errors of metabolism transmitted according to Mendelian principles (Garrod 1923) through the recognition that nucleic acids formed the hereditary material to the astonishing integration of previous data realized in Watson and Crick's (1953) revelation of the structure of DNA and the subsequent working out of the historic insight towards the current sequencing of the human genome.

Against the background of these major strategic developments to uncover the fundamental characteristics of the hereditary mechanism there has been an enormous investment in trying to trace, with the best methods available, the part that this mechanism played in creating normal and abnormal variants of human characteristics.

Twin studies of behaviour: the logic of the twin method

Surprisingly, it was Augustine of Hippo (1983) who first used the twin method for scientific ends. In an attempt to disprove the power of the planets over human destiny, Augustine noted in the fifth book of the *City of God* that even though twins were typically born with remarkably similar horoscopes, their life histories were frequently remarkably different. Augustine, however, did not appreciate the implications of the distinction between identical and fraternal twins. It was Galton (1883) who can claim to be the father of modern twin research, for it was he who first speculated that identical twins were genetically identical (although the words 'gene' and 'genetics' had not yet been coined) because they originated from the division of the same fertilized egg into two separate 'monozygotic' twin individuals. Fraternal twins, on the other hand, shared the same 'genetic' resemblance as siblings because they were indeed just that, having been produced by the fertilization by separate sperm of two separate eggs released at the same cycle, resulting in a pair of 'dizygotic' twins. Manifest ('phenotypic') differences within pairs of monozygotic twins were expected to be due to the effects of environment alone, whereas those within dizygotic pairs reflected both environmental effects within the family and those due to the Mendelian assortment and segregation of genetic differences at parental gamete formation.

In the century or more since Galton's seminal insight there have been six principal developments that have added greatly to the power of the twin method: 1) a more precise quantitative appreciation of the effects of genes and environment on twin resemblance, making it possible to formulate and test richer models for the causes of twin similarities and their development; 2) improved methods of statistical analysis that allow specific hypotheses to be tested more rigorously and permit more precise estimation of critical quantities from the data; 3) development of standardized methods for physiological and behavioural assessment; 4) the recognition of the need for large, population-based samples and the development of twin registries of many thousands of pairs to meet this need; 5) inclusion of measures of specific aspects of the individual and social environment in epidemiological twin studies; 6) extension of the twin design to include the relatives of twins, notably their parents, spouses, siblings and children. To these six trends, we should add a seventh whose implications have still fully to be realized, namely the ability to genotype individual twins and their relatives for a growing number of highly polymorphic markers at functional and other locations throughout the genome.

The basic theory of classical studies of twins reared together

Figure 31.1 summarizes three scenarios among several that can arise in typical twin studies. The scenarios each relate the pattern of similarity (assessed on the scale of correlation) in samples of monozygotic (MZ) and dizygotic (DZ) pairs to different patterns in the causes of individual differences for a measured human trait such as stature, blood-pressure, personality or ability. The correlation coefficient, sometimes expressed as a percentage, varies between zero and unity as a function of the similarity between members of a pair. Zero correlation implies that members of a pair are no more nor less alike than individuals paired at random from a population. A correlation of 1.0 (100 per cent) implies that members of a pair are perfectly similar. Intermediate values imply intermediate levels of similarity. Correlations will be negative if, on average, high trait values in one twin go with low trait values in the other. One way of interpreting correlations is to think of them as measures of the average proportion of factors affecting a trait that are shared by members of a pair. For traits that are not

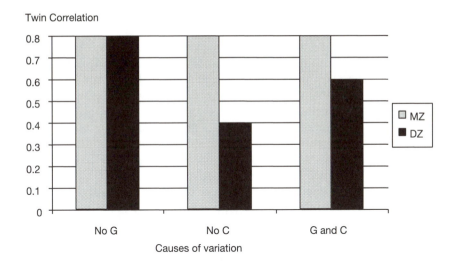

Figure 31.1 Twin correlations: three scenarios

continuous like height or weight, or that are markedly non-normal in their distribution, other correlation-like statistics may sometimes be computed that have similar interpretations.

In the absence of genetic effects ('No G') and with only effects of the shared environment of twin pairs influencing the trait, we expect the correlations to be the same for MZ and DZ twins. In Figure 31.1 the height of the bars are proportional to the correlations, so in the 'No G' case the bars for MZ and DZ twins are equally tall, indicating that, even though there are no genetic effects ('G'), there are significant effects of the shared environment common to members of a twin pair ('C'), and that one pair shares environmental effects that differ from those shared by another pair. The correlation is rarely 100 per cent even in monozygotic pairs because some unique environmental effects ('E') usually affect one twin in the family but not the other. These effects are sometimes known as the 'unique' environmental effects or the 'within-family' environment.

The second scenario ('No C') in Figure 31.1 corresponds to the alternative extreme case in which there are genetic effects ('G') but no shared environmental effects ('C'). In this case, the precise results will depend on how the genes work and how people choose their mates, but in the simplest of worlds, in which all the genetic effects are additive and cumulative and in which mates select one another at random, we expect the correlation of DZ twins to be exactly half that for MZ twins. In the real world the effects of sampling will mean that this is never *exactly* true but it is possible to test whether the ratio of MZ:DZ correlations agrees with the 2:1 ratio of the 'No C' scenario within the range of deviations that could arise by chance given the known precision of correlations based on particular sample sizes.

If genetic effects are not additive, for example if the effects of one gene depend on a person's genetic constitution at one or more other genes ('epistasis'), the DZ correlation is expected to dip below one half of the MZ correlation, although the sample sizes or non-additive effects have to be large before such effects can be detected statistically.

If mating is not random (i.e. if spouses are correlated) the 2:1 ratio will also not apply. If like tends to marry like so that trait values of spouses are correlated positively ('positive assortative mating'), the genetic correlation between DZ twins will be increased relative to that for MZ twins so that the DZ twin correlation will now be more than half the MZ correlation, a finding that will mimic the third scenario in which the effects of the shared environment as well as genes create twin similarity.

The third set of correlations in Figure 31.1 illustrates the pattern to be expected if *both* genetic and shared environmental factors ('G' *and* 'C') contribute to twin resemblance. Now the DZ correlation is significantly *less* than the MZ correlation (a reflection of genetic effects, 'G') but it is still significantly *greater* than half the MZ correlation (a reflection of shared environmental factors, 'C'). In reality there are a number of additional nuances affecting the analysis and interpretation of twin data. We have already mentioned the possible effects of non-additive genetic effects that may, under some circumstances, cancel out some or all of the apparent effects of the shared environment in twin data (Jinks and Fulker 1970). The genetic effects of positive assortative mating may also inflate the DZ correlation, giving the appearance of shared environmental effects in classical twin data (Jinks and Fulker 1970). Social interaction between twins, either competition within pairs or mutual reinforcement of one another's behaviour, affects twin resemblance and variation in predictable ways (e.g. Eaves 1976; Carey 1986).

If genetic effects are additive and if mating is random, in the absence of social interactions between twins, we may quantify the contributions of G, C and E to individual differences by simple algebra. The contribution of the within-family environment, E, can be estimated as $1 - rMZ$, where rMZ denotes the correlation for MZ twins. The (additive) genetic contribution, G, may be estimated from $2(rMZ - rDZ)$ and the contribution of the shared, or common, environment, C, estimated as $2rDZ - rMZ$. In practice, the contributions are estimated somewhat differently by more general methods that extend to more complicated models and data sets (see, for example, Neale and Cardon 1994), but these more refined approaches yield estimates that are very close to those provided by these simple calculations.

Perhaps the most challenging assumption of the classical twin study is that the environments of MZ and DZ twins are equally correlated. It has been argued, with some empirical support, that MZ twins are more often treated alike, are dressed similarly, have more frequent contact as adults, etc. Such effects could inflate the MZ correlation relative to the DZ correlation for behavioural outcomes influenced by these environmental measures. This 'equal environments' assumption has been tested in a number of ways. Typically, it is found that MZ twins do indeed share more similar environments, but it is also typically the case that such environmental effects do not have a major impact on the behavioural measures of primary interest (see, for example, Loehlin and Nichols 1976), and it is impossible to demonstrate definitively that such 'environmental' measures are not themselves influenced by the genes of the individual. In this case, we have what behaviour-geneticists term 'genotype–environment correlation', i.e. the environment that an individual creates or is exposed to depends ultimately on the individual's genotype (e.g. Cattell 1965). Insofar as the individual's own genotype influences exposure to salient environmental factors, we will expect measures of the environment to behave like 'genetic' variables in twin studies and, indeed, to contribute to estimates of genetic contributions to specific outcome variables (see, for example, Jinks and Fulker 1970). We expect the possibility of such genotype–environment correlations to be especially important in humans who have a long period of behavioural development during which small early genetic differences may be reinforced or exaggerated by repeated exposure to correlated environmental input.

Religious affiliation: a model of purely social inheritance

Armed with the theoretical background, we can explore some of the critical data that illustrate the diverse patterns of genetic and social influence upon individual differences in religion and values. Figure 31.2 presents the pattern of MZ and DZ similarity for religious affiliation in a large sample of twins from the Australian Twin Registry (see Eaves *et al.* 1990). 'Religious affiliation' is a nominal variable comprising twins' self-assignments to one of several religious denominations or none (Catholic, Protestant, Eastern Orthodox, etc.). For this reason the measure of resemblance is not the correlation coefficient, which is only appropriate for ordered continuous variables, but a 'correlation-like' statistic that summarizes the association for nominal variables. Resemblance is substantial for MZ and DZ twins. More importantly, however, DZ twins are just as similar as MZ twins. This result corresponds to the first scenario of Figure 31.1. That is, religious affiliation is a paradigm of a *non-genetic* trait in which there is substantial family resemblance (twins are very highly correlated), but the correlation between twins is purely environmental in origin. A more complete analysis (Eaves *et al.* 1990), including the religious affiliations of the parents of twins, shows that a large part of

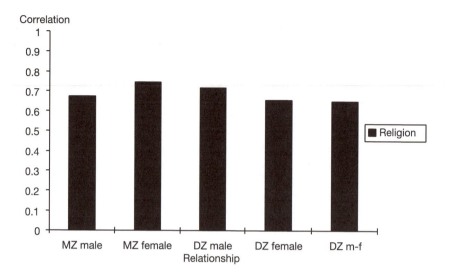

Figure 31.2 Religious affiliation in Australian twins
Source: Kirk, Maes *et al.* 1999.

the environmental influence on twins' religious affiliation derives, as might be expected, from their parents.

Testing the model: twin correlations for stature

The findings for religious affiliation are no surprise. Indeed, we would be suspicious of a method that showed there were genes that influenced whether individuals were catholic or protestant. (Actually, we can think of some ways in which genes might even do that, but we would be surprised if it were a large effect!) It would help our comfort with the twin model to see data for a variable that is more likely to be predominately genetic.

Figure 31.3 shows twin correlations for stature from the 'Virginia 30,000' study of twins and their relatives (e.g. Eaves *et al.* 1999a). Our data, like those of many other twin studies of stature, show the pattern expected from a variable in which genetic differences play the major role. As in the second scenario from Figure 31.1, the MZ correlations are very high, indicating a small effect for the unique environment, E. The DZ correlation is much lower, suggesting that genetic effects, G, play a very large role in the creation of differences in stature. Furthermore, the DZ correlation is very close to half the MZ correlation, suggesting that the contribution of the common environment, C, is negligible for stature. In practice, data on additional relatives suggest that reality is a little more complex (Eaves *et al.* 1999a) but the findings for twins tell most of the story.

290

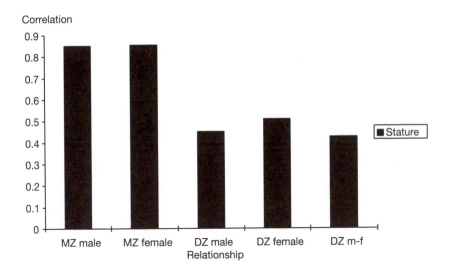

Figure 31.3 Twin resemblance for stature in the Virginia 30,000
Source: Eaves *et al.* 1999b.

Church attendance: a hint of genes?

Our real-world examples of a purely social variable (religious affiliation) and a variable that is largely genetic (stature) provide a background against which we can judge the findings for other variables of interest. Figure 31.4, for example, shows the results for large studies of church attendance in Australia and Virginia, USA (Kirk, Maes *et al.* 1999). The data for the two countries show some striking similarities and intriguing differences. Twin resemblance is large in both countries, but somewhat greater in Australia than Virginia. Surprisingly, both samples show the marks of both genetic and common environmental influence. That is, the pattern of twin correlations resembles that in the third, G and C, scenario of Figure 31.1. The DZ correlations are lower than the MZ correlations, suggesting that genetic effects are important but the DZ correlations are greater than half the MZ correlations, indicating that there are probably effects of the shared environment and/or of assortative mating. In their much more extensive analysis, in which they include the parents, spouses, siblings and children of twins, Kirk, Maes *et al.* conclude that there are slight but statistically significant differences in the quantitative contributions of genes and environment to church attendance in the two populations but that the overall qualitative findings are similar. The contribution of the shared environment turns out to come from a number of sources, including parents and other influences that do not depend directly on parents. The authors also show that the large correlation between spouses for church attendance leads to a pervasive increase in the genetic

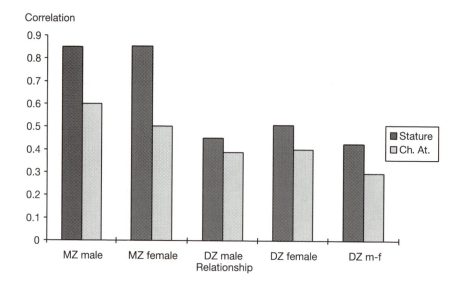

Figure 31.4 Twin resemblance for stature and church attendance in the Virginia
30,000
Source: Aggregated from Eaves *et al.* 1999b and from Kirk, Maes *et al.* 1999.

and social resemblance between family members. What surprises us,
however, is *the small but significant role of genetic factors (15–35 per cent*
of the total variation, depending on sex and nationality) in the creation of
individual differences in church attendance.

Does personality mediate the effect of genes on religious behaviour?

As might be expected, the analysis of church attendance shows small
contributions from a variety of different genetic and environmental
factors. Obviously, the frequency of church attendance is at the end of a
long chain of individual and social influences. The slightly surprising
finding that genes play any role in influencing how often people go to
church may be less disconcerting if we reflect on the variety of individual
and developmental factors that may influence whether or not someone
chooses to practise religion. Some of these may fall under the umbrella of
'personality' factors, for which there is a long-standing literature showing
the significance of genetic influences and very little evidence of shared
environmental factors.

In a recent analysis D'Onofrio *et al.* (1999) showed that there was
virtually no correlation between church attendance and the broad personality dimensions of extraversion, neuroticism and psychoticism, so clearly
these cannot be candidates for any genetic contribution to religious prac-

tices. There are, however, other more specific personality-like dimensions that may still be relevant. Bouchard *et al.* (1999) report correlations for intrinsic (IR) and extrinsic (ER) religiousness in a small sample of MZ and DZ twins separated at birth. IR and ER are independent of other major personality dimensions, but IR correlates with religious fundamentalism and authoritarianism. The distinction between intrinsic and extrinsic religiousness is conceived to resolve orientation towards 'terminal' (intrinsic) rather than 'instrumental' (extrinsic) values.

Since the twins were separated at birth, post-natal environmental differences that would normally be shared by twins in a family (C in Figure 31.1) will contribute to differences *within* twin pairs. Thus, only genetic effects are expected to contribute to twin correlations unless there are also major pre-natal environmental influences.

The sample sizes in the data of Bouchard *et al.* (1999) are very small, so the sampling errors attached to the correlation will be very large and it is almost impossible to draw any precise conclusions about the role of genetic factors. The authors, however, conclude that the data are consistent with a small genetic influence on IR (15–64 per cent of the variance) and ER (9–61 per cent). As the twins were separated at birth, it is not possible to separate the effects of the shared environment, C, from the within-family environment, E, with these data.

A larger study of Australian twins reared together (Kirk, Eaves and Martin. 1999) provides twin correlations for a measure of 'self-transcendence' from the Temperament and Character Inventory (Cloninger *et al.* 1993) defined as the 'capacity to reach out beyond oneself and discover or make meaning of experience through broadened perspectives and behaviour'. Among the 15 items selected to represent the construct in the Australian study are many relating to spiritual beliefs and experience, as distinct from those relating more specifically to beliefs in God and formal religious practice. The Australian data confirm a significant correlation between self-transcendence and church attendance.

The twin correlations are given in Figure 31.5. Statistical analysis confirms what is clear to the eye. The data are quite consistent with the 'G only' for family resemblance. Thus, although there are large within-family environmental effects (the MZ correlations are only 0.40–0.50), the DZ correlations are approximately half those for MZ twins. Thus, the data support a modest role for additive genetic effects explaining 40–50 per cent of the variation in self-transcendence and a neglible role for the effects of the shared environment. These findings are remarkably consistent with those typical for measures in the personality domain (see, for example, Eaves, Eysenck and Martin 1989) and quite distinct from those usually reported for religious practices (Figure 31.4) and social attitudes (see below). Thus, self-transcendence is a dimension that clearly has content typical of religious affect yet shows many of the hall-marks of a

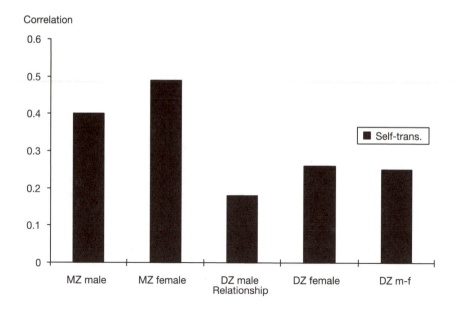

Figure 31.5 Twin resemblance for self-transcendence in Australian twins
Source: Kirk, Eaves and Martin, 1999.

'personality' variable when it comes to the causes of individual differences: moderate heritability and negligible effects of the shared family environment.

Genetic and environmental effects on social attitudes

Every politician has an intuitive grasp of the fact that human attitudes are organized around a relatively small set of principles. It is this fact that makes it possible to steer an electable course through the minefield of diverse attitudes towards a variety of issues by recognizing, for example, that 'liberal' attitudes towards topics such as abortion tend to correlate, but not perfectly, with liberal attitudes towards taxation, foreign aid, capital punishment and homosexuality.

Attitudes are inconceivable without culture. The law, economy, education, medicine, marriage and family, religion: all are so profoundly 'human' that it seems self-evident that attitudes are themselves above and beyond the reach of genetic diversity. Indeed, some of the earliest family studies of social attitudes were motivated by the need to develop models for *non-genetic* inheritance (e.g. Cavalli-Sforza and Feldman 1981). Studies of twins, adoptees and the families of twins (e.g. Eaves and Eysenck 1974; Eaves, Eysenck and Martin 1989; Eaves *et al.* 1999a and 1999b) suggest that such a view may be too simple.

Figure 31.6 presents correlations among large samples of nuclear family members (spouse, sibling and parent/offspring pairs) for a measure of general conservatism versus liberalism from the Virginia 30,000 study of 15,000 adult twins, their parents, spouses siblings and adult children (Eaves *et al.* 1999a). Participants completed a 'Health and Lifestyles' survey that included a sample of 28 attitudes on a variety of topics ranging from adult movies to capital punishment. The data suggest a series of natural ways in which people cluster their replies, but the most prominent dimension turns out to be the relatively liberal or conservative position of subjects on a wide range of correlated topics. It turns out that relatively few people adopt extremely conservative or liberal positions on a very large number of attitudes. Indeed, there is a 'bell curve' of liberalism much as there is for stature or blood pressure that can be assessed by accumulating the number of relatively liberal or conservative responses over all the items in the survey.

The figure shows quite high correlations between the attitudes of family members, suggesting that influences shared by family members play a large part in sustaining variation in attitude. The correlation between spouses is especially marked. Is this due to spouses selecting one another on the basis of their attitudes (assortative mating) or is it due to the mutual influence of spouses? It seems that most of the effect is assortative mating and not mutual influence. Certainly, there is hardly any evidence that attitudes of spouses become more similar with longer marriage and the patterns of correlations of other relationships by marriage (e.g. the spouses of twins)

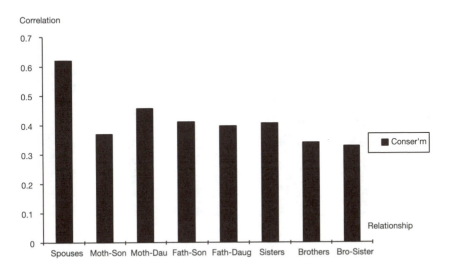

Figure 31.6 Nuclear family resemblance for conservatism in the Virginia 30,000
Source: Data from Eaves *et al.* 1999b.

seem to rule out post-nuptial interaction as a source of the high correlation between the attitudes of spouses (see Eaves *et al.* 1999a).

Although nuclear family data are intriguing because they point to the considerable impact of the family on attitude formation, they do not allow us to address the critical question of the role of genetic factors. Figure 31.7 shows the pattern of twin correlations for conservatism in the Virginia 30,000. These results are very similar to those published previously for British and Australian twin samples (Eaves, Eysenck and Martin 1989; Martin *et al.* 1986).

The data are clearly consistent with the third scenario in Figure 31.1, i.e. the correlation between family members is a mixture of both genetic and environmental effects. Indeed, quantitative analysis of the twin data alone suggests that genes, the shared environment and the unique environment contribute roughly equally to variation in conservative versus liberal attitudes. When data on other relatives are included, it is apparent that much of what seems to be due to the shared environment in twin data could well be genetic also because of the very large effect of assortative mating (Eaves *et al.* 1999a).

The basic finding of the twin data, that differences in adult attitudes have a substantial genetic component, has been replicated in other samples

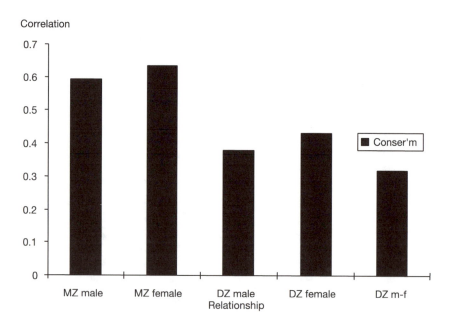

Figure 31.7 Twin resemblance for conservatism in the Virginia 30,000
Source: Eaves *et al.* 1999b.

and largely confirmed by, albeit much smaller, studies of separated twins and adoptees.

Genotype x environment interaction and developmental change

The studies summarized above point to a rich and diverse picture for the role of genes and environment in sustaining differences in religion and values. Obviously, the philosophical implications of these studies, if any, have still to be worked out. It is likely that the main surprise that the data offer so far is that genes play any role at all in producing individual differences in behaviours that are so obviously 'social'. The danger is that the data may be taken as proving too much. Genes affect behaviour. Genes are DNA. DNA is incredibly resistant to change. Therefore behaviour genetics shows behaviour is impossible to change. There are further nuances of this argument that appeal to evolution as the arbiter of what can be allowed to qualify as human.

This syllogism is, of course, rubbish. But implicit acceptance of it, and even adoption of it to underscore conservative social, economic and political values, has sometimes led to the mislabelling of behaviour genetics as oppressive science.

The role of genes in the creation of complex traits such as religiosity and attitudes is not a fixed and stable reality that cannot be changed. Rather, the path from DNA to phenotype is so tortuous and nuanced that, even if the entire individual genome were known, predictions about individual destiny would be next to impossible without knowing also the social, historical and developmental context in which the genome is located. Part of this context, indeed, is the environment provided by the genomes of others.

Our examination of the scientific context, the 'is', of religion and values concludes with three studies that hint at the role of contextual factors in the development of behaviour. One addresses the role of religion as a cultural effect modulating the expression of genetic differences on socially maladaptive behaviour. The second considers the role of social context on the expression of genetic differences of religiosity. A third considers developmental change in the role of genes and the family environment on social attitudes.

Religious upbringing modulates gene expression in the Netherlands

Boomsma *et al.* (1999) published intriguing findings for a Dutch study of behavioural disinhibition in adolescent and young adult twins. She first showed that religious upbringing was itself entirely non-genetic with the

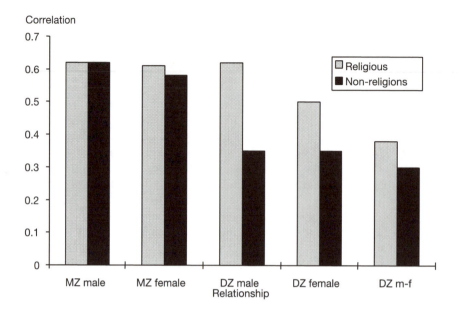

Figure 31.8 Effect of strict religious upbringing on expression of genetic differences in behavioural disinhibition among Dutch juveniles

Source: Boomsma *et al*. 1999.

expected very large shared environmental effect on twin resemblance. However, the most important result (Figure 31.8) is the pattern of twin correlations for disinhibition when the twin pairs are divided into those who have had a religious upbringing and those who have not. In pairs who have not had a religious upbringing, genetic effects (the difference between MZ and DZ twin correlations) are much more marked than in pairs who have not. Indeed, in males there was no evidence of genetic effects at all in twins who had had a religious upbringing but quite a large effect of genes in those pairs who had not had a religious upbringing. Boomsma's finding is a fascinating glimpse of the possible role of 'genotype x environment interaction' (GxE) in human populations. Her result shows that the expression of genetic differences is indeed not fixed but contingent on the environmental context, in this case family religion, in which the genotypes are embedded. The more 'permissive' environment of the non-religious family facilitates the expression of genetic effects that may still be present, but unexpressed, in the more religious family. The data do not allow us to decide exactly what features of the religious home protect against the expression of genetic differences.

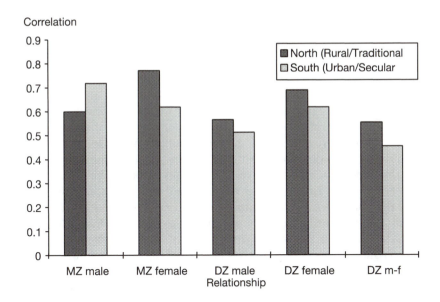

Figure 31.9 Twin correlations for religious fundamentalism in Northern and
Southern Finland

Source: Winter *et al*. 1999.

Genetic and environmental effects on religiosity are modulated by context

The Dutch study illustrates how religion can affect the expression of
genetic differences on another behavioural trait. A recent Finnish study
(Winter *et al*. 1999) examined the role of contextual factors (urban versus
rural) on the expression of genetic differences for adolescent religiosity.
Twins were divided by residence into those who were 'Northern' (relatively rural) and 'Southern' (relatively urban). The pattern of twin
correlations for scores on the Wiggins Religious Fundamentalism Scale
derived from items on the MMPI are given in Figure 31.9. The authors'
statistical analysis confirmed what is apparent from the figure. The
pattern of twin resemblance varies significantly by sex and location.
Notably, males in the rural North show the pattern diagnostic of purely
non-genetic variation whereas those in the urban South show more
marked genetic effects. Among females there is no apparent genetic influence, but the effect of the shared environment is greater in the North than
in the South.

A developmental perspective on the genetic component of social attitudes

The Dutch and Finnish studies focus on religion as a variable that both influences gene expression and is itself influenced by environmental context. A final study (Eaves *et al.* 1997) explores the role of developmental change in the expression of genetic differences in attitudes. Figure 31.10 gives the pattern of MZ and DZ twin correlations for conservatism/liberalism assessed in US twins at a variety of ages from 9 to 80. The findings are quite striking. During puberty and throughout adolescence the correlations for MZ and DZ twins increase markedly, but are virtually independent of zygosity. Thus, until about age 20, attitudes appear to be almost entirely environmental, with a major contribution from the shared environment, presumably parents, peers, teachers and shared access to media in the home and at school. As twins get older, the attitudes become more salient and the shared environmental influence becomes more marked. Relatively suddenly, at about age 20, the DZ twin correlation starts to decrease fairly rapidly, while the MZ correlation stays the same, towards the pattern shown in Figure 31.8 for adult twins in whom genetic and family environmental factors both play a role.

The data demonstrate that the effects of genes and environment on social attitudes are dynamic rather than static. The effects of genes are only expressed in adults after adolescents have acquired through their social environment the necessary cultural information to develop attitudes. Initially, they absorb the attitudes of those around them, including their parents with whom their attitudes correlate significantly, and it is only

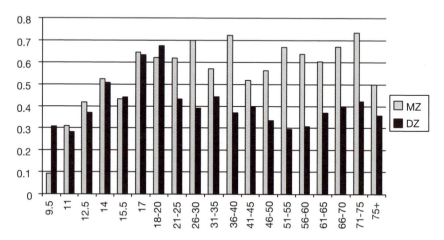

Figure 31.10 Twin correlations for conservatism: age changes
Source: Based upon Eaves *et al.* 1997.

when they have acquired the basic input from their environment that it becomes possible for genetic differences to be expressed. Lyons *et al.* (1995) suggest a similar mechanism underlies the transition from juvenile conduct disorder to adult anti-social personality.

So, what 'is'?

The above studies are chosen to illustrate the range of findings concerning the biological and social causes of differences in traits that might be regarded as most characteristic of *human* behaviour, religious affiliation, religiousness and social attitudes. They show that the truth is quite complex. Culture, in the form of the influence of family and the shared environment, plays its expected role in the determination of religious affiliation, but genes play varying roles in other aspects of religion and social attitudes. Measures of 'pure' religiousness, such as self-transcendence, reflect patterns that are reminiscent of published findings in personality research. A significant part, but by no means all, of the variation is due to genetic differences, with the major environmental effects being those unique to individuals and not shared by family members. Other measures reflect mixtures and interactions of both genetic and social factors. Church attendance, for example, and social attitudes both show the marks of genetic and social factors in family resemblance, although it was noted that the genetic effects of assortative mating may resemble those of non-genetic inheritance in most family studies.

We should not imagine that there is only one gene, or even a small handful of genes, that is responsible for the differences we observe in these complex behaviours. The number of genes is likely to be very large – there are at least 30,000 of them and a very large number of these are expressed in the brain. So it is unlikely that we will ever point to 'a' gene and say this is a gene that contributes to differences in conservatism. (Predictions like that have an unhappy propensity to turn out false!) Furthermore, the data show that as much, if not more, of the variation is due to environmental effects unique to individuals within families. These differences are responsible for part of the variation within pairs of MZ twins. Some of the environmental effects are very short term, and make even one individual's behaviour fluctuate over time. The contribution of such effects in longitudinal data on social attitudes has been documented (Eaves *et al.* 1978).

The data on the development and context-dependence of gene expression show that the effects of genes themselves are not permanent or unchangeable. The social context – upbringing and geography – exercises a significant effect on the expression of genes that affect these complex traits. We must also recognize that the early behavioural consequences of genetic differences may be reinforced by correlated environmental input that is selected or elicited by the individual, so that the behavioural consequences of genetic differences may, ontogenetically speaking, be very remote from the DNA.

When all these qualifications have been expressed, however, the studies we have discussed provide a strong *prima facie* case for some role of genes in the origin of significant dimensions of religion and values. Although the study of behavioural genetics is still in its infancy compared with what is already becoming known from advances in molecular genetics, the work described brings home the fact that one day the theoretical and explanatory power of genetics may open up new horizons in our understanding of behaviour that was once dismissed as beyond scientific study.

What does the 'is' have to say about 'ought'?

How do we construct a model of the is–ought relationship that remains true to the scientific 'facts' as they are currently perceived yet sustains a life-giving culture? The question is embedded in a powerful transcendent 'ought'. Although its precise origins may remain mysterious, it has appeared along one of the evolutionary trajectories discernible in our corner of the cosmos, namely the fragile emergence of being from non-being, life from non-life, consciousness from oblivion and science from superstition.

The question is asked more easily than answered. Among scientists and theologians we encounter a broad spectrum of opinions concerning the significance of findings such as those we have presented here. Such views are organized around two major constructs: what is regarded as scientifically necessary and what may be concluded morally. That is, the data affect our view of what 'is' and, according to some at least, they influence what 'ought' to be.

Some scientists espouse the view that the scientific data are themselves a sufficient foundation for our understanding of the human and that science has 'explained' everything, including the 'ought'. The principal outcome of this position is typically to dispense with religion or theology as unnecessary and to regard science as the agent that liberates humanity from more primitive and oppressive views of humans' place in the universe.

No one should deny the positive rallying power and heuristic value of the radical reductionism at the heart of many genetic and evolutionary models for complex human behaviour. Theologically speaking, science has a prophetic role as a counter-cultural agent. The Promethean element in science is a legitimate, faith-filled, response of the human spirit to the idolatry of religious perspectives that metastasize through lacunae reinforced by a radical disconnection between theology and the empirical sciences. Each requires the other to preclude the uncritical ascendance of either religion or science as a demonic cultural motif. Science holds culture accountable to the facts. Faith sustains the transcendence of the human spirit in the face of oppression in the name of 'the facts' (cf. Theissen 1985). A life-giving culture demands that science and faith engage and criticize each other.

Ian Barbour (1990) has made a helpful clarification of four different elements underlying the interaction between science and theology: conflict; independence; dialogue; integration. These elements are also encountered on the frontiers between and within other academic disciplines. Indeed, although some scientists and theologians might be inspired by a vision of ultimate integration, we recognize that there is a time in the history of science for creative conflict, focused independence and impassioned dialogue.

Exorcism of the demons of religious authoritarianism by the holy water of science, however, may simply clean the house for a number of pseudo-scientific devils that vie for attention. The scientific data have to be handled with great care if we are to resist two temptations. The first temptation is to claim more for the data than they warrant. The second is to claim without reflection that the data make no difference at all. Many scientists share an intuitive sense that data *do* make a difference to values and to our conception of the underlying nature of things. They are not alone. Science makes some versions of religion untenable.

The conversation about the relationship between the scientific study of values and behaviour and its implications for theology is made possible by the recognition of the provisional quality of the 'woven web of guesses' comprising the models and theories we construct to organize our encounters with nature (see, for example, Murphy 1997). If theology and science fail to adjust their epistemological claims to this postmodern perspective, they will disqualify themselves from a crucial dialogue at a critical time in the history of culture (see, for example, Pannenberg 1976).

Before embarking on a constructive task, it is important to be clear about what the data do *not* mean. Overstatement of the theological and philosophical significance of the data from biological anthropology, consciously or unconsciously, is a modern instance of the idolatrous capacity to make absolute what is provisional and claim more for a model than can be sustained by experience. Idolatry makes humans the servants of their models rather than their architects. The theological understanding of humanity as *imago Dei* reflects the qualified freedom of human agency in relation to creation. Fundamentally, we are model-builders. Models, including those of science, are a testimony to human transcendence with respect to nature. Humans transcend their models, whether they are scientific or theological. Human transcendence is a critical anthropological 'fact', without which scientific anthropology falls short of the data.

The scientific data discussed here deal with what might best be called 'penultimate oughts' not the 'ultimate ought'. The individual attitudes, values and beliefs that have been analysed in twin and family studies obviously address issues that are of profound significance to individuals and society. They certainly relate to how we treat one another and how we express our place in the universe. However, these values and beliefs show enormous diversity. Insofar as they reflect issues that concern individuals ultimately, there is no consensus. Different individuals give different weights to different tactics as part of their overall strategy for adaptation. History and evolution are still undecided about whether one or other set of common values is more adaptive than another. We are dealing with a very small slice of human history. In that slice we find that genetic diversity has a significant impact on how individuals describe themselves in terms of values and beliefs. The data show that, partly as a function of genetic differences, some people are, for example, more strongly opposed to abortion and others less so, some are more in favour of capital punishment than others. The scientific data document diversity of values and behaviour. The data also suggest some of the causes of this diversity. They do not and cannot, by themselves, support one or other set of values as 'ultimately true' against the others.

The second important issue is related to the first. Intriguing and even challenging though the scientific data are, they are based on a very impoverished anthropology. This limitation is partly forced on us by the need to measure humans briefly, reliably and in large numbers. It is likely that study participants would recognize themselves only partly in the measures that are made. Our measures are at best only crude approximations to the 'examined life'. The data may not capture the 'existential' features of moral and spiritual lives and are unlikely to compel many by the adequacy to experience of any general anthropology derived from them.

Thirdly, we must understand that 'genetic' effects *per se* do not impart some kind of special significance to the measures. It is a common misconception, even among professionals, that the demonstration that a variable has a genetic component amounts to validation. This is false. The most arbitrary and trivial measures that are in all probability devoid of any significance whatever can nevertheless 'be genetic' in the same sense as any of the measures we have employed here. Arguably, there are many genetic differences at the molecular level that are without any significance in the life or the organism. A trait does not derive its significance from the fact that it is genetic. But the fact that a significant trait is genetic may affect our assessment of its specific significance if knowing that fact makes a difference to what we might do scientifically or think theologically.

Fourthly, we need to be clear about the relationship between genetic models and determinism. It is commonly assumed that 'genetic' models imply determinism and that, for that reason, genetic models are more threatening to human freedom than environmental models. The reason for this perception needs to be examined briefly for, in truth, genetic theories of human behaviour are neither more nor less 'deterministic' than environmental theories. Determinism is a theoretical construct implicit in most, if not all, scientific theories of behaviour because they seek to explain behavioural phenomena in terms of underlying biological and social causes. Behaviourism and Marxism are as explicitly deterministic as sociobiology. It is hard to conceive of a current research paradigm in the behavioural sciences that is not deterministic in this sense. The vindication or otherwise of determinism will be decided by its heuristic value in guiding the quest for simple and coherent theories of complex behavioural outcomes. The quest has been partly but not wholly fulfilled.

The baggage associated with the phrase 'genetic determinism' has made it difficult to pick apart both the success and failure of any model that involves genetic influences on human behaviour. Genetic determinism implies scientifically no more nor less about the capacity of humans to change individuals and society than environmental determinism. Indeed, it may be that genetic disabilities are inherently more treatable than environmental disabilities if 'treatment' is the goal. However, the value of 'treatment', like the pursuit of 'truth', is itself a transcendent value that is not addressed fully by the current models of human behaviour. We may speculate that the cultural power of 'genetic' determinism, and the reasons for our suspicion of the idea, stem in part from its success in connecting complex and seemingly elusive behaviour to relatively simple and concrete causes. The matter of genetics is DNA. If behaviour is genetic, it is firmly reducible to chemistry and may be modifiable only by those with the power to dispense the arcane technology that reproduces the underlying molecular mechanism. Superficially, environmental mechanisms seem to be user friendly because access to the necessary means of change may appear more freely available.

If genetic determinism is to be attacked, it must be attacked, along with other non-genetic determinisms, on anthropological grounds. Heuristic value notwithstanding, the reasons for challenging determinism must stem from its poverty in characterizing human orientation towards the world. Current genetic studies of behaviour are bland alongside such categories as 'faith', 'hope', 'justice', 'sacrifice' and 'freedom' that exercise unparalleled power in individual and social life. It is inherent to these human characteristics that they resist the confining implications of overstated determinism and reductionism even when they are promulgated in the name of 'truth'. These and other comparable categories embody the most profound challenge to any installation of determinism at the heart of human orientation. Humans evolved their passion for freedom before they discovered the utility of determinism.

Resistance to determinism and ontological reductionism may well evolve in a species for which the future is such a consciously significant feature of the environment. Human behaviour and the human environment are profoundly 'eschatological'. That is, they are organized to serve a remote future that, in its most potent form, is captured best in terms of 'dream', 'vision' and 'spirit'. Anything less is less than human. Humans have evolved to be the most forward-looking of primates. Categories such as faith, hope, freedom and sacrifice arise primarily within this eschatological context for a species that has evolved to inhabit the most exposed of shores. The future is unsure yet lies within the horizon of our prolonged anticipation and creativity. The specific penultimate 'oughts', sacred and secular, that our family studies have addressed are incarnations of this ultimate eschatological horizon that conditions the present.

Our data have shown that the diversity of the particulars is both genetic and cultural, and that the expression of genetic and cultural differences depends on the broader context, the ecosystem, within which individuals develop. Human ontogeny and evolution constitute a dialogue between organisms and their environment that leaves the marks of history, unconscious and yet mysterious, upon the genetic code. The image and power of the gods are now encoded within us. The genetic code is a microcosm of the history that gave us life. 'God talk' strives to name and characterize this reality.

While attempts to dissolve 'ought' into 'is' typically thrive on impoverished anthropology, empirical data such as those we have presented cry out for some response from those who behave as if all theological and philosophical speculation were immune from the realities of biology.

The strange, almost paradoxical, place to which the data bring us is that the data that comprise the 'is' of our humanity simultaneously say both much and nothing about the imperative we experience as 'ought'.

The data say much because they imply that much of what we humans agonize about under the category of 'ought', much of what we experience as a 'transcendent imperative', our attitudes, values and many of the spiritual values that seem to drive and shape them, appear to be grounded in the code that is tuned by our evolutionary past and unfolds during the ontogenetic dialogue between the developing human organism and its environment.

Our present ability to analyse the 'is' through science is grounded in a transcendent intellectual and moral imperative, an 'ought', that empowers science. But that imperative, though its origins are still only dimly understood and largely unquestioned, is unlikely to be any different in terms of the biological and social forces that shaped it from any of the penultimate values whose origins have been the subject of this inquiry.

We must take care to avoid extravagant claims. Our conclusions are based on the study of differences between people. They do not necessarily generalize to values or dispositions we all share. In anthropometric terms we are studying why people differ in their heights, not why people 'have height' at all. In genetic terms we are dealing with only that small fraction, perhaps less than 1 per cent, of the total genetic material that is 'polymorphic', i.e. is not the same in everyone. It is not safe to assume that the polymorphic genes that create individual differences between people are necessarily a random sample of all the genes that create people. Natural selection is likely to act more rapidly to remove differences that are more inimical to survival. What we see could well be the more or less trivial differences remaining after natural selection has already established most of what matters.

Nevertheless, if we may assume that our studies of individual differences provide some clues as to how we come to be humans with moral passions and religious convictions, our data suggest that the transcendent ground of our being and values is both deeply within us ontogenetically yet antecedent to us phylogenetically.

From a strictly secular perspective, Richard Lewontin (1974) encapsulates well the cultural impact of evolutionary biology in his observation that evolution accounts for life in terms of immanent material processes rather than external 'supernatural' causes. Nevertheless, given the fact that so much of what makes us human is shrouded in the mists of evolutionary time and given that our individual experience of life is shaped in the preconscious silence of the genetic code, it is small wonder that humans develop models rooted in realities beyond their immediate experience of nature and express them in language and actions that appear to owe more to passion than reason. Such models still capture many of the elements of experience in ways for which adequate post-religious images have still to be found.

Acknowledgements

Some of the data analysis presented in this chapter was conducted with the support of the John M. Templeton Foundation (L.J. Eaves, B. D'Onofrio, D. Boomsma, A.C. Heath, N.G. Martin) and first described at a symposium supported by the Foundation at the Center for Theology and the Natural Sciences, Berkeley, California.

References

Augustine of Hippo (1983) *City of God: Book V*, English trans. by M. Dods, in P. Schaff (ed.) *Nicene and Post-Nicene Fathers, Vol. II*, Grand Rapids, MI: Eerdmans.

Barbour, I. (1990) *Religion in an Age of Science*, San Francisco: Harper Collins.

Boomsma, D.I., de Geus, E.J.C., van Baal, G.C.M. and Koopmans J.R. (1999) 'A religious upbringing reduces the influence of genetic factors on disinhibition: evidence for interaction between genotype and environment on personality', *Twin Research* 2: 115–25.

Bouchard, T.J. Jr., McGue, M., Lykken, D. and Tellegen, A. (1999) 'Intrinsic and extrinsic religiousness: genetic and environmental influences and personality correlates', *Twin Research* 2: 88–98.

Carey, G. (1986) 'Sibling imitation and contrast effects', *Behav. Genet.* 16: 319–41.

Cattell, R.B. (1965) 'Methodological and conceptual advances in evaluating hereditary and environmental influences and their interaction', in S.G. Vandenberg (ed.) *Methods and Goals in Human Behavior Genetics*, New York: Academic Press, 95–140.

Cavalli-Sforza, L.L. and Feldman, M.W. (1981) *Cultural Inheritance and Evolution: A Quantitative Approach*, Princeton: Princeton University Press.

Cloninger, C.R., Svrakic, D.M. and Przybeck, T.R. (1993) 'A psychobiological model of temperament and character', *Arch. Gen. Psychiatr.* 50: 975–90.

D'Onofrio, B.M., Eaves, L.J., Murrelle, L., Maes, H.H. and Spilka, B. (1999) 'Understanding biological and social influences on religious affiliation, attitudes and behavior: a behavior genetic perspective', *Journal of Personality* 67: 953–84.

Eaves, L.J. (1976) 'A model for sibling effects in man', *Heredity* 36: 205–14.

—— and Eysenck, H.J. (1974) 'Genetics and the development of social attitudes', *Nature* 249: 288–9.

——, Last, K.A., Young P.A. and Martin, N.G. (1978) 'Model-fitting approaches to the analysis of human behavior', *Heredity* 41: 249–320.

——, Eysenck, H.J. and Martin, N.G. (1989) *Genes, Culture and Personality: An Empirical Approach*, New York: Academic Press.

——, Martin, N.G. and Heath, A.C. (1990) 'Religious affiliation in twins and their parents: testing a model of cultural inheritance', *Behavior Genetics* 20: 1–22.

——, Martin, N.G., Heath, A.C. Schieken, R.M., Meyer, J.M., Silberg, J., Neale, M.C. and Corey, L.A. (1997) 'Age Changes in the Causes of Individual Differences in Conservatism', *Behavior Genetics* 27(2): 121–4.

——, Heath, A.C., Martin, N.G., Maes, H.H., Neale, M.C., Kendler, K.S., Kirk, K.M. and Corey, L.A. (1999a) 'Comparing the biological and cultural inheritance of personality and social attitudes in the Virginia 30 000 study of twins and their relatives', *Twin Research* 2: 62–80.

——, Heath, A.C., Martin, N.G., Neale, M.C., Meyer, J.M., Silberg, J.L., Corey, L.A., Truett, K. and Walters, E. (1999b) 'Biological and cultural inheritance of stature and attitudes', in C.R. Cloninger (ed.), *Personality and Psychopathology*, Washington, DC: American Psychiatric Press, 269–308.

Fisher, R.A. (1918) 'On the correlation between relatives on the supposition of Mendelian inheritance', *Transactions of the Royal Society of Edinburgh* 52: 399–433.

Fisher, R.A. (1958) *The Genetical Theory of Natural Selection*, 2nd edn, New York: Dover.

Galton, F. (1883) *Inquiries into Human Faculty and its Development*, London: MacMillan.

Garrod, A.E. (1923) *Inborn Errors of Metabolism* 2nd edn, London: Henry Frowde and Hodder and Stoughton.

Jinks, J.L. and Fulker, D.W. (1970) 'A comparison of the biometrical genetical, MAVA, and classical approaches to the analysis of human behavior', *Psychological Bulletin* 73(5): 311–49.

Kirk, K.M., Eaves, L.J. and Martin, N.G. (1999) 'Self-transcendence as a measure of spirituality in a sample of older Australian twins', *Twin Research* 2: 81–7.

Kirk, K.M., Maes, H.H., Neale, M.C., Heath, A.C., Martin, N.G. and Eaves, L.J. (1999) 'Frequency of church attendance in Australia and the United States: models of family resemblance', *Twin Research* 2: 99–107.

Lewontin, R.C. (1974) *The Genetic Basis of Evolutionary Change*, New York: Columbia University Press.

Loehlin, J.C. and Nichols, R.C. (1976) *Heredity, Environment and Personality: A Study of Twins*, Austin: University of Texas Press.

Lyons, M.J., True, W.R., Eisen, S.A., Goldberg, J., Meyer, J.M., Faraone, S.V., Eaves, L.J. and Tsuang, M.T. (1995) 'Differential heritability of adult and juvenile antisocial traits', *Archives of General Psychiatry* 52(11): 906–15.

Martin N.G., Eaves, L.J., Heath, A.C., Jardine, R., Feingold, L.F. and Eysenck, H.J. (1986) 'The transmission of social attitudes', *Proceedings of the National Academy of Sciences of the United States of America* 83: 4364–8.

Murphy, N. (1997) *Anglo-American Postmodernity: Philosophical Perspectives on Science, Religion and Ethics*, Boulder, CO: Westview Press.

Neale, M.C. and Cardon, L.R. (1994) *Methodology for Genetic Studies of Twins and Families*, Dordrecht: Kluwer Academic Publishers.

Pannenberg, W. (1976) *Theology and the Philosophy of Science*, trans. E.T.F. McDonagh, Philadelphia: Westminster Press.

Theissen, G. (1985) *Biblical Faith: An Evolutionary Perspective*, Philadelphia: Fortress Press.

Watson, J.D. and Crick, F. (1953) 'A structure for DNA', *Nature* 171: 737–8.

Winter, T., Kaprio, J., Viken, R.J., Karvonen, S. and Rose, R.J. (1999) 'Individual differences in adolescent religiosity in Finland: familial effects are modified by sex and region of residence', *Twin Research* 2: 108–14.

32

WHAT VALUES GUIDE
OUR OUGHTS?

Angela Roothaan

After a presentation of some results from twin studies, Lindon Eaves asks about the meaning of these results for human religious and moral orientation. In my reaction I will first phrase what are, to my mind, the most important conclusions of the twin studies. Then I will concentrate on one element, that is the 'personality' factor in the question of the genetic origin of human behaviour. I will try to elucidate the aspect of personality from a philosophical point of view, introducing Charles Taylor's concept of 'strong evaluations'. Subsequently, I will ask a question about the relation between values and the oughts that Eaves is looking for in the interpretation of his results. I will conclude by asking to what oughts he seems himself committed.

Personality and 'strong evaluation'

The point of comparing the attitudes and behaviour of monozygotic and dizygotic twins is to find out to what extent these attitudes and this behaviour are related to the genetic constitution of the individual. To make this point very clear, Eaves has selected surveys that concentrate on behaviour and attitudes that normally would be considered to have a weak relation to one's biological constitution, namely the ones relating to religiousness.

An interesting result seems to be that those aspects of religiousness that are more closely related to one's personality (church attendance and intrinsic religiousness) show a stronger correlation to genetic constitution than those aspects that are only loosely related to one's personality (religious affiliation and extrinsic religiousness).

Also, it is shown that the genetic factor gains greater weight over the social factor in adult life, which would point to the recognizable fact that in adult life (at least in Western culture) individuals are allowed to follow their own insights. They then follow their own 'personality', which seems to be based in their genes. At least, one can find a significant statistical correlation on this point.

Eaves would admit, I assume, that a person would explain the behaviour by referring not to his or her genes, but to values he or she believes in and is committed to. The Canadian philosopher Charles Taylor has drawn attention to so-called 'strong evaluations'. He writes: 'It is those [evaluations] which are closest to what I am as a subject, in the sense that shorn of them I would break down as a person' (Taylor 1982: 124). They seem to consist of one's deepest convictions about things, like the conviction that it is of the greatest importance to express one's personality in life, or the conviction that one should let oneself be guided by social tradition.

Such evaluations constitute, according to Taylor, one's personality, and thus they guide the 'oughts' which one holds on to. This brings us to the next question, regarding the relation between values and oughts in the interpretation of twin surveys.

Values and oughts

When reading the last section of Eaves' paper it struck me that, although he asks how what 'is' (the scientific results) leads to an 'ought', he does not commit himself to any kind of ought. The reason is not, I think, that the results of the mentioned surveys are not clear enough. The reason is that they are in themselves morally neutral. If we find that extrinsic religiousness is strongly influenced by socialization, what should we think of this? Is it good or is it bad? The answer to such a question cannot be found in the results themselves, but only in our strong evaluations and the values which they encompass, such as 'liberty' versus 'tradition'.

Eaves' paper also presents the finding that intrinsic religiousness has a stronger link to one's genes, but to what 'ought' would this lead us? Ought we to let genetic diversity express itself and therefore disavow traditional religious upbringing, or ought we to further a traditional upbringing because it suppresses potential conflicts inherent in genetic diversity? The careful avoidance, by Eaves, of moving from an is to an ought seems to support my view that such a move cannot be made on the basis of this kind of research.

If the research adds anything to this question it is that it shows that social and genetic factors alike constitute human attitudes and human behaviour. Of course, one may find good moral reasons to want to favour the genetic factor over the social or vice versa. In general, one could say, modern culture favours the genetic factor more than any other culture, and this is an interesting and remarkable fact. But even when intrinsic religiousness is shaped significantly by the genes, its free expression is not thereby morally justified.

One's own view

This brings me then to the final point. As I hope to have shown that 'oughts' do not derive from what 'is', but that they imply values to which one commits oneself, it can be interesting to ask about the commitment of Lindon Eaves himself in this matter. What should we try to further in ourselves and in others? The free expression of our natural (anti-) religiousness, or a solid traditional upbringing to make people good citizens? Or could we perhaps have both, room for our genetic differences in the context of a tolerant society that floats on the self-discipline brought upon us by a strict socialization? These, of course, are moral questions, which are not touched by 'what is', but by what we believe in.

Even if our personality and our evaluations were nothing other than the expression of our genes, we would not reach a different conclusion. Because if they were, it would mean that a pro-genes (liberal) view as well as an anti-genes (the traditional) view was an expression of someone's genes, which would mean that some people's genes would be better off by not expressing themselves, and others by expressing themselves. All the same, the persons concerned cannot avoid discussing the preferability of their views in moral and ideological terms.

References

Eaves, L.B. (2003) ' "Ought" in a World that Just "Is" ', in W.B. Drees (ed.) *Is Nature Ever Evil? Religion, Science and Value*, London: Routledge.

Taylor, C. (1982) 'Responsibility for Self', in G. Watson (ed.) *Free Will*, Oxford: Oxford University Press.

33

THE NORMATIVE
RELEVANCE OF DISPUTES
IN PRIMATOLOGY

Tatjana Visak

This contribution is about facts and norms. More precisely, it is about how normative conclusions are drawn from empirical evidence, and how the normative outlook of a scientist determines which empirical evidence to look for and accept. The investigation of some hot items in primatology shows (1) that facts about apes are meant by some scientists to be relevant to norms of and among people, and (2) that the normative engagement of the scientist determines which facts about apes he or she looks for and accepts.

These conclusions will be specified and illustrated by a number of examples. It is shown that sociobiologists and animal ethicists relate facts about apes to norms for people. Sociobiologists are prone to the naturalistic fallacy in deducing what *ought to be* from what actually *is*. They suggest that the behaviour of animals offers not only explanations but also justifications or even norms for our own behaviour. Animal ethicists focus on facts that prove continuity between humans and non-human primates. They argue that this continuity can be relevant to our moral notions on the treatment of animals. While sociobiologists and animal ethicists are scientists who relate facts about apes to norms among people, they are also scientists whose normative engagement determines *which* facts about apes they present to the public. But sociobiologists and animal ethicists are not the only scientists whose selection of empirical facts is led by their normative engagement: it will be shown that there are more engaged or even prejudiced scientists looking for and interpreting empirical facts.

Introduction

In her book *Almost Human – A Journey into the World of Baboons*, published in 1987, Shirley C. Strum criticizes (p. 106) the anthropomorphic interpretations of earlier primatologists: 'Many early interpretations of animal behaviour were unconsciously anthropomorphic, projections of human behaviour onto animals. The problem was greatest in studies of monkeys and apes, since our biological closeness to another creature influences our ability to view it in human terms.' Animal behaviour can indeed be falsely interpreted in human terms. A certain type of grin in a chimpanzee, for instance, does not have the meaning of our smile. If a chimpanzee pulls back his lips to show his teeth, it might be a sign of submission, and even fear. If a male ape mounts another, it is not usually a sign of homosexual attraction, but may have a number of different functions, such as the reduction of tension. If the species-specific manners of an animal are not known, mistaken anthropomorphic conclusions can be drawn.

Anthropomorphism, however, is only one of the possible problems. When the famous primatologist Jane Goodall gave human names to her primate research subjects and described their characters in human terms, she was much criticized for being anthropomorphic. But here the prejudice stemmed from her critics. It is true that apes can be misunderstood by drawing parallels with humans where there are none. But they are also misunderstood if parallels that do in fact exist are not acknowledged. Relevant similarities between humans and non-human animals are acknowledged by animal ethicists, denied by speciecists (who discriminate in favour of their own species) and exaggerated by sociobiologists. The latter are prone to yet another fallacy: they try to posit norms for human behaviour by drawing simplified parallels from the behaviour of apes.

Facts and norms are intermingled, if not in science then surely in scientists. Science as a method may not be neutral; scientists certainly are not. In primatology, just as in other fields of science, there are many disagreements. There are different opinions on primate infanticide, war, rape, morals, culture, language, matriarchy and personhood. There are disputes about a suitable species categorization and about the apes' evolutionary origins and relatives. In primatology more than in a great number of other sciences, new theories and findings – not to mention long-standing scientific disputes – touch upon some of our fundamental beliefs and values. In apes, especially the great apes, nature has an outward appearance that reminds us too much of ourselves. The examples from the field of primatology discussed in this paper will therefore lead to the following conclusions about the interrelation between facts and norms: (1) facts about apes are intended by some scientists to be relevant to norms of and among people, (2) the normative engagement of the individual scientist determines what is accepted, and this is presented as empirical evidence about apes.

How facts about apes are thought to be relevant to norms of and among people

What do facts about apes tell us about norms for humans? What is the normative relevance to our own behaviour of what we learn by studying apes? Or, what does scientific evidence teach us about norms? In the following section I present two answers to that question, one drawn from the field of sociobiology and one from animal ethics. As I show, the sociobiologists and the animal ethicists have completely different ways of answering the same question.

Sociobiologists try to understand human behaviour by drawing simplified parallels from the behaviour of apes. In popular literature about apes explicit mention is often made of the close relatedness between apes and humans. If primates are supposed to offer compelling insights into human behaviour, then it is necessary to decide which primates and which aspects of primate behaviour should be brought to the attention of the public. The three following examples may make this clear.

1   Richard Wrangham prefers to write about *Demonic Males – Apes and the Origins of Human Violence* (1996). Wrangham's book is about primate war, rape and dominion; about primates killing and eating their young and castrating each other. 'This book is dangerous,' comments Alison Jolly, the author of *Evolution of Primate Behaviour*, seductively on the cover of Wrangham's book. But why is Wrangham's book considered dangerous? Isn't Wrangham just describing facts? Jolly seems to fear the possible implications for humans contained within the evidence selected by Wrangham. She suggests that Wrangham's book about primate behaviour might offer us an evolutionary legitimization of, or even norms for, our own behaviour. The message seems to be that it is natural (and therefore justifiable or even good?) *for humans* to castrate, rape and kill each other.

2   While Wrangham focuses on demonic males, Meredith F. Small prefers to write about *Female Choices*. The reader is told that 'in her intriguing and provocative book about females and sex, Small concentrates on primates – whose ancestry we share – to show how females have evolved to be highly sexual creatures.' The book, praises a critic on its cover, is 'filled with fascinating and compelling ideas about human behaviour'. (It is not unimaginable, though, that other critics may find Small's book 'dangerous'.)

3   After having written on *Chimpanzee Politics – Power and Sex among Great Apes*, primatologist Frans de Waal focuses on the habit of *Peacemaking among Primates*. It happens that the bonobo is De Waal's favourite species. Bonobos are very different from the macho chimps in that they make 'love not war'. Bonobos or 'hippie apes' are, for reasons that will be stated later on, very popular among feminists. In his book *Good Natured* De Waal explores the origins of moral consciousness in humans and other animals. Apes, he claims, have capacities that are prerequisites for and ingredients of (human) moral thinking. Apes show sympathy with others, internalize social rules and

anticipate punishment. Furthermore, apes have a concept of giving, trading and revenge. They show aggression against violators of reciprocity rules in order to 'teach them a lesson', have a habit of peacemaking and avoiding conflict, show community concern and try to maintain good relationships. Furthermore, apes accommodate conflicting interests through negotiation.

With De Waal, I share the belief that the development of moral thinking has been an evolutionary process. There seems to be continuity in the capacity for moral thinking in humans and other animals; there is a similar continuity for a variety of other (human) characteristics. The evolutionary link between human and non-human primate behaviour, however, does not mean that the study of apes can teach humans what is moral. Although in their clearer moments sociobiologists seem to admit this, the exact message of sociobiologists is not always clear. In recent books by sociobiologists De Waal finds the shared belief that 'evolution needs to be part of any satisfactory explanation of morality'. He even claims that 'we seem to be reaching a point in which science can wrest morality from the hands of philosophers' (De Waal 1996: 218). This is an astonishing claim. Philosophers' searching is not so much for the origins of morality as for an answer to the question 'What is moral?' I do not see how empirical scientists could take over this normative task from philosophers.

Animal ethicists also use empirical evidence to ground their normative recommendations on how we humans should behave. In contrast to sociobiologists, however, they are not prone to the naturalistic fallacy of deducing what *ought to be* from what actually *is*. Instead, they correctly use the empirical evidence gathered by ethologists and point to actual similarities between humans and other animals. But which similarities are relevant? This depends on the moral principles or norms which are used by moral actors. If, for example, moral actors want to avoid suffering and promote well-being, they should in principle pay equal attention to all beings that can suffer or feel well. If the moral status of a being depends on characteristics such as 'personhood', all beings conforming to that definition (and only these) should be granted equal moral status, regardless of their species. Animal ethicists show that (some) animals can suffer and that (some) animals are persons. They argue that these animals should eventually be granted equal moral status, as criteria that are meant to be morally relevant (such as 'well-being' or 'personhood') should either be applied consistently or not at all. This shows that animal ethicists make use of empirical evidence. At the same time, they are engaged normatively in the world around them: as scientists they are not neutral. However, that doesn't mean that what they do is bad science.

How the normative outlook of the scientist determines the evidence

There are many examples in the field of primatology which show that engagement determines which empirical facts are looked for and accepted: it has already been stated above that sociobiologists have different preferences concerning the primates and the aspects of primate behaviour they choose to bring to the attention of the public. While the normative engagement of animal ethicists leads to a focus on relevant similarities between humans and other primates, anthropocentric or speciecist scientists try to find relevant differences. This last point can be illustrated by the disputes about primate culture and language.

When scientific evidence pointing to the existence of primate culture was found, the reaction of many scientists was to change the definition of 'culture' in order to reserve that value-laden concept for the human species. As early as 1950 the Japanese anthropologist Kinji Imanishi stated that culture (defined as habits that are not genetically transferred) is not only possible but also very likely to be found among non-human primates (Itani and Nishimura 1973). At the fourth international congress of primatologists E.W. Count introduced 'the idea of proto-culture' to distinguish *Homo sapiens* from other – less cultural – higher primates. In an article entitled 'Cultural Primatology Comes of Age' Frans de Waal discusses an investigation by nine of the most renowned primatologists which shows that there are significant cultural differences between free-living chimpanzee communities. The neatly documented free chimpanzee groups were checked for 65 different characteristics in categories involving food choices, way of eating, tool usage, greeting rituals and housing. Of course, the statistics were adjusted for given differences, such as vegetation, which necessarily influences the food choices of animals living in different areas. Despite these adjustments, clusters of significant cultural differences were found. De Waal states: 'If animal groups vary in a single behaviour, such as potato washing, there is, perhaps, not much reason to use a loaded term such as "culture" – "group specific trait" should do instead.' Recent research, however, forces even de Waal to recognize the existence of primate culture: 'The record is so impressive that it will be difficult to keep these apes out of the cultural domain without once again moving the goalposts' (De Waal 1999: 635).

Comparable examples could be given for the reaction of scientists to empirical evidence of primates using language, and of primates fitting the definition of 'person'. My intention is not to solve these disputes: I would prefer to ask why 'neutral' scientists, like obstinate football players, are manipulating goalposts. Are they changing definitions to suit their prejudices? Is it an acceptable excuse for a scientist that some concepts are just too value-laden to be touched by new evidence?

There are even more compelling examples of how one's normative outlook determines which empirical evidence to accept and look for. In the 1990s biologist and journalist Dirk Draulans joined a young biologist on her expedition to Congo (then Zaire). In his book *De Mens van Morgen*, Draulans describes the experiences they had studying the bonobo. Only a few people before them, the most renowned of whom was the Japanese ethologist Takayoshi Kano, had previously studied this species. In 1986 Kano published the book *The Last Ape – Pygmy Chimpanzee Behaviour and Ecology*, which was translated into English in 1992. One of its most astonishing aspects is the author's persistent failure to mention that females dominate bonobo society. Notwithstanding his own findings, which clearly led to that conclusion, Kano refused to identify bonobo matriarchy by name. In an interview Kano stated cryptically that among bonobos 'males and females are co-dominant, although males seem to be somewhat more dominant except for questions about their food' (Draulans 1998: 85). Recent publications of primatologist De Waal among others recognize a special dominance of females in bonobo society; Draulans concludes that some powerful women are needed in the Japanese research team to realize that truth.

Another example of engagement determining which facts are looked for and accepted is Elaine Morgan's feminist version of human evolution. In books such as *The Descent of Woman* Morgan confirms the findings of a number of male scientists who say that humans share some common ancestors with their evolutionary cousins, the non-human primates. Morgan disagrees, however, on the exact route by which the human's ape-like ancestors developed into what is now *Homo sapiens*. In Morgan's opinion, the well-known heroic story of man the hunter is just another fairy tale invented by macho men. Socio-biologist Desmond Morris, in contrast, likes the theory about male ancestors going on hunts, triggering human evolution on their way. Man-the-hunter developed the upright stance and lost his body hair. He learned to use tools, language and fire. Women, if they are mentioned at all, stayed at home passively. They developed breasts and body contours to care for the young and to please their heroic homecomers. Morgan not only attacks this 'man-made myth' by showing how vague, incomplete and implausible it really is. She also succeeds in offering a (nearly) compelling feminist alternative to it. Morgan describes the human's ape-like ancestors as living peacefully in coastal areas. In her view, the human species developed from what were previously 'aquatic apes'. Geological, ecological, biological and evolutionary evidence and viewpoints enforce her theory. Fossil finds, human adaptations, prehistoric climate changes and geology – all seem to fit together.

When climate changes forced our ape-like ancestors to leave the trees, according to Morgan, they did not inhabit the savannah, but went to live in coastal areas. There – in their search for food and to escape land predators

– they developed the upright stance by wading into the sea. The maritime environment is believed to be the reason for their loss of body hair and for their development, similar to that of other sea mammals, of a subcutaneous layer of fat. Being quite safe on the rocky coasts and in the shallow waters, our ancestors had plenty of time to develop their tool-using skills by trying to open shells with stones; after all, they would not have had time to learn to walk upright or to use tools while fending off wild beasts on the savannah. Many features of the human body can be explained by Morgan's Aquatic Ape Theory, for instance the salty sweat and tears, the fat layer under the skin, or even the female orgasm. Females play a central role in Morgan's story. In 1987 scientists from all over the world met in Valkenburg in the Netherlands for a first symposium on the subject, one outcome of which was the book *The Aquatic Ape: Fact or Fiction – The First Scientific Evaluation of a Controversial Theory of Human Evolution* (Roede 1991).

Whether fact or fiction, the conflicting stories of human evolution and the confusion about primate matriarchy all demonstrate the importance of engagement in the scientific study of reality.

Conclusion

It should be evident from these examples that scientists are not value-free: their concern goes further than describing and analysing natural processes in factual terms. Their scientific inquiry is inspired by their own *motivations* and directed towards some more or less explicitly acknowledged *aims*. As scientists, they share certain *presuppositions* about what counts as factual; and, finally, they use their findings to come up with their own *interpretations* and *conclusions*. Unlike Descartes with his pretensions, the researcher is not like a God, facing the world. As Merleau-Ponty explains, our thinking and perceiving take place from within the world and from within our body and mind. Each perception is bound to the point of view of the perceiver. Each empirical study of reality is bound to the engagement of the researcher. The above-mentioned examples from the field of primatology show that facts about apes are suggested as having repercussions on norms of and among people, and this holds as well the other way around.

References

De Waal, F. (1996) *Good Natured – The Origins of Right and Wrong in Humans and Other Animals*, Cambridge, MA: Harvard University Press.

—— (1999) 'Cultural Primatology Comes of Age', *Nature* 399 (17 June 1999): 635.

Draulans, D. (1998) *De Mens van Morgen*, Amsterdam: Atlas.

Itani, J. and Nishimura, A. (1973) 'The Study of Infrahuman Cultures in Japan', in *Precultural Primate Behaviour*, ed. E.W. Menzel, Jr, Basel: Karger, 26–50.

Kano, T. (1992) *The Last Ape: Pygmy Chimpanzee Behavior and Ecology*, translated by E.O. Vineberg, Stanford, CA: Stanford University Press.

Merleau-Ponty, M. (1997) *Fenomenologie van de waarneming*, Amsterdam: Ambo.

Morgan, E. (1985) *The Descent of Woman*, 2nd edn, New York: Stein and Day.

Roede, M. (ed.) (1991) *The Aquatic Ape: Fact or Fiction – The First Scientific Evaluation of a Controversial Theory about Human Evolution*, London: Souvenir Press.

Small, M.F. (1993) *Female Choices: Sexual Behavior of Female Primates*, Ithaca: Cornell University Press.

Strum, S.C. (1987) *Almost Human – A Journey into the World of Baboons*, New York: Random House.

Wrangham, R. (1996) *Demonic Males – Apes and the Origins of Human Violence*, London: Bloomsbury.

34

EVOLUTIONARY VIEWS ON THE BIOLOGICAL BASIS OF RELIGION

Nico M. van Straalen and Jair Stein

From a biological point of view, humans are a peculiar species of mammal. They walk on two legs, they practise a high degree of omnivory, their body is devoid of hair or other skin cover, and they have extremely large brains. Humans are also intensely social; they rely on complex behaviour for their survival, including communication by means of symbolic language. Humans have an extraordinarily long juvenile period in which behaviours and experiences are transmitted to offspring by an extensive institutionalized learning process. There is a high degree of phenotypic and genetic variation among humans; the human species is differentiated into a great number of peoples and cultures. The fact that interbreeding between populations is always possible demonstrates, however, that *Homo sapiens* as a whole is clearly one biological species.

Despite the enormous amount of phenotypic variation in the human species, there are a lot of common characteristics, not only in anatomy and physiology but also in complex traits, such as language, social behaviour, emotions and even religious inclination. It is therefore often assumed that these characteristics are biological, that is, the propensity to engage in such behaviour is determined by the genetic constitution of the human species, even though its specific expression is modulated greatly by culture. The study of these common biological characteristics, and their variable expression among ethnic groups, constitutes the research area of human biology (Stinson *et al.* 2000; Molnar 1998).

The synthetic theory of evolution has been adopted as a useful framework for human biology (Stinson *et al.* 2000). In general, evolutionary biology attempts to explain the differences and similarities among species by developing hypotheses about their common ancestry and their transformations over time by natural selection, drift and mutation. These hypotheses are tested against evidence from palaeontology, genetics, morphology, physiology and ecology. The evolutionary perspective is considered so important in biology that almost all biologists agree with the famous sentence of Theodosius Dobzhansky: 'Nothing makes sense in biology except in the light of evolution' (Dobzhansky 1973).

Evolutionists are convinced that our own species is a very recent addition to biological diversity. The first living organisms on Earth date back 4 billion years. However, *Homo sapiens* did not appear until about 200,000 years ago. According to the most popular view, *Homo sapiens* evolved from its predecessor, *Homo heidelbergensis*, in a restricted area of Africa, developed a small population that fragmented and then spread across Europe and Asia; the continents of America and Australia became colonized only between 40,000 and 10,000 years ago (Lewin 1999). This so-called 'out of Africa' theory is supported by the similarity of homologous DNA sequences among living man and the fact that the African sequences are the most variable. Another theory, which has fewer adherents, claims that the roots of *Homo sapiens* are not necessarily to be found in one place and that *Homo sapiens* evolved independently in Asia, Africa and Europe, from an earlier species (*Homo erectus*) that already lived there (Wolpoff *et al.* 2001). In addition to *Homo sapiens* there may have been six other *Homo* species (some of which coexisted with each other), as well as seven species of 'ape-man', usually assigned to the genus *Australopithecus*, which were bipedal but did not have the brain size of *Homo*. There is discussion about the correct genus names of these thirteen hominine species, and about the way in which they transformed into each other (Wood and Collard 1999). Anyway, it is commonly assumed that the hominine clade separated from a chimpanzee-like ancestor about 5 million years ago (Tattersall and Matternes 2000). The evolutionary evidence suggests that properties of our present brain began to evolve while our ancestors lived in hunter-gatherer societies in the savannah of Africa. The biological basis for the complex behaviours of present-day man, such as religiousness, could date back to evolutionary processes in primitive human societies starting about 200,000 years ago.

The chapter by Lindon Eaves in this book (Eaves 2003) considers studies of genetic variation for traits related to religious affiliation, religiousness and social attitudes in present-day man. The analysis greatly depends on the concept of heritability, which is technically defined as the amount of additive genetic variation relative to the total amount of variation of a certain trait in a population. Heritability can be estimated from similarities of traits among monozygotic and dizygotic twins. The statistical analysis of twin data by Eaves shows that the variability among individuals of certain aspects of religious behaviour has a significant genetic component. The inter-individual variability also has a great environmental (cultural) component, which is often larger than the heritable component; in some cases there is an interaction between genetic and environmental effects, which means that the expression of genetic differences between individuals depends on the environment; for example, the religious tradition in which children are brought up influences the expression of genetic differences in propensity towards disinhibitive behaviour (Boomsma *et al.* 1999). The author then discusses the implications of these findings, with reference to the question of whether human religious values might ultimately be understood in the same material terms as any other aspect of human biology.

The aim of the present chapter is to reflect on Eaves' text and to add some biological comments. We briefly review some ideas that have been proposed by biologists about the evolutionary significance of religion, and then proceed to make some critical remarks on the chapter by Lindon Eaves.

The adaptive significance of religion

Several biologists have developed theories about the adaptive value of religion. A common line of reasoning to explain the biological basis of complex behaviours such as religion is the following. Among the first *Homo sapiens* that existed there was a certain degree of genetic variation for traits that determine aspects of an individual's social behaviour. Within a given environment, some behaviours were better than others in the sense that the persons exhibiting such behaviours left more children, either by increased survival up to maturity or by greater reproductive success. Since the behaviour had a genetic basis, a greater share of the next generation displayed that behaviour. That is why the majority of people today have a propensity to exhibit such behaviours. To explain why there is still polymorphism (variation between individuals) of complex behaviour, it must be assumed that selection was not so strong that it eliminated all suboptimal behaviours, or that selection varied over time or space, owing to variability in the environment. The importance of the environment, in particular geographical and historical factors, in shaping spatially differentiated cultures was emphasized by Diamond (1998).

We want to point out here that there is a difference between the concept of heritability, which is essentially a property of a population, and the concept of genetic determination, which is a property of an individual. To say that a certain trait has a significant heritability means that there are genetic differences between individuals. For example, if the heritability of fingerprint ridge count has a heritability of 0.8, it means that 80 per cent of the differences in fingerprints between individuals in a population is due to differences between their genotypes (and 20 per cent is due to other influences, including environmental effects). On the other hand, to say that a certain trait is genetically determined means that its phenotypic appearance depends on the genetic constitution of the individual. For example, we can say that the development of the disease phenylketonuria is genetically determined by the presence of a defect gene coding for the enzyme phenylalanine hydroxylase. Genetically determined traits may or may not be heritable and their heritability may change if the environment changes or if the composition of the population changes. Genetically determined traits will have a heritability of zero if there are no differences between the individuals of a population.

Evolution depends on both heritability and selection. For selection to act, there should be an adaptive value for the trait under consideration; that is, it should confer an advantage to its bearer. This argument is not without difficulties. The thesis that every trait can be seen as an adaptation and is a product of natural selection is obviously false (Van der Steen 2000). The question to be discussed here is, in the evolutionist line of reasoning: what is to be considered as an advantage of religion? Many authors have discussed this question before. We summarize here some of the better-known theories. This should not be taken to imply that we agree with what all these authors say. In fact there are many dubious and speculative arguments in the theories.

Not only biologists but also other scientists have developed theories about the evolutionary origins of religion. An example is the recent book by Boyer (2001), who approaches the subject from a psychological point of view. In the present chapter we will limit the discussion to evolutionary biology.

Acceptance of authority

Waddington (1960) emphasized the importance of learning in human evolution. A great deal of the success of the human species is due to the fact that knowledge obtained through experience during the life of an adult is transmitted to children during the extended juvenile period. Selection could act on flexibility of the brain during childhood, in such a way that children who were better at absorbing knowledge from their parents, or other experienced adults, had a higher chance of survival later in their life. According to Waddington it is necessary, for educational transmission to be optimal, that the child accepts some sort of authority. Any propensity to accept authority had an adaptive value because this facilitated learning. If this theory is correct, the belief in a supernatural power and, ultimately, religiousness could be considered as a correlate of the propensity towards accepting authority.

The ideas of Waddington are similar to Wilson's theory about the evolutionary advantages of religion. Wilson (1975) argued that natural selection has developed a 'capacity for culture' in primitive human societies. This would include a tendency to develop rules and to subordinate to the interests of the group. The core of understanding religion, he says, is the fact that humans are so very easy to indoctrinate. The argument is mainly based on a mechanism of group selection: groups consisting of individuals practising conformism to group rules would be superior to groups consisting of non-conformists; the latter groups would be less keen competitors because of internal struggles among selfish individuals. The mechanism of group selection is supposed to be reinforced by individual selection; the personal advantage of being a member of the group outweighs the disadvantages stemming from subordination to group rules.

In a manner comparable to that of Wilson, Alexander (1987) explained religion as a form of institutionalized moral. Religion can be viewed as a system by which norms and values are imposed on a group by means of a super-human authority. These imposed rules of conduct would make it easier to co-operate and to live together in a group consisting of many individuals. In the evolutionary history of man, groups that adopted such rules could increase in size and would therefore be better competitors with other groups. Alexander (1987) emphasized that it is unique for the human species that other social groups of the same species constitute the most important life-threatening factor. Competition between groups, in his view, is to be considered as a major factor in the evolution of the human brain, the adoption of moral systems and ultimately the evolution of religion.

Sublimation of passions

Another line of reasoning explains religion as a consequence of man's inclination to adhere to rituals. This is basically an ethological explanation. According to the ethologist Lorenz (1966), rituals have arisen from the necessity to sublimate strong and basic passions such as hunger, sexual desire, fear and aggression. In cases where a direct expression of these passions would hurt or otherwise disadvantage the individual, they were diverted into ritual behaviours. There are many examples among animals of such sublimated behaviours; for example, a posture of attack can evolve into a ceremonial mating dance. In this way, the originally aggressive behaviour received a new, symbolic meaning, which is often completely unrelated to the original meaning of the behaviour, just as the jawbones of reptiles obtained a new function as inner ear bones in mammals.

According to Lorenz, adherence to rituals has an adaptive significance for many animals. Animals often cannot understand the logic of causes and effects in the natural processes around them. Therefore it is highly advantageous to adhere to behaviours that have proven to be successful and without danger. If the animal cannot exactly tell what caused the success of certain behaviour, it pays to copy that behaviour with great precision. In man successful behaviours were transmitted to offspring by means of education and culture. Learned behaviours could therefore become separated from the original experience on which they were based and so develop into rituals.

Explaining natural phenomena

The third line of reasoning we want to discuss briefly has its origin with Charles Darwin himself. In his book *The Descent of Man* (Darwin 1871) a few pages are devoted to the evolution of religion. According to the author, modern religions of the 'civilized world' stem from animistic traditions in primitive societies. The origin of animism is related to the evolution of higher brain functions. In evolutionary history, increased intelligence had empowered man with functions such as wonder, imagination and curiosity, which to a certain extent allowed him to control his environment. From his capacity of logical thought, primitive man would feel the need to explain the phenomena occurring around him and their relation to his own existence. One of the simplest ways to explain the world was to assign a soul or spirit to natural phenomena. Religion would thus originate from a projection of human characteristics on to the environment.

The views of Darwin are not at all outdated. In a textbook on evolution Strickberger (2000) devoted a chapter on religion and provides an explanation that resembles very much Darwin's argument. Strickberger argued that religion first developed as a form of behaviour through which man sought to deal with aspects of his environment that he could not control or understand. By assuming that such aspects could nevertheless be human-like, they became subject to appeal and thus indirectly to control. The belief that natural forces and spirits could be influenced stimulated the development of rituals. At the same time, it gave primitive man a feeling of control over his environment and removed concern and fear. Since this contributed to personal stability, there was an immediate advantage to the individual.

The significance of heritability of religiousness

This very short overview of biological theories on the origin of religion (there are many more!) shows that evolutionary biologists have proposed a great variety of mechanisms by which primordial forms of religion could have originated in the societies of primitive man. The question as to which of these theories is most likely is not relevant for the present discussion. The point is that mechanisms assigning adaptive value to religion are easy to formulate but can hardly be tested. The fact that we observe genetic variation among humans in behavioural traits related to religiousness cannot be taken as an argument that religion was subject to natural selection. In fact, if selection was purely directional, it should have removed genetic variation. Conversely, neither can the existence of genetic variation be taken to imply that there was no selection at all. So what evolutionary theory can say about complex human traits might after all be less obvious than is often thought in human biology (Stinson *et al.* 2000).

While it is relatively easy to develop arguments for why religion could arise through evolution because it was an advantage to the individual or the group, it is not so easy to explain why genetic variability among individuals in religious behaviour should persist today. This is the topic of investigation in the chapter by Lindon Eaves. Viewing the chapter from the perspective of population genetics and evolutionary biology, three main comments can be made.

Can religiousness be considered a quantitative trait?

The methodology used by Eaves to analyse twin data and estimate heritabilities was originally developed from animal breeding practice (Falconer 1981). Traits considered were those that the breeder wanted to improve, such as milk production, fat accumulation and body weight. Such traits are called metric or quantitative because they can be expressed in scores or numbers. It is assumed that many genes are involved in the expression of these traits, each contributing a small additive part. Genetic variation is then assumed to stem from inter-individual differences in these genes, be it on the structural or the regulatory level. In the case of complex traits such as religious inclination, the causal chain between DNA polymorphisms and variation in personality scores that ultimately determine religious values is extremely long. Heritability of a complex trait may depend strongly on how that trait is measured. Of course, any score from an interview or a personality test can be treated as a metric variable and subjected to statistical analysis. However, the reduction of a multidimensional concept such as personality to a one-dimensional score raises the question of whether its essence is still there. One might also consider the term 'religiousness' as covering a heterogeneous collection of phenomena that happen to be indicated by the same word but cannot be considered as a single trait at all. Heritability was originally defined for variables that can be measured on a metric, one-dimensional scale. Can religious inclination be considered as such a variable? We believe it is a serious simplification.

Is religiousness an evolutionary by-product of something else?

The observation that there is genetic variation among humans in religiousness does not imply that religiousness itself was subject to selection. It is easy to imagine that the genes involved will have strong pleiotropic effects; that is, the gene product (a protein) will have more than one biochemical function in the human brain. For example, if a gene encodes a receptor for a certain hormone, the area in the brain where that gene is expressed will be susceptible to the action of that hormone. If the action of the hormone is related to a behavioural pattern of the individual and that behaviour carries a fitness advantage, selection might operate on the expression of the gene. However, the same receptor protein might be expressed in another area of the brain and there be tied to another function, due to the different neural circuitry in that area of the brain. The same hormone might elicit another type of behaviour there. So selection for one type of behaviour may indirectly favour or suppress other behaviours, which are connected to each other in a 'co-adapted gene complex'. The consequence for studies of heritability would be to make it necessary to look at a variety of traits at the same time and analyse their genetic correlations, in addition to their heritability. Viewed in this way, religiousness might well be considered as an evolutionary by-product of something else, rather than as something under primary selection.

Is, ought or so what?

The question can be raised: does it make a difference if we know that religiousness is partly inherited and that the differences in religious behaviour among people are partly due to differences in their genetic make-up? We argue that the ethical implications of data like the ones discussed by Eaves might be less far-reaching than is sometimes considered. As is argued by Van der Steen (2000), evolutionary theory cannot be a foundation for ethics. The question is comparable to the discussion about 'brain sex'. If we accept that there are major differences between the brains of men and women, initiated in the six-week old embryo, and that as a consequence men and women have different behavioural patterns, does this imply that boys and girls should behave according to stereotypical sex roles? Nobody agrees with such a statement because genetic determination of behaviour does not impose rules of conduct in human society. Likewise, boys and girls in present society do not seem to have a problem with recognizing that they are biologically different. In the same spirit, we argue that the data discussed by Eaves only show that there is genetic variation for complex personality traits in human populations. This fact does not imply that religiousness is genetically determined in the sense that an individual's genes tell him what to do, nor does it detract from the value of religious experience. Eaves argues that genetic determinism must be attacked where it can. The problem is that investigators of human behaviour will often find themselves in a position where they have to fight the ghost of genetic determinism that they released themselves.

Acknowledgements

The authors are grateful to Wim van der Steen, Ger Ernsting and Kees van Gestel for comments on an earlier version of the manuscript.

References

Alexander, R.D. (1987) *The Biology of Moral Systems*, New York: Aldine de Gruyter.

Boomsma, D.I., de Geus, E.J.C., van Baal, G.C.M. and Koopmans J.R. (1999) 'A religious upbringing reduces the influence of genetic factors on disinhibition: evidence for interaction between genotype and environment on personality', *Twin Research* 2: 115–25.

Boyer, P. (2001) *Religion Explained: The Evolutionary Origins of Religious Thought*, New York: Basic Books.

Darwin, C. (1871) *The Descent of Man*, Oxford: John Murray.

Diamond, J. (1998) *Guns, Germs and Steel: A Short History of Everybody for the Last 13,000 Years*, London: Random House.

Dobzhansky, T. (1973) 'Nothing in biology makes sense except in the light of evolution', *American Biology Teacher* 35: 125–9.

Eaves, L.B. (2003) " 'Ought' in a world that just 'is' ", in W.B. Drees (ed.) *Is Nature Ever Evil? Religion, Science and Value*, London: Routledge.

Falconer, D.S. (1981) *Introduction to Quantitative Genetics*, New York: Longman.

Lewin, R. (1999) *Principles of Human Evolution: A Core Textbook*, Malden: Blackwell.

Lorenz, K. (1966) *On Aggression*, New York: Harcourt, Brace and World.

Molnar, S. (1998) *Human Variation: Races, Types, and Ethnic Groups*, Upper Saddle River: Prentice Hall.

Stinson, S., Bogin, B., Huss-Ashmore R. and O'Rourke, D. (eds) (2000) *Human Biology: An Evolutionary and Biocultural Perspective*, New York: Wiley-Liss.

Strickberger, M.W. (2000) *Evolution*, 3rd edn, Sudbury: Jones and Bartlett.

Tattersall, I. and Matternes, J.H. (2000) 'We were not alone', *Scientific American* 282 (January): 38–44.

Van der Steen, W.J. (2000) *Evolution as Natural History: A Philosophical Analysis*, Westport: Praeger.

Waddington, C.H. (1960) *The Ethical Animal*, London: George Allen & Unwin.

Wilson, E.O. (1975) *Sociobiology: The New Synthesis*, Cambridge, MA: Harvard University Press.

Wolpoff, M.H., Hawks, J., Frayer, D.W. and Hunley, K. (2001) 'Modern human ancestry at the peripheries: a test of the replacement theory', *Science* 291: 293–7.

Wood, B. and Collard, M. (1999) 'The human genus', *Science* 284: 65–71.

35

ON PATTERN RECOGNITION, EVOLUTION, EPISTEMOLOGY, RELIGION AND EVIL

Mladen Turk

Pattern recognition and searching order are fundamental cognitive activities. Mathematics is the most efficient way of recognizing patterns. Religions too are about discerning order. In this chapter I will explore the idea that the relation between religious perceptions of order and our pattern recognition capacity is similar to the relation between mathematics and pattern recognition.

Pattern recognition is hardwired in our brain. We cannot perceive without finding patterns in what we perceive. If we perceive patterns mathematically, it is not because we have a choice of doing so, but it is necessary. If the religious sense for order is akin to our sense for mathematics, we do not have a choice of perceiving order non-religiously.

Pattern recognition

What is order? Where did order come from? From nature or from us? Questions like these have vexed the human race for a long time.

In order to illustrate the relevance of order and pattern, let me use some recent works on mathematics and biology. In several popular works we can read about the connection between mathematics and biology in general and neuroscience in particular (Dehaene 1998; Herrnstein Smith and Plotnitsky 1997; Stewart 1997; Stewart and Cohen 1997). The authors argue that mathematics is important for biology. They also offer speculations on how mathematics itself works. According to Dehaene, mathematics is conditioned by the biological and neurological constitution of humans. The structure of the human brain is the place to search for answers to questions about the origins of mathematics. For Stewart, mathematics infinitely extends the search for patterns, and only with mathematics can we describe patterns that we can observe.

Our mind evolved in order to recognize patterns, to search for patterns and to create patterns. We can understand patterns; without patterns we cannot know anything. When we look at a carpet or a wall, or listen to an off-channel radio, after a while we will see familiar shapes and hear patterns in the noise. This is because our mind searches for patterns and order (Blackmore 1999: 74–81; Stewart 1995). Those patterns are not random; they are the product of how physical reality presents itself to us.

Let us take the example of our perception of colours. Across cultures we name at least a few different colours. But as far as physics is concerned, light involves a continuum of wavelengths. Our discrimination of wavelengths is arbitrary in a way, but it can be found across different species that 'recognize' different colours. The pattern of colours is very important for our perception, yet at the same time it seems arbitrary and, according to modern physics, is not intrinsic to nature.

Where in this order is the place of human beings and their sense for order? Humans are not apart from nature by virtue of their knowledge. Maybe the answer to the question posed by the title of this book is that nature can be evil for the very reason that humans can be perceived as being evil. Since we cannot remove human beings and their products from nature, how could we remove being evil from nature?

Our knowledge is the product of the same evolutionary processes that have formed our brains and that have formed the brains of our animal relatives (Rescher 1990; Cosmides, Tooby and Barkow 1992). Just as life has its basis in inorganic DNA, our sense for pattern and order has its basis in our brains. If we take this claim further, we can say that we are the products of natural processes and we are those natural processes themselves, and in that sense everything that humans do is natural, a part of nature.

Even though we think we know what is evil, it is sometimes hard to describe and define clearly what evil is. In evolutionary biology there is an ongoing debate about the evolutionary origins of morality and our sense of good and evil (Alexander 1987; Ridley 1997; Sober and Wilson 1998). Perhaps we have problems defining evil for the very simple reason that evil can be seen as a pattern, or maybe the absence of a pattern, that our mind has evolved to search for.

Evolution, epistemology and order

The question remains open as to which came first: the pattern or the brain that can recognize the pattern? If human beings use their brains in order to study human brains, and if our brains tend to find patterns in everything, it is, in a way, obvious for us to find patterns in our brains. Since mathematics is the method of science, is it not obvious that we will find mathematics in our brains and everywhere around us? This is a restatement of the classical epistemological problem, and it seems that it is not self-evident that nature is intelligible.

Conundrums aside, if we take Darwinian evolution seriously as far as human beings are concerned, patterns that we can recognize and the mathematics underlying our descriptions of those patterns must be attuned to nature because, as Rescher puts it, mathematics 'itself is a natural product as a thought instrument of ours: it fits nature because it reflects the way we ourselves are emplaced within nature as integral constituents thereof' (1990: 60). Humans as evolutionary products of nature use mathematics as a tool in their attempts to describe their environment and this should be evolutionarily advantageous. Just as humans are predisposed to enjoy fat and sweet food, so are we predisposed to express mathematically the patterns we observe.

Nature that has produced the human mind and its cognitive capabilities, including mathematics, must be well attuned to the mind that it brought about. Evolutionary processes are possible because there is a certain amount of regularity and predictability in nature (Cairns-Smith 1996: 55–7; Rescher 1990: 68). Those evolutionary processes have produced an intelligence powerful enough to look back at its origins and describe regularities in those origins by means of mathematics. Mathematics devised by human intelligence must be powerful enough to be capable of describing regularities that we can find in evolutionary processes.

If we understand religion as being composed of a number of interdependent elements, some of which are beliefs, narratives, rituals, codes of conduct, religious experiences, social aspects of religion, psychological aspects of religion, ideological aspects of religion, etc., then we can say that religion cannot possibly be explained as an adaptation in the biological sense (Hinde 1999; Lincoln 1999). For something to be understood as adaptation in the biological sense, it needs to have a clear function (Williams 1966). But if we understand religion as a pattern-seeking activity, an attitude that can help us find patterns and bring order into our experience, then maybe we can speak about the adaptive function of religion. Searching for patterns and finding them in mathematics is similar to providing patterns, and we can say that religious teachings, feelings and attitudes are another form of providing patterns in our environment. The human brain appears to be hardwired for mathematics because we can find patterns within it; we have a 'number sense'. Maybe the human brain is hardwired for religion because we have a sense for order, and because religion provides order in our experiences.

It seems that almost all religions deal with order at least to some extent. Religious narratives describe our place in nature. If we follow the rituals and other types of behaviour described in those narratives, the order is believed to be preserved. Disorder can be represented in religious narratives as well. Together with beliefs about the genesis of disorder, we are told the way to re-establish order. The beliefs, rituals, narratives and codes of conduct we need to follow in order to perceive the pattern that surrounds us in a way that is coherent with our religious narratives determine to a great extent what is good and what is evil.

The mechanism by which we recognize a religious pattern is the same mechanism that we use to recognize any pattern. The question still remains as to whether there 'really' is a pattern in nature or whether we apply patterns in our brain to everything that we experience. In order to settle the question of the objectivity of our experience of patterns, there are many ways in which to proceed. I shall list some of those possible ways in order to illustrate the issue and show the relationship of this problem to the biological understanding of religion.

If a non-human conscious intelligent being, say an 'alien', were to experience patterns in a similar way, we might be convinced that the patterns are objective. If we were to encounter aliens with whom we can communicate, we could ask them if they experience patterns in the same way. Alternatively, their perception of patterns could be completely determined by the way in which they evolved. We would also find out whether our experience of patterns is real and objective, if we were to create a computer powerful and intelligent enough to consciously perceive patterns. Then we would be able to ask this computer to confirm the validity of the patterns we observe.

Another way to argue that our experience of pattern is real and objective is a very well-known, traditional way. Religions claim that there is some sort of inherent guarantee that the order perceived is in fact an objective order. Religious beliefs, narratives and rituals point us to the criterion of the objectivity of our perception of order.

Are mathematics and religion reducible to biology?

With the reintroduction of religion we enter another level of the epistemological circularity mentioned earlier. For example, if we have evolved certain features that enable us to think mathematically and to search for patterns through mathematics, then whatever we find as a pattern is preconditioned by the mathematics that is hardwired in our brains. Much in the same way, if we have evolved certain features that produce religion, and one of those features is the need for a recognizable order in patterns, then we cannot tell religion apart from all other activities that we do.

In the case of understanding God as a creation of the human brain, we cannot be sure that humans created God once we have a concept of God that reveals God-self to human beings. Since the concept of a self-revealing God has entered human brains, we can understand God as the one who has produced the need for order and the ways in which our brains are hardwired for the detection of patterns. This is in my opinion almost as intricate a situation as the famous ontological proof. More generally, what we in religious beliefs, rituals and narratives recognize as patterns would not be recognized as such unless it was understood as something relevant for the survival of the species.

It seems to me that there are some fundamental parallels between how we can understand mathematics biologically and how can we understand religion biologically. To say that religious phenomena can be explained by reducing religious phenomena to biological ones is as wrong as it would be to say that mathematical phenomena can be reduced to biological ones, while explaining this very reduction of mathematics to biology via a mathematical proof.

One way to escape from this circle is to understand religion through evolution, not necessarily biological evolution but the evolution of concepts. The human brain evolved through the complex processes of biological evolution, but it also contains information that has some features of replication on which natural selection can operate and that can be understood through the theory of evolution. The usual name for those units is memes. Memes were selected by natural selection. But once selected, memes can bring about what is usually called downward causation (Popper and Eccles 1977; Van Loocke 1999; Blackmore 1999; Prigogine 1984). Namely, memes can ensure the survival of a brain by ensuring their own survival. Brain size and the evolution of language are today the most debated issues in memetics (Blackmore 1999). But in the future the importance of religions as a case study in memetics should become more recognized and accepted. As memes may have a downward causal influence, processes taking place at higher levels fill in indeterminacies at a lower level. One of the functions of pattern recognition is the construction of models of various parts of the environment (Van Loocke 1999). Among the models constructed by human brains are religious models, which thus may have valuable features

References

Alexander, R.D. (1987) *The Biology of Moral Systems*, New York: Aldine de Gruyter.

Blackmore, S. (1999) *The Meme Machine*, Oxford: Oxford University Press.

Cairns-Smith, G.A. (1996) *Evolving the Mind: On the Nature of Matter and the Origin of Consciousness*, Cambridge: Cambridge University Press.

Cosmides, L., Tooby, J. and Barkow, J.H. (1992) 'Introduction: Evolutionary Psychology and Conceptual Integration', in J.H. Barkow, L. Cosmides and J. Tooby (eds) *The Adapted Mind: Evolutionary Psychology and the Generation of Culture*, Oxford: Oxford University Press.

Dehaene, S. (1998) *The Number Sense: How the Mind Creates Mathematics*, London: Allen Lane.

Herrnstein Smith, B. and Plotnitsky, A. (1997) *Mathematics, Science, and Postclassical Theory*, Durham, NC: Duke University Press.

Hinde, R.A. (1999) *Why Gods Persist: A Scientific Approach to Religion*, London: Routledge.

Lincoln, B. (1999) *Theorizing Myth: Narrative, Ideology, and Scholarship*, Chicago: University of Chicago Press.

Popper, K. and Eccles, J. (1977) *The Self and Its Brain*, New York: Bantam Books.

Prigogine, I. (1984) *Order out of Chaos*, New York: Bantam Books.

Rescher, N. (1990) *A Useful Inheritance: Evolutionary Aspects of the Theory of Knowledge*, Savage, MD: Rowman & Littlefield.

Ridley, M. (1997) *The Origins of Virtue: Human Instincts and the Evolution of Cooperation*, New York: Penguin.

Sober, E. and Wilson, D.S. (1998) *Unto Others: The Evolution and Psychology of Unselfish Behavior*, Cambridge, MA: Harvard University Press.

Stewart, I. (1995) *Nature's Numbers: The Unreal Reality of Mathematics*, New York: Basic Books.

—— (1997) *Life's Other Secret: The New Mathematics of the Living World*, New York: John Wiley & Sons.

—— and Cohen, J. (1997) *Figments of Reality: The Evolution of the Curious Mind*, Cambridge: Cambridge University Press.

Van Loocke, P. (1999) *The Nature of Concepts: Evolution, Structure and Representation*, London: Routledge.

Williams, G.C. (1966) *Adaptation and Natural Selection: A Critique of Some Current Evolutionary Thought*, Princeton: Princeton University Press.

INDEX